THE VOICE OF SILENCE

THE VOICE OF SILENCE

Discourses on Mabel Collins' *Light on the Path*

OSHO

JAICO PUBLISHING HOUSE

Ahmedabad Bangalore Bhopal Bhubaneswar Chennai
Delhi Hyderabad Kolkata Lucknow Mumbai

Published by Jaico Publishing House
A-2 Jash Chambers, 7-A Sir Phirozshah Mehta Road
Fort, Mumbai - 400 001
jaicopub@jaicobooks.com
www.jaicobooks.com

THE VOICE OF SILENCE
ISBN 978-81-8495-018-2

First Jaico Impression: 2010
Third Jaico Impression: 2012

Printed by
Snehesh Printers
320-A, Shah & Nahar Ind. Est. A-1
Lower Parel, Mumbai - 400 013

Contents

Introduction

Every few thousand years an individual appears who irrevocably changes the world around them in ways that are never immediately apparent, except to the most perceptive.

Osho is one such individual: his spoken words will resonate for centuries to come.

All those words have been recorded and transcribed into books like this one, written words that can carry a transfor-ming message to the reader.

For Osho, all change is individual. There is no "society" to change – it can only happen to each one of us, one at a time.

So, no matter what the subject matter of the book, the thread that runs through all Osho's words is like a love song that we can suddenly, mysteriously, hear at just the right moment. And strangely, no matter what the words seem to be referring to, they are really only referring to us.

And this is no ordinary love song, more an invitation to open our hearts to hear something beyond the words, beyond the heart...a silence beyond all understanding. Where we all belong.

I

AMBITION

PART I

These rules are written for all disciples: Attend you to them.

Before the eyes can see,
they must be incapable of tears.
Before the ear can hear,
it must have lost its sensitiveness.
Before the voice can speak
in the presence of the Masters,
it must have lost the power to wound.
Before the soul can stand
in the presence of the Masters,
its feet must be washed in the blood of the heart.

1. Kill out ambition.

Ambition is the first curse:
the great tempter of the man
who is rising above his fellows.
It is the simplest form of looking for reward.

Men of intelligence and power are led away from their higher possibilities by it continually.
Yet it is a necessary teacher.
Its results turn to dust and ashes in the mouth; like death and estrangement, it shows the man at last that to work for self is to work for disappointment.

I called you and you have come. To come outwardly is very easy but until you also come to me inwardly, your outer coming or not coming does not have much meaning. One who can come outwardly, who has a thirst and longing, can also come from the inside too. The outer coming is a proof that you are searching, but that proof alone is not enough. It is an indication, and it is a good indication; it is necessary, but it is not enough. You have to come inwardly too. And before that inner journey can begin, it is necessary for you to understand a few things about yourself – because it is you who will make this journey. No one else can make this journey on your behalf. In this world, it is not possible to see with someone else's eyes, nor is it possible to walk with someone else's feet. Here, you have to die for yourself and you have to live for yourself. Here, nobody can take your place.

That is why it is necessary first of all to understand a few things about yourself – because if there is a misconception about that, then even a right path will take you to a wrong place. If you do not have the right understanding about yourself, you will turn even a right path into one that takes you to the wrong destination. And if you have a right understanding about yourself, then there is no path that will not take you to the right place. Even wrong paths can reach to the right destination; what is needed is the right traveler. It all depends on the traveler. It is not the path that takes the traveler to the destination, it is the traveler who reaches.

The path changes in accordance with you. As you are, so becomes the path. That is why there are no ready-made paths on which you can walk blindly.

The first thing is to have the right understanding about yourself, because it is out of *you* that the path will be born, and in the end the destination will also arise from you.

You are everything – you are the seed and you will also become the tree. And when the flowers bloom and the fragrance emanates from them, then it is you who will be in those flowers and in that fragrance. If you have the wrong understanding about yourself, then all your hard work will go to waste.

The first thing: the first thing for you to understand about yourself is that you don't know anything. If you did know, then there would have been no need for you to come to me. If you are able to catch hold of even one ray of sunlight, then the whole path which reaches to the sun has opened up because by catching that ray you can reach to its original source, the sun. And if you are able to taste even one drop of the ocean, then you have tasted the whole ocean. If you know even a little bit of life, then there is no need to ask anyone anything. With the help of that little bit that you know, you can keep moving on ahead.

It is as if a man takes a small lamp and walks in the darkness, and the way is lit for only two steps; but when he has taken those two steps, two more steps are lit up and then when he has taken those two steps, two more steps are lighted. With a lamp which can shed light on only two steps, you can complete a journey of a thousand miles. There is no need to light up the whole thousand miles. Even if you have a small lamp in your hand, even then, the journey along the longest of long, dark roads can be completed. Two steps are enough.

If you knew even a little bit about yourself, then there would have been no need for you to come to me; there would have been no need for you to go to anyone. So the first thing is that you understand this rightly: as yet, you don't know anything about yourself, and whatever you may know is just words. But words have no life and no meaning. In this world, there is nothing more false than words.

Experience, yes – experience has meaning. I may talk as much as I want, but I cannot put my experience into words. Nobody has ever been able to do it and nobody will ever be able to do it – because whatever I know is *my* experience. And when I put that into words, what you hear is not the experience, but empty words.

I say *God* and you hear it, I say soul and you also hear it, but there is no meaning in the words *soul* or *God*. What you are hearing is just words, and by hearing them again and again an illusion is created that you have understood. The knowledge of words is another name for foolishness.

You don't know anything. Please let this be clear; this is fundamental. Because if a person who does not know starts to think that he knows, then all the doors to knowing close for him. If a sick person believes that he is healthy, then the search for a cure stops. If an ignorant person thinks that he is wise, then this so-called wisdom will lead him much farther astray than his ignorance would have.

If you can understand that you don't know anything, then that is the first ray of wisdom. Now you have become honest. Now you have at least accepted one truth: that you don't know anything. You have put your scriptures aside and you have left your words behind. You have become honest. You have become authentic with yourself in seeing that you don't know anything about your soul or about salvation; you don't know what life is all about. This acceptance of your ignorance is the first step of wisdom.

If any wise person happens to have come here, please go back. I will be able to work only with those who are aware of their ignorance. Your knowledge will become a barrier for you. And if you already know, what is the need to make unnecessary efforts here? And please understand this rightly – only if you are sick will I give you medicine; only if you are ignorant will I try to take you towards wisdom; only if you are in darkness will I show you the path to light. But if you are already standing in the light, then don't waste your efforts and mine. It is very easy to wake a man who is sleeping, but it is very difficult to wake a man who is pretending to be asleep.

The second thing: the life of every person is a search for only one thing – how to get rid of suffering, how to attain happiness. There is only one thirst, one search. Even if a tree is rising out of the ground towards the sky, it is on this search. Every bird that flies, every animal that moves, every man that lives...they are all this same search. In existence, the inner search of even a stone is for happiness. So the second thing to keep in mind is, what are you searching for?

Many people go straight into the search for godliness, but that search is difficult. It is difficult because there is no deep inner thirst for it. If you follow your thirst, then one day perhaps that thirst may ripen into the thirst for godliness – but it is not yet the case. Understand this rightly, that right now your search is for bliss. Maybe this search will take you farther – maybe the Ganges coming out of this little Gangotri will move farther on.

Slowly, slowly, as your search deepens, you may realize that bliss is another name for godliness; you may realize that bliss is one of the attributes of godliness. And you may come to know that your search is not only for bliss, but for something greater. But the initial search is for happiness, not for godliness.

Some people get involved with godliness right at the start; then it becomes difficult. Their effort to become a tree begins without first becoming a seed. Then there will be problem. Then there will be much running around, but with no result – and when no result comes, they are disappointed and in despair.

So one thing is that you have come here in search of bliss. Drop this God. There is no hurry. Start your journey with the search for bliss, and it will end with your attaining to godliness. But don't begin with it. It is appropriate to start the climb from the first rung; the beginning should be from *a*, then to *b* and then to *c*. Everyone understands bliss, even if he is an atheist. Whether he is a Hindu, a Mohammedan, a Christian or a Jaina; whether he believes in God or not; whether he has faith in religion or not; he may be anybody but the search for bliss is universal. So let us begin with that which everyone is searching for.

In this world, if we could only accept this universal search, there would not be disputes between so many religions. Hindu, Mohammedan and Christian would not fight each other; there would not be any contention between Hindus and Jainas. But instead we begin our search for God, and we don't know anything about godliness. We have no strong desire to search for it, nor do we have any reason to do so. So we fight about words, so we make different wordy interpretations about a God whom we don't know at all. Then there is conflict between these different interpretations; then temples, mosques and *gurudwaras* come into being, and man unnecessarily suffers.

Begin with bliss: then there is no problem or conflict even for the atheist. Then whether you are a Hindu or a Mohammedan, there is no question – because if you are searching for bliss, you are searching for the thing that every living being is searching for. About this, everyone agrees. And slowly, slowly, as the search becomes deeper, you will come to know that the search for bliss has become the search for godliness.

The third thing to keep in mind is that you want to search for bliss, but what will you give for it? What will you pay for it – with what? What do you have that you will give in return?

In order for a man to take even one step, he has to leave the piece of ground on which he was standing; only then can he go forward. There is no progress in this world if he is not willing to leave something behind. Without sacrifice you cannot take even one step. If your hands are full of mud, pebbles, stones, and you want diamonds, you will have to let go of the stones. To grasp the desired object, your hands at least should be empty; you will have to let go of the useless things. So what do you have?

Please don't become afraid. I will not tell you to renounce your wealth – because no one has any wealth, no one at all. In this world, even the richest man is a pauper. Nobody has any wealth.

There are two types of paupers: one is a poor pauper and the other is a rich pauper – but all are paupers. Up until now I have not seen a rich man. You can see many people who have money, but they are not rich. They are also in the rat race to grab as much as they can, just as the poorest of the poor are. Like a beggar holding on tightly to whatever he has got in his hand, just like that, the man who has the biggest safe is also holding on tightly to whatever *he* has. The tightness of their grip is the same, so their poverty is also the same.

So you don't have wealth – no one has – and that is why I don't insist that you drop it. How can you let go of what you do not have? I don't tell you to give up your life, because even that is not yours. How can you have a life that you are not even aware of? And each moment you are trembling with the fear of death. If you are life itself, why are you afraid of death?

Life has no death. How can life ever become death? But you are trembling with the fear of death; each moment death is surrounding you. You are trying to save yourself in whatever way you can so that you don't disappear, so that you don't die and you don't come to an end. And you don't even have life! That is why I will not tell you to give up your life. How can you give up what you don't have?

I will ask from you only that which you have. And I will ask for that which everyone has. Just as I said that everyone's search is for bliss, in the same way there is one kind of wealth that everyone has – and that is their suffering. You have plenty of that, you have more than you need. For many lives you have not collected anything else; you have collected piles of it! Even Mount Everest will seem small compared to the piles of troubles that you have collected; your problems are so big that even Mount Everest will feel embarrassed in front of them! And perhaps even Hillary and Tensing would not be able to climb the mountains of your sufferings – they are so big.

They are your efforts from many lives; you have not earned anything apart from your suffering. Even now, you are earning it.

I would like you to let go of your suffering, to renounce your suffering. Nobody ever asks for your suffering – but I do. And if you can give up your suffering then the path to happiness can be opened up. If you can manage to let go of your suffering you will come to realize that what you thought was suffering was nothing but an illusion; that suffering was not holding onto you – you were holding onto it. But you will only come to know who was holding on and who was being held when you let go.

You are always asking how you can get rid of suffering. From your questions it appears as if suffering has got a hold on you and you want to be released from it. If suffering is holding onto you, you cannot possibly become free from it because the grip is not in your hands but in the hands of suffering. Then you are helpless. And if after so many lives you still haven't managed to become free, how can you suddenly become free now?

I say to you that suffering is not holding onto you, you are holding onto suffering. And if you can agree to look into what I am saying, you will come to understand it for yourself. Not only will you come to understand it, but you will experience a letting go – and you will come to know how suffering can be dropped. And when you become good at the art of letting go of suffering, then one day you will realize that you were dragging it around with you – and no one except you was responsible for this. Whatever suffering you experienced, nobody else was to blame. It was your wish, you wanted to suffer. Whatsoever we wish for comes to pass. And whatsoever you are is the fruit of your wishes. Neither God is responsible, nor luck; no one has any investment in causing you trouble.

The truth is that existence is always eager to make you blissful. This whole existence wants your life to become a celebration – because when you are unhappy you also throw unhappiness all around you; when you are unhappy then the stink from your wounds reaches to the whole of existence. And when you are unhappy existence also feels pain. This whole universe feels pain when you are unhappy and rejoices when you are joyful. Existence has no wish for you to be unhappy: that would be suicidal for existence itself. But you are unhappy, and to become unhappy you have developed a certain system. Until this is destroyed, you will never be able to open your eyes to happiness, to bliss.

What is this system? What arrangement has man created to accumulate suffering? How does he collect it? Try to understand this a little – then perhaps it will be easier for you to let go of it.

Beginning tomorrow morning, we will start some experiments. If you want to weep sometimes… A small child wants to cry: psychologists say that the act of crying in a child is a catharsis. Whenever tension builds up in the child, then by weeping he throws out his tension. You too were a small child once. A small child is feeling hungry, he is not getting his milk on time, so he cries because he is filled with tension and he needs to let this tension out. He will cry, the tension will be released and he will feel lighter. But we teach him not to cry. We try to find all sorts of ways to prevent him from crying. We put toys in his hands so that he forgets; we put something artificial in his mouth, or we put his thumb in his mouth so that he mistakes it for his mother's breast and he forgets. We begin to rock him to and fro so that his attention is diverted and he doesn't cry. We try everything to prevent him from crying. That tension which could have been released by crying collects – it isn't released. In this way we let it accumulate. Who knows how much pain and tears each person accumulates? And he sits on this collected pile.

Who knows how much tension you have collected? You have never wept heartfully nor have you ever laughed totally. Because you have not cried, something has become stuck in you; because you have not laughed, something has become stuck in you. You have never been wholeheartedly angry nor have you ever forgiven someone completely. You have become half-hearted. Your branches want to grow all around you, but they have not been able to. Leaves want to sprout from all sides, but they have not been able to. Your tree has been left bare. The name of this accumulated pain, this unreleased pain, is hell – and you are dragging it around with you.

I have called you here so that your hell can be thrown out. And only *you* can throw it out. In this camp you should become like a small child. You should forget that you are cultured, that you are very educated, that you are in an important position, that you have wealth, that you are respected in the city. Drop all that! Become like a newborn baby who has no reputation, no education, no position, no wealth, no prestige. If you want to save your prestige and reputation, then before tomorrow morning please run from here as fast as you can and don't even look back. I am not here to support these things. Save your prestige and position, your wisdom and your respectability, and run away. Don't stay here.

I am here for those who are ready to become simple, like children. Only then can I do something – because only children can be taught something, only children can be changed. A revolution can occur only in the lives of children.

In the meditation experiments which will happen here, cathart, throw out all the suffering that you have in your heart. If you have anger, throw it out into the sky. If you have violence, throw it out into the sky. You don't have to be violent with anyone; just release it into the open sky. Suffering, pain, anguish – whatsoever is inside has to be thrown out. You have to throw it out with as much totality as you can. Use your total energy, so that whatever pain is inside you is expressed.

You should understand that until you express the pain you have buried in your unconscious, it will not leave you, it will remain buried. Express it, bring it to the conscious. Pull out whatever is buried in darkness inside; bring it to light.

Some things die in the light. If you pull the tree's roots up from the darkness, they will die. They need darkness; they live in darkness, in darkness is their life. Just like roots, suffering lives also in darkness. Expose your suffering to the light and you will find that it is dead. If you keep on burying it inside, it will remain your constant companion for many lives. Unhappiness has to be brought to the light.

Understand one more thing: you have taken your pain into you from the outside; please return it to the outside. Pain is not inside. All your pain is brought in from the outside.

When you are born, there is no suffering in your self-nature. There is no pain; pain is brought in from the outside. If a man has abused you and you have become unhappy, then you have brought the abuse in from the outside. Now you will accumulate this pain inside, you will let it grow. You will repress it, and then it will expand and poison each and every pore of your body. You will become an unhappy person. We bring suffering in from the outside – it is not in our intrinsic nature.

That is why I say that you can become free from suffering. You cannot become free from your self-nature, but only from that which is other than your self-nature. You can become free only from that which is not yours. There is no way to become free from that which is yours.

Pain has to be thrown out. During these coming days, throw out as much pain as you can. And as you go on throwing it out, the understanding will grow that this was a strange madness you were nurturing! This could have been thrown out very easily, it was in your hands to do so, but you unnecessarily stopped yourself.

And the second thing is that as you throw out the pain, as you throw it from the inside back to the outside from where it came, bliss will begin to arise from within you.

Bliss is within. No one gives it to you from the outside. It doesn't come from the outside; it is your nature, it is you. It is hidden within, it is your soul.

If this rubbish which has been collected from the outside is thrown out, then the soul within begins to expand, it begins to grow. You begin to see its light and you begin to hear its soundless sound; you start to become immersed in an inner music. But this will only happen if you release the rubbish so that an inner sky is created, some space is created. Then that which is hidden inside can expand into this space. Pain has to be thrown out so that bliss can expand inside. And when bliss begins to expand from within, it is necessary for you to understand a second thing too: that if you repress pain, it grows. If pain is repressed it grows; if you express it, it diminishes. With bliss it is totally the opposite: if you repress bliss it diminishes, if you express bliss it increases.

So the first thing is this: you have to throw out the pain, because it becomes less by being expressed. Don't repress it, because it grows through being repressed. And when you have the first glimpses of bliss from within, then express that bliss...because the more you express bliss, the more it grows inside. Fresh layers of it will begin to unfold.

It is just like when you keep on drawing water from a well: new springs from fresh sources keep refilling the well. The spring of bliss is within, so don't become afraid that if you draw from it, it will diminish. Pain is reduced by being expressed because its source is not found within. It was brought in from the outside, so if you throw it out, it will get less.

If you want to hold on to the pain, then keep this technique in mind: never throw it out. If you want to increase your suffering, if this is what you are set on doing – and it seems that many people are set on doing just this – then never express your suffering, don't manifest it. If tears are welling up, swallow them; if you feel anger, repress it. If any trouble is welling up inside, repress it – it will increase. You will become one big hell.

If you want to reduce pain then throw it out. If you want to increase bliss, then express that too; because bliss is within and new layers will keep on revealing themselves. And as you keep on expressing bliss you will begin to have more and more glimpses of a purer bliss.

Bliss increases when it is shared.

That's why Mahavira and Buddha ran away to the forest when they were in pain – because pain has to be released. It is good that they released it in solitude, so that no one was affected by it. But when they became filled with bliss, they went back to the marketplace because now they had to share it, and when you have something to share, it is right to do so in the marketplace. Perhaps someone will be touched by it, perhaps someone will hear the music, perhaps someone will start to dance. Perhaps it will touch the veena of someone's heart and that veena will begin to play.

So keep it in mind that whether it was Christ, Mohammed or Buddha, whenever they were in pain they went into solitude. Pain had to be released – and it was the right thing to do, to release it alone so that no one else knew about it. And when they were filled with bliss they returned to the world, because now sharing had become a joy – and the more bliss is shared the better it is.

Pain has to be released. And when you start to have glimpses of bliss, those too have to be released. You have to become like a small child who has no worry about the past nor any concern about the future; who doesn't even know what others are thinking about him. Only then will that happen for which I have given you the call, and the journey I want you to go on will begin.

A little courage is required, and the treasures of bliss are not far away. A little courage is required and you can drop your hell. Just as when a man who has become dirty from the road comes home and takes a bath and the dirt is washed away, in the same way meditation is a bathing, and pain is the dirt. And when the dirt is all washed away and you feel fresh from bathing, the joy, the bliss that comes to you then is your self-nature.

Now we will take up the sutra.

This small booklet of Mabel Collins', *Light on the Path,* is a beacon. It is one of the few very valuable books in the history of mankind. Mabel Collins is not the author. This booklet is born out of those few essential words which man discovers again and again, and loses again and again. It is difficult to safeguard truth. Truth is revealed only when an individual has attained to the highest peaks – only then. Only those who are standing on the highest peaks of human consciousness can glimpse truth. They talk, they write it down, they try in a thousand and one ways, that the glimpse which they have attained can become the wealth of everyone, the inheritance of everyone. But people who are not at those same heights can never understand the words rightly. Whatever they do understand will be wrong, and whatever they interpret will also be wrong. Slowly, slowly, that first ray of truth is lost and only meaningless words are left in our hands. Sometimes even the words are lost, and then those essential words have to be searched for again and again.

Mabel Collins says that she is not the author of the words which are collected in this booklet, that she has only seen them in the depths of meditation. She says, and rightly so, that these words are from a lost Sanskrit booklet. It vanished, it was lost; man lost touch with it. She has had a vision of this booklet and she has written it down exactly as she saw it in the vision.

In this world there is fear of losing whatsoever is valuable, but there need be no fear of it being totally lost, because whenever someone reaches to those same heights, anyone, then it can be rediscovered. Many scriptures of the world have been rediscovered again and again like this.

The Koran was revealed in this way. When for the first time Mohammed heard the command to read – and Mohammed was illiterate, uneducated – he replied, "How am I to read?"

During meditation some words were swimming in front of his eyes, and a voice was coming from within, asking him to read. So Mohammed said, "What should I read? ...because I don't know how to read or to write!" The voice said that there was no need to be educated in order to read the words, he should simply read them. Mohammed was very puzzled by what was happening. Was it an illusion, a dream – or had he gone mad? He returned home, hid under a blanket, and went to sleep. He became feverish; his whole body started shivering.

His wife asked, "What has happened to you?" But for three days he did not tell even her, because he himself did not believe that what he had seen could be true. And as he couldn't believe it himself, how could his wife? She might say that he had gone mad, that he had a brain fever, that she should call a doctor and have him treated. He held himself back for three days, but the voice came again and again telling him to read. And the same words were repeating themselves again and again. Slowly, slowly, Mohammed began to recognize the words, and the lines of the Koran began to descend on him. This was how the Koran was born.

This booklet, *Light on the Path*, descended on Mabel Collins in the same way. Each and every verse of this booklet is valuable. This is the distilled essence of thousands and thousands of people's search over thousands and thousands of years. Listen to each and every word very carefully.

These rules are written for all disciples:
Attend you to them.

They are not for everybody, but only for the disciples. What is the meaning of this? These rules are only for those who are ready to learn. These rules are not for everybody because there are many people who are not willing to learn.

That's why I said if you know that you are ignorant, then stay here – otherwise escape, because only the ignorant person can be a disciple. Someone who is ignorant and knows that he is ignorant is qualified to be a disciple, is ready to learn. Knowledgeable people are not ready to learn. That is why they remain ignorant, because they are not ready to learn. Ignorant people become wise because of their readiness to learn, and the art and skill of learning is called discipleship. These rules are for those who are disciples.

What does it mean to be a disciple? A disciple is someone who is willing to bow down, who understands wisdom to be more valuable than his own ego; someone who says, "I shall bow down my head, I will put my head on the earth if I can have even one ray of light. I am willing to lose everything, I am willing even to give myself up."

To be a disciple means to be in deep humbleness. To be a disciple means bowing down so that the heart becomes a receptive bowl.

If the river is flowing, and you are standing beside it – thirsty but not willing to bow down – the river will not leap up into your hands. The river is not angry with you; at each and every moment it is ready to quench your thirst. But you have to bow down, you have to bow down and cup your hands…then the river will come into your hands, that is all. Wisdom also cannot be gained without bowing down.

So these rules are for those who are willing to bow down. Just being thirsty is not enough. They are for those who can cup their hands and bow down, for those who say that even if they have to die – no matter. They want to be able to understand the mystery of life. "Even if I have to lie like dust at your feet – no matter. I want to be able to taste the essence of life, its meaning, its purpose; why I am here." These rules are not meant for those who are bent upon protecting themselves, for those who have no desire at all to bow down.

So think about it, and if you have the spirit of a disciple in you, only then will you be able to understand these rules. And if you can understand them, only then will you be able to use them.

Every day I see people coming who want knowledgeability; they don't want to learn. To know *about* something implies knowing without having to pay anything for it. But to learn means to give oneself in return. The meaning of learning is to bow down in humbleness. And the meaning of knowledgeability is "We will see..."

A friend came to me and I asked him... He had written to me many times that he wanted to come, so I asked him, "You have been repeatedly writing to me saying that you want to come – but what is it about?" He said that he wanted to discuss and exchange ideas. So I said, "If you are absolutely sure that you have something to say, then I am willing to learn from you in the spirit of a disciple. But if you are not absolutely sure – and I am absolutely sure that I have something – then please be ready to learn in the spirit of a disciple. There is no point in having the exchange you suggest. Either you give me what you have, or I will give to you...if you are ready to learn. What is the point in an exchange of ideas? If you have it, and I also have it, then too, the matter is over. What is there to exchange? And if both of us have nothing, then what will we exchange? If one of the two of us has it, then there can be a give and take." So I said, "Let us first decide on this."

He became very uneasy. He couldn't say that he had it – and he *didn't* have it. He couldn't acknowledge this much because it would have hurt his ego. He would not accept that he had something to learn from someone. So he said, "I will think about it and then I will come back."

I said, "If you have it, then what is there to think about? And if you don't have it then, too, there is nothing to think about...because the matter is clear!" I said to him,

"You will not be able to come back if you think about it." And until now he hasn't come back.

He just wanted to exchange ideas. But those ideas would have been false: like two blind people trying to show each other the way. That is what an exchange of ideas means.

Once Mahavira and Buddha were staying in the same *caravanserai*, but they didn't meet. It seems strange; because we think if two wise people meet, it must be a good thing ... so many people kept wondering why they didn't meet. Those who have no real understanding of religiousness must think that ego kept them from meeting each other. Jainas think, "Why should Mahavira have made the effort to meet with Buddha? – he is all-knowing! And if Buddha had wanted to meet with him, he could have come and met him."

Buddhists think, "Why should Buddha have made the effort to meet with Mahavira? He is all-knowing. If Mahavira had wanted to meet with him, he could have come and met him."

But the reason why Mahavira and Buddha did not meet is different – there was no sense in meeting, there was no purpose. There is no sense in the meeting of two ignorant people and similarly there is no sense in two wise people meeting either. If an ignorant and a wise person meet, then something can happen; otherwise nothing meaningful occurs. What is the use of two wise people meeting each other? There is no use, no meaning. What is the use of two ignorant people meeting each other? There is no use, no meaning. Only through the meeting of an ignorant person and a wise person can some revolution come about.

These rules are written for all disciples...

The meaning of this sutra is that when you go to a master, when you go to someone who knows, if you truly want a revolution to happen to you, then go with the attitude that you do not know. These sutras are for such people. Only then a revolution will take place, only then a transformation will happen.

...Attend you to them.

Before the eyes can see,
they must be incapable of tears.

Your eyes are so full of tears that you will not be able to see. You are so full of pain – how will you be able to see? Your pain will distort everything. Let the tears flow from your eyes, let them be released. Let your eyes weep and come to the point where there is nothing left to weep for.

What you don't know is that when all the tears have left your eyes, they will become so bright that you will have no need for a third eye. Or put it like this: your two eyes will have become so clear that you will have discovered the third eye in them.

This is not only true in the case of your eyes – your whole body, if it is freed from suffering, will become transparent. If your hands become empty of pain, their touch will have the same magnificence as the touch of the divine. But being full of pain, you are closed from all sides. Your eyes appear to see but they are blind. They are so burdened that you cannot see with them. Your hands touch, but that touch is lifeless. The life-giving force which could have come from within you and made that touch alive, has been blocked by the pain of unhappiness – so it cannot reach to the outside.

In these eight days make your eyes free from tears. The way to make them free from tears is not by repressing them, because by repressing you will make them even more full. What it means to free them from tears is that you let the tears flow. Don't stop them. Tears are marvelous, they are alchemical, they have a mystery. There is a reason for the freshness and innocence which appears in the eyes of young children. Small children are able to weep wholeheartedly, they are able to empty their eyes.

Jesus has said that until you become like small children, you will not be able to enter his father's kingdom.

Weep, and see.

The sutra says:

Before the eyes can see,
they must be incapable of tears.

No tears should be left inside. And when no tears are left inside and no feeling to cry remains, when no amount of accumulated pain is left, then you have become ready. Now you can see something.

Here, this very moment, if your eyes have become empty of tears you can see that which you have been missing for many lifetimes. This very existence – these pebbles and stones, these plants, the stars in the sky; you, and the people sitting all around you – inside them all, that very phenomenon of ultimate bliss is throbbing, that ultimate life force is flowing but blind eyes cannot see, and your eyes are blind because they are full of suffering. Empty your eyes. The eye is only a symbol; you have to empty yourself of suffering.

Before the ear can hear,
it must have lost its sensitiveness.

As you are, you hear much, but as yet you only hear what you want to hear. As you are, you do not hear that which is; you do not hear what is being said, you only hear what you want to hear. Your ears make a choice; they select what they like and they leave out what isn't relevant to them. They catch whatever fulfills your purpose. Whatever doesn't fit in with your purpose they leave out, they do not even hear it...or they hear it and then they ignore it.

Before the ear can hear...

Can hear what? Before you can understand the voice of whosoever it is you have gone to learn from, your ears should have become deaf.

...it must have lost its sensitiveness.

Your structures and habits of hearing – your choosing, your efforts to insert your meanings, your structure of thinking in terms of your own vested interests – should all be destroyed. Those ears which you have considered to be your ears up until now, should become deaf. As they become deaf, your ears will also become pure – just like your eyes. Then whatever is said will be heard without any distortion.

One night it happened that Buddha said to his disciples, "Now go and do the last of your work for the night." That day a thief had come to listen to him. Buddha told the monks to go and perform the last of their work. The last of their work for the night was the last meditation of the night: before sleep came, they were to drown themselves in deep meditation. So the monks got up to go and meditate. And the thief thought, "You have reminded me! Midnight is approaching, now I should go and do my job."

The thief thought that Buddha was an amazing man: How does he know that I have to go and do my job? – "Go and do the last of your work." And a prostitute had also come. She also heard the words – they were the same – but she thought to herself that it was time for her to get up and go to her workplace in the market. Later Buddha would often say that he had said only one thing that night, but people had understood it in many different ways.

You take the meaning that you want to take. The ear of the thief hears one thing, the ear of the prostitute hears something else, and the ear of the *sannyasin* hears something totally different. But the ears which attach their own meaning are not right; those ears need to become deaf, only then will you be able to hear what the master is saying. Otherwise, you will derive your own meaning even from the master's words, and you will understand what you want to understand from them. This is very cunning, because in this way you put the responsibility onto the master, and at the same time you also fulfill your own purpose. And you will start following something on the basis of what was never said, and which was not the master's meaning. If you get lost you will blame the master for it. You will never say that you heard wrongly at the time. If you do something wrong you will say that the master had told you to do it, that is why you did it. You will not understand that your ears interpreted wrongly. That is why the sutra says:

Before the ear can hear,
it must have lost its sensitiveness.

Whatever your ways and habits of hearing were up until now – which you may have brought with you here – put them aside. Now hear clearly. Don't interpret, don't attach any meaning. As I speak, don't be calculating about it. For example, when I said, "Until your eyes have become empty of tears, you will not be able to see," many of you must have thought that you don't have any tears inside you, so this must have been said to somebody else. I said, "Before you come to know anything you will have to bow down." Your mind must have said, "But I always bow down! – I touch the master's feet, I go to the saints, I serve the monks. All this I have done, right from the start – this must have been said to someone else." If this is so, you have avoided the point, you have protected yourself from what was said, you have not heard it. Whatsoever is being said here is being addressed to you and to no one else. So do not even think about someone else. Just think about yourself, and even when you think about yourself, be honest about it.

Before the voice can speak
in the presence of the masters,
it must have lost the power to wound.

To speak in the presence of the masters there is a condition: don't say anything to the master until your voice cannot wound. Until then whatever you say will be wasted. Until then whatever you say will only increase the distance between you and your master; it will not bring you closer.

We commit great violence with our speech, and if we want to, we can even do it with silence. We are good at committing violence. Sometimes you don't even speak, and you do not speak because your not speaking will hurt. Even when you do speak sometimes, your manner of speaking has a cutting edge. Superficially your words may be sweet, but from the inside they are poisonous. In your laughter, in the way you move, in your gestures, in your eyes, there is a tendency to wound, to be violent.

This sutra says that you are behaving in such a way everywhere else, and that is alright, but in front of a master only speak when you have got rid of this tendency. Only then will you be able to come close to the master by speaking; otherwise it is better to remain silent. Listen, but don't speak. And this too is right, because you will gain only by listening, not by speaking. But people are very strange...

One man used to come to see me, and he would talk to me for an hour, two hours. He would talk about all sorts of things. All I had to do was to nod my head in between, and that too I had to do in order that it wouldn't appear to him that his talk was useless. All his chatter was complete rubbish, there was no sense in it, and it did not even have anything to do with me. But in order for him not to feel that I thought his talking was useless, I would nod in between and say, "Yes, yes."

Before leaving, after two hours of unloading all his rubbish from God knows where, he never once forgot to say to me, "I immensely enjoyed everything you said to me today." He would tell me as he was leaving that he had very much enjoyed my talk. And I had not spoken a single word – in fact I was not even given a chance to speak! He would talk and I would listen. But as he left he would always say to me, "All that you said was of immense value."

And he wasn't lying, it didn't feel like that. It was not as if he was being deceitful; he would say it with great feeling and respect. There was no reason to deceive – this must have been his perception.

If you go to a master in this state of mind and keep saying whatever you feel to, then you are just wasting your time,

time which could have been well spent in listening. And instead you are just moving farther away.

The words which come from the master's side bring the master and disciple closer, and the words which come from the disciple's side create a distance. The union which takes place between the disciple and the master comes from the words of the master and the silence of the disciple. And a time comes when even the master puts his words aside. When the silence of the disciple has deepened, then the silent communion can take place. But the disciple should begin with silence.

So this is the condition: until your words have become free from the tendency to violence. You have to recognize this. It is very complicated because you do not even know which of your words do violence!

I was a guest in someone's home. The father called his son and said to me, "Please meet him – he is my 'good son'!" "Good son" is a good phrase, but the way he used it, it meant 'bad son'!

"Here stands my 'good son'," he told me. Then he said to his son, "Why are you standing there like a dummy? Touch his feet!"

Sometimes you cannot even inflict wounds with a knife the way you can with words. This son will never be able to forgive his father. It is very difficult to forgive your parents, it is very difficult, because parents don't know what they are saying. And they have no fear. Who fears a child? They say whatever they feel like saying. You do not realize what you are saying to your wife, what you are saying to your husband, how you are speaking to your servant, the manner in which you are speaking to your friend – what you are doing all around you.

There is a real need to become aware of this.
It will be good if you can keep silent during the period of this camp. And when you speak, think about the words so that no one is hurt by them. You will find that the quality of your words has changed, and you will find that the state of your inner being is changing. Just make a decision that you will speak as few words as possible.

Only if you have to, if you really have to, will you speak. If one sentence will do, then you will speak only one sentence. And if one word will do just as well, then make do with just one word. If a sign with your hand serves the purpose, then don't use any words. And if silence can serve the purpose, then that is the best. But if you still *have* to use words, use only as few as possible so that there is the least chance of hurting someone.

Someone is standing and meditating.... You pass by and laugh at him. Inside, you are saying, "What madness is he up to?" You have committed violence. And maybe that man is not very mature and is influenced by your thought and picks it up. And so what was going to happen in his life may not happen now. You will be responsible for this – you have committed great violence.

People say just about anything to each other. Someone says, "What type of madness have you got yourself into? Does meditation ever happen this way?" as if meditation has happened to him and he knows all there is to know about it. But no, people say whatever they want to.

Speak with caution and thoughtfulness. Consider every word before you speak. Then you will be able to see how your mind is occupied with violence. And this sutra says that until you have reached the stage where there is no violence in your words, until then, don't speak in front of the master.

Before the soul can stand
in the presence of the masters,
its feet must be washed in the blood of the heart.

It is only right that you wash your soul with your blood before you are able to stand in front of the masters. It is only a metaphor. It is essential to take one's own life through all kinds of fire so that one is purified, so that all the rubbish is burned away and only the pure gold remains. Then, and only then, the readiness to stand in front of the masters.... One should stand in front of the masters as if one is not.

That's why in Tibet the disciple makes a salutation at the feet of the master hundreds of times each day. Whenever he sees his master, he bows down to him, he prostrates himself at his feet, and only then goes on his way.

One young man came to me and said that he was learning meditation from a Tibetan lama. One thing he didn't like at all was the need to prostrate himself at the master's feet so many times. I told him, "Forget about the need – come back after three months of bowing down there, and then see me."

He said, "But what is the use of doing this?"

I said, "You will have wasted three months, that's all. As it is, you have already wasted thirty years of your life, so just think of it as wasting three more months. But first go on with the bowing down, and then return. And while falling at his feet, don't think. Just put your head down on the earth wholeheartedly, as if your head has become dust."

Three months later the young man returned and said to me, "What have you done? I used to think that all this was useless, that it had no meaning, that it was merely an exercise. What could happen by bowing down again and again? But for three months continuously.... Then it came to my mind that this ego, this pride searches for ways and means to escape. It says, 'What is the use of all this?' But after three months of falling at his feet, the ego inside me fell down too. I was able to understand the words of my master, which I could never understand before. And what I could never hear before, although he had always been saying it, I was able to hear it then."

Let yourself dissolve, burn away and be erased so that you can become empty, and in that emptiness you can relate to the master. This sutra is saying let these things become a part of your understanding.

Kill out ambition.

This is the first thing that the master will say. If all the preceding steps have been taken, then what all the masters of the world have always said is contained in this sutra:

Kill out ambition.

What is ambition? It is the desire to be something. It is the desire to be somebody – to become a president, to become a prime minister, to be a Rockefeller, to be an Einstein or a Buddha or a Mahavira – the desire to be someone, the madness to be somebody.

The first sutra is:

Kill out ambition.

Why? Because if you want to become something, you cannot be that for which you are born. If you wish to be something, you will not be able to realize your own self-nature – because you already are your self-nature, you don't have to become it. And what you wish to become will be a deception, will be an escape from yourself, will be an avoidance of yourself. Think of it like this: a rose wants to be a lotus flower. It cannot become one, but it can live in the illusion and thereby destroy itself. And in this destruction it won't even be able to be a rose; what to say about becoming a lotus flower!

Existence accepts you as you are; otherwise you would not exist in the first place. Existence accepts you whatever you are; otherwise it would not have created you. It does not repeat, there is no repetition. No matter how beautiful Buddha is, even so, existence will never make him again. Only those artists whose genius is so limited that they cannot come up with something new repeat themselves. Existence makes everyone unique and new. It makes each and everyone unparalleled. Rama may be very beautiful – but a repetition of him? And think: if many Ramas were born they would become meaningless and boring too! Now you would like to see Rama but in that case you would feel like running away from him. Enough – one Rama is sufficient! With more than one, things become stale. Existence doesn't like staleness.

So you have not been born in order to become a Rama, a Krishna or a Buddha. You were born so that you could come to be that which only you can be, and no one else; that which no one could become before, and no one will be able to become after. If you miss this, then this opportunity, this moment is lost for ever. Only you can become that which you are; apart from you, no one else can fulfill this destiny.

Drop ambition so that you can be rooted in your self-nature. Ambition makes you run around imitating someone else. It wants you to become like someone else so it says, "Run, hurry, do something!" All this doing will be false. It will only be on the surface, it will only be a cover – it will be false. You, as you really are, will remain hidden inside as a seed, and on the outside you will have pasted paper flowers.

Kill out ambition.

Just forget the idea that you have to become somebody else. You should think of only one thing: that you have to know that which God has made you. You don't have to become it – you already are it. Just keep one thing in mind: that you have to discover that which you already are. You don't have to become anything else. No ideals are required, you don't have to follow any blueprint.

The search for spirituality is not a search for ideals; the search for spirituality is to discover that which is already within you, to allow it to unfold.

Whatever you need is already there. And whatever you can become you already are – this very second. Not even an iota has to be added to it – rather something has to be just taken away. Whatever rubbish has been collected has to be removed. Nothing has to be added. There is a diamond hidden within the pile of rubbish.

And don't copy anyone else, don't try to become like someone else. This effort to be like someone else is ambition.

Kill out ambition.

**Ambition is the first curse:
the great tempter of the man
who is rising above his fellows.**

It is the simplest form of looking for reward.
Men of intelligence and power
are led away from their higher possibilities by it
continually.
Yet it is a necessary teacher.
Its results turn to dust and ashes in the mouth;
like death and estrangement,
it shows the man at last that to work for self
is to work for disappointment.

I have told you about one face of ambition. There is yet another face which, though it is secondary, keeps us very tightly in its grip. We are thrown around in its whirlpool quite a lot. That is the ambition to get ahead of others. One is the ambition to be like someone else, the second is the ambition to get ahead of others.

The second aspect of ambition is that which asks: "How can my house be bigger than my neighbor's, how can I become more famous than my neighbor, how can I outdo my neighbor?" You are always comparing yourself with someone. While you are thinking of yourself in comparison with someone else, you are not respecting yourself, you are insulting yourself – because you are not alike, so there cannot be any comparison between the two of you. All comparison is an illusion, and it is wrong. And you are not here to be like somebody else, you are here to be yourself. And what can happen even if you do get ahead of others? Because by the time you get ahead of one person you will find that someone else was already ahead of him. In this world one never reaches to a place where there is no one ahead of you.

Life is very complex. Even if you become the president... It can happen that while walking along the road, seeing a sweeper cleaning the road, an ambition may arise in you – because you don't have such a healthy body as he has. Seeing an ordinary man, jealousy may arise in you, even if you are the president, because you don't have such a beautiful face. Someone or other is always ahead of you in one way or another. There are a thousand ways to be ahead in life, and no one can ever be ahead of everyone in everything. This pain is always there.

Only the man who drops out of the race to get ahead attains to bliss. Only the man who says to himself, "I am completely fulfilled where I am – there is no question of getting ahead. I should become totally what I am; the question of comparing myself with anyone doesn't arise. Whatever I am should not be left incomplete; my flower should bloom fully, whatever kind it is. No matter if it is a simple grass-flower, it should bloom fully. Whatever way God has made me, I should become complete in that."

In this there is no comparison with anyone else. When a roseflower blossoms, another, bigger rose may have also blossomed in the neighborhood. But even if the first rose is a small flower, it is equally blissful and accepting of itself – the whole existence accepts it. It is dancing in the winds just as the big flower is.

There was a Zen monk, Bokuju. Someone asked him how he could become like him. He replied, "Please wait. Let the people go away first."

The man waited the whole day. He became tired, he became fed up – someone or other was always present. So by the evening when everyone had left, he said, "Now please don't delay any further. I have been sitting here all day long. Now tell me, how can I become like you?"

So Bokuju said, "Come outside with me."

There were many trees outside – some were small, some were big. Bokuju said, "See, this tree is small, this tree is big. I have never heard these two trees discussing the fact. The small one has never inquired from the big one how it can become big, nor has the big one ever asked the small one how it can become small....Because the flowers that bloom on the small one don't bloom on the big one, and they are very fragrant. The big one reaches high into the sky and the small one is not as tall. But these two never ask anything of each other, nor do they compare themselves with each other. For many years now they have been near my window: I have never heard any conversation between them, any questioning. And they are equally blissful; here is not one iota of difference in their joy, because each one has accepted itself. Whatever it is, it is so.

"If you really desire peace you also should not ask me this. Don't even ask me. You are whatever you are. And when I am not asking how to become like you, why are you asking me how to become like me?"

The man said, "I am asking because you are so peaceful and blissful, and I am so unhappy and worried. That's why I am asking how to become like you!"

Bokuju said, "I am telling you the knack, but you aren't even hearing it. I was telling you the method...that once I too was worried and unhappy because I was also trying to be like someone else. Once I accepted myself, the whole trouble disappeared."

In comparison lies unhappiness, jealousy and violence – so drop comparison! Don't assess yourself in relation to anybody. There is no meaning in it, and there is also no way to become the other. Become accepting of whatsoever you are. You should concern yourself with only one thing – how to manifest whatever you are totally.

Here, our search will be for the same thing. I don't want to make you into a Buddha, a Rama or a Krishna. There is no need – they have already happened. I want to make you into that which you can become. Only that seed which is within you should sprout. And I don't want to compare you by putting you in front or behind anyone else. No one is behind or ahead of anyone; everyone is in his own place. You will blossom from where you are, the fragrance that is hidden within your heart will be released. I want to make you just you.

Tomorrow morning we will do the meditation.
There will be four stages of ten minutes each.

In the first stage of breathing, let it be as intense and fast as you can make it, like the bellows of a blacksmith. Breathing, and only breathing, should remain.

The second stage of ten minutes will be for the catharsis of emotions. Whatever is lying repressed inside – pain, tears, screaming, shouting, anger, violence – all this has to be thrown out. And you are not only to think about it but to throw it out through the body. Let your body do whatever it wants to do in the moment, so that the weight of all this falls away from you.

In the third stage use the mantra "Hoo." Do it so loudly that it reverberates with a great echo. You have to throw the sound of "Hoo" outside. The effect of this sound "Hoo" is like a hammer on the kundalini. When the kundalini energy is hit inside, it begins to rise upwards. You will experience it for yourself. As the kundalini is struck, you will feel as if powerful storms of energy inside you are beginning to rise upwards. And with their rising, you begin to enter into another world.

In the fourth stage there will be silence for ten minutes, complete silence, in which the meeting with the divine will take place.

Now we will meet in the morning.

2

DESIRE FOR LIFE

2. Kill out desire of life.

3. Kill out desire of comfort.

Work as those work who are ambitious.
Respect life as those do who desire it.
Be happy as those are who live for happiness.

Seek in the heart the source of evil and expunge it.
It lives fruitfully in the heart
of the devoted disciple as well as in the heart
of the man of desire.
Only the strong can kill it out.
The weak must wait for its growth,
its fruition, its death.

The law of life is very paradoxical. It brings contradictory outcomes. For example, someone who wants to run away from his shadow finds out that while running away, his shadow is moving alongside him. There is no way to escape from your shadow by running away from it. If you stop, the shadow also stops. If you run, the shadow will chase you with equal energy. There is only one way to get rid of the shadow and that is to realize that it is a shadow, that it is not something substantial. Then whether it is there or not makes no difference. Running away from your shadow is not the way to save yourself from it – the only way is to become aware of the shadow's reality. Then, realizing that a shadow is just a shadow, you drop the effort to save yourself from it; after all, why try to save yourself from something that doesn't exist?

And the moment you drop the effort to escape, you are saved. This is the paradox. As long as you wanted to escape, you couldn't and as soon as you no longer want to, you can.

In the same way a living person may drown in the river, but a dead body won't; a dead body will float on the river. A living person drowns, a dead one floats – and this appears to be very contradictory. The laws of the river seem to be very illogical. The living person should be saved because even if the dead one drowns it doesn't matter – but it is the living person who drowns, and the dead one who doesn't. Perhaps the dead person understands the laws of the river better; he seems to know how to be with the river. But whatever the living person does, he gets into trouble.

What is it that the dead body knows that the living person doesn't? The dead body knows the art of leaving itself in the hands of the river and letting the river do what it wants to. If you can do that, the river will not allow you to drown, it will help you to float. The living person struggles with the river and in that very struggle he is destroyed and drowns. The river doesn't drown him; the person destroys himself through his own struggle and drowns. If the river can help a dead body float, it can also help *you* to float. And if a living person behaves in the same way with the river as a dead one, it will be impossible for the river to drown him. But to do this is extremely difficult.

To behave as if he is dead – that is the quality of a sannyasin. And the day a living person starts to behave like a dead body, he attains to the ultimate life. Life goes on slipping away from the hands of anyone who tries to save it by grabbing hold of it.

Jesus has said that if you try to save your life you will lose it, but if you are willing to lose it you will have abundant life, a full life.

These sutras point to this very paradox.

The first sutra says:

Kill out desire of life.

But why? Why should you kill out the desire of life? So that you may have life, so that you may attain to life, so that you may know it and live it, so that you can know what life is.

Those whose minds are filled with a desire for life cannot know life. This is contradictory. It should be that those who desire life get it – but they don't. They get only death, they only die, and their time is just spent in dying.

But someone who lets go of the desire for life, who says that he has no worry about life, no desire – "Even if death wants to come right now, let it come. I am not worried, I am willing to die" – that person comes to know that which is deathless. It is contradictory, but there is a reason for this contradiction. Only when it is very dark, and dense clouds have gathered in the sky, can the lightning be seen. If there is a background of darkness, blackness, then the lightning is bright. If you want to see the lightning then a background of black clouds is necessary.

For those who want to see life, it is necessary to accept the background of death. The spark of life shines bright for someone who has accepted death. The one who is afraid of death, who is terrified and tries to save himself from it, cannot see the spark of life. The acceptance of death and the realization of deathlessness are simultaneous. We are all afraid to die, but it is not as though this fear is going to save us from death! Death will come anyway, but because of this fear we don't see the life which is just here. As long as we remain afraid of dying, the life that is given to us passes us by. Our eyes are forever focused on death and life passes us by.

Life is here and now. To live life there is no need to go anywhere into the future. Life means *you* being here and now. You don't need to turn back, you don't need to go forward. You already have life, but your mind is either moving towards moments that have gone by in the past, or into future worries. It is lost in making plans for the future, in moments which have not yet even arrived. And in this way, the delicate stream of life keeps on flowing by, and you never become acquainted with it. You are never able to bathe in it, it never becomes possible for you to develop a relationship with it.

Kill out desire of life.

Why? So that you may have life.

A desire for life means the future. All desires are related to the future, no desire occurs in the present. This is a very strange thing: you cannot immerse yourself in any desire if you are *in* the present moment. Desire is always for the future, it is always in the tomorrow. For desire, time is needed; for its fulfillment time is needed, space is needed. Whenever you desire something, that very desiring is in the future.

If there is no future then the desire dies, and if there is no desire then the future comes to an end.

There are two possibilities: either the desire has to be dropped and then the person can be in the present, or, if the person moves into the present then too the desire is dropped – because there is no way to generate a desire here and now, in the present. What do you need right here and now? Think about it a little. What desire can you have in this moment? As soon as you desire you have moved into the future. There can be no connection between desire and the present. The moment you desire, you have left the present. You have removed yourself to tomorrow, to the coming day; your mind has run away.

So the meaning of "desire of life" is also that you are searching for life in the future. But life is here and now, life is you. You are standing in the middle of it, but your eyes are on tomorrow. That is why the present day cannot be seen, it is overlooked. That is why the sutra says to remove the "desire of life" – so that you can get to know life itself. Drop the desire for comfort; so that comfort may be yours.

Everyone is unhappy, comfortless – not because it is in the nature of life to be unhappy but because we do not know the art of being happy, being in comfort. We know the art of making ourselves unhappy, uncomfortable – to an unimaginable degree. We seek suffering. The man who desires for the future, and all desire is about the future, is bound to fall prey to unhappiness because the future never comes, it only appears to be coming. What actually comes is the present; what never comes is the future. No matter what you do, what you get is the present. And if your mind is in the habit of living in the future, then today you will live in the future, tomorrow too, and the day after. Whatever day comes, you will stay in the future. And how can you get what you want in the future? If the future never comes, when will your future wishes be fulfilled? The result will be unhappiness. That is why the fruit of desire is always unhappiness.

Life is not unhappiness, desire is unhappiness. The more desires there are, the more suffering there is. If you are very unhappy, don't think it is because existence is angry with you. If you are very unhappy that only indicates that you are full of desires. And when those desires remain unfulfilled, then wounds of unhappiness grow in your heart.

If you are very unhappy, don't try to drop unhappiness. Instead, drop desires – because unhappiness is only the fruit. It is desire that is the seed. The one who has sown the seed has shot his arrow. The arrow can be stopped only up to the point until it is released from the bow. After releasing it there is no way to stop the arrow.

Whosoever desires, suffers. He has sown the seed, he has planted the seedlings and now he will have to harvest the fruits. Whatever you are suffering now is because of the seeds of desire you have sown in the past. And if you do not want to suffer in the future, in the days ahead, then don't sow any seeds of desire today, because whatever seeds you are sowing now will bear fruit – if not today then tomorrow.

This is also worth understanding: your sufferings are in equal proportion to your desires. If you want more suffering, then desire more. If you *really* want happiness, then never ask for happiness. Then no one will ever be able to make you unhappy, no power on earth will ever be able to make you unhappy. Then, even if this whole world is against you, it cannot cause you one iota of suffering.

If you don't ask for happiness, then you step outside the circle of unhappiness. The moment you ask for happiness you enter into the world of unhappiness. However much happiness you ask for determines how much unhappiness you get.

This calculation never occurs to us, this paradoxical rule never occurs to us. That is why we suffer so much. We ask for happiness but what we get is unhappiness. We all put our efforts into trying to be happy but we make a fundamental mistake: happiness is not related to the effort, happiness is related to not asking for it.

Lao Tzu says, "No one is as happy as I am because I have never asked for happiness." Pearls shower on you when you do not ask. Someone who never asks for anything gets everything and the one who asks, loses everything. In this world, one who lives like a beggar lives unhappily and the one who lives like an emperor lives happily.

But who am I calling an emperor? I call that person an emperor who asks for nothing, not even happiness; and I call the person a beggar who, even if he asks for nothing else, asks for happiness. So those people we normally call emperors are actually beggars, because they are asking for happiness. And it sometimes happens that a beggarly-looking person is an emperor inside. We have seen Buddha – he goes begging on the road with a begging bowl but he is a real emperor. He is not asking for anything, he has given up the desire for comfort. And such a person becomes happy.

Experiment with this a little. During these days that you are here with me, don't nourish any desire for happiness, and then see how your heart becomes filled with happiness. Don't have any desire for peace, and see how the turmoil within you vanishes. Don't beg for contentment and see how contentment showers down on you. Please try this – only then will you understand.

This is the deepest experiment of life. And whatever has been discovered in regard to life, this is the most significant finding of all: don't ask for happiness if you want to be happy, don't ask for peace if you want to be peaceful. Whatever you ask for will be lost. Whatever you do not ask for you will get. You have asked many times and seen that you do not receive it. Now try not asking and see. There is no need to believe me; there is a need to experiment.

What can happen by my telling you this? Even if you understand it intellectually, it will bear no fruit – you will have to experience it. For the few days that we have, make a decision that at least during this time you will not ask for happiness, you will not ask for peace, you will not ask for contentment – and see what happens.

If you experience just once that you attain happiness by not asking for it, then I don't think you will make the mistake of asking for it again, because nobody wants unhappiness. If this much is realized, that it is through asking that you receive unhappiness, then asking can be dropped. There is no intrinsic need to ask – nobody feels good about asking anyway. But only if this extraordinary sutra is experienced will you understand this.

Work as those work who are ambitious.

Let go of ambition, but work hard like those people who are ambitious. Have you watched ambitious people and how madly they work? Someone has to become a member of the legislative assembly, someone has to become a member of the country's parliament, someone has to become a minister in the government – how madly they work for it! Just see their rat race! They never sleep, they never rest: for twenty-four hours a day they have only one concern. What devotion they have, what feelings they have for their cause!

The sutra says drop ambition, but work as hard as the people who are ambitious. The way the ambitious man runs madly after money, after power, after prestige – this madness has a quality to it, and it is worth learning from this type of madness. Have you seen the concentration of a man who is in search of money? When you sit for meditation, you sit down with the attitude, "Okay, if it happens it happens, and if it doesn't happen it doesn't happen." But when you run after money, you don't say to yourself, "If it happens it happens, and if it doesn't happen it doesn't happen." Instead you stake your life on it, you stake everything that you have.

In the search for dirt, man stakes all that he has. In the search for nectar he doesn't want to stake a thing.

Learn something – even from a person who is mad after money. Don't be mad about money but at least imbibe the madness. That madness will be useful. If you can put that same kind of madness into the search for truth, no one can keep it from you.

Look at Majnu, how crazy he is for Laila! If you can become love-struck for God in the same way, who will be able to stop you? What wall can hinder you? But many people become Majnus for Laila, many people go madly after useless things, but no one goes madly after something worthwhile. As far as the worthwhile is concerned, they show great prudence.

People come to me... I have a friend who is in politics and who is forever in search of political posts. He came to me and said, "Please help me so that meditation can happen to me."

I told him, "When you want meditation you ask for my help, but when you want to become a government minister, you work hard for it by yourself. Perhaps this word *help* is a cover-up? This is just a trick of yours, just something you want to get for free. You know that if you want to get ahead in politics you will have to work hard at it. But when you want to progress in your meditation you think that someone else will do the job for you. Perhaps you don't really want to go into meditation? You work hard to get where you want to but when you don't want to go somewhere, you just play with words and talk." But then I said to him, "Keep in mind that the day you become sincere about meditation and are ready to work hard for it, on that day, help will also come."

Help does not come for free; it has to be earned, you have to take steps towards it. And only those who are not miserly about helping themselves receive help. Only those who apply themselves receive grace – and that too is not for free. Nothing is for free, so how can the search for supreme truth and supreme bliss be free? This sutra says to let go of ambition, but to work as hard as the man who is ambitious.

Respect life as those do who desire it.

Let go of the desire for life, but don't let go of the quality which those people who are mad for life and who want to live at any cost have. Let go of your desire for life but have respect for all life.

Be happy as those are who live for happiness.

But do not desire happiness. Don't ask for happiness, live in happiness. This is worth understanding.

People ask how they can live happily – I tell them to live this very moment happily, and not to ask how. Breathing, breathe joyfully; if you raise your hands, do it joyfully; if you walk, sit, do it joyfully. Whatever you do, do it joyously so that your every action becomes a waterfall of happiness. Don't wait for happiness and don't even ask how. Whatever you may be doing, even the smallest of small jobs… If you are sweeping outside your house, do it joyously too – enjoy it.

Whatever you have to do, wherever you may be, don't do anything unhappily, because then, even if you enter heaven, you will enter unhappily; there too you will always manage to find reasons for being unhappy. You will be always looking for unhappiness, and there too you will generate darkness. Even if God himself is present, you will find that something or other is wrong, so that you can remain unhappy.

Whatever you are doing, do it happily. Don't ask for happiness. During these camp days, be mindful of this. *Live* happily, don't ask for happiness. Whatever may be happening, seek out where and how you can find happiness in it. Then even a dry crust of bread can give you happiness – if you know how to find it. If you know how to be happy, even ordinary water can quench you deeply. If you know how to be happy then even the shade from an ordinary tree will put palaces to shame. If you know how to be happy then just the song of the birds in the morning, or the sun rising, or the beauty of the stars at night, or even a small breeze, can shower you with happiness. Don't ever ask for happiness – live happily. The moment you ask, you have already begun to live in unhappiness.

Seek in everything around you to find where happiness lies. Happiness *is* there. And drink so deeply from it that not a moment goes to waste, not a moment is without it. Squeeze it. Whatever the source of happiness, squeeze it! When you drink water, when you take your food, when you walk on the road or sit under a tree and just take a breath, even then, live in happiness. Make being happy the art of living, and not asking for and desiring happiness.

There is so much happiness that you won't be able to gather it all. There is so much happiness that all your pockets and containers will seem too small. There is so much happiness that your heart will be overflowing – and not only will you become happy but whosoever sits near to you will be moved by the presence and dancing energy of your happiness. Wherever you go, an atmosphere of happiness will follow you: whosoever you touch, will feel the glow of your happiness. When you look at someone, flowers of joy will blossom there. You will have so much happiness inside you that you will be able to share it, it will start being shared.

Happiness, joy begins to share of its own accord. It begins to spread all around you. Waves of happiness will arise in you, and songs of joy will emanate from you. But happiness is not a demand; happiness is a way of living.

Please understand this difference correctly. Happiness is not a wish, happiness is the art of living. The moment you demand it, you have missed. Learn the art, start with this very moment. What is lacking in this moment? Everywhere around you birds are singing, the sun's rays are showering on you, life is blooming, you are alive. At this moment where is the shortage of joy? This moment is full of joy.

But if you desire, then you will become unhappy this very moment. Don't desire. Emptiness, silence…then who can be happier than you? The sutra says:

Be happy as those are who live for happiness.

Although all *they* get is unhappiness. People who live for enjoyment can never find happiness. But don't worry about them – *you* be happy.

Seek in the heart the source of evil and expunge it.
It lives fruitfully in the heart
of the devoted disciple as well as in the heart
of the man of desire.
Only the strong can kill it out.
The weak must wait for its growth,
its fruition, its death.

The mind has been conditioned through many lives, and for many lives you have done nothing but collect suffering. And this conditioning is pushing you again and again into the cycle of suffering. Sin has only one meaning and it is this: living with an unhappy attitude. This may sound a little strange. You may not have heard this definition before, that sin is to have an unhappy attitude. Why is this so? It is because a man who is himself unhappy inevitably enjoys making others unhappy. That is why it is a sin. Sin means causing unhappiness to others.

But before you can cause unhappiness to others you must have become an expert in the art of making yourself unhappy. How can you cause in others what you yourself do not have? If you are not unhappy how can you make others unhappy? You must first be unhappy yourself – and not in an ordinary way. You must be a great expert at it, because then you will know all the tricks and strategies of being unhappy in many different situations. Then, even if heaven is flowing all around you, you will still manage to find a corner of hell – because only then will you be able to be unhappy. And heaven is present and flowing all around you, but you still manage to discover a hell in it!

To cause suffering in others you need to be unhappy yourself. To make others suffer is a sin. So the fundamental meaning of sin is to cause suffering to yourself. Someone who does not make himself suffer will never cause suffering to others. He won't be able to do it, he won't even be able to think about it. And someone who does not cause suffering to himself will be so full of happiness that he will want to share it with others – because the more you share happiness, the more it grows.

Why do we want to cause suffering to others? – because we are very unhappy. And whenever we are able to make someone else suffer more than ourselves, we get a little thrill of happiness. That is our only happiness, that is the only happiness we know. If somebody is more miserable than you are, you feel a little thrill of happiness. This is not happiness – but relatively speaking it is because when you have managed to create more unhappiness in someone close to you, your own suffering appears small in comparison.

That is why we go on creating so much suffering all around us. An unhappy husband will make his wife unhappy; he will not feel happy until he can make her really miserable. An unhappy wife will make her husband unhappy, an unhappy father will make his children unhappy, unhappy children will make their father unhappy. Our whole society is a web of suffering in which we are all making each other unhappy. And when we have created pools of suffering all around us, standing in the middle of them we breathe a little more easily, thinking, "Never mind, we are not as unhappy as so many others are!"

And then while we busy ourselves causing suffering to others, we forget our own suffering. We don't even remember that we are unhappy. We become so occupied with causing suffering to others that we forget our own worries. That is why people who are busy causing suffering to others seem happy in a way, they seem not to worry about themselves. This is a way of forgetting yourself.

It is a sin to cause suffering to others and it is a sin to cause suffering to yourself.

The sutra says:

Seek in the heart the source of evil and expunge it.

Whenever some feeling of unhappiness takes a hold of you, throw it out – that very moment. Don't say yes to it, don't flow with it, don't identify with it. Whenever some feeling of unhappiness catches hold of you, immediately throw it out and look all around yourself for joy. If you are spared from becoming unhappy, you will be spared from hurting others. Then there will be no sin in your life.

Bliss is virtuous. And whenever you are blissful you become a virtuous soul.

That is why I don't say that you will become a virtuous soul by giving to charity. I don't say that if you build temples, mosques, *gurudwaras*, you will become a virtuous person. It is not necessarily so. It may be that this too is coming from your natural tendency to hurt others. You may be building a temple in order to cause unhappiness to someone. If your neighbor has donated one hundred thousand rupees, then you may donate two hundred thousand rupees – because until your ego becomes bigger than your neighbor's, you will not be able to hurt him.

I have heard about a very charitable man who had never ever donated even a single paisa. But he was very charitable – his charity was known all around – and he had never donated even a single paisa. If anyone in the village ever wanted to make a collection for a charity, they first had to go to him. This charitable man used to promise one hundred thousand, two hundred thousand, half a million rupees – and because he never had to give the money, he would promise liberally. And when he had written down half a million rupees, then the minds of all the other rich people of the village would become inflamed with jealousy and they too had to give. He never gave anything. He would write down half a million rupees, and sign his name – and this was his sole contribution to charity. And then all the wealthy people of the village would have to give something because their pride was hurt.

You can find these types of charitable men in every village. And those who collect for charity are fully aware of the fact that there should always be two or three names already on the list. Then, if you approach someone, his pride is stung and he has to give something. Even an ordinary beggar knows this and before he goes out begging he will put a few of his own coins into the bowl, because then, when he shakes and clinks them, you will think that someone has already given him something – even though you would not be willing to give him anything if your ego were not being put to the test. If someone has already given something before you and then you don't give anything, you will feel like a pauper in front of the beggar – and this hurts your pride.

Even the beggar knows not to approach you when you are alone, but in front of four people he will beg and touch your feet, because in front of four others it becomes a question of pride. In order to cause jealousy and suffering to others, you will even give to charity. You will even build a temple to cause suffering to someone else. You can do anything to make others unhappy, but then everything you do becomes a sin.

Bliss is virtuous because when you are blissful, whatever you do, bliss flows from it. Until whatsoever you are doing creates bliss, know that you have no idea of virtue. And if you do not destroy the very roots of sin, there can be no virtue– because the rocks of sin obstruct the spring-waters of virtue.

So remember one thing: whenever you feel that you are falling into an attitude of suffering, for whatever reason, don't hesitate – destroy it immediately, throw it out. Don't befriend it, even for a moment, because if you pause for just one moment, suffering will enter and spread its roots within you. So great courage is needed.

The sutra says:

**Only the strong can kill it out.
The weak must wait for its growth,
its fruition, its death.**

We feel very weak. We feel weak even about throwing out our own suffering. What is the reason for this? – because it would appear that if we don't want to suffer we should be able to throw out anything which causes us suffering. But no, we befriend and become intimate with our old sufferings; they become our family.

You may not be aware of this, but man's mind is very complicated. If you have an ailment and you feel it is a major disease and then you visit a doctor and he tells you that it is nothing but a cold, your mind will feel very hurt. The visit was futile! The mind doesn't like it when the doctor says that there is really nothing to worry about. A minor ailment for such a great person as you? A great man should have a great disease! The mind feels hurt.

If all your diseases were taken away from you at once, you wouldn't like it, even though if you were asked, you would immediately say that you are willing to let go of them all. But think about it again, and you will see that you wouldn't like it – because how could you live without your diseases? You would become very empty. What would you do? What would you cry about? What would you complain about? What excuse would you have to bite off your neighbor's head? What flag would you wave if all your diseases were taken away from you? You would become totally useless and empty – unoccupied, unemployed. All your business would come to an end. You would suddenly feel that without having any disease this world seems pointless. Without having anything to complain about, what will you do?

Right now you have plenty to complain about, so the day passes easily. Until now you have taken a great interest in discussing your troubles. Have you ever thought about it? – that you would not be willing for all your diseases to vanish suddenly with the wave of a magic wand?...Because you think that you are the sum total of all your diseases and that you might also disappear....

If someone's hands are chained for too long, the chains begin to feel like ornaments. Diseases also become a way of life, they become an occupation. A sick person tries to hold onto his diseases; the sufferer looks after his suffering. It becomes a kind of wealth.

And while I am telling you all this, keep in mind that it relates to you all. This is the law of the mind. So don't start thinking that "It may be true about some madman or other but as far as I am concerned I really want to get rid of my diseases." If you really wanted to let go of your sufferings, you could have done so a long time ago. You are holding onto them, so you must have found some way to take care of them. Otherwise, who is holding you back? You could have thrown them out a long time ago. No one is stopping you, no one is making you suffer, but there is some kind of complexity in your mind that protects your suffering.

Now psychologists say that there is even an investment in suffering, that you are invested in your suffering. A small child sees that when he falls sick his mother sits beside him and soothes his forehead. When he is sick his father, too, comes to visit him and pats his head. When he is sick no one scolds or nags him, everyone showers love on him. When he is sick he gets sympathy and understanding from all around. So one thing stays in the mind of the child: that when he is sick, everything is nice and good but when he is well, no one comes near him or pats him on the head – his father doesn't care about him, his mother doesn't worry about him – everyone is busy scolding him and trying to improve him. Then the whole world seems to be hard.

So the child's experience is that there is something wrong in being healthy. Perhaps there is something good in falling sick! When you are sick the whole world is friendly but when you are healthy the whole world becomes a stranger. So the idea of being sick starts to be attractive to the child's mind. From now on in his life, whenever he is in difficulty and begins to feel that the world is cold and hard, he will unconsciously want to become sick; and whenever he feels he is losing out in the world, that he has been left all alone without any friends, he will want to fall sick. And whatever one wishes happens.

Psychologists say that out of one hundred diseases, ninety of them have been invited by us; and because of these ninety, the remaining ten will find a way in too. Basically, whosoever you invite will come. No guest comes to your home uninvited. It is possible that you may not be aware of when you sent the invitation, you may not recall that in your sleepiness you sent the invitation. Or you may have sent the invitation many years ago and the guest has only just arrived – you may not be aware of the connection.

Whenever some disaster descends upon you and you want sympathy, pity, love – you fall sick. If a person falls sick in order to attract sympathy, he will never want to recover. He may go to the doctor, but unconsciously he will want to remain sick. He has an investment in his sickness.

Have you ever thought about it, that a person might not want to be sick if he did not gain anything from it? If a child falls over and his mother is there...he looks all around for her. If she is not close by, he doesn't cry. This is a very strange thing – but now to cry will be useless, there is nothing to gain from it, there is no investment in it. He will not profit from it, because the person who could have given him something is not there. So the child has a look around; he doesn't cry from the fall unless his mother is there. If she is present then he cries uncontrollably. If she is not around, he ignores the incident.

What does this mean? It was useless to cry, there was no sense in crying just then. It was not the right occasion, nothing could have been gained from weeping – he was not hurt by the pain. Suffering is a part of our nature, and we want to profit from that too! If he had spotted his mother he would have started crying immediately because then something could have been gained from it.

You must have seen women happily sitting at home, chatting away. When the husband comes home, their faces change they develop a headache, a back pain, a stomachache. Some trouble or other starts to brew! So many troubles start brewing in wives with the arrival of their husbands in the house! And it is not as if they are consciously or falsely creating these illnesses. It is an unconscious investment – and they are created just by seeing the husband!

The wife wants to be loved, and no husband shows love to his wife unless she is sick. If the wife is sick, love has to be shown to her. If he doesn't show it, then he feels guilty. So the wife falls sick to create that guilty feeling: "See, I am so sick and you are off to your club! I am so sick and you are engrossed in meditation. Here I am, sick and bedridden, and all you do is read the newspaper or your book – and I am so sick!" Deep down in her unconscious she is demanding love. Now it is very difficult to make her healthy because it is not just a matter of sickness. It is a matter of her clinging to her deep, unconscious suffering because she profits from suffering.

You are miserable because you gain something from it. And as long as you see some profit in your suffering, it will continue. But there is nothing to gain because it is suicidal. And if any tendency towards suffering surfaces, no matter how tempting it may be, no matter how much gain it promises – get rid of it, throw it out! All these promises are false and are deceiving you.

If a person continues to get rid of the desire for suffering in this way, he will soon find that where there was once suffering now springs of happiness bubble up.

Happiness is just near at hand – inside you are full of it. But until you drop this habit of suffering and your ways of enjoying suffering, these springs of happiness will not become available to you.

3

A SENSE OF SEPARATENESS

4. Kill out all sense of separateness.

Do not fancy you can stand aside
from the bad man or the foolish man.
They are yourself, though in a less degree
than your friend or your Master.

Remember that the sin and shame of the world
are your sin and shame;
for you are a part of it;
your karma is inextricably interwoven
with the great Karma.
And before you can attain knowledge
you must have passed through all places,
foul and clean alike.

As man has become more civilized, more and more educated and cultured, he has also become more anxious, restless and troubled. Why is this? As man's intellect grows, why does his unhappiness also grow? The reason for this growing unhappiness is because the whole development of the intellect is based on the idea and the feeling of duality. Intellect dissects, intellect separates; it analyzes, it draws boundaries, it defines.

The heart unifies. It shatters boundaries, it demolishes definitions and the mystery is born. The more heart there is in life, the less anxiety; the more intellect there is, the more anxiety.

Intellect divides. It is just like a prism: as the sun's rays pass through it, it breaks them into seven parts, and seven colors become visible. The same ray that was white before passing through the prism now divides into seven parts – it becomes seven-colored.

Sometimes in the rainy season, a rainbow forms in the sky because the drops of rain function like a prism, they break the sunray into seven colors. Intellect works just like a prism. Whenever you look through the intellect, things are broken down and separated into parts.

This is the danger of the intellect, but it is also its usefulness. If you have to define something, if you want to know something correctly, what it is, then you will have to dissect it., otherwise nothing will be known, because as far as existence is concerned, everything is one whole. So in fact, it will only be possible to know a single thing when the whole is known – which is an impossibility. Even a small pebble is connected, joined to the whole of existence; the whole of existence has taken part in the creation of even that small pebble. The sun has contributed, the sky has provided the space, the earth has given substance to it

– together they have made that piece of stone. The infinite has given life to it in infinite ways. So until we have understood the whole, we will not be able to understand that small piece of stone.

But this is extremely difficult. This means we will have to wait until all is known. And how is it possible to know about the whole? – it is so vast. In order to know even one small thing in this world, many other things need to be known first. So this means that ignorance becomes eternal…that we will never come to know.

The intellect helps us to know. It can do so because it can break things down and divide them into categories. It says that it is not necessary to know everything at once; one can also come to know something by breaking it down into parts. Science can stand on the strength of intellect. But there is a danger – and this is that the intellect also breaks down whatever is unified. It divides what is by its very nature an integral whole, into many parts. That's why whatever you learn with the help of the intellect can never be the ultimate knowing. It has to be a half-truth because so many parts remain unknown, so many basic aspects remain undiscovered. That's why science says that all its knowledge is only temporary, it can never be permanent. That's why science has to change and update its knowledge every day. Science keeps on changing every day.

Religion asks: what is the value of a knowledge that changes every day? What is the value of temporary knowledge? This means that what was understood to be knowledge yesterday becomes ignorance today – although it was ignorance yesterday too, but we didn't know that. What is knowledge today becomes ignorance tomorrow. As we come to know more, our knowledge will become ignorance. So then, what is knowledge?

Religion says that until we come to know the whole as the whole, we will remain ignorant. To try to know the whole by dividing it into parts is an illusion. It is useful, but an illusion. Illusions can also be useful. Science is one such illusion, it is very useful. Religion searches for another form of knowledge – real knowledge, knowledge which once known can never again become ignorance because it is eternal.

What do we have to do to attain this eternal knowledge? Just as science divides and breaks down, if we want eternal knowledge we must learn the art of synthesis. This first sutra points towards that very art. It says:

Kill out all sense of separateness.

There should be no duality, no sense of two. Only one should remain. And the day there is no distance remaining between you and existence, when you no longer even feel, "I am the knower and the universe outside is the one to be known," the day there is no distance between even the knower and the known, when all duality disappears, all barriers fall and you become one with existence – just as a dewdrop falls from the lotus and becomes one with the pond – the day when there is such a meeting between you and existence, only then what is worth knowing becomes known. Only on that day will what is known not be lost again.

Only that which is known brings liberation. Science bestows power, but not liberation – because science can only give us facts, which are useful, but it cannot give us eternal truth. There is only one process in the search for eternal truth, and that is to experience oneness.

But it is very difficult because all our ways of perception are based on the intellect. From wherever we look, everything turns into two. Now, I am talking, you are listening: this is one phenomenon. The speaker, here, is at one end and the audience, there, is at the other – but the phenomenon is one. What is happening here is one single phenomenon. Talking-and-listening is happening here, but it is not two things. At one end talking is happening and at the other end, listening. These are two poles of the same experience – the experience is one. But as you start to think, the speaker and the listener become separate.

At the moment of listening, when your mind is not at work but is silently listening, then there are not two. At the moment of talking, when the mind is not doing anything, is not thinking about anything, when pure speech and pure listening meet – only one remains. Neither the speaker is there, nor the listener is there; this is the point where understanding and dialogue happen. But where the speaker is separate and the listener is separate, then there will be only arguments...arguments will keep moving around inside.

In fact, the deeper we go within, the more we realize oneness. But the moment we return to thinking, it appears that things have become divided again, that they have become two, and that they have become separate. The one who is speaking and the one who is listening become different.

When two people are deeply in love or in a deep friendship, then there are not two in their love. Only love remains; the lover and the beloved both disappear. And only when this disappearance happens is love born. Until this disappearance, love is not born. But as soon as we start to *think* about love, the lover is separate and the beloved is separate.

When the devotee is engrossed in his devotion, no distance separates him from existence. If some distance remains, then the devotion is incomplete, it is not true devotion. In devotion, both the object and the devotee disappear and only a presence remains – both shores merge, leaving only one existence. But when we start to think about devotion, the object of devotion is separate and the devotee is separate.

But forget this example. Perhaps you have not even experienced love, because even the experience of love has become very difficult. And you certainly can't have had an experience of devotion, because that has become almost impossible. In a society where it has become difficult to experience even love, the experience of devotion is impossible. How can those who do not even know love know devotion?

Love is the only ladder in the world by which a person can ascend to the temple of devotion – but those who have not even loved in their life will never be able to understand its nectar.

This does not mean that love is devotion, but rather that love is a preparation for devotion. It means that if there is any phenomenon in the world which comes the closest to devotion, it is the love between two people. Why? – because in the deep love between two people non-duality is glimpsed. One gets only a glimpse, but that is enough.

When it is dark, when there is absolute darkness all around, even a single flash of lightning reveals much. It disappears again because lightning is not a lamp you can hold in your hand to seek the way, but on a dark night, if there is even one flash of lightning and you catch a glimpse of the road, your vision changes and your fear is overcome. Now you know that the path exists.

You have had just a glimpse of it, but you become fearless, knowing that now you can seek it out, now you can grope your way along. Now, even if you make a mistake and lose your way for a while, you will not lose your trust because you have had a glimpse of the way, and you know it is there. You may make a mistake in the dark, you may get lost, it may take time, but you will reach your destination because the path is there! Now a trust is born.

Devotion becomes possible in the lives of those who have had an experience of love. There is a trust – at least they have experienced two identities melting; a moment came when two could merge. Such a moment was possible for a second – it struck like lightning and vanished, but in that moment they could see that there were no longer two, and only oneness remained. From that moment the possibility of the divine and the devotee becoming one is substantial – it can be trusted, it can be depended upon.

That is why I say that devotion has become so difficult, because the possibility of love has become so difficult. But one thing needs to be understood – the phenomenon of the disappearance of duality. Let us look at it from a few other sides. Perhaps you may also have felt that in some moment you disappeared. No matter how that moment may have come about, from where it may have come; if there was even one such moment in your life...

Maybe it was an experience of beauty – you were sitting near a flower, and just looking at it your identity disappeared, the flower also disappeared, and only the fragrance of the flower, the beauty of the flower remained with you. Both poles vanished and only a perception of transparent beauty was left. Then you may get an idea of what this sutra is hinting at. Or perhaps there was a moment while listening to music when the listener and the musician were forgotten, and only the music remained. That may give you an idea of what the experience of non-duality is like.

And you will only come to know what this ultimate experience is like when it happens to you. But in the meanwhile, if there has been any moment of beauty, of love, some feeling of exhilaration in your life – when you felt that the knower and the known were no longer two, when you felt that the observer and the observed vanished and only a wave of experiencing remained – a wave in which both shores disappeared and only oneness remained... If you have ever had such an experience, it will be easy for you to understand this sutra.

If you have not, then meditation is a way to have such a realization. Try to immerse yourself in meditation in such a way that you are not even aware of meditation, that you do not even have the idea that you are meditating – not even the thought remains that you are meditating on something or someone – and you become so blissful that the concept of duality vanishes.

This is possible in the afternoon's *kirtan*, the devotional singing and dancing. If you become totally absorbed in the dance, the dancer vanishes, the outer world vanishes and one's "amness" also disappears. Only the act remains, a pure act of dance, of bliss, of great celebration. At such a peak point, in such a moment, all experience of duality vanishes and only one remains. This oneness is vast – all is contained in it. These trees close by are a part of it; the sky, too, is a part of it, and this earth. The whole of existence is included in it. Nothing is outside this experience; all becomes one in it.

Meditation is this kind of a realization. And when such a realization becomes so deep that it cannot be lost whether you walk, or sit, or eat, or drink; whether you are in the world or in a monastery, whether you are in a shop, or in a temple – when there is no way to lose this realization, when no matter what you do, it remains intact – then this very realization becomes samadhi.

We are undertaking a journey for this *samadhi*. That is why it is necessary to understand this sutra quite rightly.

The sutra says:

Kill out all sense of separateness.

Do not fancy you can stand aside
from the bad man or the foolish man.
They are yourself, though in a less degree
than your friend or your Master.

Remember that the sin and shame of the world
are your sin and shame;
for you are a part of it;
your karma is inextricably interwoven
with the great karma.
And before you can attain knowledge
you must have passed through all places,
foul and clean alike.

Many things have been said here, and they are worth considering. If it is true that existence is one – that I am not separate from it, that I am not an island – then my boundaries are only functional, and I do not end at these limits. Then, there is no "other"; then, whatever is happening to the other is also happening to me – perhaps at some distance, but it is also happening to me.

When Mahavira said no even to killing an ant, this is what he meant. The whole philosophy of non-violence is based on this feeling of non-duality. Not killing an ant does not mean that you should take pity on an ant, or even that it can be pitied; it simply means that whenever you are hurting someone, or causing suffering, or killing, you are unaware that you are being suicidal.

All types of violence are suicidal. If I am one with the whole of life, then whenever I inflict pain, I hurt myself. So keep this in mind: whenever you inflict pain on others, whether you know it or not, that pain also reaches to you, because the other is not different from you. There may be some distance between you; the other may be far away and the journey may take a long time – but we are all joined to one another. That is why if you cause suffering to anyone, you will also have to suffer. Without causing suffering to yourself you will never be able to cause suffering to others. That is impossible.

Just try making someone unhappy and you will also become unhappy. And the reverse is also true. Just make someone happy and watch: you will find that happiness starts echoing in your heart in many ways. If you remove even a small thorn from someone's path, many thorns will be removed from yours. If you put just one small flower on someone's path, you will find a carpet of flowers is strewn on yours – because whatever you do goes on echoing endlessly all around you. And it can echo endlessly because you are connected with the whole, you are one with it.

If even one small thought arises in you, the whole of existence hears it. Even one small feeling in your heart can be heard reverberating all through existence. And it is not as if this will only happen today; it will be heard for eternity. Your form will be lost, your body will fall apart, your name will disappear – it will become difficult to be sure that you ever even existed – but whatever you desired, whatever you did, whatever thoughts, whatever feelings you had will all keep echoing throughout existence. You may no longer be here but you will appear somewhere else. You may be lost to this world, but your seed will sprout again in some other place.

What we do and what we are is never lost, because we are part of a vast, infinite whole. The wave vanishes but the ocean remains intact; and the water from that wave also remains in the ocean.

It is necessary to understand this from many angles, because it will have a far-reaching effect on your life, your behavior and your future. If this can be deeply understood by you, you will become a totally different person. You have made one type of life for yourself based on the understanding that you are a separate entity – and that is why man is anxious, troubled and unhappy. In reality you are not a separate being; all your attempts to separate yourself fail. And in the end you discover that you have failed to separate yourself.

What is death? Death is nothing except the shattering of your false belief that you are separate. Death takes you back into non-duality. If you were able to go into non-duality on your own, then death would not happen to you. But as you are, death is absolutely necessary for you because on your own you seem to have no desire to return to the experience of non-duality.

You were in a state of non-duality before your birth, and after death you will return to that same state. Just for a while, in between, there is this wave with all its sound and fury, its momentary rising and its dance in the sunshine. And so for a time the wave gets the idea that "I also exist." Each wave must feel that it is separate from the ocean, it must. And it must also feel that all the waves rising around it are separate from it. It must feel like this – and there is a logic behind it. If the wave has its logic, if it has its own intelligence, then it will wonder, "How can I be one with the other waves?" It may think, "Some waves are so small, some are so big. We are all so different – how can it be that we are all one?" It will also wonder, "Some waves are falling, while I am just beginning to rise, so how can I be one with the falling waves? If I were one with the falling waves, I would be falling too. Or if a falling wave were really one with me, it would also be rising, like I am."

You look around and you see that someone is dying and you are young; someone has grown old and someone else is a child – how can we all be one? If we were all one, then when you die, they should all die with you.

But we know that even if one wave is rising and the other wave is falling, all waves are one, they are all joined at the center. And the falling wave is going back into the same water that the other wave is rising from. At the depths there is no difference between these two waves – all this is just the play of one ocean. Just for a little while the wave has taken a form; then the form is lost and only the formless remains.

We too are nothing more than waves. In this world everything is a wave. A tree is a wave, a bird is a wave, a stone is a wave and so too is man. If all are waves in the same ocean, then this leads us to a very far-reaching conclusion. And that conclusion is in this sutra:

Do not fancy you can stand aside
from the bad man or the foolish man.

Do not think that the bad man is bad and you are good, because the bad man is also connected with you. And the truth is that if the bad man were banished from this world, that very same day the good man would also disappear. If there were no devil in this world, nothing ungodly, if there were no thieves, no murderers, no dishonesty, the saint would also vanish along with them. How can the saint live without the devil? Have you ever thought about it? The godly lives side by side with the ungodly; they are two faces of the same coin. The man who is good, who is a nice man, a religious, pious man, only exists because of the irreligious; he cannot exist without the irreligious.

There is no way for Rama to exist without Ravana; no way either for Ravana to exist without Rama. So people who only look superficially think that there is great enmity between Rama and Ravana. Those who can see more deeply know that it is difficult to find a deeper friendship than the one that exists between these two – because how can we call what we need in order to exist, an enemy? What we cannot exist without is our true friend. How can you call someone who makes your very existence possible, who is a part of your very foundation, an enemy? And if this is the case, then you will have to completely change all your definitions of an enemy: an enemy is even closer than a friend.

Can Rama exist without Ravana? Have you ever thought about this? If you cut Ravana out of the story of Rama, it becomes immediately pointless. The dynamics of the story only exist because of Ravana. Rama's whole dignity exists because of the presence of Ravana. Rama's goodness only becomes clear in contrast to Ravana's evil. Without Ravana, Rama would be just like white chalk writing without a blackboard: if the blackboard is removed the white chalk also disappears. Those white letters stand out not only because they are white, but because they are written on a blackboard. The blackboard has a hand in their whiteness. They stand out so clearly only because of the blackboard. If the blackboard were removed, the white letters would also vanish.

It is a curious fact of life that if the desires of the so-called saints were fulfilled, and the whole world were to become saintly, then they themselves would disappear. Without realizing it, they are busy trying to efface themselves, but so far they have not been successful. And they will never succeed, because they cannot exist without the unsaintly. Just as it is not possible for the day to exist without the night, just as darkness cannot exist without light, and birth is not possible without death, so all opposites are connected.

No intelligent person should think he is separate from the retarded. No beautiful person should think that he is separate from the ugly person, no healthy person should think that he is separate from the sick. We are all connected. Deep down we are all connected.

If this connectedness is understood, then the intellectual's ego will drop away – because what is this intellectual man's ego in the first place? His ego resides in the thought that he is not retarded. But without the retarded person, his intellect has no meaning.

Intellect only exists in relation to retardedness. What kind of power does this give the ego? Is there anything in this world more impotent than the ego? The ego of the intellectual is just this: that he is not retarded. But his intellect is dependent on the existence of the retarded.

The leader thinks that he is not a follower – but can there be a leader without followers? He is only a leader because there are followers. If a great man thinks he is great, he is not really great. He is simply forgetting that it is only in relation to the ordinary people that he appears to be great. The truly great man sees this point: that he appears great only in relation to the ordinary man. Then even greatness becomes ordinary, because how can a greatness which needs ordinariness as a buttress be called greatness? And this applies to both sides.

If the intellectual can only see that the idiot is just the other side of the same coin, his insulting attitude, his disregard for the idiot will disappear and a feeling of brotherhood will be born. If the saint can only see that the unsaintly are just the other side of the same coin, his condemnation of them will come to an end; a deep friendship and love will arise in him even towards the unsaintly. And until such compassion is born in the saint, know well that he has no idea of non-duality.

The moment you have experienced non-duality, the opposite also becomes a part of you. Then, the religious person knows the sinner is his other side, the religious person knows that as long as sin is happening on this earth, he is a part of it. This is a little complex, so it has to be understood.

As long as there is sin on the earth, I am a participant in it – whether I sin or not. If I sin, then of course I am a participant, but even if I don't sin, I am still a participant because I am a part of this world's consciousness, and if this consciousness commits a sin, I am a participant.

Buddha has said somewhere that as long as even one person is still tied up in the chains of ignorance, how can anyone know liberation? If even one wave of the ocean is polluted, how can another wave become pure? It could only happen if the waves were separate – then one wave could be pure and one remain impure. But if all the waves are a part of one ocean, then we have to give up the duality of pure and impure, we have to give up differentiating between the holy and sinful; we have to realize that they go hand in hand. Someone who understands this, who perceives that they go hand in hand, transcends both. And someone who goes beyond both is a religious man.

Let us look into it a little more deeply. The holy man is the opposite of the unholy man, and the unholy man is the opposite of the holy man. There is no opposite to the religious man – that is why we make a distinction between buddhahood and knowledgeability. Knowledgeable people and ignorant people are opposites. But someone who understands and treats both knowledgeable and ignorant people alike, and sees that knowledge and ignorance are connected has attained to buddhahood. We say that he has attained to wisdom.

Real knowledge is not the opposite of ignorance; it is actually a transcendence of both knowledge and ignorance.

This is a little difficult to understand: to be relieved of ignorance and become wise – this much we can understand. Not to sin and become holy – this we can understand. To drop a bad character and become a good man – this too we can understand. But this perception is based on duality, and it has no relationship with true religiousness. This type of understanding is childish! This kind of knowledge is full of ignorance. On the surface it appears to be knowledge, but underneath it is only ignorance – because all that seems to be opposite is connected underneath.

This then means... Gurdjieff used to say that the more emphasis you put on having a good character, the more incentive you are giving to the bad character to grow. This seems a little difficult to understand, but Gurdjieff is right in what he says, because the proportion of both will always remain constant. That is why the more morality there is in the world, the more immorality there is.

People generally believe that there must have been an age when only morality was prevalent. This is not so. There could never have been such an age; there could never have been a time when morality and only morality prevailed. It can only mean one thing – that there was so little of either, that the presence of immorality was never felt. Today, both of them have increased tremendously. Today, morality is at its peak and immorality is also at its peak. That is why both of them are clearly visible. Today, the difference can be very clearly seen because both have reached the extreme. Both rise and fall at the same time.

Look at it this way: a small mountain is bound to be surrounded by small valleys. If a mountain is high, touching the sky, the valleys surrounding it will have to be deeper. You are just being foolish if you think that a mountain can be high without having any valleys, because this can never happen.

Nietzsche has said that the tree that wants to touch the sky must extend its roots deep into the earth. The more a tree rises upwards, the deeper its roots will have to go underground. If you think that a tree can touch the sky but have no deep roots, you are deluding yourself. No seasonal plant can touch the sky because its roots are not capable of going deep enough. The more it rises upwards, the more it has to go downwards. This is life's balance.

So if you want society to be very moral, you will also have to be prepared for an equal amount of immorality. If you want society to become very intelligent, unintelligent people will also have to be born in the same ratio; if you want very intelligent people, you will have to accept idiots as well. There is no way to avoid it. This is the law of life and nothing can be done about it. If you want very beautiful people, you will also have to tolerate very ugly people, because beauty can exist only in contrast to ugliness. The wise can exist only in contrast to the ignorant – there is no other way. If you want no sin in the world at all, you should be prepared to let go of all virtue as well. Then sin cannot be committed. If you want no ugliness in the world you should drop all criteria of beauty, you should forget about the notion of beauty. Then no one will be ugly because without the criterion of beauty how will you assess what is ugly? If you want no fools in the world, you will have to get rid of all the intelligent people. If you don't want the unholy, you will have to say goodbye to the holy men. They come together, all opposites move together.

But there is a way out: not to choose between the opposites. That is what this sutra is saying – do not choose between opposites. Just know that they are one. The beautiful and the ugly exist because of the same criterion. The wise and the foolish exist because of the same criterion. Rise above them both. We call someone who transcends both a religious man, a great soul. We call someone who transcends both an awakened one – cause only he comes to know truth. Anyone who is lost between the two, this way or that, will never realize truth, because truth contains both.

And in choosing, you choose only one and reject the other; but where will the other go? The other also exists. You say that godliness is light; then what will happen to darkness? You like light, so you call godliness, light. This only indicates your choice, but then what will happen to darkness? Darkness also exists. And if there is a god of light, then there will be two gods – a god of darkness too. Then there will be trouble! These two gods will fight and no one can win. This war will be endless and pointless. It will be a false war because for light to exist, darkness is needed, and for darkness to exist, light is needed. So this war will be a false and meaningless fight.

It is just like most of your wrestling; in reality the game is rigged, they only pretend to fight and there is a lot of hullabaloo. They make a big fight out of it and the spectators are very impressed, very excited. But everything has been settled beforehand; even who will win and who will be defeated has been settled beforehand. In one competition one wins, in the next, the other one wins; and fighting in yet another town, again, the first one wins. It is a partnership.

Similarly, there is a partnership between light and darkness; there is no fight between the two of them. And those who see a fight are getting unnecessarily excited, they are getting worried for no real reason. You can transcend both. In the state beyond both, they are one. The divine is both and neither; it is neither light nor darkness – it is both. And so we cannot call it light or darkness – it is transcendental.

The sutra says:

Do not fancy you can stand aside
from the bad man or the foolish man.
They are yourself, though in a less degree
than your friend or your master.

You may well think that someone is very, very close to you, but it is not exactly so. And no matter how far away someone may be, all distance is only another form of closeness. The opposite is also true: no matter how close you come to someone, all closeness, however deep, is but another name for distance. No matter how close you come to someone, the distance always remains. Even if you embrace each other, a distance remains. That which is closest is still a form of distance. The distance may be small, but what is the difference between small and large? Distance is distance – what does it matter? Whether the distance between you and me is a mile or an inch – what does it matter? Distance is distance.

That which is near is also far, that which is far is also near, because near and far are measured on the same scale: distance. Both are a way to describe distance. Near and far away are both ways to describe distance. A friend will be near, an enemy will be far away. Whatever appeals to you seems to be very close; that which you dislike remains at a distance. But if you look a little more deeply, you will see that these are only relationships. And relationship as such happens only between distances. You cannot have a relationship when you have become so close to something that there is no distance left. You need distance for a relationship. You say "this is my wife," "this is my beloved," "this is my son," "this is my father." All these are only ways to describe distances. A relationship happens only between distances.

If two banks of a river come close, so close that no distance remains, there will be no need to build a bridge between them. And if the river's banks come so close that no distance remains, the river will be lost. It will not be possible for two banks to exist; what remains will be one.

All our relationships are just names for the respective distances between us, or simply tricks to cover up the distances. After we have given a name to a relationship, we mistakenly feel that now all distances have ceased to exist. We say to someone, "This is my wife," and this makes us feel that all distance has vanished. But a husband and a wife are as far away from each other as anyone can be. The distance never disappears. In this world distances can never be erased, they will always remain. But someone who can raise his consciousness beyond this world will suddenly discover that all distances have vanished; then the river becomes the bank and the bank becomes the river – there is no gap. The boat becomes the river, and the river becomes the boat; all distances disappear, because in all opposites he has experienced a oneness.

These rules, these sutras are to help you to perceive the oneness that exists in opposites.

Remember that the sin and shame of the world are your sin and shame...

In this world if anyone feels proud of being a religious man, you can be certain that he still has no idea of what it means to be a religious man. And if someone tells you that he is a very pious man and you are a sinner, know that he is deluded and ignorant. Anyone who has come to know even a small part of life's truth will immediately see that he is a participant in whatsoever is happening anywhere. If there is a war raging in Vietnam and men are being butchered there, if a war is raging in Bangladesh and men are being slaughtered there; or if there is a famine, a massacre, violence or looting somewhere – he too is a participant in it.

Certainly he has not done anything directly; he has not gone to Vietnam to take part in the fighting, he has not killed anyone in Bangladesh – so how can he be responsible? How is he involved? But he *is* a part of this world, and so he has a hand in whatever is happening in it, whatever is being manifested in it at this moment. He is in this world and just that fact makes him a participant. By just being here he becomes a participant. And knowingly or unknowingly he must be doing many things which have a hand in this violence, even though the end result is happening far away from him.

If he says that he is a Hindu and not a Mohammedan, he is creating strife in the world; even if he does not take part in the Hindu-Muslim riots. Maybe he even tries to bring about a settlement when Hindu-Muslim riots take place. He may even sing songs about Rama and Allah being one. He may try to reconcile people, but just by saying that he is a Hindu and the other is a Mohammedan, and that they are separate, he has a hand in the riots even though he may not take part in them. He may not take part in the wars in China, Vietnam or Bangladesh but if he asserts that he is an Indian, then he is dividing the world. He sees the earth as divided into so many parts, and in seeing that, he is participating in the war. Whatsoever may be happening in world politics, directly or indirectly, he has a hand in it. There is no escape from it. Sartre has said somewhere that man cannot escape, no matter how hard he tries.

Two people are standing for election in your village and you don't vote for either. But don't start thinking that you have got out of it – because not casting a vote is as decisive as casting one. Because you have not voted one person has won, whereas if you had voted, the other one might have. So if you vote, one person wins, and if you don't, someone else wins. You cannot escape, you cannot run away. You cannot say that if you don't vote you are not a participant – because by not voting someone else can win. So you have become a participant in it – maybe from a distance – but still, you are a participant. Even if you keep silent and you don't say anything, still you are a participant. Your silence may become a support. While you are living in this world there is no way to escape from it.

Someone who feels that he is an integral part of this world, and that all its sins and good deeds are attributable to him, is moving towards true religiousness. He has no condemnation for anyone – because to condemn the other is to condemn himself. He does not single someone out for praise, because all praise is self-praise. Such a person is able to step aside and see life beyond the struggle between praise and condemnation. Only then one attains to the state of being a witness.

Once you experience that there is no way to be freed through your actions, only then can you become disidentified with the doer and become a witness. The witness means that "I am simply a watcher, and whatsoever is happening I am also a participant in it – because I exist. That is why I will not say that you are a sinner – because I am also here. Nor will I say that you are virtuous – because all these differences are just superficial, illusory and dangerous. So I will say just this much: that whether it is virtue or sin, good or evil, war or peace, I am a witness to both, a watcher of both."

One who has attained the state of simply witnessing enters non-duality.

…you are a part of it;
your karma is inextricably interwoven
with the great karma.
And before you can attain knowledge
you must have passed through all places,
foul and clean alike.

Whether good or evil is happening in this world, they are both a training for the disciple. One has to go through both sin and virtue, and grow through both. You can make use of them both to help you transcend. You can turn both sin and virtue into stepping stones.

And if there is some evil in you, you can put that to some creative use, you can learn something from that too. And even through the pain and suffering of it, some growth will come to you; you will become more aware. You may burn in it, it may cause you pain – but that too will be helpful in your awakening. And that pain will stop you from repeating the same mistake again. In this world everything can be used.

Such an understanding is called *sadhana*, spiritual discipline. Spiritual discipline does not mean to drop evil and grasp hold of virtue. Spiritual discipline means to rise towards ultimate truth through both good and evil. Do not choose between good and evil; extract the essential experience from both, and let them both mature you. Let both go deep into your understanding and expand your heart. Steer your boat between the two; let your river flow between the two and out to the ocean. Let sin and virtue become your banks.

Don't choose. If you choose sin you are still choosing one of the banks and you will not be able to flow with the river. If you choose virtue you are still choosing one of the banks and you will not be able to flow with the river. Whether the bank is of sin or of virtue, it is static, it does not reach to the ocean. It is the river, which makes use of the banks and flows between them, that reaches the ocean. If there is some evil in your life, make use of it. There is no need to be afraid of it; make use of it.

A friend came to me and said, "I don't think I will be able to meditate. I am a drunkard, and the habit has taken such a hold of me that I can't drop it in this lifetime. Now I will have to wait until my next life to do it." He had tried in many ways to drop the habit, but all had proved futile. Now he had even given up trying, because after so many failures he had also lost his resolve. He had faced so many failures that he had lost all hope that he could fulfill any pledge. So he asked me not to ask him to drop drinking. "If there is a way in which I can meditate irrespective of my drinking, please tell me," he said.

I told him, "You are drinking because you are in search of meditation."

He was startled to hear this. He said, "It's true what people say – that you are a dangerous man and I shouldn't have come to you! I thought you would definitely give me some method to help me drop my drinking and assure me that I could do it. But you say that drinking is a search for meditation!"

I said, "Try to understand. If you can understand that drinking too is a search for meditation, then it can be dropped. After all, why do you drink? Forget about the drinking itself...tell me, why do you drink?"

He said, "I drink to forget myself."

I told him, "The desire to forget oneself is the desire of the meditator too. To lose yourself, to drown, is also the desire of the meditator. You have taken up drinking by mistake. You want to drink meditation and instead you are drinking alcohol! So I won't ask you to give up drinking, instead I will ask you to learn the art of losing yourself of drowning yourself, from alcohol. And once you have learned the art of drowning, of forgetting, you won't have much trouble giving up the support of wine. If you can drown and forget yourself without the help of wine, the habit of drinking will also disappear. You are not a drunkard, you are a meditator; it is only that you have adopted the wrong type of meditation."

So then he asked me, "Can I come to learn meditation? – but I will still continue to drink."

I said to him, "Don't mention wine to me! I am going to give you a new type of wine – drink that! If this new taste suits you, the old will become tasteless. Until you have begun to like the new wine, it is foolish to drop the old one – and there is no point in it either. First have a good experience with the new wine, see if it has some substance.... And if meditation does not have enough substance even to make someone drop drinking, there is no point in hoping that it will lead him to the divine. After all, if one can't drop a small thing like drinking, meditation must be weaker than alcohol. And you should always choose strong friends. What is the use of choosing weak ones?"

So he came along. He was skeptical, but he became really immersed in meditation, more immersed than people who have never even touched alcohol. This was because he already knew how to let himself be drowned. Those who have never drunk wine don't know how to drown themselves.

Now, by this I do not mean that you should start drinking. That is not necessary; you can go into meditation without having ever drunk wine. But if you have tasted wine, it is good to make use of the experience.

It is not good to waste any experience in life – its essence should be extracted.

This man immersed himself deeply in meditation, and the alcohol disappeared. But then he came to me saying, "You deceived me! If you had warned me before that it would be like this, I would never have come. You never talked about dropping alcohol. I assumed that 'This man is okay because he never asks me to stop drinking – instead he makes me meditate, so I have nothing to lose.' But now I am so engrossed in meditation..."

But you will be surprised to know that his wife came to see me and said, "What have you done? He was better off as a drunkard!" Can you see how strange life is? The wife said, "He was better off as a drunkard because at least he was afraid of me. Now, after becoming a meditator, he is not afraid of anyone! When he was drinking, I had a hold over him: coming into the house he used to tremble – and feeling very guilty, he would ask for my forgiveness. Now the whole situation has turned upside down. Before, when he drank, I could make him agree to a thousand and one things and he had to listen to me. Now, I have to give in to him and agree to whatever he says."

So don't believe if a woman says she wants her husband to give up drinking, that she really means what she says; or that if a father asks his son to stop stealing, he really means for him not to steal. Life is very complicated. Only if you drop some bad habit will you come to know how much trouble it causes around you.

Everywhere in the world people say, "Be good," but they only say this because they know you can't be – and by saying it they can criticize you and put you down. It is a way of dominating one another. And if by some chance you really become good, the very people who were harassing you to be good will be the first ones to be unhappy with you, because they lose their hold over you. The person who was once under their thumb has now become free.

So there are power politics going on inside all the people who are urging you to become good. No one is really interested in seeing anyone else becoming good, because when you see someone else as good, you feel inferior and see the other person as higher than you. Such is the complexity of life.

But it is important to keep one thing in mind – wherever you are, whatever you are, the road to the divine leads exactly from there. There is no place from where the road to the divine exists. So make use of whatever place you may find yourself in, and turn all experiences towards the divine.

Even the most evil experience can be turned towards it; and even the most sinful experience becomes virtuous the moment it is turned towards the divine. And all this will be easy to do if we keep one thing in mind: that we are not separate in this vast universe, we are all part of one consciousness; we are all the waves of one vast ocean.

4

DESIRE FOR SENSATION

5. Kill out desire for sensation.

Learn from sensation and observe it,
because only so can you commence
the science of self-knowledge,
and plant your foot
on the first step of the ladder.

6. Kill out the hunger for growth.

Grow as the flower grows,
unconsciously, but eagerly anxious
to open its soul to the air.
So must you press forward
to open your soul to the eternal.
But it must be the eternal
that draws forth your strength and beauty,
not desire of growth.
For in the one case
you develop in the luxuriance of purity;
in the other
you harden by the forcible passion
for personal stature.

Bliss is very subtle. The voice of the divine is a whisper. Only those who have freed themselves from the pull of useless voices, who are no longer attracted by them, can hear it – but we live in the noisy crowd. The flavor of the divine is very subtle, only those whose capacity to taste has not been destroyed by running after stimulation will be able to experience it.

But all our senses are restless for stimulation. And the law of the senses is that the more stimulation they are given, the more their need for excitement increases. It is just like a man who drinks one glass of wine today and becomes unconscious; tomorrow he will need two glasses – one will not be enough. He has developed the capacity to absorb one glass of wine, so now one will not be enough to create the same effect. Tomorrow two glasses will be needed, and the day after tomorrow even two will not be enough. The body will be able to absorb their effect, so now three glasses will be needed. And a time may also come when wine becomes just like water and doesn't affect him at all. Then more intoxicating poisons will be needed.

In Assam there is still a small Tantric sect which keeps a pet snake. Other types of poison no longer create intoxication in these people, only if the snake bites them on their tongues is there some degree of intoxication.

Slowly slowly, in this mad race for stimulation we lose all sensitivity. The stronger the stimulants we use, the more the capacity of the senses to feel and experience decreases – in the same proportion. Then more and yet more stimulation is needed, and there is no end to it. Finally, the senses are completely numb.

If you prefer foods which strongly stimulate your senses, your capacity to taste will quickly disappear. Then, no matter how many spices you add, you will find the food is tasteless. What is this interest in spices? They have strong stimulants that wake up your taste buds. But what we take for stimulation starts having a deadening effect. Then if you eat food without spices, it will taste like mud. You will have lost the sense of what food should taste like; your ability to taste will have diminished. This seems paradoxical: in your efforts to increase the sensation of taste, your ability to taste has decreased. You cannot taste food in the same way as Mahavira or Buddha would have done.

That is why I keep saying that it is difficult to find people who are enjoying more than those whom we call renouncers, because whatever they experience is very pure. The taste Buddha experiences from drinking water – you will not be able to get even from drinking your wine, because the less the senses are stimulated, the more capable, finely-tuned and subtle they remain.

If you are used to listening to loud rock music, you will not be able to hear the soft voices of the birds – but they too have their song. You will not be able to make out the voice of the cricket in the stillness – but it too has its song. The winds which pass through the trees have a song in their whispering – but you will not be able to hear it. And this much stimulus is certainly enough to prevent you from hearing the echo of the song arising from within your own heart. You will never be able to know the music of *omkar* which resounds in the depths of your innermost sky. And someone who has never heard the music of his heart has not heard anything at all. He has remained deprived of the supreme melody.

So before we go into the sutra, the first thing to keep in mind is this: that the more intense your rush for excitement, the less your capacity to experience. That is why there is a lot of excitement in the world today, but very little experience. Never before have so many different kinds of pleasure been available in the world. Even in the ancient scriptures, the descriptions of heaven do not mention such a wealth of pleasures. Everything imaginable has been realized; science has made our dreams come true. There are so many different methods to experience so much – but the experiencer, the man, has become totally insensitive.

Just a few days ago a young American girl came to see me. She told me that she had read my book, *From Sex to Superconsciousness*. After reading it she came to me and said, "I don't have any interest in meditation, nor am I searching for God. But I don't feel or get any enjoyment out of sex, and I am worried about this. I don't experience any kind of enjoyment, I don't feel any sensation whatsoever. I have been treated by doctors, I have been analyzed by psychologists, I have already wasted thousands of dollars, and I still don't derive any pleasure from sex at all.

Since you have written this book, I thought I should come to you."

So I asked her what different experiments she had tried with sex.

You may not have heard about this, but it has become very popular in America: they have made a mechanical penis, a vibrator, in the shape of a man's penis, which operates with a battery or electricity. So this woman had been using a vibrator. Now, if you use a vibrator your sexual senses will become totally insensitive because no man's penis can have the same power as an electric vibrator. So I told her, "You don't have any problem other than this vibrator. It has destroyed you, so drop it." Whichever sense organ it may be, if you fall into a mad rush for more and more stimulation – and certainly the vibrator is very stimulating – that sense's capacity will be lost.

You will be surprised to know that Tantra has experimented to produce subtle experiences even with sexuality. It has found that even friction between the sexual organs is unnecessary. Instead, the sexual energy which arises at the sex center can be felt without the presence or help of another person. That is even more subtle and its enjoyment is even deeper. But even by the time the sensation has reached your sex center, there is already too much excitement – because your energy has already created to an inner friction; the other is not present, but a subtle friction has started inside you. Even that is gross! So Tantra experimented with feelings: there should be no resonance in the body, just the experience of sex energy in the feelings. That is even more subtle, but there is still a friction...so then not even in the feelings! Tantra took the experience beneath the layer of feeling to where the unconscious lies – where we do not even know what is going on. The depth of experience in sex that has happened through Tantra has not been attained in any other way, anywhere in the world. You go on taking the experience deeper and deeper and deeper...

If you know something about the science of mantra, then you will know that it starts with intoning a sound, for example, *Om*. So you intone *Om* but that becomes a stimulus, and friction is created – your sound collides with the atmosphere and the whole thing becomes gross. So the right way is to start intoning with your lips closed, letting *Om* continue to echo inside. Nothing is heard outside, but inside you start enjoying it. But the friction is still there even inside, so slowly slowly, you drop the intoning of *Om* even inside – you don't *do* it, you just try to hear whether there is an echo of *Om* inside. And there *is* an echo of *Om* inside. It can be heard only when we are not doing it. We call that *ajapa jap*, meaning the soundless sound. We are not creating the sound but it is happening.

As we descend deeper into subtleties, we will have to drop our attachment to excitement. There is a place inside which is devoid of any excitement, which the Buddha has called *shunya*, the void. It has been called a void because no excitement exists there. And until you have had an experience of this, you will not be able to experience bliss at all.

Now try to understand the difference: happiness is born out of sensation, and bliss is born out of non-sensation. In happiness there is a friction involved; in bliss there is a void, peace.

That is why, in the search for happiness, every happiness turns into a suffering – because you need a greater and greater sensation of happiness. Today a woman appears to be beautiful, but after being with her for a few days she no longer appears to be so beautiful. After being with her for a few more days you will need an even more beautiful woman, because your senses have in the meantime become used to that level of arousal – so now you need a greater stimulus.

A friend came to see me; there was great struggle between the husband and his wife. After I had heard both sides, I felt that there no longer existed any meeting point between them. I asked them, "Please tell me honestly… do you even look at each other?"

The husband told me that since I was asking him to be honest, even when he was making love to his wife he was actually thinking of some film actress. Without visualizing some film actress, he could not make love to his wife. The husband thought that this was only happening to him, but then his wife said, "Now that the matter is being discussed… to be honest, unless I can imagine him to be the man I was in love with before I was married, I cannot make love to him."

Do you know what all this means? Neither one of them loves the other. And there are not two people in that house but four: the two fantasy figures are standing between husband and wife. And because of those two figures there can never be any meeting between them. And both of them are helpless, because now there is no excitement left between them.

With experience excitement dies – that is why happiness turns into suffering. That which you have not yet experienced still appears to promise happiness, but when you get it, the same experience becomes suffering. The moment you have it, it becomes unhappiness. Happiness becomes unhappiness because the experience of excitement demands a greater and greater stimulus. And with each experience your sensitivity goes on decreasing until a time comes when you cannot experience anything, because all your senses have become completely dull, they have all become numb. And then you begin your search for the ultimate experience.

When a man becomes old… I call a man old not because of his age but because he has numbed all his senses by running after excitement. This can even happen in youth, in childhood. Today in America it is already happening in childhood. Nowadays it does not take very long; there is no need to wait until old age. If, as a child, you are given so many ways to experience excitement, your senses will be dulled. And after that has already happened man sets off in search of bliss: "Where is the soul? Where is the universal soul?" Then it becomes difficult, because on this search you will need a pure sensitivity.

Mahavira and Buddha leaving their palaces and escaping was only superficial. The deeper truth is that they were renouncing the place of excitement so that the natural purity of their senses could be regained. They made their way to the forest, which means they moved towards nature, towards naturalness, so that the rubbish that had accumulated, which was blocking the inner doors of experiencing, could be removed. Only when that has been done do we start to become sensitive again. Only then are we able to hear that which can only be heard by the finest sensitivity. Only then are we able to see that which can only be seen with the subtlest of vision. This sutra relates to all of this.

The first sutra:

Kill out desire for sensation.

Drop the desire for sensation. This does not mean that this sutra is against the senses. The truth is that your desire for sensation is the death of your senses. This sutra is about purifying the senses; it is not against them. If you refine your sense of taste, the sumptuous food of kings will not compare with the taste of a dry crust of bread you may be eating – because taste does not depend on the bread, on the food, it depends on the one who is tasting. It depends on you, how much you can experience, how deeply you can immerse yourself in the experience.

Without first getting rid of the desire for sensation no one can enter into the world of meditation, because meditation means leaving behind all that is gross, and going in search of the subtle. But it is you who will search for the subtle! So are you capable of experiencing the subtle or not, do you have the capacity to imbibe the subtle?

If you do not – if your eyes are blind and you cannot see – then even if the subtle appears right in front of you, you will not be able to see it. You have to keep on purifying yourself. You have to become so pure that you are aware of what is happening even at the center of your innermost core. Try to understand this.

Those senses to which we give too much excitement become jaded, and because of this we have to give them even more excitement, which deadens them even more. A vicious circle is born. Then every day a new taste or sensation is needed, every day a new woman, a new man is needed, every day a new house, a new car is needed – every day something new is needed. But for how long can this newness last? For a while it seems to be something fresh, because we have not experienced the excitement of it before; so for a while it seems to be good. Then after some time it too becomes stale. Everything which was new becomes old. And the more dull the senses become, the quicker an experience becomes stale. That is why nothing satisfies; instead everything leaves us dissatisfied. So what is the way to fulfillment?

The way to fulfillment is not through paying attention to outer things but rather to your inner capacity to experience. Then even small things – even a smaller number of things – can give you much fulfillment. Even with nothing you can feel bliss.... Because one thing you can see is that having everything doesn't necessarily bring bliss, so it is possible to conceive of nothing bringing bliss.

Diogenes, who lived in Greece and was a great thinker, gave up everything. He was the only man in the West to live naked – like Mahavira, he lived naked. All he kept was a begging bowl, for begging and drinking water. One day, while passing through a village, he saw a villager drinking water by cupping his hands, so he immediately threw away his begging bowl. The villager asked him, "What have you done?"

He replied, "I never knew that one could drink water by cupping one's hands – now why should I be deprived of such a joy? The begging bowl is only a dead thing, and when I fill it with water I feel nothing from it. When I fill my hands with water, they feel the connection with the water, its coolness, its life-giving energy. My love also enters the water through my hands, and it becomes alive. So I will be drinking that too."

The first time Diogenes cupped his hands and drank water from them, he started dancing! He said, "What a fool I was to use a dead vessel to drink water from, because it made the water dead too. The energy from my hands, the heat of my hands, could not pass through to the water. And this was also insulting to the water."

That is why I am telling you this incident about Diogenes – because all our senses have become numb like his begging bowl. Whatever we receive through them becomes dead. While food lies on the plate it looks beautiful; the minute it enters your mouth it becomes ordinary. Your mouth makes it ordinary. Music becomes mundane when it enters your ears. Flowers lose their beauty when seen through your eyes.

We make everything ordinary – whereas everything in the world is extraordinary. The flower you see on a tree has never blossomed before. It is absolutely new. It is impossible to find another flower like it on this earth. It has never existed before, and it will never exist again in the future. Our eyes turn the existence of a unique flower into something mundane when we say, "It's okay – we've seen thousands of roses like this before." Because of the thousands you have seen, your eyes have become blind and you cannot see what is there, present, in front of you. What have those thousands of flowers got to do with this one?

Emerson has written that upon seeing a rose it came to his mind that the flower has no idea of the existence of thousands of other flowers – neither of the flowers still to come, nor of those which have gone before. This rose is present, here and now, offering itself to the divine. It is joyful because it does not compare itself with any other. But when he sees it, the thousands of others which he has seen get in the way. His vision is blurred, and the unique experience of this flower goes to waste. He doesn't perceive its beauty; the strings of his heart are not moved, nor are his senses stirred.

We are living in a unique world. The divine is being manifested here in so many ways all around us. The highest beauty is happening here, supreme music is resounding here – there is no end to the dance. But we pass through all this as though we were deaf and blind. Nothing touches us – we are like corpses, we have made a grave of our senses. We are enclosed within them, enclosed within as if we were in a coffin. We are only passing through life – nothing touches us, we feel and experience nothing. And then we ask, "Where is bliss, where is godliness?" – and it is present all around us! Inside, outside, there is nothing other than godliness. And there is no moment which is not a moment of bliss. But someone is needed who is capable of experiencing this. Through abusing our senses, we kill the one who could experience it.

My definition of renunciation is the science of supreme enjoyment. And only someone who knows how to let go is able to experience. Let go of the meaningless so that you can realize the meaningful; let go of sensations so that you can perceive the subtle.

There is a saying in China that after a master musician has attained to the supreme music, he breaks his musical instrument and throws it away. It is true. Those who said it must have spoken from a very deep understanding – because even the strings of a musical instrument create excitement. And when someone has attained to the supreme music, even the strings of the instrument become a hindrance to his music. Then he breaks it, throws it away, and he begins to listen to that music which is ever-present, which does not have to be created, which is resonating all around us – there is no moment when it is not there.

But we are not able to hear it, so we have to create it on musical instruments. Because of our dulled senses, we have to seek help from the strings of the *veena*. The strings do not produce music, they only create noise, a systematized noise. But because we have become insensitive and cannot hear anything, we give our attention to the music made by strings and instruments.

In Japan the Zen masters give a particular kind of meditation to their disciples. They say, "Try to hear the sound of one hand clapping." They make them meditate on this for years. Everyone has heard the sound of two hands clapping, but Zen masters ask their disciples to meditate on the sound of a single hand clapping...the sound for which two hands are not needed. It is total madness! Has one hand ever made a sound? But the Zen master says, "Listen, and keep on listening, and one day you will hear it."

There is a sound which is born without friction. We have called it *omkar*. In it, the sound is not made by two hands, it is not made through any impact, it is not created from friction – it is ever-present, it is in the very nature of life, it is resonating with life. But for us it has become very subtle. We are only aware of sound when two things strike each other. If nothing is striking anything else, we feel as if nothing is happening. But a lot is happening...silently.

The deep things in life happen in utter silence. The seed is being cracked open underground...and there is no sound. The plants are growing...there is no sound. The stars are moving... there is no sound. The sun rises...there is no uproar. In the very fine, subtle realms of existence, everything is silent. This silence has its own music, but to experience that our senses have to be refined.

Kill out Desire for sensation.

Learn from sensation...

Learn what? Not to kill the senses, but rather to let them come alive, to let them become more sensitive. The divine can be experienced through any one of the senses if that sense is capable of the purest experience. And then it becomes possible to taste even the ultimate reality, to taste godliness.

To taste godliness may seem absurd. You will say, "What are you talking about?" We have always maintained that God can be *seen*, but that does not mean that godliness cannot also be tasted. The reason we talk about *seeing* God is that the majority of seekers have searched for godliness after purifying their capacity to see – that is the only reason. They talked of seeing God because they sought godliness through purifying their vision. In India we have called the ultimate realization of the search *darshan*, seeing. But this is because of the eyes – man is visually oriented.

This is not only the case in India, but throughout the whole world. In the West they also call someone who has experienced realization "the seer," the one who sees. But why? Nobody calls him the one who tastes, nobody calls him the one who hears, nobody talks about the perfume of the ultimate reality. If you usually talk about "seeing" the ultimate reality, all this will look strange to you. But if the eye can see it, then why shouldn't we smell the ultimate reality? If we feel no problem with the idea of seeing the ultimate reality, then what is the problem if I talk about its taste? The only reason is that all of man's other senses have dulled more quickly than the sense of sight.

The ability to see is the most fluid sense in the human body. Understand it like this: the eye is the least material part of the body, it is ethereal. And that is why, when we look into someone's eyes, we can see right through that person. That is why a deaf man does not lose out that much, but a blind man loses a lot. With the loss of sight, eighty percent of one's experiences cease. All the other senses put together give us only twenty percent of our experiences, while eighty percent of our experiences come through the eyes. That is why you don't pity a deaf man as much as you do a blind man. The reason is that he is losing so much – with the loss of his eyesight he loses eighty percent of all experiences. That is why, being visually oriented, we say, "*seeing* the ultimate reality."

But this is not necessary. If you can purify your sense of taste, you will also know the taste of the ultimate reality; if you can purify your sense of touch, you will also experience the touch of the ultimate reality. If you purify any sense, you can realize the ultimate reality through it. If you can purify all your senses, the ultimate reality pours into you from everywhere.

Meditation is purification of the senses. And the sutra for purification of the senses says:

Kill out desire for sensation.

Learn from sensation and observe it...

What can we observe? – that the greater the stimulation, the more the senses die. The less the stimulation, the more lively, alert and awake they become.

...because only so can you commence
the science of self-knowledge,
and plant your foot
on the first step of the ladder.

What we want to experience is hidden within, and the search for sensation is on the outside. So the greater our sensory stimulations, the farther we move away from ourselves. It is a strange thing that man has landed on the moon but he is not at all bothered about landing inside himself. Going to the moon – that too is the search for sensation. But whatever type of sensation it may be...

The desire to land on the moon is very old. Ever since man has been here, he has had the ambition to reach to the moon. Even small babies try to reach out towards the moon. From time immemorial man has been thinking about reaching the moon. But do you know what happened? When man first landed on the moon there was great excitement throughout the world – especially in America, because it was their man who had landed on it, so there was even more excitement. Everyone was glued to his television set! But after two hours the excitement had already died down. Man had landed on the moon – and people switched off their televisions. Then their routine, their daily grind started again. The news was hot for twenty-four hours, and then it came to an end! The thing that had excited man for thousands of years was over within two hours. Man had reached the moon – now what? For a moment it seemed as if a great event was taking place; then everything became normal, the world went on its way. Such a long journey to victory, one which had been dreamed of for so many eons – even that becomes old in two hours!

Man's mind turns everything into the old. And no matter how far away we go... The farther away we go, the more difficult it becomes to experience that which is within.

The first lesson of the science of self-knowledge begins with the experience of the senses: if you don't go in search of sensation, you come closer to yourself. If you don't search for the distant, you will be able to know that which is near.

Kill out the hunger for growth.

The ambition to grow is just as fatal as the ambition for more sensations, perhaps even more so. It may appear strange to you, because you think that even spirituality is after all a desire for growth. Whether we desire bliss, whether we desire liberation, whether we desire the divine...these too are desires for *growth*. But it is necessary to understand one fundamental difference: there is one type of growth which comes through your desire, and another which does not; which comes when there is no desire in you.

There is one type of growth which comes from your efforts – and a growth which comes from your efforts cannot be greater than you. It *cannot*; your action cannot be bigger than you. The deed is always smaller than the doer. Whatever you do, the deed will always be smaller than you. It will always be so. How can you perform an act that is greater than you? When you are the doer your act cannot be greater than you. No matter how great the deed is, you will always remain greater than it is.

No matter how beautiful the painting of an artist, he will be greater than the painting. No matter how harmonious the music someone makes, the musician will remain greater than his music. What you do cannot be greater than you: the deed is always smaller than the doer.

Now this creates a very difficult situation. It means that even if you make some spiritual progress, it cannot be greater than you. It will be smaller than whatever you are. And this means you are caught in a trap. You cannot be free of yourself – you will be there and you will always remain greater than whatever you attain. Even if you attain to the ultimate, to the divine – please note, I am saying that even if *through your efforts* you attain to the ultimate – it will be smaller than you. It has to be, because it has been attained by your efforts; it cannot be bigger than you. This is the reason you cannot attain to the ultimate through your efforts – it is greater than you. But there is another way to attain to it: by dropping the effort.

The sutra says:

Kill out the hunger for growth.

Grow as the flower grows,
unconsciously, but eagerly anxious
to open its soul to the air.

You don't even come to know when a bud turns into a flower, but it is *...eagerly anxious to open its soul to the air.* The bud is only eager to blossom, it does not make any *effort* to blossom. No exercises, no yogic postures, no breathing techniques – the bud does not do anything. It is only eager, it has only a deep longing that whatever fragrance it may have is released to the winds. Neither does that eagerness become an effort; it only remains an awaiting. The bud only waits: the sun will rise in the morning, and the winds will be there and the bud will become a flower. But it makes no effort to become a flower, it is not admitted into some school, it goes to no guru to learn something, to find some way, some plan, some technique, some mantra. No, it does not do anything like that – it only waits.

So must you press forward
to open your soul to the eternal.
But it must be the eternal
that draws forth your strength and beauty,
not desire of growth.

Understand this difference. Don't make any effort from your side to attain to the eternal; only prepare yourself, so that if the eternal wants to enter, you do not create any hindrance. Only keep the door open so that the eternal does not knock and find the door closed, so that the divine does not come looking for you and find you not at home; so that it does not find you have gone out somewhere and no one knows of your whereabouts. Don't let it happen that the divine wants to enter your heart and finds a big crowd gathered there with no space for it to enter; that there is no room for the guest to stay, there is no opening through which the divine can enter; that your doors and windows are closed. Just don't let this happen.

Don't try to search for the eternal. How will you do this? You don't know anything about it – where will you search for it? You can only search for it on paths which are familiar to you; and you would have already found it if it were there. How can you do something beyond your limitations? Whatever you do will be bound by your finiteness; and that will not connect you to the infinite.

But it must be the eternal
that draws forth your strength and beauty,
not desire of growth.
For in the one case

you develop in the luxuriance of purity;
in the other
you harden by the forcible passion
for personal stature.

So don't try to grab the eternal in your fist. Your fist is too small, the eternal will not fit into it. And the more tightly you clench your fist, the more the eternal will defy it. Your fist will remain empty. You will find that no one except yourself can fit in your fist.

So there are two ways to grow. One way is the way of effort, resolve, labor. There, you are the master. Whatever you do, you are the planner. Then whatsoever you attain is nothing but your own game. Much can certainly be achieved through effort, through labor and resolve. But whatever you attain will be smaller than you. And whatsoever you attain in this way is called the world. What you get through resolve and labor is worldly. Your ego is strengthened by it – it is a search for your own ego.

There is another way to attain – through surrender, through letting go, through waiting, through prayer; not through labor but through relaxation. It happens when you are relaxed, it happens when you are in prayer, it happens when you surrender yourself at the feet of the divine, it happens when you don't swim but float along with the current of the river. It does not happen because of you, it happens because you keep yourself open. It is something bigger than you which makes it happen – you are simply not creating any obstacle. Essentially, spiritual search is not an effort, it is a non-effort.

Zen masters have called it "effortless effort" and they are right. It is not a practice. You have to leave yourself in the hands of the divine; then wherever it takes you, whatever it does – it may efface you or save you – you are in agreement with it. You have only a deep willingness to meet it, and that deep willingness is your preparedness. You will not stop it, you will not put obstacles in its way. You become like an iron filing, so you can be pulled by it as though it were a magnet. The iron filing does not move towards the magnet – it cannot. The magnet pulls it. It is enough that the iron filing does not create a hindrance. It should be willing to be pulled – that is enough. When pulled, it rushes towards the magnet – that is enough. And anyway there is no way for the iron filing to rush on its own. The divine is a cosmic magnet. Become like an iron filing.

The sutra says, don't have any ambition for growth, have only a longing. Don't ask, don't shout and scream for it, don't make plans, don't project your desires, don't tell existence what it has to do. Only do this much: tell existence that whatsoever it wants to do, it can. You are in agreement. Your agreement alone is your spiritual discipline. And then growth happens. In fact, *only* then the growth that is bigger than you happens.

Whatever you may achieve in the world is smaller than you are. In the spiritual realm whenever something is attained, it is greater than you. That is why devotees say that it has been attained by the grace of existence, and not through their efforts. The sole reason for saying this is that we cannot attain anything greater than ourselves by our own efforts; whatever we attain will be smaller because we are insignificant. It is attained through the grace of existence, through its compassion.

There is meaning in what the devotees say. Actually all they are saying is, "What can happen through our efforts? We have not achieved it through our efforts." But in fact, they *have* made an effort. So just because of their statement, don't start thinking, "Okay, so I will get it when I get it," because if that were the case you would have attained it already – since you have never made any effort anyway. No, don't start thinking that you don't have to do anything – because that non-doing is also a doing in a way; that letting go of yourself is also a doing; to surrender is also a spiritual discipline. So don't think, "Okay, it's fine then." There are many people who start thinking like this, who stay exactly where they are, thinking, "So when it wants to come to me, it will come. I am sitting lazily." That is not the meaning of this sutra.

The meaning of this sutra is that although you won't attain to it through your effort, at least you will have to make this much effort: not to create any hindrance. Otherwise, as you are, you are creating a hindrance; as you are, you are standing with your back to the divine. Right now your situation is like this: the sun has risen but you are sitting locked inside your room with all your doors and windows shut. The sun is not rising because of your effort, and you cannot bring the sun inside through your effort, but you can close the door and make it stay outside the house. You don't have any power in your hands to bring the eternal inside but you are capable of making it stay outside; you can keep your door shut.

And the eternal is not aggressive: it will not break down your doors and come inside. It will wait; it waits on your doorstep so that whenever you open the door, it will be right there. And you can go on sitting like this, life after life. So keep the door open.

And it is not as if it will enter just by your opening the door. But if your door is open, then there is a possibility of its entering. So don't open the door and start saying, "The door is open and it hasn't come yet!" You are only creating the possibility that when the moment is ripe, if the door is open it will not turn away.

Nothing happens before the time is ripe. When that moment comes and your door is open – the eternal is at your door, and you are keenly awaiting it, eager – when your waiting is total and the door is fully open, it will happen. Even if your door is open and you think "The door is open but the eternal is not coming," then know that either the door is not yet open and you are only dreaming that the door is open, or maybe you have opened the door a little bit, but you are not yet eager for it to come in. Perhaps deep inside you are scared that it may actually turn up! We are afraid, because if it comes into our life, then our life will not be as it is now, it will change completely.

In Sri Lanka an enlightened Buddhist monk had been preaching to people for fifty years. His time of death was coming closer, so he said, "I have been trying to make you understand for a long time. Now my day of departure is near. I have repeatedly told you what to do, but you never do anything. So before I die I will give you one last chance. I won't tell you what to do to attain nirvana, rather, if there is anyone among you who is eager to have it, I will give it to him right now. If there is such a person, stand up!"

Thousands of his disciples were gathered there because their master was dying, and everyone was looking at everyone else to see who would stand up. They had never thought that nirvana would suddenly appear without a warning, like a calamity at their door! Only one man raised his hand slightly and said, "Let me tell you straight away: not now, not today. Just tell me the way...who knows, I may need it some day! I definitely want nirvana one day – but not now. Now I have plenty of things to do; so many jobs are still unfinished. I have to fulfill so many promises, to get the children married – and besides, my wife is sick – so not now. Please try to understand! But one thing I can tell you absolutely: one day I will definitely need nirvana, so please show me the way."

You would be worried if you could have nirvana today, here and now. Just a moment before, you were worried about how to attain to it – because it is not so easy. You were happily worrying about it. But if you could have it right now, you would be caught up in another type of a worry: "My God, now I am caught! How to get back home?"

If the eternal is attained right now, what about the web you have woven and left behind? Would you like to take care of that first? And that web seems to be more important to you than the eternal. You will choose it. You will ask, "What is the great hurry to attain? This is an eternal matter. And besides, there are still so many lives left, I can attain any time – what is the rush? But all my other concerns are not eternal matters. Either they have to be accomplished soon, while there is still time, or they will be gone forever. Those things belong to the world of time; as for you, you are timeless, eternal. I can always meet you again." So your effort is needed for just this much – a negative effort – that you don't create any obstacles.

All the experiments in meditation which we are doing here are experiments to destroy the obstacles. Methods as such are only to destroy the obstacles; there is no method to attain to the divine. Godliness cannot be attained through any method. What kind of godliness will this be – which can be attained through a method?

Godliness cannot be attained through any method. It is in the realm of non-method, it happens in the method*less*. But your obstacles can be destroyed by methods. The locks on your doors can be destroyed. The rusted keys have been lost because the doors have been locked for so long. Now they are like walls; they don't even feel like doors anymore, because we have never opened them. You have thrown the keys away in a place where, even if you searched for them, you would not be able to find them – because you are scared that you might find the key and the door might unintentionally open! All methods are negative: they are meant to destroy something.

People ask me, "What will happen through all this? Even if someone does deep breathing for ten minutes, dances around like a madman and shouts 'Hoo, Hoo' – can he attain to godliness by doing all this?"

No, you will not attain through all this, but you will be effaced by doing all this. And that is the prerequisite for godliness to happen to you. Through these methods you will disappear. It is a way of effacing you, of attaining to godliness – because it is only when you disappear that godliness can be attained. That is why these methods are needed.

So all these methods I am making you go into like a madman are to destroy you, so that your knowledge ability disappears, your so-called wisdom is erased, your ego dies, your insensitivity is dispelled; so that what you have made of yourself is annihilated, melts; so that you vanish; so that you become simple, with open doors. Then one day, at the right moment, the eternal comes.

5

DESIRE ONLY THAT WHICH IS WITHIN YOU

7. Desire only that which is within you.

For within you is the light of the world –
the only light that can be shed upon the path.
If you are unable to perceive it within you,
it is useless to look for it elsewhere.

8. Desire only that which is beyond you.

It is beyond you,
because when you reach it you have lost yourself.

9. Desire only that which is unattainable.

It is unattainable,
because it for ever recedes.
You will enter the light,
but you will never touch the flame.

With these sutras the journey deepens.

The language of religiousness is a little puzzling. It has to be, because religion has less to do with facts and more to do with the mysterious. A fact is something that can be understood. And that which can be understood a little but which also remains not understood we describe as mysterious; only this much can be understood – that it cannot be understood. Fact is that which is below the level of the intellect; the mysterious is that which is above the level of the intellect. Intellect can measure the depths of fact, but when it tries to fathom the depths of the mysterious, the intellect itself is dissolved.

Ramakrishna used to say that if a figure made out of salt tries to fathom the depth of the ocean, it will fail. It will begin the search but it will never reach to the destination, because it is after all made of salt – and as it falls into the ocean's depths, it is dissolving, becoming absorbed. By the time it has reached a certain depth it will be gone – nothing will remain, nothing can return and say how deep the ocean is.

Yet only salt can come to know the depths of the ocean. If you throw in a stone it will reach to the depths, but it will remain untouched by the soul of the ocean. How can something which cannot dissolve feel the ocean's soul? How can something which cannot disappear, which cannot be absorbed, measure the real depth of the ocean?

The ocean has one kind of depth that can be measured in feet and miles, and it has another depth, an existential, oceanic depth, which cannot be measured in that way. Only salt will be able to measure that depth because it is willing to be dissolved, to merge, to lose itself. It will become one with the ocean through being absorbed. In that very absorption it will come to know the ocean. But then there will be no way to return and talk about it.

The mysterious means something that you may search for, but the time it is found you have already disappeared. We can hold a fact in our fists, but it is the mysterious in whose hands we are.

Now these sutras become deeper, now the river deepens. Only if you pay attention will you be able to understand.

The seventh sutra:

Desire only that which is within you.

It is very paradoxical, paradoxical in two ways. One is that we only wish for, we only desire, what is not within us. That's what it means to desire something – a longing for that which we do not already have. We only desire what we feel is lacking. So to desire means to want something which we do not yet have, but which can be had tomorrow. What else is desire but this thirst?

This sutra is saying:

Desire only that which is within you.

The first implication is, do not desire what is not within you. But all our desires are for things which are not within us; we only desire what we do not have. It seems logical that we should ask for what we do not have; why should we ask for what we have already? So the first thing is, desire does not arise for that which is already within us; hence this sutra seems very paradoxical.

And this sutra is very meaningful and paradoxical in a second way: in life we can only attain that which we already have. We can never attain that which was not already inside us. No matter what we attain on the outside, it will never really be attained. It can be taken away from us.

No matter how much wealth a person may accumulate, it can be stolen, you can be robbed of it – and even if it is not stolen, even if you are not robbed, even if the state does not become communist, even if none of all this happens, still death will snatch it away. Whatsoever you desired and accumulated will, at the moment of death, drop from your hands. It was with you, but it did not become yours. If it had become yours, then no one could have taken it away from you.

That is why, in the eyes of religion, *wealth* means that which cannot be taken away from you. That which can be taken away is just a trouble – because of all the problems involved in having to protect it. First you take it from others, and then you suffer the problem of having to protect it. First the problems of snatching and taking it from others and after doing all this you remain afraid and trembling, twenty-four hours a day in fear, in case someone else takes it away from you. And in the end it *is* taken from you anyway! So religion says that only the foolish call it wealth – it is actually a misfortune.

Real wealth is that which cannot be taken away from you; only then can it be yours, only then is it meaningful to call it yours. But what kind of wealth is this that cannot be taken away from you? If this kind of wealth does exist, it must be something within you – only then can it have such a quality.

Whatever we can accumulate from the outside can be taken away. Only that which belongs to our intrinsic nature cannot be taken away from us. That which dwells in our very soul cannot be taken away from us; and that which cannot be taken away is what we call the soul.

Many people do not have a soul. When I say this, you may be very shocked, because we start with the belief that everybody has a soul. That is correct; it is correct in the sense that everyone could have a soul – but not everyone does. If you take an inventory of everything that you possess, does it include anything that cannot be taken away? In answering this question you will come to know whether you have a soul or not.

Just make a list of all your wealth, of whatsoever you have; then sit down, and with a red pen start ticking off whatever can be taken away. You will find that the whole list is covered in red – not a single thing is left which cannot be taken away. So this means you don't have a soul. If you come across anything in your life which cannot be taken away by anyone, not even by death, only then can you know that you have a soul.

From reading the scriptures everyone gets a wrong idea: that the soul is something which we already have. We certainly do, but what is the point of something existing or not existing if you know nothing about it? And if you don't have any experience of something, then even if you have it, what will you do with it? It is like having a diamond buried under your house but not knowing where it is or whether it is even there at all. What value can such a diamond have in the marketplace?

You may say that even though you don't know its where abouts, the very fact that a diamond exists under your house makes you an emperor. But in reality you will still have to go on begging, because you do not have the diamond in your hands. And until you have found it, how can you be really sure that it is actually buried there? Until you have unearthed it, even to say that it is buried under your house is meaningless.

Are you going to say that it is meaningful because it is written in the scriptures?Does the assurance of your scriptures make any difference? You have no idea! You don't have a map, you don't know what the soul looks like, you don't have its name or address or anything. You have only heard that there is a soul; you don't know whether such a soul exists or not.

The sutra says:

Desire only that which is within you.

Why waste your time and energy in desiring things outside yourself? Even if you get them, they will be lost and all your efforts will vanish like lines drawn on water – before you have finished drawing them, they are already erased. All your wealth is just like this: you have hardly taken hold of it, and it has already begun to disappear. If you have to desire something, then desire that which does not prove to be like lines drawn on water. And that wealth resides within you.

Man is born with this wealth. In existence no one is poor; existence makes everyone an emperor. We become poor through our own doing. Poverty is something which is created; we earn it through our great efforts. We are born wealthy. A kingdom is our very destiny, it is hidden within us.

Yet even that which is hidden within us has to be attained, because we have forgotten about it, we have no memory of it. We have deliberately diverted our attention to a road where the memory of the inner has been lost. Our attention has been diverted to the outside, and we have forgotten how to turn our attention inside.

There are reasons why we focus on the outside – and this has not happened because of some bad deeds in the past. There are natural reasons for our attention going to the outside. It is necessary for survival. If a child is born with his attention only turning inward, he will not be able to survive. The child needs to pay attention to the outer. He needs to be alert to the outside for the sake of his body, for the sake of his life, for the sake of his safety. When he is hungry, food will not be provided from within – it will have to come from the outside. So when the child feels hungry his attention goes to the outside, from where he can get his food.

That is why, whether you know it or not, women's breasts hold an attraction for men even when the men have become old. This is the first experience of childhood and it is hard to let go of it. The first relationship that the child had with the world was through his mother's breasts. The very foundations of his whole life and security are in the breasts. Breasts were the child's first world. The breasts were his first contact with the outside world, and a pleasant contact, through which he was able to grow, develop and survive.

That's why even when a man becomes old, his fascination with a woman's breasts doesn't leave him. In films, paintings, and statues, man has paid a lot of attention to the breasts. It is a memory from childhood which does not leave him. The day it does, know that you have been freed from the world. The breasts were your first world, for you the world began from there. They became the basis of your first contact with the world.

So when the child feels hungry his attention goes to the outside, and when he feels thirsty his attention goes to the outside. All his needs are fulfilled from the outside. The soul is not a need and you do not need to look for it on the outside. It is already there – inside. And because we do not need to look for it, we forget it. We only keep in our remembrance what is needed.

You must have noticed how when a thorn gets stuck in your foot, you become aware of your foot, or if there is pain in your head, you become aware of your head. Are you aware that you have a head when there is no pain in it? Whenever you are aware of it, it is because of pain; without pain you are not aware of your head. Only a sick man is aware of his body; a healthy man does not think about it.

This is the definition of health: bodilessness is the definition of health – when you are not aware of the body. If you are aware of the body it means that it is diseased. You only come to know of it when it is sick – because in sickness you need to give it attention. While the thorn is stuck in your foot, all your attention is on the foot because your first need is to remove the thorn. So all your attention goes there, and only then can the thorn be removed. If your attention did not go to your foot, the thorn would remain and its poison would spread. So if your head is in pain, all your attention will go there.

That is why medical science has found ways.... When there is pain it is not actually removed by giving you a tablet. The only thing that happens is that the communication channel through which you register pain is interrupted; so then you don't feel the pain. The pain is not removed by the tablet – that is a fallacy – it only disconnects the transmission of your attention to the pain, it deadens the nerves in between so that the message cannot get through. So even if your foot is going to be amputated, you will not be aware of it. An injection is given: it does not stop the pain, the pain is there, but it does not allow your attention to reach to the pain. That is why the pain is not felt. Your whole body can be cut open, and you will not even be aware of it. There is only one way of becoming aware of it, and that is by your attention reaching there; and your attention *will* go there – wherever there is pain your attention will go.

There is no pain in the soul; that's why there is no way for your attention to reach there. The soul is always blissful – that's why there is no need for it to call for your attention.

The body is always in some trouble or other. The body is a vast mechanism, it is very complicated. So far we have not been able to make any machine on earth as complicated as the body. Scientists say that if we wanted to duplicate the workings of an ordinary body, a factory covering at least ten square miles would have to be built. There would be such a noise and clamor in that factory – but in the body of man everything is happening so silently.

Man is a vast phenomenon. In his body, in the body of an ordinary man there are some two trillion cells. There is a crowd of two trillion cells in your body and they have a society, they have regulations, and their regulations are unique. So far, man has not been able to create an organization like this. The biggest of our biggest states are not regulated and systematized as well as those two trillion cells in your body.

You have no idea how they work: if you did, you would be amazed. A small wound, and some work is activated. With the intake of a little bit of food some work starts. Even when you are doing nothing the big machine is operating. And whenever there is even a little problem in this complicated machine, it is necessary that your attention immediately goes towards it. If this attention is not given, you will die.

So if a child were born inwardly attentive, he would not survive. That is why we say that those who have attained to the ultimate in meditation are not born again. And there is a reason for it: there can be no birth because those who have attained to the ultimate in meditation are absorbed within. With this inward absorption no relationship can be established with a new body. Even if a relationship were made, the child could not survive because he would not be able to fulfill the body's outer needs. He would not be able to face the outside challenges.

It is because of the needs of the body – life's need – that attention goes outwards. And there are so many pains in the body, so many complications, that there is a constant call for attention. That is why we come to know of the body, of the senses, of the world; and yet there is one thing that we don't come to know about – that which we are! For one thing, there is no pain there; there has never been any pain there and there will never be any pain there. From this, try to understand why there is this self-forgetfulness in man. Self-forgetfulness is there because you do not feel the need for self-remembrance. Those who feel the need for self-remembrance attain to it at once.

Who are the people who need self-remembrance? Try to understand this: who are the people in whose lives the need for self-remembrance arises? The need to remember the body is there in everyone's life, but there are very few people in whose life the need for self-remembrance is born. When is that need born?

It is born when, having gone through all the experiences of the body, you realize that no matter what arrangements you make for it, sufferings of the body will remain. No matter what outer means you provide, there is no way to obtain happiness. No matter how many plans you make on the outside, no ray or note of bliss can be felt. When someone begins to realize this and his whole outer life has turned to suffering...

Remember that even if you are only suffering from one thing it will not make any difference – because your hope for happiness from something else remains alive. If you have ten different kinds of suffering, then the hope for ten kinds of happiness appears alongside them, and you will keep on running here and there. You let go of one kind of happiness because it has turned into suffering but you start seeking another kind. It is only when the whole of one's outer life feels like a suffering – that is why Buddha has said that life is suffering – it is only when the whole of life feels like suffering, that you suddenly realize that since there is only suffering on the outside why not search within and see what is there? When everything becomes meaningless without a person begins to turn within. A child is born outwardly oriented. It is only once in a while, after having gone through the deep experiences of life that someone turns within. This sutra is for this turning inwards.

Desire only that which is within you. Only then is there a possibility of ultimate bliss and ultimate liberation. Desire only that which is within you. And yet even when we appear to desire what is within, it is really only pretending to be about the inner – actually the desire is for the outer.

People come to me and ask, "If we meditate will we have more material comforts and fulfillment?" There is a desire that meditation should increase one's material wealth. People come to me and ask whether, if they start meditating, they will have success in the world. They don't know what they are saying!

Meditation means that now the world has failed for you. Realizing that success does not exist is the beginning of meditation. Meditation starts only when you have come to know that there is no wealth worth speaking of in the outer world. The question of getting or not getting it does not arise; wealth does not exist there, there is only an illusion of wealth. When someone's illusion is shattered, then the question of meditation arises.

But for these people the illusion has not yet broken. They have tried on the outside in every possible way and they have not found this wealth. But the idea that wealth is possible from the outside still remains, so they start thinking that perhaps it can be obtained through meditation – "Let us give meditation a try." But their interest is not in meditation, their interest is in wealth.

As long as your interest is in the outer, as long as your desire is for the outer, you can make no progress on the spiritual journey. That is why you need to keep this sutra in mind.

Desire only that which is within you.

For within you is the light of the world –
the only light that can be shed upon the path.
If you are unable to perceive it within you,
it is useless to look for it elsewhere.

Whatever is worth having is within you. You may call it light, you may call it bliss, you may call it God, you may call it liberation, you may call it nirvana – but whatever is worth having, is within you. The Mahaviras, the Buddhas, the Krishnas, the Christs – whatever they attained is also within you. But we are seeking it outside ourselves. We are even seeking that which is within us on the outside. Our very search runs outward. We know of only one way to seek, and that is outward. This pattern has been born out of life's needs, but if you don't break this pattern, you will continue to run around on the outside.

And in the race outside many times you will feel that happiness is just close by, near at hand; that it is only a matter of time before you catch hold of it. And every time you reach to that point, you will find that it has disappeared like a rainbow. Rainbows *appear* to be very beautiful – but this is so only from a distance. If you come closer, they disappear. Some distance is needed to see them. It is an illusion created by distance; as you come closer, the illusion disappears. All happiness is like a rainbow – it is far away.

If you are begging on the roads you will think that happiness is in the palaces, because the palaces are far away. And yet whoever is sitting inside the palace is not feeling any happiness at all. It may be that he is even more miserable than the beggar – because at least the beggar has the hope that there *is* happiness in the palace. He can hope that at some time or other he will reach the palace – at least he can live in this hope. But the hope of someone who has already reached the palace has been shattered; even in his palace he cannot feel any happiness. Even he hopes and thinks that maybe there will be happiness in a bigger palace. Happiness seems to be wherever we are not.

And it is not as if this is only true in relation to palaces. It also happens that a person who is fed-up with living in a palace sometimes starts wondering whether people living in huts are not happier. People living in cities think that people living in villages must be very happy, and the people living in villages are running to the city! If you tell some villager that he is living in ultimate bliss, he will not believe you, but there are people in the cities who think that bliss is raining down on the villages! They write books and poems about the great joy to be had in the villages – although they don't ever go to them, and continue to stay in the cities. If they went to the villages, they would find there is great suffering there. And those who do go return immediately.

It is very strange. Happiness seems to be where we are not, and where we are, we find suffering. But someone else is there, where we are not, and we don't bother to ask him how he feels there! And he too is dissatisfied with where he is.

We seek outside. Yet we will never find what we want on the outside because it is not to be found outside so there is no way we will get it. What we are searching for has been lost within, and we have lost it because of the demands of life. Our attention has gone to the outer and is occupied there for twenty-four hours a day. We have become unaware of the inner; all our attention has gone to the outer. If this can be remembered, it is possible to turn our attention inside.

That is why I ask you to become just like a dead body in the last stage of the meditation. Whatever may be happening, become just like a dead person; otherwise you will take the energy which arises in meditation outside – it will go out instantly. If you are given a chance to keep your eyes open, the meditative energy which has arisen will immediately start flowing out through your eyes. You will waste it on something useless outside. You may see some women standing nearby, or someone dancing, or someone looking as if he is mad. You will not know what you are doing, but in that moment your eyes will still be fresh from the meditation born within – and you can destroy this meditation in a second! What is born out of hours of effort can be lost in a second.

That's why I tell you to keep your eyes closed, so that the meditation which has just been born does not leave through your eyes. That's why I tell you to let your body be as if it were dead, not to move it even slightly, because even you are not aware of your cunning ways.

Sometimes you may feel that your foot hurts, sometimes you may feel to alter the position of your hand a little bit, you may feel an itch somewhere on your head – and even if your head is feeling a little itchy, what is the harm in feeling like that for another ten minutes? You have your whole life left to scratch it! And even if your foot is feeling a little uncomfortable for ten minutes, what great harm will it do – you will not die. And if an ant has begun to crawl up your foot, what harm can it do to you? It can only bite you. It is not as if a snake were climbing up you...only an ant is crawling on you! Yet even an ant is enough to trouble you. But the ant is not the problem – it is just an excuse.

The meditative energy which has arisen within you is seeking an excuse to move outward. If you remove the ant with your hand you will not even be aware of how, through such a small action, you have discharged the energy.

That is why I say that when the energy of meditation arises, stop – in every way. Become just like a stone. During these ten minutes the outside world should no longer exist for you. Only then, some day, at some moment, is there the possibility that meditation will knock. There will be no way for it to move outward, and so it will push its way inward. And in that moment you will have a glimpse of the inner. Once you have a glimpse, you have had a taste of it – and then you will easily move inward.

But you are ready to lose this energy in small things, in very insignificant things. If you think about it, even *you* will feel what petty things they are, and that there was nothing in them that was worth losing the energy for. What would have been lost by remaining still? Standing up you became tired – so what? But I can see how you are able to deceive yourselves.

You immediately sit down. I say, "Stop!" and you immediately sit down! I say, "Stop! Stay just as you are" and you immediately sit down and adjust your posture. You don't even know what you are doing. Who are you trying to deceive? You are not deceiving me! What will be the point in deceiving me? You have exerted yourself so much for thirty minutes, and now you are losing it all in just a second because you are paying attention to the external, the outer.

Energy can leak out through a small hole. Don't think that because there is only a small hole in the boat it does not matter, and you will still be able to cross the river. The question is not that there is only one hole. If there is just one hole, that is enough. One hole can sink the boat. And these dishonesties become holes.

Desire only that which is within you.

If you are unable to perceive it within you, it is useless to look for it elsewhere – because it is not outside.

The eighth sutra:

Desire only that which is beyond you.

This is also worth thinking about: *Desire only that which is beyond you.* We always desire that which is within our grasp. We only want what we feel sure we will be able to get, we only want what we feel sure we are expert in.

This means that you will never be able to grow bigger than yourself. You will remain exactly as you are. You should always wish to go beyond yourself: only then can progress be made, only then can you grow – because in attaining to that which is beyond you, you grow up.

But what is beyond you? There is nothing in this world beyond man. Man can attain to everything – you too can have everything. Certainly Alexander achieved much. You may be a smaller Alexander who cannot achieve as much as he did, but if he carved out a big kingdom, you can make a smaller one – nothing is impossible. If you become just as mad and crazy as Alexander was, if you can become just as intoxicated for riches, then you too can manage it.

One thing is certain, whatever Alexander achieved can be achieved by anyone. There is nothing he did which is beyond man. A Duke, an Andrew Carnegie, some Rockefeller earns billions – but you can too. Nothing is beyond you. If you can earn a single penny you can also make billions, because the difference between a billion and a penny is only quantitative, it is not qualitative.

Why shouldn't someone who can earn one penny be able to earn two? One penny and then one more...all together they will add up to a billion. So the difference is not qualitative but quantitative. So if I have earned one penny, I have earned the wealth of the whole world; or I could, because by earning one penny I have got the basic skills in my hands. Now it does not matter whether I make one billion or two billion. By earning the first penny the way is paved – I can earn that much, it is not something beyond me.

This sutra says:

Desire only that which is beyond you.

What is beyond you? You yourself, that which is hidden within you – that is beyond you. Everything else is within your reach, everything else is easy. No matter how difficult it may appear to be, it is easy; everything else is insignificant. Only the wealth which lies hidden within you appears to be beyond you, and you cannot seem to find a way to get there. You cannot see the path leading to it. You cannot stretch your hands towards it, because hands reach outwards, nor can you open your eyes to it, because eyes open outwards, nor can you lend your ears to it, because ears listen outwards. All the senses reach outwards, and you have to look for it within. The mind goes outwards, and the search has to take place within. Only that wealth within is beyond you.

Your being is beyond you. This means that you are made up of two parts: one is your outgoing face – your senses, your body, your mind, your ego. The ego is the sum total of all of these; it reaches outwards. And beyond this ego lies your actual nature, your soul. So if you have to desire something, then desire only that which is beyond you.

It is beyond you,
because when you reach it you have lost yourself.

It is beyond you because in reaching it you will be dissolved. Try to understand this sutra.
Attaining anything in which you do not become dissolved is not going beyond yourself. Attaining anything for which you do not have to drop your ego is not going beyond yourself. Only that which you have to pay for with your ego is beyond you. And the day a man attains to his true self, the old self with which he started his journey drops away from him just like the old skin drops away from a snake. The day you attain to yourself, you will be really surprised to discover that the "I" who started the search has disappeared.

Kabir has said, "O my friend, seeking and searching Kabir has been dissolved!" In the search Kabir has disappeared, and then the union has happened. Of the one who went on the search, nothing is left – and then the union takes place!

Kabir has said a very beautiful thing: "I went out in search to find it. While *it* was not, *I* was. And when it was found, I saw that the seeker has disappeared."

And he has also said another strange thing, that when he disappeared, he found that God was beseeching him from all sides, calling out to him, "Kabir, Kabir! Where art thou?"

"When nothing was left of me, God himself started calling me, started looking for me and shouting 'Kabir! Kabir!' As long as I existed, as long as I was asserting my existence so strongly, I could not see him. And now that I have vanished he comes running after me, calling, 'Kabir! Kabir!'"

What has vanished is being shown so much respect...but as long as it existed, nobody could have cared less!

The day you efface yourself completely, you will be recognized. Your splendor will be fully revealed the day you are not. Only after the seed has broken can the plant be born. When the river loses itself it becomes the ocean. That which is vast is hidden within you, and it is beyond your worthless ego.

The ninth sutra:

Desire only that which is unattainable.

Desire only that which is unattainable. What is the use of desiring that which you can attain? Why ask for something that you will get anyway? If you must ask, if you must wish, then desire that which you cannot attain.

It is very strange. If it *cannot* be attained, then what is the point of asking? If it is definitely unattainable, and you cannot have it, then what can possibly come to you from desiring it? And if it *can* be attained by desiring it, then why call it unattainable? It was attainable in the first place, that is why by desiring it you attained.

So you will have to understand this sutra. What is unattainable? That which can be found is not unattainable – then what is unattainable? There is one thing which is unattainable because you already have it and there is no question of having to attain it. The question of not attaining it does not even arise.

You can attain only that which you don't already have – but you already have your inner being. It is not unattained, it is already attained. That is why it has been called "unattainable" – there is no way to attain it, there is only a way to uncover it. There is no need to attain it, there is only the need to recognize it. Realization, recognition, remembrance – that is enough. You don't have to do anything else to attain it, simply move the curtain aside and it is there. It has always been there, it has always been present within.

When Buddha became enlightened, someone asked him, "What have you attained? Please tell us."

Buddha said, "Nothing has been attained. Yes, plenty has been lost but nothing has been attained, because what has been attained was already there. I was ignorant, I did not know about it. I lost much: I lost my self, I lost ignorance. All the dreams, all the desires and all the wishes were lost.

But I cannot say *what* was attained because it was already there. I attained to that which was already attained."

That is why the sutra says, "unattainable."

It is unattainable,
because it for ever recedes.

It is unattainable in another sense: as you approach it, it keeps on receding.

You will enter the light,
but you will never touch the flame.

It is also unattainable in the sense that you will never be able to hold it in your fist because as you keep journeying within, *you* will begin to disappear. You will never attain to it. Before you can attain, you will have disappeared – "O my friend: seeking and searching, Kabir has been dissolved."

Before attaining it you will have disappeared. That is why you will never attain to it. It is unattainable for you. *You* will enter its light but you will never touch the flame. It is just like when a moth is pulled towards a lamp. It enters the light, it enters the light of the lamp, and as it gets closer and closer, it comes nearer to the moment of disappearing. And when it gets very close to the flame and touches the flame, it dies. It never attains to the light, it disappears before that.

If we take this symbol a step further, the body of the moth dies but its soul must become one with light. When we go within, our ego drops away like the moth and then our soul...

But the way we know ourselves right now – from our present face, from what we have understood to be our name, our address, our occupation – this "I," this identification of ours, can never attain. It enters the light...this ego certainly climbs the stairs of the temple, but it dies outside the temple. And what enters is not the ego.

It is like when you take off your shoes before entering the temple; it is just like that. Your "I" will also fall away outside the real temple. Your existence as you know it now is also a layer, a covering, and that too will fall away outside the temple.

You will certainly enter the temple, but you have no idea about the you that will enter. That "you" is not the one you know. The "you" that is known to you will drop away outside the temple. And the "you" which you do not know will enter the temple and will become one with the flame. And this is another reason why the sutra calls it "unattainable."

Desire only that which is unattainable.

6

DESIRE OF SELF-MASTERY

10. Desire power ardently.

And that power which the disciple shall covet
is that which shall make him appear as nothing
in the eyes of men.

11. Desire peace fervently.

The peace you shall desire
is that sacred peace which nothing can disturb,
and in which the soul grows
as does the holy flower upon the still lagoons.

12. Desire possessions above all.

But those possessions
must belong to the pure soul only,
and be possessed therefore by all pure souls equally, and
thus be the especial property
of the whole only when united.

The tenth sutra:

Desire power ardently.

And that power which the disciple shall covet is that which shall make him appear as nothing in the eyes of men.

First of all it is necessary to understand the difference between a desire and a longing. The dictionary gives the same meaning for both, but in the book of life there is a great difference. A desire and a longing appear to be the same: for a while they appear to be the same and then they part ways. In English there is no alternative word for *desire*. That is why Mabel Collins has used *desire* for both states.

It is very difficult to find a word in another language approximating *abhipsa*, because the yearning for such a state has hardly happened in another culture. Actually the meaning of both words is to want something. But *ichchha* is the wish for something which we do not have, and *abhipsa*, yearning or longing, is the wish for something which we intrinsically already have within us. In desiring there is a demand, and there is restlessness attached to that demand. As long as you don't get it there will be unhappiness. But in the form of desire that is a yearning, while there is also a demand, along with that demand there is a feeling of great fulfillment. Even if you don't get what you want there is no anxiety. If there were such a thing as a peaceful desire that's what longing is, and that's what I am talking about. It seems very paradoxical – like saying "cold fire" – because desire does cause worry; its very meaning is: "I am discontented, I am not satisfied with whatever I have. I need something else in order to be satisfied."

The meaning of this longing, *abhipsa*, is "something more should be there, but as things are I am already content." Understand this difference.

In desire I am discontented, and I will remain discontented until my demand is fulfilled. If the demand is fulfilled, then there will be contentment. So this means that my contentment is conditional; if one of my conditions is met, I will become contented. That is why a man who is full of desires is never content: his conditions are never fulfilled. By the time one wish is fulfilled, twenty-five more have been born. The fulfillment of each wish gives birth to new wishes.

The man who longs becomes content because he is contented in the first place. There is no way to make him discontented. He is happy with what he has. A longing is being born out of this contentment – to be even more content. So remember, it is being born out of contentment and when this longing is fulfilled he will become even more content.

It is necessary to take into account one more difference: desire is never fulfilled, but longing is – because the minute a desire is fulfilled, it will generate ten more, different types of desires. A desire is self-generating. But longing is like a barren woman who cannot bear children. When longing has been fulfilled it does not go on reproducing.

Understand another difference: in desire there is always a pull towards the outer, towards objects. It may be towards wealth, towards fame, towards status, but there is something outside which is pulling you. So the mad outer race is born through desire. Longing is also a pull, but towards the inner. It is also a race, but it does not take you away from yourself; on the contrary, it brings you closer to yourself.

In the dictionary they have identical meanings, but in the book of life the meanings are very different. India was able to discover a word like *abhipsa*, longing, because we have not had only ordinary wishes, we have wished for some extraordinary things too. *That* kind of wishing is exactly the opposite of desiring. That is why we have had to create a new word – *abhipsa*.

The sutra is:

Desire power ardently.

Desire power ardently. So it is necessary to understand the second point which relates to power. There is one type of power which is gained through outer means: you are powerful if you have wealth, you are powerful if you are armed with a sword. If there is strength in your body you are powerful, if you are wealthy you can purchase someone, armed with a sword you can make someone bow down to you. But by yourself you are not powerful. The power is in the sword, and if the sword breaks you become impotent. Power resides in your wealth and if that wealth is lost you become weak. A politician derives *his* power from the people who vote for him. Just by their not casting a vote his power disappears.

So there is a type of power which is gained through outer means, but this is not real power – because *you* remain weak. You are surrounded by power, but you are weak. And this power may be snatched away from you at any moment: the man sitting on a throne can become a beggar at any moment. When those people whose names make the headlines every day in the newspapers no longer hold office, we don't even know whether they are dead or alive. They leave no trace. Many politicians quietly disappear, and then one day, the day they die, some news about them appears in a small corner of the newspaper. Only then do you come to know that "Oh! He was still alive!" In between no trace is left. And when they were in power, in the seat of power, it seemed as if the newspapers wrote about nothing else except them.

So this means that power achieved through outer means does not get rid of your weakness. It only hides it, conceals it with veils. These veils are all beautifully decorated, but you – you remain as helpless as you ever were before.

That's why once a man has reached a certain position he doesn't want to let go of it. He holds onto it with all his might because now he has had a taste of power, he has enjoyed power – in spite of his remaining weak inside. Now, if he loses his position, he will once again become helpless. And this second type of helplessness will bother him much more than the first, because in the first instance he had not tasted power; now he has had a taste of it. In the first instance he did not know how helpless he was; now he does.

It is just like when you are walking on a road on a dark night. It is dark, but you can still find your way a little. Then a car speeds by with its lights full on. The glare of the bright lights shines in your face but still, for a moment, everything is lit up. But when the car has sped away, you find that the road has become darker than it was before; now you cannot see anything.

Once a man who holds high office loses it, he is left standing on just such a dark road, a road which has now become even darker. That moment of brightness did not give more light but rather caused even more blindness. That is why once a man has reached an important position, he doesn't want to let go of it. He wants to hang on to it at any cost.

It is a very strange thing. First, people stake their lives to reach a certain position, then they stake their lives to remain there. And if you want to remain in an important position, there is only one way, and that is to keep trying for an even higher office. To maintain a position it is necessary to keep on making efforts in the race to get ahead, because people are trying to pull you down all the time. Hundreds of people are competing for that same office.

Politics is the search of the weak, the journey of the impotent. So the more impotent you are inside, the more you will try to gather ways of being more powerful on the outside. But please keep one thing in mind: I call all those things political which give you outer power. Then whether it is wealth or knowledge gained from the scriptures, you remain weak. You have learned the Gita by heart, and when the need arises you start quoting the Gita. But you are not a Krishna; this Gita is not something which has been experienced by your inner self. This has been poured into you from the outside, it does not come from within. If it did, you would be very strong. And if by bringing it in from the outside you think that you have become very strong, then it is only an illusion of power.

This sutra says:

Desire power ardently.

Which power? Definitely not that power which comes from wealth, position, scriptures or borrowed knowledge. Long for that power which is not dependent on anything but is born from within you, which cannot be obtained but is inborn, which cannot be bought from the market but which is the flowering of your soul. And it flows outward, from the inner, not to the inner from the outer.

Now you will be able to understand the connection between desire and power in this sutra.

Longing means a desire for the inner. And power is also hidden within, that too is born there. Only through this kind of power will you really become strong. That is why we have called Vardhman, "Mahavira" – the great warrior.

It is not as though Mahavira would have won if he had fought the wrestling champion, Gama. It is nothing like that. Still, we cannot call a man like Gama, "Mahavira" – because although his physical body is strong, the soul within is very weak. And how long will the body last? Gama died of tuberculosis and his last days were very painful.

You will be surprised to know that in the end, all wrestlers die from very dangerous diseases and that their last days are very painful – because whatever strength they had was in their bodies. They mistake the strength of their bodies for their own, and when their bodies start to wilt away they feel they have been cheated. And the body *will* wither away. The wrestler's body loses its strength much faster because he has misused it. All forms of wrestling are a misuse of the body. What happens in the name of exercise is not exercising, but pressurizing.

So a wrestler is pressurizing his body. By doing so, by exerting so much pressure on his muscles, he is forcing the blood to circulate so that his muscles bulge. That is why no wrestler lives to be old; he dies early. A body which could have been of service for sixty years will now last for only forty years. You have used up twenty years of energy violently.

Bodybuilders die early, and the last days of these "strong men" are very sad and painful. As old age dawns they begin to realize that they were actually weak people and the illusion of power that was coming to them was coming through the body.

We have called Vardhman, "Mahavira" – the great warrior. We have called him that because his life energy is arising from such a place that it can never be snatched away: it is arising from within. It is not dependent on any means – neither wealth, nor position, nor the body. It is not at all dependent: it is ours, it is free. This we have called the power of the self. That which is ours is the power of the self. Whatsoever we get from someone else in any way, whatsoever is dependent on another's help, is a false power.

Desire power ardently.

Desire this power ardently and remove your attention from all other types of power, because paying attention to those types of power will prevent this power from developing. And while you remain dependent on others, you will find that you are becoming weaker day by day. All dependent people become weak. Dependence, no matter what type it is, brings weakness.

We are all dependent, and we have created various ways and means through which we get the false impression that we are powerful. Dependence is a deception. It brings a *feeling* of power, but power is never attained.

There is only one power, the one which you are the master of, and nothing outside you can decrease it or increase it. Nobody can snatch it away from you or destroy it. Even if your body is coming to the end of its life, it does not make one iota of difference to your power. Your inner flame will go on burning just the same, your inner light will continue to shine just as brightly, your inner life-giving force will not be the tiniest bit weaker. Nothing can extinguish that life force. That life force is eternal and endless. To desire power ardently is to search for that eternal source.

And there is another very interesting thing. Naturally the power which you get from the outside is manifested on the outside. Inside you are weak, but outside people look at you with star-struck eyes. After you have become president everyone bows down to you, everyone begins to sing your praises. All the people start believing that you are powerful, and inside you are absolutely helpless and weak. Deep inside you know that there is no such power, but the whole world is seeing the influence of power. People can feel the influence of that power which has been gathered by outer means, because it is something that they have given to you. You are a mirror which is simply reflecting their power, which is returning their power to them. They can see what they have given you.

But the power which is born inside cannot generally be seen by others. It can be seen only by those who have had some experience of the inner self, otherwise not.

If Mahavira passed by, don't ever think that you would be able to recognize him. But if Gama came by, you would be able to recognize him immediately. If an emperor came by, you would have no hesitation in recognizing him. If a Buddha came by, you would not be able to recognize him, because the Buddha's power comes from the source and you do not have the eyes to see it. It will be just the opposite: if Buddha passes by you, you will think, "This man is nothing, of no significance." You will have great difficulty in recognizing him, because this kind of recognition implies that your whole life has to be transformed in order for you to recognize him.

That is why it is not so easy to recognize Buddha. To recognize a Buddha you have to change yourself. In order to recognize him, you cannot remain your old self, you have to be new – only then can you recognize him. But who wants to take that much trouble? So we say: "What is the need to recognize a Buddha if in the process I have to change?"

The way we are, we will not be able to recognize Buddha, we will miss him. But yes, we will be able to recognize politicians, wealthy people, generals. The way we are, we can recognize them, because there is no difference between them and us. We are part and parcel of the same world. We speak the same language – our personalities are the same. And whatever they have has been given to them by us. We know that very well; that it belongs to us.

So this sutra says:

Desire power ardently.

And that power which the disciple shall covet
is that which shall make him appear as nothing
in the eyes of men.

It is very necessary that you understand this correctly. If you feel that you have a desire for spirituality, but hidden inside that desire is a wish that people will touch your feet when they see you, then you are wrong. If you wish such things you are nothing but a politician in the guise of a monk. Your nature is that of a politician. If you think that the day you attain to spirituality and become a wise man, you will show people what you are made of, they will witness your miracles – if you have any such wish hidden inside you, you are making a mistake in treading the path of religion. It would be better for you to go into politics. That would be more honest and clear.

I see monks, I see holy men: their search is also fundamentally political. They are also interested in people coming to know of their power. They are not just interested in attaining inner power – their interest is in people knowing about it. Even if they have no such power, they are satisfied if people talk about them.

When the birth of real power takes place only a few people can recognize it. Whether it can be recognized or not is of no concern to the seeker. If people can recognize it, it will do them some good; if they can't, that is their misfortune. But the seeker himself is not at all concerned with all of this. He is only concerned with how his search can make him powerful: "What I am in the eyes of other people is the concern of other people's eyes. That is their problem, it does not concern me." And if the seeker keeps this awareness he will become a nothingness. People will not be able to recognize him from the outside, because the things that outer-oriented people recognize will not be present in him.

What can outer-oriented people recognize? They can recognize if you have money pouring out of your pockets. People come to me and say, "There is never a shortage of money at such and such a holy man's place – even if thousands of people come, there is never any shortage of food, even if hundreds of thousands of people come, there is never a shortage." These people have returned not impressed by the holy man's spirituality, but by the extent of his wealth.

People come to me and tell me that when they visit such and such a holy man, amulets appear in his hands, holy ash appears. These people have returned impressed by a magician, not by spirituality. The deep desire behind this power which is producing amulets and ash is not spiritual; nor is the reason people are impressed spiritual. They are all being impressed by an exhibition of power. If we are impressed when a sick person gets well after he touches a holy man's feet, that is not spiritual, it is something else. We understand the language of the outer world.

But we will not be able to recognize a person like Buddha. A sick person does not become well by touching his feet, nor does he heal a sick man by touching him. Even if by some chance this does happen, Buddha does not say that he has done it. He just says that perhaps it was a matter of chance, and that the fruits of the other's own good actions may have hastened the healing. He does not say, "I have done it." He just says, "It happened to be like this, but don't pay too much attention to it." No wealth, no position, no miracles – so then how will you recognize

Buddha? All the ways in which you normally recognize someone are not there.

I was on a journey. There was one other man in my compartment – there were just the two of us. Naturally it became difficult for him to stay quiet, he wanted to make some conversation. But I only nodded a yes or a no, so that a conversation couldn't get started. Then he took out a packet of betel leaf, and asked me to help myself, but I said thank you, I didn't chew betel leaf. So then he took out some cigarettes, and asked me if I wanted to have one. I said thank you, but I didn't smoke.

Then he said to me, "Please tell me if there is any way to be friendly with you" – because if I had taken the betel leaf or a cigarette, a friendship would have developed. I asked him whether, apart from betel leaf and cigarettes, he knew of any other way to be friendly. His methods of communication were exhausted – whatever ways he knew were all finished, so it seemed that now no relationship could be established.

How will you establish a relationship with Buddha? The language of power is useless – that is unless you consider emptiness also to be a power, unless you know that someone attaining to a state of emptiness is the biggest miracle in this world. To become nothing is the biggest happening in this world...because even a very ordinary person believes he is something. Even an ordinary person believes he is something. In this world to believe you are something is a very normal state of affairs. But to have experienced that you are nothing, an emptiness, is the greatest miracle.

The Jewish mystic, Baal Shem, was the founder of Hasidic mysticism. Somebody came to his village and inquired what it was about Baal Shem that was so miraculous and why he should be given such prominence that he was even worshipped – when there was another rabbi in their village who was known to perform great miracles.

The people of Baal Shem's village said, "First let us decide what a miracle is. If Baal Shem asked God to perform something, and God did it instantly, would you recognize this as a miracle?"

They replied, "Certainly, this is a miracle. This is exactly what our rabbi does: whatever he asks of God, God fulfills it."

So then the people of Baal Shem's village said, "Our Baal Shem too performs miracles, but his miracles are of a different sort – whatever God asks him to do, Baal Shem does. Baal Shem doesn't even ask. If you consider this to be a miracle, then our Baal Shem is miraculous! Whatever God says, whenever he says it, Baal Shem obeys him. So far he has not asked anything of God; that's why we don't know anything about the first kind of miracle. And even when we tell him to ask, he says, 'Who am I to give commands to God? I am nothing. If his command is fulfilled, that is enough.'"

The power that the spiritual seeker is looking for is the power of emptiness. The power that you are seeking in the outer world is not the power of emptiness – it is a power dependent on some outer resource, a search for something material, some wealth or position. But when someone is prepared to be nothing, in his state of being nothing a seed sprouts and flowers from within his soul. Ardently desire *that* power.

The eleventh sutra is:

Desire peace fervently.

The yearning for peace is mentioned immediately after the sutra on power. Whatever power comes from the outside brings worry with it. Wealth bestows power, but worry also comes in its wake. It is very difficult to find a rich man who is also peaceful. Sometimes you can find a poor man who is peaceful, but a rich man who is peaceful – never! And those who wanted to become peaceful renounced their wealth and became poor. The man who holds a political post can never be peaceful – he simply cannot. Power, whenever it comes from the outside, brings with it the shadow of turmoil. So if you want to live peacefully, there will be no way to have outer power.

I have a friend who is a government minister, and now he wants to become the chief minister. He always comes to me and asks me how to become peaceful. So I tell him, "First, become the chief minister. Right now you should ask me how to become worried. Right now don't even ask me how to become peaceful, because if you find a way of becoming peaceful, one thing is certain: you will never become chief minister. So first be certain whether you want to be chief minister or not; only then will I tell you how to become peaceful. Otherwise don't come to me and then tell me later on that I spoiled everything, that I ruined your life. It is better that you become chief minister first and then, when you are really troubled, the thirst to become peaceful will arise."

When a man has worked hard, he starts to feel hungry. In the same way, when a man has become really troubled, he hungers for peace. I said, "Right now, even your hunger is not real. Right now, even your hunger comes from reading books; peace is just an idea, it is just your greed. Right now, you want to become chief minister and you also want to become peaceful."

I told him that if he searched honestly within himself he would find that he only wanted peace in order to help him become chief minister. He replied, "How did you know? It is just as you say. I have to do so much running around that if my mind were to become just a little more peaceful, I could succeed. My mind becomes so restless that I can't sleep at night; I become so tense that I become sick – and so the others are getting ahead of me. They have no problems sleeping, they don't become sick. In the morning they start again, fresh for the race, and I am dead tired! That is why I have come to you – so that you can tell me a way to become peaceful so that I can really take on my opponents."

We want to use even peace in the service of anxiety! We want peace so that we can worry more effectively, so that our worrying becomes even more efficient. We want peace so that we can draw power from it. But power brings worry.

So take this as your criterion: the power which brings turmoil is outer and is not worth longing for, and the power which creates peace in you is inner and is worth longing for. Outer power means turmoil, inner power means peace.

That's why this sutra follows immediately after the sutra about power:

Desire peace fervently.

But to want power alone is dangerous. You can deceive yourself, thinking that you want inner power, but in fact that may still be a desire for outer power. That may still be a contest, a competition. That may still be a way to prove yourself to someone who is really enlightened: "How is it possible that while I am not enlightened another person can be? Now I will show that I too can attain."

A very rich man, the richest in the town, came to see Mahavira. He came to him and said, "I want to buy meditation – and I am willing to pay any price you ask."

Mahavira said, "That is impossible, meditation cannot be bought. A person who always thinks in terms of buying and selling cannot understand meditation, let alone attain to it. All your wealth will not be able to buy it."

The rich man said, "Perhaps you don't know how much wealth I have. Ask any price and I will pay you double. Just tell me how much it will cost."

That man must have known only one language – the language of money. And it was not his fault either, because everything he had acquired in his life was with money, so he could be excused for thinking like that. He had bought everything. If he wanted a beautiful woman, he paid some money and he had her. If he wanted a big palace, he bought it. If he needed a good doctor, he paid for him. What can't be bought with money? He had always bought everything, so he must have thought, "What's so great about meditation that it cannot be bought with money? When everything else can be bought, then I must be able to buy this too."

But actually, attaining to meditation was not the problem. A poor man of the village had attained to meditation, a poor man of the same village! And Mahavira had confirmed that this man had attained. It was this that was creating the problem.

Mahavira came to know what the rich man's problem was, so he said, "Do this: go to the poor man in your village who has attained to meditation, and purchase it from him. He is a poor man – perhaps he will be tempted by the money. Perhaps he will sell it, and you can buy it from him."

The rich man replied, "There is no problem, that's very easy. If he refuses to sell meditation, I can buy him out. There will be no problem."

Now what he said is completely right, because if a poor man can be bought out then what is so great about any meditation he may have? But even if you buy the poor man out, meditation cannot be bought. If you seize that poor man, put him in chains, and throw him into your house – even then meditation cannot be seized. The difficulty lies in the language: the rich man understood only the language of money.

He went to the poor man and said, "Look, I am willing to pay anything, you just name your price, but you must give me meditation. And if you refuse to hand over meditation, I have brought soldiers along with me – they will take you away."

The poor man said, "Take me away – that will be easier. How can I give you meditation? Is meditation a commodity which I can give to you? Meditation is an experience. You can take me away, but how can I give you what I feel? You will have to experience that for yourself."

There is a power which others can give you, and there is a power which can be found only through one's own experience. The power that others give you will never give you peace, because fear is always a part of it. What is given to you by another can also be taken away from you by him. And what another has given me is simply not mine – whether I have gained it through stealing, or through persuasion, or through charity, or by force. It is not mine – it belongs to another, and what belongs to another remains his. That is why it always instills fear. Fear keeps following silently in your footsteps.

Fear gives birth to turmoil, anxiety grows out of that which can be taken away. And then the more outside power accumulates, the weaker you seem to be inside. This creates anxiety.

That is why no poor man can feel his poverty as much as a rich man can – that is, if he is intelligent. If he is a fool, without intelligence, then he isn't even aware of it. A poor man will never feel his poverty to the extent that a rich person with even a little bit of intelligence does, because for the poor man there is no contrast, there is no comparison. A rich man accumulates great wealth, and then he looks within and finds a begging bowl in his heart – there is nothing inside. A poor man has a begging bowl in his hand, and a begging bowl within. There is no contradiction in the comparison, so he doesn't realize how poor he is. Only when a man has become rich does he realize how poor a man can be.

That is why I always say that the poverty which Mahavira experienced after giving up his kingdom, or which Buddha experienced when he left his throne and became a beggar on the road, can never be felt by a common beggar. Wealth has a big hand in their poverty. Their poverty is royal, it is a poverty enriched by the experience of having been an emperor. And after becoming emperors they came to realize they could not get rid of the poverty that lies within; in fact now they could see it more clearly. The more you accumulate outer power, the more you come to see your inner helplessness. This creates anxiety – and remember, a poor man can never be as worried as a rich man.

If America is the most worried and tense country today, it is not because its morality has declined in some way, but only because it has become richer than other countries. Anxiety is a part of life in America. You are all trying to make your countries rich – and that is how it should be, but you must remember that all this anxiety will become yours too. With wealth comes worry. There is a carefree quality in poverty, because it creates no awareness of the real poverty. I am not saying that you should remain poor. All I am saying is that if you become aware of the poverty within, that awareness will give birth to spirituality. What I am really saying is: to be rich is a must in order to become religious. The more affluent a society is, the greater the possibility of its becoming religious.

A poor society cannot become religious – there is no way. A poor man's desire for religion is only the desire for outer power. Even if he prays, it is for money; his worship is just for the sake of wealth. When a poor man prays and worships, his demands are materialistic. A rich man is materially satisfied; there is no question of his asking for more, he already has enough. Now there is no sense in adding any more to what he has. And from this arises a great worry, a deep anxiety: now what?

That is why no nation on earth today is in as much anguish as America is. But this is fortunate, because this madness shows that wealth simply highlights poverty, power simply highlights helplessness, education simply brings our inner ignorance to light.

If what we have attained in the outer world is the opposite of what we experience inside, then a tension arises, an anguish is born. Whatever we achieve in the outer world will give birth to a restlessness. Hence, along with the longing for power, a deep longing for peace should also be there. Only then can your power become an inner power.

Your search should always be for power and peace. And wherever you find that your power is working against peace, understand that this power is wrong. Let go of it. Let peace be the foundation. Whenever your power begins to interfere with your peace, let go of the power and hold onto the peace. Make peace your sutra, let it become the touchstone for testing the outcome. Understand that the power which passes this test is authentic and as pure as gold. And as for the power which does not pass this test – throw it away like dirt. Don't let it hang around you, even for one moment.

If you always keep this criterion of peace in your mind, you will never be lost. Peace works like a compass. Whichever direction peace points to, know that this is the right one. And wherever the needle of peace does not point to is not the right destination; leave it. You need to take peace as the criterion so that power doesn't give you false illusions.

The peace you shall desire
is that sacred peace which nothing can disturb,
and in which the soul grows
as does the holy flower upon the still lagoons.

The peace which you shall desire is that sacred peace which nothing can disturb... Remember, if someone can disturb it, it is not peace. It is necessary to understand this.

Often people complain that their peace has been disturbed. But if someone can disturb your peace, then that peace has been given to you by someone else – because only that which has been given to us can be disturbed, otherwise we cannot be affected. If you are sitting quietly and a child is making a noise, and you say that he is disturbing you, this means that if he sits quietly he will give you peace and if he makes a noise, he will disturb your peace. This peace doesn't belong to you – it is the child's.

You say that the noise from the market hinders your meditation: then it is not meditation. What is the value of a meditation that can be disturbed by the marketplace? It is not worth a penny. It has been given to you by the marketplace. You say that in the mountains meditation really flowers. This is not meditation, it is a gift from the mountains. What has been given to you by the mountains is not yours. What the marketplace can take away from you is not yours.

So you may sit for years on end in the mountains, but you will be living in illusion, because when you leave the mountains you will find yourself in turmoil again – and you will be in even more turmoil than you ever were before. If you have something which can be disturbed, it does not belong to you.

Search for a peace that no one can disturb. This means when you search, don't avoid disturbances – rather search in the midst of them. If your child is not making a noise, go and collect all the children from the neighborhood, ask them to make a lot of noise and then meditate amongst them. The day you feel that you can meditate even though the children are making a noise, you will know that meditation is yours. Don't search for mountains, the Himalayas, rather meditate sitting down right in the middle of the marketplace – because the mountains can deceive you. The mountains give you peace, that's why they can be deceptive. Avoid the mountains, search for peace in the marketplace. The day you find peace even in the marketplace, from that day on, no one can take it away from you, because now you have found it in the middle of the very thing which could have taken it away from you.

So don't run away from your home. Your sannyas is only true if you can become a sannyasin while being a householder. If you were to become a sannyasin after leaving your house, your wife, your children and your wealth, that sannyas would be false, a conditional, imposed sannyas. If your wife were given back to you, she would take away your sannyas in just one night – even sooner than that! It wouldn't take much time.

That is why the so-called sannyasin always remains very fearful. He is afraid a woman may touch him. Why is he so afraid? Where will this fearful sannyas take him? What will be the fruits of such an impotent sannyas? Will the soul become weak or strong through it? We never consider all this.

A man is afraid to touch a woman and we think he is very religious. And he is afraid to touch a woman! If a woman touches him, his celibacy will be destroyed! This is the height of helplessness – what can such a helpless soul achieve? He goes around preaching that a woman is nothing but a bundle of skin and bones, but he is scared to even touch her! So all he is saying is superficial; it is nothing but a method to convince himself. Inside, his interest is very present. If he touches the woman the interest will be kindled, and once that happens he will begin to feel that he has fallen.

But no woman creates an interest in a man, and no man creates an interest in a woman. If the interest is already there, she brings it out. This will help your search: if desire is inside you, the presence of a woman will bring it out. So the woman only works as a mirror, the woman is only providing a diagnosis of what lies hidden within you. Why run away from it? It is good to keep her always beside you, so that you can remain aware of what lies hidden within you. And if your sexual desire vanishes while she is with you, only then have you attained real celibacy, only then have you attained to an inner power.

If you attempt to live avoiding the pull of opposites, you will become like a hothouse plant. You can make a greenhouse and provide it with air conditioning – and then any plant can be taken care of inside it. But don't ever take this plant outside by mistake into the air and sunshine: it will die.

Your so-called sannyasins are such hothouse plants. They have created a certain structure and their sannyas survives within this framework. You only need to place them just a little outside this framework, in the real world, and they will prove to be made of mud. They are mud lions – a little water can wash them away. They are so afraid of water that they cannot be real lions. A real lion will enjoy being in the water, he will find it invigorating, he will become more powerful.

You should learn the art of becoming enriched through opposites. Escaping the opposite is a sign of weakness.

So don't ever desire a peace which can be disturbed by someone. This kind of peace is of no use, in fact it will be trouble. The truth is that it will become the cause of even greater turmoil.

That is why, if someone in a family becomes religious, like these so-called sannyasins, he becomes a source of disturbance to the whole household – and remains disturbed himself. If you start to meditate, it becomes a trouble for the whole family, because now you will use meditation as a pretext for criticizing everyone. Now, even a small thing disturbs your peace and you will blame someone or other. Why did a utensil make so much noise when it fell? Why did the child shout? Why is someone crying? Why has someone put on the radio? You wanted to be peaceful but you have managed to gather around you the very set up which will keep you in turmoil!

Radios go on playing, children cry and laugh, utensils continue to fall – you will have to have a deep sense of acceptance towards all of this, you will have to become peaceful in the midst of all of this. Don't be afraid of disturbances; see them as a part of the vast world of meditation. Then the peace you attain will be your own, you can rely on it. If you really become religious in the truest sense, then because of *you* your home will become more peaceful. If you become a pseudo-religious man, and this country is full of them, then each and every home will become troubled. If one member of a household becomes pseudo-religious he can drive the whole family mad.

A lady came to me and said, "Please, you have to save me! My husband has become religious and our whole house is in trouble." Her husband too was not an ordinary person; he was a *sardar*.

I asked her, "What is he up to? What has happened?" She told me that he was getting up at two in the morning and doing loud devotional singing, so that no one else was able to get any sleep. The children's exams were approaching, they were all beating their heads – but this religious man would start his *kirtan* at two every morning.

So then I sent for her husband. I asked him, "What are you doing?" He told me that he performed *kirtan* at the auspicious early-morning hour of the *brahman*, the divine. Two o'clock in the morning is the auspicious hour of the *brahman*!

He said, "Everyone should be awake by the hour of the *brahman*; the question of there being any disturbance doesn't even arise." He told me not to be taken in by all those heretics who were trying to disrupt the *kirtan* and make problems for such great religious work.

Now he was blaming the whole household – and whoever he would ask to perform *kirtan* at the hour of the *brahman* did not have the courage to ask him to stop – because who likes to be known as an irreligious person? So I told him, "Listen, no need to stop, but move the hour of the *brahman* a little forwards. Two o'clock is also a little too early for the divine – make it three o'clock. Then move it to four o'clock and then to five, and *then* do your kirtan."

He replied, "What are you saying? How far do I have to move it?"

I said, "I call the hour of the *brahman* the hour when the divine in you opens its eyes. I can't call it the divine if any device is used to make this happen. Right now you are using an alarm clock to get up, so this is not the auspicious hour of the divine, rather it is the alarm's auspicious hour. Stop this. When that divine which lies hidden within you wakes up from sleep, then *that* is the hour of the *brahman*."

He said, "You will lead me astray! I can't get up before nine o'clock."

So I said, "If you can't get up, then think a little bit about your children. You have been kindled with spiritual fire, they haven't yet, so why are you bothering them? And because of you, these children will be put off religion for ever. They will never be attracted to religion, even mistakenly, and you will be responsible for it because you are ruining their lives. Whenever anyone talks about religion, they will be reminded of two o'clock in the night, the hour of the *brahman*: 'Let's not get caught up in all this.' You are blaming them, but it is you who is mad. You say that they are disturbing the peace, that they are causing a disturbance, but it is you who is destroying their peace."

Almost all insane people are attracted to what goes on in the name of religion. You just cannot imagine how easy it is to hide madness under the guise of religion. Under the guise of religion people hide a thousand kinds of sickness. If you enjoy being dirty – and the psychologists say there are certain people who delight in having a dirty body – there are many paths available for you to choose from. You can become a Jaina monk, who is forbidden to take a bath – and so on. Then, what a delight you can take in being dirty! If a clean person approaches you, you can look down on him – because according to you, one who takes a refreshing bath is indulging himself because he is adorning the body. Bathing and washing are an unnecessary adornment of the body. Remaining dirty, not brushing your teeth, having a mouth reeking of bad breath – these are pious deeds!

In the West such types of mad people are medically treated. Here, they find some way to be religious. In the West if anyone behaves so foolishly he will be immediately taken to a doctor to be treated. He will be taken to a psychiatrist; they will say that something has gone wrong with him. But here, there is nothing wrong in it. Here, such a person will be accepted.

Jung has said that there are so few mad people in India because the mad have other avenues for their madness. They can remain mad without being thought of as mad. If a person is shitting while he is eating we call him "The Supremely Enlightened One"! Anywhere else in the world he will be immediately locked up. But we say that this man has attained to supreme indifference, non-duality; that he is the wise one, he is beyond discrimination. This man is mad, he is in need of treatment! He has lost his mind. He has not transcended mind, he has fallen below the mind – but we will honor him.

Always remember that a pseudo-religion will make you more anxiety-ridden, it will promote insanity. And a pseudo-religion will always put the blame on others: you are always right, others are always wrong. But a true religion doesn't blame anyone. Others are what they are.

They have a right to be what they are, they have the freedom.

A child has the right to sing, to dance. This is the child's right. Your need is to meditate, but the child's need is to dance, to shout. You enjoy your meditation. The child doesn't say that your meditation is disturbing him, that your sitting down to meditate is getting in the way of his playing. So then why are you saying that his playing is disturbing your meditation? You meditate – and let the child play. Just forget this idea that someone can disturb your meditation. By dropping this idea you will start moving in the right direction of meditation. Whenever you feel that someone is causing a disturbance, immediately understand that it is *you* who is making some mistake – otherwise no disturbance is possible.

That is why this sutra says:

The peace you shall desire
is that sacred peace which nothing can disturb,
and in which the soul grows
as does the holy flower upon the still lagoons.

Just as a lotus blossoms in a peaceful lake, the lotus of your soul will blossom only in a peaceful state of meditation. There is no need to try to make it blossom, it will blossom of its own accord. Only two essential conditions must be fulfilled first: a peace that is free from the outer, and a power that is free from the outer. Then the lotus of your life will begin to bloom.

The twelfth sutra:

Desire possessions above all.

But those possessions
must belong to the pure soul only,
and be possessed therefore by all pure souls equally,
and thus be the especial property
of the whole only when united.

Desire possessions above all.. Self-mastery! That is why the Hindus have chosen to call their sannyasins *swami* – one who is the master of himself. But what type of mastery? – of a house, of wealth, of a shop? No, because all of that is only a deception: actually you become a slave, but you think that you are a master. You become a slave and you think that you have become an emperor.

I have heard…

The Mohammedan saint, Farid, was passing through a village. He saw a man who had tied a rope to his cow and was taking her to his house. So Farid stopped – he was in the habit of doing such things – and he said to his disciples, "Go and surround this man and his cow; I want to teach you something."

The man was a little startled. He said, "Why are you surrounding me?"

Farid replied, "Keep quiet. We aren't concerned with you, I just want to teach my disciples." He confirmed, "My disciples, I ask you: of these two, which is the master? – the cow or the man?"

The disciples said, "What are you asking? It is quite clear that the man is the master because the cow is his property and he has put a rope around her neck."

Farid said, "I'll ask you a second question. Suppose we cut the rope and the cow runs away: will the cow chase the man or will the man run after the cow?"

They said, "Certainly it is the man who will run after the cow."

"So this means that the cow will not go searching for the man, the man will search for the cow," said Farid. "If this is so, then who is the master?" And he added, "This rope which you see around the neck of the cow is actually around the man's neck."

Possessions put a rope around our necks. We become the slave of what we own. You will become the slave of whatsoever you own.

Just think a little! In India husbands call themselves masters. Can you find greater slaves than they are? They are masters? When their wives write them a letter they may address them as "master" and in the end they may write "your slave" and so on, but everyone knows very well who is the master and who is the slave. No one has even the slightest doubt on this subject. The woman is clever – she says, "Okay, what does it matter if it is only a matter of writing 'your slave' and so on. It hardly matters." But in reality who is the master? The husbands will remain slaves as long as they have this notion that they should be the masters. As long as they think that they should be the masters of their wives, they may be the master in name but actually they will remain slaves.

Anyone who tries to be a master over someone else becomes a slave. All types of possession in the outer world bring slavery along with them.

So what type of mastery is the sutra hinting at? It is hinting at the inner mastery. You can only be master of yourself. You simply cannot be the master of somebody else. Never make this mistake. Outer mastery is impossible, it is only a deception. And whenever you fall into that deception, you discover that you have become a slave, you haven't become a master. And in the end you will find that the castles of mastery that you have built have become prisons of slavery and you are trapped inside them.

There can be only one mastery – and that is of oneself. And remember: how can someone who is not a master of himself be the master of another? There is only one way to be a master of yourself: he who wishes to become his own master stops possessing others.

This sutra says: Desire self-mastery above all, so that you don't become satisfied with a deception. Desire self-mastery above all – desire the *real* mastery. Don't become satisfied with a deception. By possessing falsities don't think that you have become a master. Until you have become your own master, keep your longing for it alive.

This seems contradictory. We have called those who have left everything behind and dressed in the clothes of roadside beggars, masters. Only Buddha did not call his disciples "masters" but "beggars." There was a reason for doing so. Both approaches have an interesting significance.

The Hindus called the sannyasin *swami*, master, because he has dropped all ideas of mastery in all areas of his life and is concentrating on becoming the master only of one thing: his own self. He is his own master – that's why the Hindus have called their sannyasins, swami, a master.

Buddha called his sannyasins *bhikkhu* – a beggar. This seems to be very contrary, but Buddha called his disciples a beggar because in this world everyone has the idea that he is a master. Here everyone seems to be a master of this or that. The word had become polluted. So he said, "I will call you a beggar. I will address you as a beggar because in this world everything seems to be topsy-turvy. Here, all beggars are calling themselves masters. That's why I will call a master a beggar."

Buddha said that in this world, because everything seems to be on its head and people are standing upside down, he will make all his disciples stand the right way up, on their own feet: "Here, every beggar is calling himself a master, so by calling you a master a great misunderstanding will be created. That is why I will call you a beggar. You are the master of yourself. Beggars are calling themselves masters, that's why it is appropriate that a master should call himself a beggar."

But it is one and the same thing, the intention behind both the names is the same – that an inner self-mastery can be attained.

Desire possessions above all.

7

SEEK OUT THE WAY

13. Seek out the way.

Pause and consider awhile.
Is it the way you desire, or is it
that there is a dim perspective in your visions
of great heights to be scaled by your self,
of a great future for you to compass?
Be warned.
The way is to be sought for its own sake,
not with regard to your feet that shall tread it.

14. Seek the way by retreating within.

15. Seek the way by advancing boldly without.

The whole nature of man must be used wisely
by the one who desires to enter the way.
Each man is to himself absolutely the way,
the truth, and the life.
Thus seek out the way.

Seek it by study of the laws of being,
the laws of nature, the laws of the supernatural.

Steadily, as you watch and worship,
its light will grow stronger.
Then you may know
you have found the beginning of the way.
And when you have found the end
its light will suddenly become the infinite light.

Be not appalled and terrified by the sight;
keep your eyes fixed on the small light
and it will grow.
But let the darkness within
help you to understand the helplessness of those
who have seen no light,
whose souls are in profound gloom.

The thirteenth sutra:

Seek out the way.

Pause and consider awhile.
Is it the way you desire, or is it
that there is a dim perspective in your visions
of great heights to be scaled by your self,
of a great future for you to compass?
Be warned.
The way is to be sought for its own sake,
not with regard to your feet that shall tread it.

There are many things to understand in this sutra.
The first: the way is not already given to you, you have to search for it. But every person is under the illusion that it is already given to him. And if there is one thing that has

played a major role in destroying religion throughout the world, it is the illusion that the way is already given.

The way is not given to us by birth. But all the religions have created a system so that as soon as you are born, you are given a religion as well; along with your mother's milk you are given a religion. When a child has not yet developed his intelligence, when he does not yet think about anything, when he still does not have a mind, when he still does not have any understanding, we instill a religion into the depths of his unconscious. The parents instill their way – which is not their way either; that too was given to them by their parents. So then you are born as a Hindu, a Mohammedan, a Jaina or a Christian. From your very birth you are connected with some path which has been forced upon you.

No one is born a Hindu or a Mohammedan; no one can be. A person can be born into a Hindu house, but no one can be born a Hindu. He can be born into a Mohammedan house, but he cannot be born a Mohammedan. When a man is born he does not have a religion, a way. The way is forced upon him as a child by his parents, by the family, by the caste, by the society. And they are in a great hurry to enforce it, because if the child begins to understand, he will oppose this forcing. That is why it is enforced when he is not yet fully alert.

All religions are in a great hurry to grab children by the neck; a little bit too late, and it will be difficult. Once the child emerges from an unconscious into a conscious state of mind, he knows how to take care of himself and then you will not be able to enforce your religion – the child will seek it out for himself. It may happen that a child from a Hindu household feels that Christianity is his way. A child from a Christian home may have a preference for Hinduism. Now this will create a great disturbance. To prevent a child from turning away from your religion, in your unconsciousness you commit a sin with him – you wrap your conditioning around his neck. Of all the sins that man has committed so far, this is the greatest of them all.

Why do I call it the greatest sin? – because we give the child a false religion which is not of his own choosing. And religion is such a thing that unless you have chosen it for yourself it will not be of any value. Only when *you* have chosen it – as an outcome of the search from your own being, from your own pain and thirst – can you be religious. The religion which has been given to you by others remains superficial, and because of it your own search is hindered.

That is why while Buddha or Mahavira or Mohammed or Christ is alive, the light of religiousness shines out and there is a revolution in the lives of the people who go to them; but once they are gone, the light slowly begins to fade. The people who went to Buddha to be initiated had made their own decision to follow him. Through reflecting, through experiencing, through considering, through practicing and experimenting, they felt that Buddha's way was the right way for them too, and so they began to follow him. This was their own personal choice, this was their own surrender. This commitment had not been forced upon them by someone else. They had chosen it themselves so it had a totally different flavor. They could put their whole lives at stake for it – because one puts one's life at stake only for something that one feels oneself is right.

But their children will be Buddhists by birth – it will not be from their own choice. They will not have made their own decision, they will not have even thought about it. The Buddhist religion will have been forced upon them.

Bear in mind that whatever *you* choose, even if it is hell, will turn out to be a heaven. And even if heaven has been forced upon you, it will turn out to be a hell. Hell is in the enforcement. If something has been thrust upon you from outside, even if it is bliss, it will be a suffering. Forcing causes suffering, and whatever is forced upon you becomes a prison.

So on the earth today there is no real Hindu, there is no real Mohammedan, no real Buddhist: today only prisoners exist. Someone is in a Hindu prison, someone is in a Mohammedan prison, someone is in a Jaina prison...

I call it a prison because you have never thought about whether you wanted to be a Hindu, a Mohammedan, or a Jaina. You did not choose. Your religion is your slavery but the slavery is so subtle that you are not even aware of it, because it was instilled in you when you were not conscious enough. When you were not yet aware of what was happening, this slavery, this chain was put around your wrists. By the time you became conscious you found your hands chained. And it was not called a chain either. Your parents, your family, your society told you that it was an ornament that needed to be carefully guarded, so that no one could destroy it. This was an ornament, and a very valuable one, and for its sake you would stake your life.

And a very interesting thing has happened. If the Hindu religion is in danger you will give your life for it. For the Hindu religion, for Christianity or for Islam...you can die for the sake of whatever your religion is, but you are not ready to live for it. If you are asked to live your life as a real Hindu, you will not be ready. If you are asked to live your life as a real Mohammedan, you will not be ready. But if there is a riot between the two, you are willing to die! The man who is willing to die for Hinduism is not willing to live for Hinduism. What has gone wrong?

There is a disease somewhere, there is a sickness somewhere. You have no zest for life at all. You are very eager to fight: when someone attacks your religion you lose your senses – a part of your unconsciousness is being attacked.

Whenever Hindus and Mohammedans are fighting, don't think that they are aware of what they are doing. They are fighting in a state of unconsciousness. In that state of being they are Hindus or Mohammedans, but they are not conscious. That's why if anyone hurts their unconscious mind, they just go mad. Hindus and Mohammedans are not fighting: it is mad people who are fighting. Some mad people are branded Hindu, some Mohammedan – there is a difference in brands, but they are all mad.

Religion is instilled in you when you are not capable of logical thinking. That is why I say that this is the greatest of sins. And while this sin continues, as long as we do not allow the freedom to each and every person to find his own way, the world can never become religious. Because each person needs to make the decision to be religious for himself, because for religiousness to happen, it needs to be each individual's own choosing.

It will be easier if we understand it like this...

In the past – and in India until even very recently – there used to be child marriages. Neither the husband nor the wife was at all concerned about the person to whom they were getting married. They were such small children that they had no idea of what was going on. In their innocent state we made them a husband or a wife; they were not fully in their senses, they were not aware of what was happening. Just as one gains a sister, a mother and a father at birth, so too in their unawareness they acquired a wife or a husband.

One benefit of child marriage for the society was that it was very difficult for the couple to break up. Because it was their unconsciousnesses that were being joined together, because it was not their conscious choice – there was no question of any conscious choice – how could there be any question of their separating? The people who first introduced child marriage must have been very clever. What it meant was that the marriage would never break up, because two people who have not come together consciously cannot consciously choose to part. So the marriage would last, it would be stable.

But the phenomenon of love can never happen in such a marriage. Keep in mind that by staying together, by living closely, by staying with one another, a type of friendliness develops – but this is not love. Love is a madness, love is a rapture. In a child marriage love just doesn't happen. Actually the very intention behind child marriage is to prevent love from happening. Because love is dangerous, everything is done to prevent it from happening.

Marriage is safe, love is dangerous. Love ascends to such heights that there is a danger: if you fall down from those heights, you will end up in a ditch of the same magnitude. No such fall can take place in a marriage because it never climbs to those heights. The journey is on even ground. There are no peaks, there are no valleys – it is safe, it is stable. So marriage is an institution, but love is a happening. A happening is something unplanned, an institution is always planned.

They were clever people. Love can be dangerous – it has to be. It is difficult to live at such heights forever; you will have to climb down. Love takes one to such heights of imagination, it creates such dreams, that it is possible for only a few dreamers to live with those dreams. Most people will fall back down to earth – it is difficult to live at such a peak. And when they fall, they will be in great pain. Remember that the greater the happiness you aspire to, the deeper the ditch of suffering that is present at its side. So the people who instigated child marriage set up a very clever arrangement; they removed the danger of love so that then there was no fear of a fall.

When you yourself have not chosen to get married, there could be no question of a divorce either. You cannot undo what you have not done. Can you divorce your sister? Can you ask your mother for a divorce? These are situations given by nature, how can you undo them? What could it possibly mean if you were to say, "Now I divorce my sister, now she is no longer my sister"? There is no way you can do this. Even if they become your enemies, whatever they do – a sister remains a sister, a father will always be a father, a mother will always be a mother. We have created exactly the same mold for a wife.

In life there is only one chance to choose and that is in a love relationship. A father is given by birth, a mother is given by birth, brothers and sisters are given by birth. It is only in the relationship of a husband and wife that there is the freedom to choose. In all other relationships we do not have that freedom. So this one opportunity to exercise freedom can be dangerous, because freedom is dangerous; hence we took that away too. We made marriage into an institution and made it a part of the unconscious. The danger was removed, but so too was the romantic flight of love. The elixir of love vanished along with the danger.

We have done exactly the same with religions as we have done by having child marriage. We have made them a part of the unconscious too. When the child grows up he discovers that he is a Hindu. He doesn't even know that when he was born he was not a Hindu. As he grows up, he finds out that he is a Hindu, he is a Mohammedan. It never occurs to him that all his conditioning is borrowed, that someone has instilled it, injected it into his mind, that he was not born with it. Now he will go through his whole life believing that he is a Hindu.

And he can't possibly have much interest in what he has not chosen for himself. If we look carefully we can see that he doesn't have any real connection with it. It is an imposition which he will somehow carry around with him, it is a formality. At times, when it is necessary to visit the temple, he will oblige; he will find himself in church on a Sunday; he will take part in some festival as a formality. Religion will become a part of his social structure.

But religion is not a part of the social structure. Like love, religion is dangerous – even more dangerous than love. Like love it is dangerous because there is no way to know where it will lead, no prediction can be made about the outcome. Religion is even more dangerous than love. Love takes you along unknown paths, but religion takes you onto even more unknown paths. Religion is an inner revolution. By making religion a social institution no avenue is left for the inner revolution.

So our minds build up a resistance to what has been imposed upon us. They have to. And we relish destroying what has been imposed on us. Why? – because when we destroy it, we feel as if we are becoming free from it.

Freud has written about an incident that happened when he went for a walk in the park with his wife and child.

"...As we were returning from the park and just as the gates were being shut, we realized that our child was missing. So I asked my wife, 'Where is our child?' My wife became very frightened; the gates were being shut, the park was miles long and the child could have been anywhere.

"Then I said, 'Don't worry, just tell me: did you forbid him from going to some particular place? If you did, then that is the place where we should look first. If he has even a little intelligence, that is where he will go.'

"My wife replied, 'I told him not to go to the fountain.'

"I said, 'Come, let's run to the fountain.' And there we found our son sitting with his legs dangling in the water."

Freud's wife then asked him how he had guessed that their son would be there. Freud said, "There was nothing to guess. If the child had been really stupid, only then could a mistake have been possible. But if there is even a little intelligence in him, then naturally he is interested in what is forbidden."

What has been forbidden is what becomes inviting. Tell someone not to do something, and you have made him interested in doing it.

If you see so much immorality in today's society, it is because of the moral preaching of those who have now become your gurus. Your priests, your so-called saints, your mahatmas are ninety percent responsible for this immorality, because they create the interest in you. They say, "Don't do this, don't do that" – and wherever they say, "Don't do this," we suppose some mysterious treasure is hidden there. When so many wise men are bent on dissuading us, there must be something in it! Something must be there, otherwise why should so many wise men waste their time saying, "Don't do this"? The mind feels it must find out and so an unhealthy curiosity is born.

You know if a film is labeled, "For adults only," you will see small kids queuing up wearing false mustaches trying to get in: they feel that there must be something really juicy in the film, which is not to be missed! It is very difficult to ignore something that is forbidden.

So man begins to take delight in destroying whatever has been imposed upon him. The reason for so much irreligiousness is that religion has been forced upon you; it is not of your own choosing, it was not your own personal wish.

It is better to be irreligious than to carry someone else's religion on your back, because if you do, you will never become religious, you will always remain pseudo-religious. It is better to throw away borrowed things. And no harm can be done if you live without such a religion for a few days.

But no man can live without religion for too long, because without religion there is no way to experience bliss. And that is the reason why I am not afraid to say that it is better to be without any religion than to have an imposed religion, which is dangerous. Because of that imposed religion a kind of resistance towards religion will be born in your mind. Your religion remains only on the surface –

deep down there is resistance and you become divided in two. Then you don't even bother to seek. Then whenever the subject of religion comes up, you feel everything is fine, you already know what religion is. This borrowed, imposed, instilled religion – this is not the path for you. It has even more dangers.

One thing: religion should never become an organization. Religion is a revolution and each person should choose his own religion, should choose his own way – because how can a path given to you by someone else make you free? Just think: if the very first step of something through which you intend to attain to the ultimate liberation is rooted in slavery, how can it ever take you to ultimate liberation? If someone says, "You will be liberated, but first let me handcuff you. Liberation will be yours but first let me imprison you. You will be given freedom but first let me hang a stone around your neck," will you agree that, yes, you are being helped towards supreme liberation? No! You will say, "As it is, I am quite liberated! What you are telling me will only become even more of a slavery."

Liberation can be attained only when you have freedom. The first step towards freedom will also have to be taken in freedom. And the first freedom that is essential is the freedom from a religion given by others.

Seek out your own way – that is the meaning of the sutra. Have no fear, don't become afraid. The religion which you have been born into, the conditionings that have been layered upon you, will not necessarily be of any use to you.

It is not necessarily so. It may be that not only will they be of no use to you, they may even become dangerous. They can become obstacles, because.... Think about it a little.

Look at Meera: she dances, she sings; her enlightenment has become her dance. Can you think of Mahavira dancing – a dancing Mahavira? It will seem very odd. Even to think about it seems odd. It doesn't sound right, it is difficult even to imagine. So far nobody, not even in his dream, has seen Mahavira dancing, let alone with a crown of peacock feathers on his head! He would look very odd, very hilarious. And if Meera did not dance, but sat down like Mahavira under a tree like a statue, this too would seem strange. Meera's personality is different from Mahavira's. Her liberation will only come through dancing, and Mahavira's will only come through silence, peace, and stillness. Both paths will lead to liberation, but in their own separate ways.

If you stand Krishna and Christ side by side and think about them, you will be in a great difficulty. Those who follow Jesus say that he never laughed. Because there is so much pain and suffering in the world, how can he smile, how can the messiah laugh? But here is Krishna merrily dancing away, playing the flute and having fun and celebrating life with his girlfriends, the *gopis*!

A follower of Jesus can never imagine Krishna as a savior, a messiah, because so much happiness doesn't suit a messiah. And a follower of Krishna can never imagine that this sad and long-faced man called Jesus can be enlightened. Such sadness, being hardly alive, does not fit with being an enlightened being. An enlightened one should be full of joy.

But Christ also reaches through his own way. The one who can identify himself with the pain of the whole world – who takes upon himself the pain of the whole world, who forgets himself and becomes one with the pain of the whole world – he too reaches. This is also a way to attain.

And he who forgets about the pain, who is so lost in bliss that he doesn't know any suffering in the world, who becomes one with the celebration of creation, who is totally lost in the dance – he too attains. But the paths are separate.

I am putting it like this because if dancing is your way, and you are born into the home of some of the followers of Mahavira, you will have problems. You will not find any rapport with anyone there. If you are born into a family of people like Meera then it will be all right; but otherwise you will have no rapport with anyone in your family. You will always find that there seems to be some uneasiness. In your conscious mind you will think that you are a Jaina, but the whole structure of your personality is that of a devotee, so you will be in constant trouble.

And if you have the personality of Mahavira and are born into the home of the followers of Krishna, on the surface everything will seem to be all right but inside you will feel everything is wrong. So you will become a hypocrite. Whatever you do won't fit with your personality, that's why it won't be true, real. And you won't be able to do what you want to do, because it will be contrary to your conditioning.

If the whole of mankind today has been made confused, then this is the reason. A study of all the religions is needed, but you must make your own choice – no one else should decide for you. Then a good world can come into being. Equal time should be given to the teaching of all religions, and a person should be left to decide for himself the way in which he will conduct his search. And whatever decision he makes should be respected.

This will have lasting results. If this happens, then there will be no reaction against religion, then there will be fewer atheists in the world. Atheism is born out of a reaction against a belief that has been enforced, so there will be less atheism in the world. This chronicle of disharmony will disappear from the world. Everyone will choose only that which is in harmony with him. A new interest will be born, a love will be born. What a person has chosen will be his own individual discovery. And everyone is interested in what he discovers for himself, everyone takes joy in his individual discovery. One can put one's whole life at stake for it. And until we reach a place where we can stake everything for our religion, no revolution can ever take place in our lives.

Thirdly, in every house there will then be people belonging to many different religions, so fights and riots between communities and religions will come to an end in the world. There is only one way for this to happen and that is by homes having people of different religions living in them. There is no other way – the father a Christian, his son a Jaina, his wife a Mohammedan, one daughter-in-law a Buddhist, another daughter-in-law a Confucian – if there are people of different religions in a home, there won't be riots. With whom will you fight?

If Hindu-Mohammedan riots take place, what will you do? Your wife is a Mohammedan – she will support the Mohammedans; your son is a Buddhist – he will support the Buddhists; your brother is a Jaina – he will support Jainas. How will you partition a Pakistan in your own house? It will be very difficult.

As long as every home only has one kind of religion in it, the world will never be free from riots, because you can easily find an excuse for them. Everyone you are connected to belongs to your religion; those you are in love with, whom you are related to, all belong to your religion. But if there are ten religions in your home, and if you love your wife but she happens to be a Mohammedan, then you won't be able to fight Mohammedans.

No matter how much someone proclaims that Hindus and Mohammedans are brothers or talks about all religions being equal, it is all useless. No good is going to come from such idle talk. When each family has a milieu of love shared by different religions it will not be necessary to say that Hindus and Mohammedans are brothers, because they *will* be brothers anyway! Right now, we have to say that because they are not. All such slogans are false; they are absolutely meaningless, just superficial. And they are deceitful – mere politics and nothing else.

This sutra is very revolutionary:

Seek out the way.

The way is not within you; it is not given to you at birth, it is not given through any conditioning. You will have to seek out your way. You will make mistakes – let them happen. If you become lost, then be lost! A living insecurity is better than a dead safety. It is better to be lost, because only through being lost will you begin to search. Without risking, without being lost, anything that may come your way for free from someone else will not take you anywhere. There will be many obstacles in finding your own way...

While you are sitting here, whenever I say something to you, you are constantly checking inside whether it agrees with your religion or not. The search cannot be done this way. The question is constantly going around in your head: is it stated in the Gita or not, does the Koran say this or not, did Lord Mahavira say this or not? If so, then it is okay. If not, then it is wrong. What then will you seek? You have already made up your mind about what is right and what is wrong! You have already decided, and when your mind is already made up, what will you search for?

Only a person who has not already made up his mind can search. If I, or anybody else for that matter, is saying something, you need to listen with a very unbiased attitude. First you should try to understand it and to put your preconceptions aside so that they don't get in the way –

because if they come in the way it will be impossible to understand.

Putting them aside does not mean that you have to agree with whatever is being said. There is no need to agree, just try to understand. And after you have understood it fully, then weigh them both up. And while weighing them up, stand aside from them. Don't say, "This is my opinion and this is yours." Then you won't really be able to weigh up both sides in an unbiased way because you will be making sure your opinion wins. You will cheat – and then you cannot be a judge, because you are related to one of the parties. If you are a relative, you will not be able to be just.

The person who is seeking his way needs to remain open to all ways. If he is a Jaina, he has to set that aside; if he is a Mohammedan, he has to set that aside. Understand fully whatever you are seeking, see it in the light of experience – and then weigh up both sides. And while weighing them, don't favor either side; while weighing them stand far away from them both. Then if you feel what the Mohammedan is saying is correct, follow it.

Remember, in this way it has become your own discovery. The person who is born into a Mohammedan home will not necessarily come to realize that to be a Mohammedan is not right. He may realize that it is fine to be a Mohammedan. And a person who has been born into a Hindu home will not necessarily forsake the Hindu religion; it may be that the Hindu religion is his way. But if he seeks with such an openness, the religion he was born into can also become his very own. He has rediscovered what was given to him by birth, and found that the Hindu religion was actually meant to be his way. This rediscovering changes the quality of the whole thing. Then it is no longer a religion given to him by his parents; he has found it to be right for him too. But this requires a lot of honesty.

Don't rush through the search – deep down carrying the idea that you know the Hindu religion is right and just superficially leafing through the Koran or looking at it a little bit here and there, and then coming to the conclusion that Hinduism is right. Such hurry won't do. Not being dishonest is a prerequisite of the search.

But we are very clever. And those whom we think are very good people are at the pinnacle of such cleverness. Many books have been written along these lines. Dr. Bhagwandas has written a book on the synthesis of all religions, the essential unity of all religions. Dr. Bhagwandas was a very scholarly man and he has written it after a lot of research. Of all the books written in India about the concept of the essential unity of all religions, this is one of the most valuable. Everybody, from Annie Besant to Mahatma Gandhi, was impressed by it.

But the book is dishonest. It is dishonest because whenever Dr Bhagwandas searches in the Koran, he only looks for what is also in the Gita. His deepest, innermost feeling is that the Gita alone is right. But if the same thing has also been said in the Koran, then the Koran is also right. If the same thing has been said in the Bible as in Gita, then the Bible is also right. But his basic search is for that which is a reflection of the Gita. It is the Gita which is right; the Koran can also be right – if it says the same thing as the Gita.

This has no meaning, he is not seeking fundamental unity – because there are many things in the Koran which are not in the Gita and he ignores them completely, and there are many things in the Koran which are contrary to the Gita, and he leaves these out totally!

If a Mohammedan were to write this book, it would be totally different, because he would use the Koran as the base. And if what is in the Koran were also in the Gita, then the Gita would be correct. His decision would be absolutely different. There is a lot of difference between the Gita and the Koran. You would understand this if you were to see Jainas making a selection from the Gita.

The Jainas would take out all those passages from the Gita which are of value, because they are all contrary to the concept of non-violence. The basic message of the Gita is not to be afraid to fight, because such a thing as death never occurs, so why be afraid of violence? Nothing dies, nothing comes to an end. Even the body cannot be destroyed. Even if it is cut, that which is within remains intact – so you should not be afraid. This will create trouble for the Jainas. They will choose those parts from the Gita which are in accordance with the sayings of Mahavira. But in doing so the basic teachings of the Gita will be left out because they create trouble, they cannot fit in with what Mahavira says.

I call this choosing dishonesty, because deep within, you assume your religion to be the right one and you are simply showing a little sympathy for the other. You are tolerant, so you show a little sympathy for the other. There must be something right in his way too, so you pull it out and say, "This too has something good in it. In fact, we are the ones who are actually right, but he is not *totally* wrong. There is also some sense in what he is saying, and we are bringing it to your attention. But the essence of what he says is exactly what we have been saying all along."

You will not be able to find the path this way. You can only find the path after you have developed a neutral attitude, the attitude of a witness, and are able to see everything from a distance. And your final decision will be that you will choose what is true and not what is yours. You will not choose something just because it is yours, but because of its truth. But what we do is we assume that what is ours is the truth. The real seeker takes what is true as his. If one keeps this difference in mind then this sutra can be of immense value to the seeker:

Seek out the way.

The fourteenth sutra:

Seek the way by retreating within.

The first point: "Seek the way." The second point: "Seek the way by retreating within."

Even if from the outside a way feels to be the right one, don't make a final decision yet. Experiment with it inside too. Keep returning inside and experiment with it until it has borne fruit in your life, until you can affirm it through your own experience, until you can say from your heart that this is the right choice, until it can be proved by your experience. Until then, know that you have not found the way.

People come to me and they say that they are afraid of this type of meditation. Somebody comes and says, "This meditation is pure madness – it cannot be right."

I tell them, "Do it and see. Don't make up your mind until you have done it. Perhaps it is madness, but first do it and see for yourself. Only say it is mad if the madness within you increases. If it decreases then don't say this, because my experience is that even if mad people do it, their madness decreases."

These days, a lot of experiments are being done in the West. And they say that if a mad person is given an opportunity to get rid of his madness, his madness decreases. Society does not let him throw it out, it prevents him in every way, and so it goes on accumulating inside him. When it has become vast, it explodes – and then we lock him up in a madhouse.

Nowadays a lot of psychologists in the West are saying that we have been ill-treating mad people. They feel that "First we make them mad and then we lock them up in a madhouse! We don't let them release their madness. If they try to release their madness it is troublesome and if they don't, ultimately they go mad and we start punishing them!" We punish them in a thousand ways. This whole web is certainly very strange.

So there are people who are always ready to comment from a distance that something is wrong. No, keep quiet! Don't say something is right or that something is wrong until you have experimented with it inside yourself, because life is not so simple that it can be known from a distance. You have to dive deeply into it; only then can it be known.

If a person who has no experience of love says something about love, what value can it possibly have? And it often happens that those who have never experienced any love in their lives discuss love a lot. There is a reason for this: discussion gives them some intellectual fulfillment. There is no love in their lives, so they manage to get a little bit of enjoyment by discussing it.

Very often the people who write love poems are the very ones who have never had any experience of love in their lives. The poems are a substitute. What they wanted to do in love, what they have not been able to do, they do in words. After reading a love poem, don't ever meet the poet or you will be very disappointed: you will find a totally different sort of person.

If life could be understood simply through intellect, from a distance, then even spectators would know life; then there would be no need to live life, no need to taste life. Then even a passerby would come to know life by just standing on its banks; there would be no need to immerse oneself in life and become one with it. But passersby never comes to know anything. Those who are standing on the banks simply see what is on the surface; their eyes miss all that is happening underneath.

So once it has become clear in your mind, once your unbiased intelligence has understood a particular way to be the right one, it is still not enough. Take refuge within and seek out the way. Whatsoever you have found to be right, immediately take it inside; let it become your life, let it be transformed into your inner journey. And until you begin to experience it there, keep quiet; don't judge. A lot of stupidity could be avoided in the world if people would just stop passing judgment without knowing. Even without knowing, people pass so many judgments but they don't even realize that they are making a mistake, that they are committing a crime. People go on passing judgment without knowing. A person who passes judgment without knowing is a complete fool. Not only is he a fool, but he is also helping to make others into fools.

Except for experience there is no other criterion. Ultimately only your *own* experience is the criterion, and until you have tested it against that criterion, you should remain silent and not say that this is the true way.

And the fifteenth sutra:

Seek the way by advancing boldly without.

Now let that which has become an inner experience flow out into your living too. Seek it in your outer life too –

because whatever seems to be true within can still be a dream. Inner truths can be imaginary. What seems to be an inner truth can be a personal illusion, because there is no one else inside from whom you can seek confirmation, there is no one else from whom you can seek support. There, inside, there is no other touchstone. You are alone.

Just think about it. You can see a light inside; you are meditating and you see a light inside, you experience great bliss. But this light may be just a figment of your imagination, a projection. It may only be a projection of the mind, you may be just creating an illusion in the mind. Because you have read somewhere in the scriptures that a light is experienced, the idea may have taken root somewhere and may be manifesting now!

It is a very strange thing that if a devotee of Krishna meditates, he will see only a manifestation of Krishna and never of Christ. If he is a follower of Christ he will never see Krishna. So perhaps that manifestation is a reflection of a feeling he is carrying deep down in his unconscious. How will you examine what is happening inside? What is occurring inside may be self-delusion, self-hypnosis. Inside, you may be conjuring up something and deceiving yourself with it. In that case, the search for the way is not yet over. So far, whatever you have known inside, whatever you have found to be right within yourself, is only subjective, personal.

And with the personal there is a danger.... All dreams are personal. The beauty of a dream is that it *is* personal. You cannot enter the dream of even your closest friend, you cannot be a partner in another's dream. You and I cannot see the same dream. There is no way we can – all dreams are private. There is no way to externalize them either, no way to create a partnership and go into them.

So, is this experience you are having a dream? In the final analysis the criterion is simply this: whatsoever is happening inside you...if you are becoming peaceful inside, then that peace should start manifesting itself in your outer behavior too. If you say that you are feeling very peaceful inside, but outwardly you are full of anger, then your peace is just imaginary. If you say that your life is very blissful inside, but outwardly your life is full of lust and desire, then it is proving something else – because a man who is blissful cannot be full of lust and desire. They belong to a man who is full of suffering. The meaning of lust and desire is, "I am miserable, I want happiness." If I am blissful then the question of my wanting any sort of happiness does not arise. It is like a man who has a Kohinoor diamond asking for pebbles. Why should he?

So whatever has happened inside you – according to the sutra: Seek the way by advancing boldly without. Bring out whatever you have experienced inside. It will take a lot of courage, because if you put into practice what you have known inside, your outer network of relationships will change completely.

A woman came to me and said, "I read your books and listen to your talks. Now a very strong feeling is taking hold of me inside that I should also start experimenting practically with what you are saying."

She comes from a very respectable family.

"Should I start experimenting as well? I have only one fear – that by practicing it, it may do some harm, that it may create unnecessary problems in my home, my family and my married life."

So I said to her, "Nothing bad will come from it, but many good things will come from it, and *they* may cause problems! Just forget this idea that only something wrong creates trouble – even goodness causes problems."

She said, "I don't understand. Why should goodness cause problems?"

So I told her, "First do the meditations and then see. Then you will know how goodness can cause problems."

If your wife is very bad-tempered, a fighter, over time you adjust to it. If she then begins to meditate and her quarrelsome nature disappears, it will be as if you have remarried – now you will have to readjust. The whole affair will have to begin again; again you will face new anxieties. It is just as if you have moved into a new house, or bought new furniture for your home, or a new car which then creates difficulty for the driver. You will have to make new adjustments.

Even with a new wife there would not be so many problems, because you will accept that she is new and that it will take some time to adjust, that some minor quarrels will arise, that there will be a little noise before the engine runs smoothly – if she is a new wife. But she is the old one, and if she starts behaving in a new way, she will cause even more uneasiness and disturbance.

And inside all of us there are even hierarchies regarding such things. If the wife is nasty and bad-tempered and the husband is peaceful, or if the wife is peaceful and the husband is quarrelsome, the wife will consider herself superior and her husband useless, or the other way around. If the husband becomes peaceful, the hierarchy will change – now the husband will consider himself superior. And it is easy to tolerate a bad husband, but it is very difficult to put up with a superior husband... because your ego is not hurt by a bad husband, but it is hurt by a superior husband.

If the husband is an alcoholic, it does not create such a big problem. Why? – because a drunk husband is afraid and trembling, and he considers his wife to be a goddess. All drunkards treat their wives as goddesses – otherwise there is no real reason to think her so! The husband is trembling and he says to his wife, "You are a goddess. How to describe your sacred purity? And I am such a sinner." But if this husband were to stop drinking and start meditating, if he were to begin immersing himself in prayer, the relationship between him and his wife would go completely haywire.

Now the wife will have to consider him as a god, which will be very difficult; it creates a problem. The unconscious part of the wife's mind will say that he was better off as he was before – the unconscious part. Outwardly she will appear to be very happy that such a good thing has happened – it is all for the best, everything is just perfect! But inside she will be worried and afraid.

So I told the woman, "Go home and think it over and then come back – because even goodness can be problematic. And sometimes it can create more problems than evil can."

That is why the sutra says:

Seek the way by advancing boldly without.

Practice whatsoever you have begun to experience within in the outside world too, so that all your old patterns undergo a change. All the structures of your outer world, which you had created in a state of unawareness, will not be of any help to you. Now you will have to change everything.

I used to stay in the house of a friend's family. I was a little surprised that he never talked with his children, the servant or his wife. Once inside the house, he would pass quickly through it. If by chance his children were around, he would pretend he hadn't seen them, and walk straight into the house with no expression on his face. I used to be a little surprised, because whenever he met me he always greeted me with great affection – and I was only his guest.

I told him, "I am a little surprised by the way you walk in. If the children are standing there you don't even bother to look at them, if the servants are present you don't even give them so much as a glance!"

He replied, "That would be a very dangerous thing to do. If I show even a little bit of affection to the children, they will start demanding money. If I look kindly upon the servant, he will start to pester me at once for a raise in salary. If my wife is shown some love, she will respond by announcing that a new type of sari has just arrived in the market. That is why I finally made up my mind not to behave lovingly with anyone, but just to remain aloof, even if there is no reason to be so arrogant. That is why the children don't bother me, the servants don't bother me – not even my wife bothers me! Everything works peacefully."

Now if this person were to begin to meditate, there would be a problem. If he were to become loving, if his arrogance were to vanish.... If his arrogance disappeared all the barriers he has erected around himself would fall down. He would find himself in trouble.

Life consists of everyday routine, and the deeper a man enters within himself, the more his daily structure changes. The more dead you are, the more fixed your structure. One who is more alive, like a flowing river, his structure changes daily. That is why everything will become a chaos. That is why this sutra urges you:

Seek the way by advancing boldly without.

The whole nature of man must be used wisely by the one who desires to enter the way.

This is very deep – understand it.

The whole nature of man must be used wisely by the one who desires to enter the way.

The whole nature! It is not intelligent to reject any part of your nature. To leave anything out from whatever has been given to you by nature is to be incomplete; you will never become whole. If there is anger within you, if you have lust inside, if you have greed – they have been given to you by nature. There is nothing shameful about it, there is nothing to get worried about. They are – because nature has given them to you.

A wise man brings his anger with him to his meditation. He does not reject it. The person who takes his lust with him into his meditation makes use of it, and turns the poison into nectar. A person who doesn't reject or discard anything, who absorbs the whole of his nature in its entirety on the path of meditation, attains wholeness.

If you reject anything, that part will always remain rejected. That is why I say: don't reject anything. It is anger which becomes compassion. If you reject anger you will always be deprived of compassion. It is that very same sex which will lead to celibacy. If you have closed the doors on sex, you will never be able to attain celibacy.

These are very complex things and create problems for people, because we think that the meaning of celibacy is to discard sex, to burn it, to make it disappear; we think that only then does celibacy become possible. Celibacy has never been achieved this way, and it never will be – because it is the sexual energy itself which turns into celibacy.

If impotence were the same as celibacy, by totally rejecting sex we would achieve celibacy. Then there would be no need for meditation; minor surgery would do the trick. All you would have to do would be to go to a doctor and ask him to remove your reproductive organs! But the type of person you would become would not be a celibate.

You can see this difference in an ox and a bull. It would be the same situation. An ox can be harnessed because now it is impotent. You cannot harness a bull, because his sexual energy is very potent. But there is life and beauty in the bull and an ox has no spirit – it has no life or beauty.

So your so-called saints and holy men are in the same situation as an ox. This is what will happen if you reject and discard any aspect of yourself. What is needed is transformation. The energy should not be destroyed, it has to be channeled upwards, it has to be taken upwards. The downward flow of sexual energy has to be turned upwards – but the energy is the same. So whoever fights sexual desire can never attain to celibacy. He will always remain in the grip of sexual desire and a part of him will always remain stuck, like a dead weight. There will be no joy in his life, only a fear. And where there is fear the flower can never blossom.

A flower needs joyfulness. Only when everything is accepted can a flower bloom. And when the flower of your whole life blooms, then your sexual energy will have been transformed into celibacy, your anger will have been transformed into compassion, your hardness into kindness, and your hate into love. The difference between hate and love is only of direction: the energy is one and the same.

This sutra says:

The whole nature of man must be used wisely
by the one who desires to enter the way.
Each man is to himself absolutely the way,
the truth, and the life.

Inside you is hidden the way, the truth, the life. You are complete in yourself. Although your life has all the notes, it lacks music. You have to arrange the notes – that is the whole spiritual discipline you have to learn. It is just as if a *veena* is lying there: it has all its strings, and all you have to do is adjust them and tighten them. You have to tune all the strings to a harmony and then the *veena* will be ready to play. Every person is a God – but as yet untuned.

Man is just like a child's jigsaw puzzle. If you arrange the pieces of wood in the correct order a beautiful shape takes form; maybe a palace, maybe a boat. You muddle the pieces up, and the child goes on putting them back together again. Everything is there – an entire boat, an entire shape – but the pieces are still separate. The pieces have to be put together, and they all have to be arranged in such a way that the muddle is sorted out and the shape comes into being.

Every man is like a jigsaw puzzle until everything has fallen into its right place. The day that happens, the jigsaw puzzle vanishes and God is manifested.

Thus seek out the way.
Seek it by study of the laws of being,
the laws of Nature, the laws of the supernatural.
Steadily, as you watch and worship,
its light will grow stronger.
Then you may know
you have found the beginning of the way.
And when you have found the end
its light will suddenly become the infinite light.

Be not appalled and terrified by the sight;
keep your eyes fixed on the small light
and it will grow.
But let the darkness within
help you to understand the helplessness
of those who have seen no light,
whose souls are in profound gloom.

If you find your way, if you integrate your way into your experience and let it mold your behavior, then that light will be born inside you too. The lamp which will later become a beacon of light is lit.

But this won't happen if you just sit around. This won't happen without your making some effort. And it is right to begin from the beginning. Don't walk on a borrowed path, because if you take the first step wrongly, the last step cannot be in the right place. And there is no way to arrive if you have made a mistake with the very first step. That is why one needs to take the first step very carefully, because the first step is half way to the destination. If the first step lands in the right place, then the destination is not very far away, because the first step is the beginning of the destination. With that you have connected yourself to the destination. It will take a little time – but you are on your way.

But we are very careless about the first step, and very anxious about the final destination. We are very anxious to have bliss, godliness, liberation, but we are not concerned that we may be taking a wrong first step. We are absolutely adamant that we have already taken the first step and are on our way. We think that the whole way is lying clearly ahead and that the only question is about the final goal.

Seek the way. Test it through experience. Whatever you have known, test it in your day-to-day living so it is not a dream. *Then* the goal is not far away.

The goal is always nearby – all that is needed is the right first step.

8

ATTAINMENT OF THE WAY

Look for the flower to bloom
in the silence that follows the storm;
not till then.

It shall grow, it will shoot up,
it will make branches and leaves and form buds,
while the storm continues,
while the battle lasts.
But not till the whole personality of the man
is dissolved and melted –
not until it is held by the divine fragment
which has created it, as a mere subject
for grave experiment and experience –
not until the whole nature has yielded
and become subject unto its higher self,
can the bloom open.
Then will come a calm
such as comes in a tropical country
after the heavy rain.
And in the deep silence
the mysterious event will occur
which will prove that the way has been found.

The opening of the bloom
is the glorious moment when perception awakes; with it
comes confidence, knowledge, certainty.

When the disciple is ready to learn,
then he is accepted, acknowledged, recognized.
It must be so, for he has lit his lamp,
and it cannot be hidden.

These written above
are the first of the rules which are written
on the walls of the hall of learning.
Those that ask shall have.
Those that desire to read shall read.
Those who desire to learn shall learn.

Peace be with you.

People ask: If everyone's nature is godliness then what is the need for the world? And if everyone already has a soul then how do we become involved in this ignorance? Why are there such complications? If everything within is so natural and truthful, then why is there so much trouble without? And if we are to achieve that which we already have, then all these wanderings in between, this journey in the middle, does not seem to have a meaning. If *brahman* is everyone's nature, then why does the world exist?

Many attempts have been made to answer this question, but almost all of them have been near-failures, because no matter what the explanation, the fundamental question remains untouched. Someone says that you are wandering because of your past lives. But this answer is very childish, because even if we say that the wandering of your present life is because of your previous lives, then what could be the reason for going astray in your very first life? So there are some people who, to avoid the flaw in this answer, say that there is no first birth and that you have been wandering for an infinite length of time.

This is also the viewpoint of the Jainas; that you have been wandering forever, since eternity. But even with this understanding the question remains: why has the soul been wandering since eternity? Why is the soul homeless? What is the reason for this eternal wandering?

If you say that it is a wandering for no reason, then there can be no way of attaining liberation. If the wandering is without rhyme or reason, then for what are you seeking liberation? If this wandering has no reason, then there can be no reason to be free of it either. If there is a reason for wandering, then that reason can be taken away – and then redemption, freedom, and liberation are possible.

Some say that it is all God's play. But then the play seems to be very hard, it seems to be an absurd joke. What type of play is this, in which man has been made to suffer meaninglessly and without a reason for so many lives? A God who delights in causing such suffering seems to be a sadist, a tyrant. Otherwise, why does he continuously send so many souls through so many lives of wandering and suffering?

And in any case if he is the almighty, then he has the ability to redeem everyone. Such a long way...and that too of so much suffering! Certainly he must be taking some delight in putting people through such pain and suffering. His play is like that of a small child who has taken hold of a frog and is torturing it. Why catch hold of a man's neck like this and trouble him?

There are some who say that all that we see is just a dream, an illusion. But even those who call all this an illusion try their best to find a release from it! If the world really is a dream, then what is the need to escape from it? What is the point of trying to escape from a dream state? Why be afraid of it? But the very people who call it an illusion are those who run away from the world. Obviously, they must be finding it a reality, otherwise they would not be running away. Will you run away from something if it does not exist? What is the point in running away from it? And if the world is an illusion then *all* renunciation is useless – because what will you renounce? Can you ever renounce something which is false, can a dream be renounced? How can you renounce what does not exist?

If the world is an illusion, then sannyas is meaningless. What could it mean? Only if the world is real will sannyas have some significance. And if the world is an illusion, liberation also becomes an illusion, because when the chains are an illusion, how can liberation be true and meaningful? If my prison is a false one, how can my release be a true one? The release depends on the prison being a real one. If the prison is not real, then my liberation is also false.

In this way many answers have been put forward, but not even one touches upon the question. And every answer creates a problem. Basically every answer seems to be an effort to explain, but it does not reveal the truth. And this is exactly the difficulty.

This sutra gives an answer which, to me, comes closest to the truth. It gives a scientific answer, not a philosophical one. It says that all experiences of life are dependent upon their opposite. This sutra does not bring any God into the picture, it does not talk about *maya*, it doesn't hide behind any philosophical principle. It says that all the experiences of life are dependent upon their opposite.

If you want to experience peace, then scientifically speaking, you will also have to go through turmoil; otherwise you will have no perception of what peace is. You may be at peace, but you will only know the feeling of peace when you have also been through turmoil. If you have never known turmoil in your life, how will you recognize peace? There is no way you can. A background of turmoil is needed for peace to be felt.

If you want to experience life, then death is compulsory – and not because of any play on God's part. Death is compulsory precisely because life cannot be experienced without the background of death. Death is the soil, and life flowers from that soil of death. Death does not destroy life; on the contrary, it gives birth to life. Nothing can be experienced without its opposite. If there were no words, how would you experience silence?

The sutra says that if there were no worldliness, you would not be able to have any experience of godliness either. So this world is not merely a play, an illusion, but a process to experience godliness – and a necessary process. You could have been one with God already; you were, you are even now, you can never be outside of God, but it is necessary to be thrown into the world in order to come to understand that you are one with God.

Put it this way: if you were a fish in the ocean, it would be necessary to take you out of the ocean at least once and throw you onto the shore. Only then would you become aware of the ocean.

As a fish you live in the ocean, you were born in the ocean. You have never had so much as a glimpse of what is beyond the ocean, you have never been out of it, so you will never become aware of the ocean. The ocean is so close to you, so much a part of you, that you have never taken even one single breath without it and you will never become aware of it. To know the ocean, to become aware of it...and this will sound a little strange, you will not understand it, but when the fish is thrown out onto the sandy shore for the first time, only then does it realize that there is such a thing as an ocean. The suffering it will feel on the sandy shore, the pain of being separated from the ocean, that same pain will become its urge to be one with the ocean.

A fish that gets caught once in a fisherman's net but manages to escape into the ocean again...that fish will not be the same fish as the one who was in the ocean before. Now, the ocean will be a bliss. Now it knows that the ocean is its very life. Now it knows the mystery of the ocean, now it knows what the ocean is all about! It has experienced its significance.

So existence is not some sort of sadist that is making you suffer, existence is not doing anything at all. But it is compulsory, a part of life, the law of life, that without having gone through the opposite you cannot experience anything.

Nirvana and the world are opposites. Nirvana happens only after you have passed through the world. You arrive at the same place as you originally were, but now you arrive as a different being. You attain that which you always had, but now you have regained it after having lost it. That losing in between is of prime importance. No experience of nirvana is possible without it. That is why the world is a learning, and a compulsory one.

This law is the same as the laws of science. The scientist says that water is made from the combining of hydrogen and oxygen. If two atoms of hydrogen and one atom of oxygen join, water is made. If you ask him "But how? Why can't water be made from three atoms of hydrogen and one of oxygen?" the scientist will say, "There is no question of any 'why' – I am only saying how it is. It just so happens that two atoms of hydrogen and one atom of oxygen make up water. There is no question of any 'why', it is simply the way it is."

Science does not give answers to why, it answers how. It does not say why it is so, it just says that it is like this. That is why science never loses sight of the facts, and philosophy very often gets lost in trying to answer why. Why! These sutras are very scientific, and their emphasis is on how and not on why. This sutra does not say why it is so, but that it *is* so.

Without experiencing the contrary there cannot be any experience.

If you keep this in mind, and rightly understand this great law of opposites, then your whole way of looking at things will change. Then you will be able to remain happy even in the midst of suffering, because you will understand that without suffering there can be no understanding of happiness either. And you will be able to maintain your calm even in the midst of turmoil, because now you know that turmoil is a necessary part of learning peace. Then you will accept even death joyfully, because you will understand that the flower of life blossoms in the soil of death.

Then, you will gladly tolerate misfortune, because there is no blessing without it. You will also accept an insult with a smile, because you will know that it is also the door for respect. Then, you will not run away from ignorance, you will not be afraid of it; instead you will stand up to it with your eyes wide open, because that very confrontation, that very looking at ignorance in the face will become the key to the temple of wisdom. You won't be disturbed by the paradoxes of life; all life's contradictions will appear to lead you to a worthwhile and meaningful end.

Nothing is useless, nothing can be useless. You may not grasp its meaning, that is something different, but whatever exists has a meaning, and its meaning lies in exactly this: that it is taking you towards its opposite. Now, let us understand this sutra:

Look for the flower to bloom
in the silence that follows the storm;
not till then.

A storm is necessary for the existence of silence. And he who wishes that there were no storm, only calm, his silence will be dead, it will have no life in it.

This is a very strange phenomenon: that calmness rests inside a storm. By itself, calmness is of no use. It is of no use until there is a storm raging all around it. The storm puts life into it. Only a storm can give birth to silence, can make it come alive. Only a storm can create the presence of joy in silence – a storm, which appears to be just the opposite. If you have experienced the storm with full awareness, then you will know that there is nothing to compare with the calm that follows.

But you may become so disturbed by the storm, that when the calm follows you are still agitated. The natural sequence of the storm will unfold, but you may miss it.

You may miss out on the fresh energy that follows suffering. The wave of health that comes in the wake of a sickness will not strike you. You will remain so lost in the old sickness that you will miss out on what is happening now. There is nothing like the taste of the happiness that comes after a time of suffering.

We become so preoccupied by suffering, so disturbed by it, that long after it has gone we are still engrossed in worry. And we miss that subtle moment after suffering, when we could have had a taste of happiness, when for a moment the door to the heaven that is happiness opens. Our eyes remain lost in the old troubles.

After every happening, there comes its opposite moment. Present behind every action is its opposite, because there is nothing in this world that is without its opposite. Wait for it. When unhappiness surrounds you, don't be too distressed by it. Be unhappy, but don't be distressed. Understand the meaning of distress. Unhappiness is in itself enough suffering but as it is, first we suffer from unhappiness, and then we suffer for being unhappy. These are two different things. To suffer unhappiness is pure. But then we become unhappy about the fact that we became unhappy! We become unhappy about why there is suffering in the world in the first place; we suffer because we have the idea that there should be no suffering. This second type of suffering is philosophical and dangerous. Beware of it: it is not real, and it destroys the ray of happiness that would have followed the pure suffering.

It is very interesting how man entangles himself! You are worried – and there is nothing wrong in that – but then you worry about the worry, and *that* is bad. There is nothing wrong in being disturbed and worried, it is part of learning. But when you worry about being worried, then you get into trouble, because now you are caught in a vicious circle which has no end. It is endless. I say it is endless, because no matter how agitated you become, you will never experience a moment's peace from being agitated.

Put it this way: I am disturbed and then I become disturbed about why I am disturbed. Then I can become even more disturbed about why I became disturbed about being disturbed. For example, I say not to be disturbed about feeling disturbed. You can carry on in your old way and add this instruction to what you are already doing. First you become agitated, then you become agitated about this habit of becoming agitated, and now you hear me and so add the third agitation – that there is no need to become agitated over being agitated. Now, this is the third agitation and all this is endless. You can go on like this forever, and not a single moment of peace or happiness will ever come out of it.

Real disturbance has a moment of peace after it, but there is no peace behind imaginary disturbance because imagination is not reality and so the laws of nature do not apply to it. It is merely a play of your mind. So always remember: even unhappiness, if real, is not bad. Even happiness, if imaginary, is bad – because you are roaming around in a dream. Real suffering has a beauty of its own because it is inevitably followed by a moment of real peace. It cannot be otherwise.

But if you get involved in the second and third types of suffering – the false suffering, that because of suffering you create new types of mental sufferings – then you will become so drowned in them, so covered in dark clouds, that you will miss the ray of happiness which inevitably follows suffering. After the dark night comes the dawn. But if you become so afraid of the night, so terrified of the darkness that you sit with your eyes shut tight, thinking it is useless to open your eyes because the darkness is so immense, then you will miss out on the dawning of the day which always follows the night.

For calmness to be experienced, the background of a storm is needed.

Look for the flower to bloom
in the silence that follows the storm;
not till then.

We can attain to two types of peace: the one which comes naturally after a storm, and the second, which is brought about through effort, without a storm.

People constantly tell me that they have never come across my type of meditation before. People generally meditate with their eyes shut, sitting quietly in the lotus posture. What type of meditation is this where people dance, scream and jump around as if they have gone mad? I tell them that this is the silence which comes after the storm.

Those who sit down and shut their eyes are avoiding the storm, and without the storm there can be no experience of silence. And even if those who avoid the storm experience silence, that silence is hollow, lifeless, cultivated from without. The storm will go on raging inside them. Jump into the storm, become one with it! What is there to be afraid of? Live out the storm! It will pass, but it will be followed by a moment of silence. And if we are awake in that moment, then the door to the eternal will open.

So there can be two types of peace. It can be cultivated; you can sit down like a statue and practice it. Please understand: you see Buddha sitting under the bodhi tree, but perhaps you don't realize that six years of fierce storms preceded this. We don't have any statues from that time, because the sculptures were made by people who had no understanding. Otherwise the first statue of him would have shown that, would have captured the moment of Buddha's storm. For six years Buddha lived through fierce storms. We have forgotten this! We have only focused on the other end when Buddha has already attained peace.

So what do we do? Right from the start we go and sit down under a tree like Buddha! Our buddhahood is totally false and imitative; it is a joke. It cannot be real, because the real moment, the valuable moment, the first part is missing. Where is the storm that has to precede the birth of the Buddha, the storm that has to rage before the birth of this tranquil consciousness under the bodhi tree, the storm that has to pass before the birth of the unwavering flame of the lamp, the storm that has to precede the descent of the great light and the immense silence? Where are those six years of Buddha's wandering like a madman, knocking and searching at each and every door, surrendering himself at the feet of every master he can find, trying out each and every path, facing all kinds of anguish and suffering – where is all this? If you immediately sit down under the bodhi tree, nothing will happen and you will be just a fake Buddha. You *can* sit down; everything is possible through practice. You can practice sitting down quietly – but inside? Inside there will be no peace.

It can also happen that inside too you may experience a certain amount of peace, that you may succeed in creating a kind of stupor – but this is not peace. It will be a type of a self-hypnosis, but you will be lost in a kind of a sleep. This sleep may be very pleasant, you will at least get some rest out of it, but it is not a spiritual peace. There is no aliveness in this sleep; it is merely a rest, and that too an enforced one, born through practice. It is not a spontaneous peace coming from within, it is a peace imposed from the outside.

We can create this kind of a peace, but then there will be no joy in our lives, no dance, no beauty. Life will not have the freshness of the morning dew, it will not have the silence of the stars in the night. And our eyes will not shower with flowers, like those which blossom spontaneously on the trees. This will not happen. We will become rigid, like stone statues with no movement; with no turmoil but with no peace either.

Keep this in mind: you cannot bypass anything that is a part of life's natural process, you cannot bypass any experience of life. If you leave any experience out, you will have to return and complete it. There are no shortcuts in life, you cannot bypass certain things and still grow. Avoid the storm, and you will never be able to know the peace which follows it.

The sutra says:

Look for the flower to bloom
in the silence that follows the storm;
not till then.

Even if you manage to make some flower bloom before that, it will be a paper flower; it will not be a flower of the soul, it will not be a real one. You can have a flower in full bloom, there are plenty of paper flowers available in the market. Nowadays, you can even get plastic ones; they last even longer. Once you have purchased them, they last forever. The flowers which you get from the scriptures are paper flowers. You may even put them close to your heart and go and sit under a bodhi tree, but no flower will bloom within you. The flower will simply not bloom without the storm. Only storms and tempests can give birth to such a flower; it derives its energy from the power of the storm, and when the storm has passed, then the energy that it leaves behind is what becomes the real flower.

So don't be in a hurry. And don't try to escape from the storm, don't run away from the world; only then can the flower of nirvana be born. This may sound paradoxical. This is why it is very easy to misunderstand what I say. But I say to you: this is not paradoxical, this is the essential law of life.

Don't escape from the world. If you are looking for real nirvana, don't run away from the prison but live through the experience of it. The deeper the pain of the prison chains, the more bliss you will experience when they drop away. Experience the suffering of the prison to the full. This suffering will purify you, will refine you, will wash you clean. After going through this suffering you will become like gold; the impurities will have burned away, and you will emerge as pure, solid gold. The liberation that you will experience when you leave the prison cannot be experienced by someone who has fled from it. He can be out of it, he can be free from the chains, but he cannot experience liberation. He will have to return to the prison.

Those who try to attain to nirvana by running away from the world have to return to it again and again. One of the fundamental reasons why you return to the world again and again is because you have always tried to avoid its experiences. You are just like those children who try to avoid going through all the steps of a mathematical sum and instead look up the answer in the back of the textbook, and memorize it. The answer is perfectly correct, but for the child it is absolutely wrong. There is nothing wrong with the answer, the experts have written it – but only after solving the mathematical question for themselves. But the child did not go through all those mathematical steps, so even if he gives the correct answer it will be a false one, a fake.

The answer which arises from going through the complete process, the peace which comes after living through the storm, the nirvana that comes after living through the world, the sannyas which comes after all this, is the real one. But we behave just like those naughty children; we steal answers from the scriptures, and think the answers are ours! And it is true that those answers are correct but even then, they are not right for you. Your answer is correct only when it has come out of your own experience.

Now I am not saying that the scriptures are wrong. Those answers which have been written down at the end of the mathematics textbook are absolutely right. In the same way the scriptures are right, but they are right for whosoever went through all the necessary mathematical steps, through the whole process of solving the question, and then arrived at the answer – and did not peep at it first! On the day you arrive at the answer, *then* it is important to turn to the back of the book and look up the answer, because then the answer at the back of the book will assure you that you have arrived at the truth. The book will bear witness to it.

When you have had your own experience, *then* if you read the scriptures you will feel that what they have to say is correct, that the path you are walking on is the right one. Others have done likewise, and the scriptures are a witness to it. But don't ever steal from the scriptures, don't learn by memorizing; otherwise the whole thing will become useless.

Don't try to avoid the opposite. This does not mean that you become lost forever in the opposite. This is being said so that you can transcend the opposite.

Look for the flower to bloom
in the silence that follows the storm;
not till then.

Waiting! You don't have to do anything, all you have to do is to go through the storm thoroughly, and when the storm is over, drop worrying about the storm. That which has become the past is gone. You don't have to do anything now. In the silence which dawns after the storm only waiting is needed – and the flower will bloom.

That is why the type of meditation which I am giving to you here has the essence of this sutra in it. For thirty minutes you have to go through a fierce storm. Become as mad as you possibly can. And after thirty minutes you have to do nothing; you have only to wait in complete silence. If you have been able to generate a real storm in those thirty minutes, then a peace will descend, unlike anything you have ever known before. But if your storm was weak and feeble, the peace which follows will have the same quality. If your storm was half-hearted, not real, then the peace will also be false. The quality of your silence will depend on the quality of the thirty minutes of storm.

A friend has told me about someone who was simply a spectator, who did not take part in the thirty minutes of storm but just stood around silently watching everyone else while they were in the throes of the storm. And later on, when everyone closed their eyes, he also closed his eyes. And then he sent word to me that nothing had happened, even though he had remained with closed eyes for those ten minutes.

Who has told you that something will happen if you close your eyes for ten minutes? You have skipped the storm and kept your eyes shut for ten minutes – that is all. And you think that because it is happening to everyone else, it will automatically happen to you too!

Nothing will happen by simply shutting your eyes. What happens is because of those thirty minutes of storm. The depth of peace will be in proportion to how authentic the storm inside you was. The depth of the valley of silence you enter will depend on the heights of the storm you reached. The proportion is always equal.

That is why it all depends on you. Even a little withholding during those thirty minutes will ruin everything. That's why I observe that many of you shake and move as if you would rather not have had to do it. No doubt you would have liked it if I had told you not to shake at all.

But you can't even do that! When I do tell you not to make any movement whatsoever, somebody feels like coughing, someone wants to scratch, somebody wants to do this or that. This happens because you have not let the storm rage fully during those thirty minutes, and some of it is still left inside. When it is time to give vent to it, you withhold. When it is time to stop, it begins to come out.

What problems you manage to create for yourselves! When I tell you to do whatever you feel like doing for thirty minutes; to jump, to shout, to dance – whatever you feel like doing – then *do* it, don't stop! Let each and every pore of your body dance, let each and every part of you go mad. Then you won't have to create the calm which follows; it will be the natural result of the storm, it will be its reflection. And all you have to do in that silence is wait – simply wait. In that silence the flower will bloom; not before it.

It shall grow, it will shoot up,
it will make branches and leaves and form buds,
while the storm continues,
while the battle lasts.

When you are passing through the storm, don't think that it is the enemy of the flower.

It shall grow, it will shoot up,
it will make branches and leaves and form buds,
while the storm continues,
while the battle lasts.

Then the seed of peace begins to sprout. It doesn't happen suddenly. During the storm the seed has also been growing.

But not till the whole personality of the man
is dissolved and melted –
not until it is held by the divine fragment
which has created it, as a mere subject

for grave experiment and experience –
not until the whole nature has yielded
and become subject unto its higher self,
can the bloom open.

Even during the storm, the seed is growing. Buried in darkness, it lies within the earth's womb. Then it begins opening up, sprouting, rising towards the sky, growing branches and forming leaves. But the flower will bloom only when the storm has melted down and dissolved your personality completely, when the storm has shaken you up completely. Whatever sickness you had inside you, whatever anguish, whatever violence and anger, the storm has to carry all that away with it – it has to cleanse you completely. Whatever sickness you had inside you has to be dissolved and destroyed in the storm. Then, in the final moment, the flower blooms.

You don't get destroyed in this storm. Only the lower reality in you, only that falls away and is destroyed. In this storm it is not your soul that is destroyed. It is your ego. And it is the ego that is the hindrance in the storm.

Just think about it: when you believe that you are a university professor, or a minister of some state government or a well-known doctor, or a big industrialist – how can you possibly dance? You think, "I have a reputation to maintain, how can I go around shouting, crying and weeping? How can such an intelligent person as I am do such childish things? A respectable person like me cannot perform these mad acts."

Now who is creating obstacles? It is the ego putting obstacles in the way of the storm. Why? Because the ego is afraid that the storm will burn it away. *You* won't disappear, but your ego will. Your reputation, your respectability, your position, your titles – they will all be carried away by the storm.

Your ego is afraid. That lowest part, your personality, is afraid of the storm. That lowest part is the one that tells you to keep on sitting quietly and let the flower bloom by itself. It knows that the flower will not bloom that way, no matter how long you keep on sitting. No matter how long you may sit, the flower will not bloom that way. For the sake of the flower, you need to put that lowest part, the personality, at stake – because it is precisely the personality that is the obstacle.

The storm will carry away all that is false in you. And after the storm, only whatsoever is best in you, whatsoever is eternal, will remain. And what will remain is the blooming of the flower.

Then will come a calm
such as comes in a tropical country
after the heavy rain.
And in the deep silence
the mysterious event will occur
which will prove that the way has been found.

Then a calm comes, a calm like the one that descends in a tropical country after the heavy rains. And in that deep silence occurs the mysterious event which proves that the way has been found. There is no way to prove this occurrence until it has actually happened.

People come to me and ask how they will know that they have actually had the experience if it happens to them. If the state of fulfillment is reached, if their meditation comes to fruition – if it is complete and self-realization is attained – how will they know that it has actually happened?

So then I ask them, "When a thorn gets stuck in your foot, how do you know whether a thorn is stuck in your foot or not? Only your pain bears witness to it."

It is just like when you feel pain if a thorn gets stuck in your foot, and with the removal of the thorn you feel a release from the pain. Both of these experiences are purely personal, they happen to *you*. When the inner happening occurs, it is just like this: all of life's anguish is extinguished, all burdens disappear. You have wings and become as light as a butterfly. Nothing remains, no past and no future; no worry, no pain – only pure existence. You won't need to go and ask someone else to confirm whether it has happened to you or not. When it happens, you will immediately know that it has happened. Then, even if the whole world tells you that it has not happened, you can laugh at it.

Keshav Chandra came to meet Ramakrishna, and began to argue against the existence of God. He was an intellectual, a great believer in logic.

Ramakrishna kept on smiling, saying, "Whatever you say is logically very correct, but what can I do? I am experiencing God. If I had not had the experience, then I would probably also say the same thing as you. And I still say that as far as logic is concerned, what you are saying is absolutely correct. But my problem is that I have already had an experience of God. And an uneducated person like me cannot even refute your arguments. Where you are standing today, I once stood. There was a time when I also doubted whether God existed or not. And then all your arguments would have sounded right to me. But I have a great problem, Keshav Chandra," said Ramakrishna. "I have a great problem, because I have experienced God. Now what can I do? Now, no matter what you say, or what the world says, I cannot falsify the experience. It has happened to me – God *is*. Now, there remains only one way out, and that is that you too seek the experience of God."

So when Keshav Chandra began to leave, Ramakrishna said, "One thing is certain, and that is that you too will begin to seek this experience, if not today, then tomorrow. Because for how long can such an intelligent person as you remain caught up in words and logic?"

Keshav Chandra wrote in his memoirs that he could never forget these words – Ramakrishna saying, "For how long can such an intelligent person as you continue to remain caught up in words and logic? You will definitely experience God."

"His saying this," Keshav Chandra has written, "destroyed all my logic. He did not refute me, he did not refuse me; he accepted me wholeheartedly. And at the same time he said, 'such an intelligent person as you.' He said that my presence had assured him even more of the existence of God, because how could such an intelligence be born without God? '...Seeing someone like you who is speaking against God, I now have total faith in God, because how can such an intelligent flower bloom without him?'"

He who has had the experience does not have to go to ask anyone for confirmation. The experience proves itself, it is self-evident. The day this kind of deep peace comes, the door to the supreme mystery opens up. And that is the proof that the way has been found.

The opening of the bloom
is the glorious moment when perception awakes;
with it comes confidence, knowledge, certainty.

The opening of the flower means a trust. Look at a flower: the sun rises in the morning and the flower blooms. Why does the flower bloom in the morning? So that it can drink fully of the sun – so that it can absorb the sun fully, so that it can open the doors of its heart to the sun. The bud is closed, it cannot drink. The flower blooms to take in the sun.

A bud is closed, a flower is open. Flowering is exposing the heart of the bud, its delicate interiority, to the sun. Its opening is an act of deep trust, of faith, a confidence that "You are life; your coming inside me means the beginning of eternal life. Without you, darkness dwells in my heart; without you I remain closed, I am dead. You will become my dance, my fragrance. Only you will take me away from myself and beyond myself. I will be dissolved in you. My physical body will be gone, but my non-physical fragrance will be released far and wide to the winds; it will touch the furthest reaches of infinity."

Inside us, it is exactly the same. That is why again and again we have chosen the metaphor of the flower. Inside, when that unique phenomenon called peace occurs, when that peace that follows the storm manifests, then the flower of the heart opens out towards the divine, faces that almighty sun with a trust – inviting it to come inside. Now it trusts that it does not need to remain closed. Now it will receive the divine, now it will become a womb to the divine. Now it says, "Come, enter me. Now I don't want to keep any nook or corner of my heart from your presence.

"I have lived in darkness for long enough, I have remained closed for long enough. And I was closed out of the fear that some calamity might happen, that if this vital place inside me were left open, someone might harm it, someone might destroy it, something wrong might enter it. That is why I had barred all the doors and windows, erected walls on all sides and kept myself safely locked up inside. But now that moment has come when I can open myself up fully."

This is the meaning of receptivity.

"Now I shall not hold myself back even an inch, now I will stand fully naked in front of you. Please enter this naked heart of mine. Please come into my innermost core. I am eager to become a temple for you."

When the disciple is ready to learn,
then he is accepted, acknowledged, recognized.
It must be so, for he has lit his lamp,
and it cannot be hidden.

When the disciple is ready to learn...

This is the deepest meaning of the capacity to learn. Opening up is the capacity to learn. Becoming totally receptive is the capacity to learn. Opening wide all the doors and windows of your heart and having a feeling of total acceptance is exactly what disciplehood is. And the day this happens, the day you open up like a flower, that supreme master accepts you.

Existence is the supreme master. That is why for those who have seen existence in their master, their seeing has a meaning. There is a significance in seeing existence in the master, because in the final analysis existence *is* the master. The beginning is in seeing existence in the master, and the end is finding that existence is the master. At that very moment the supreme master accepts you.

It must be so...

It does not happen otherwise, because the day you are open and willing, existence is ready to give. While you remain closed, its hands are incapable of giving. Its hands are always ready to give, but because you are closed there is no way to give. From the day you open up, its love starts to pour in.

The master accepts, because now the disciple has lit his lamp, and the flame from such a lamp cannot be hidden. You will be surprised to know that in the esoteric discipline of religions, this has a very deep meaning.

If you are really totally surrendered and receptive to the master, your whole aura changes. It changes at that very moment. People come to me and say, "Please give us initiation, please accept us into sannyas." But very few of them are really receptive. The aura around receptive people's faces is different, the glow in their eyes is different – as if a lamp is lit within.

There are some people who come to be initiated for other reasons. There is no light in them, no glow within; there is no aura around them. Even if they are initiated, it will be useless, because their hands are not open to receive. I initiate them, because okay, there is no harm in it. They decided to be initiated, even though it was for the wrong reasons, but it is not good to disappoint them. Perhaps tomorrow they may understand and drop the wrong reasons, and then the initiation will become real. As it is, there is no harm in initiating them because if the person is wrong, he will remain wrong after the initiation too. He won't become worse, he will just continue to be as wrong as he was before. So there is no harm in it, and the possibility opens up that he may change, that he may transform himself.

But if a person is really receptive, then he is already initiated. To initiate such a person is just a formality, a mere acknowledgement that will fill him with joy; an acknowledgement which will make him firm, an acknowledgement that will deepen his trust and improve his self-confidence. But as far as initiation is concerned, he is already initiated. Receptivity itself is initiation.

And as soon as someone becomes receptive, light begins to glow all around him. That light can actually be seen. If you sit down quietly next to a receptive person, you can feel that light. Of course, the master can perceive it very naturally. It can be seen. When a person comes to him, he brings his light or his darkness with him.

A person who is closed, whose bud is totally closed, who is not willing to surrender at all carries a circle of darkness around him. A person who is open, whose light has manifested, moves in an atmosphere of light, of joy. And when there is darkness around you, there is a burden on your head. When there is light around you, your head feels weightless.

These written above
are the first of the rules which are written
on the walls of the hall of learning.
Those that ask shall have.
Those that desire to read shall read.
Those who desire to learn shall learn.

Peace be with you.

"Those that ask shall have..." Engrave this sutra deeply in your heart.

Those that ask shall have.
Those that desire to read shall read.
Those who desire to learn shall learn.

Jesus has said, "Knock, and the doors shall be open unto you. Ask, and it shall be given to you."

But we are so poor that we won't even knock at the door! We are so poor that even if we ask, it is for the trivial, never anything that has a touch of greatness. Even when we go to the gates of the divine, we make goodness knows how many trivial demands! We go and ask for something which can already be found in the world, something for which there was no need whatsoever to go to the door of the divine. And the person who goes to the door of the divine asking for worldly things never actually reaches its door. For him, even the temple is a marketplace, a shop; the temple is also the world. He visits the temple as a ritual and continues to live in his world.

If someone asks only for godliness, his request is immediately granted – but preparation is needed for this asking. Even to ask we need an empty space in our hearts, so that if our request is granted we will have room for it inside. Receptivity is needed.

That is why this sutra comes after those earlier ones – so that he who is blooming like a flower in the silence which follows the storm can ask. Whatever he asks for, he will get. And that means only one thing for him now, and that is the ultimate wisdom, the ultimate liberation, godliness.

He will only ask for that which is life's ultimate – after which there is nothing left to ask for.

And there is no need to put that asking into words. His opening heart is in itself the asking. The process of the heart opening is in itself the prayer: "Now come inside me." There is no need to give any name to it. Words have disappeared with the storm, this will be a silent thirst. This will be the longing of his whole being. He will only want to read what is written on the walls of the supreme shrine of life, that ultimate peak of life on which are laid down all the secret sutras of life. This is just imagery. If he wants to read them, he will. If he wants to learn the ultimate secrets of life, he will.

In this moment, the moment when the flower blooms; in this moment whatever his heart desires will be fulfilled. In this moment, when the flower blooms, it is as if you are standing under a wish-fulfilling tree and whatever feeling you have will immediately become a reality, will materialize.

But only *after* the storm has passed. If even a little bit of the storm is left inside you, your demand will be for trivial things, and they will be fulfilled. Your demands will be for the meaningless, and they will be fulfilled.

Tolstoy has written a small story about a man who managed to appease a ghost. It took many years to appease, and when the ghost was finally appeased, it said, "I will grant you three wishes."

The man replied, "I don't know what to ask for right now, but as you say you will fulfill three wishes of mine, I will definitely ask as soon as the need arises."

So the ghost said, "Alright, but don't forget, only three wishes, not four!" The man thought that even three would be sufficient. With three wishes you can have the whole world– all three worlds!

He went home wondering all the way what he should ask for so that no wish would be left out. As soon as he arrived home he had a fight with his wife, so his first wish was that she would die – and she died! He immediately began to worry about what would happen to the children. And the neighbors would come to know, and now his wife was dead....

Then he remembered that although she quarreled, she used to love him too, and it crossed his mind that to remarry at his age would be asking for more problems. He had passed the age for marrying, he was well past sixty, and at that age where would he find a girl? He decided he had made a mistake, so he said, "O Ghost! Bring my wife back to life!" And she came alive again. Two wishes were gone. Now he was in great trouble because only one wish was left. This made him so mad with worry – thinking, "Should I ask for this or should I ask for that?" – that he could not sleep at night. And now only one wish was left! Now one more fear arose: if during some heated exchange with his wife, he blurted out the wish for her death again, then there would be no way to bring her back to life.

For three days he became so preoccupied with this, he worked himself into such a state, that he said, "O Ghost, please take back my third wish, and make sure I never ask for it again, because it will kill me. I am so bewildered that I don't know what to think." And that third wish was taken back.

If there is trivia inside you, then even if you are granted wishes, what will you do with them? This trivia will come out.

The storm has to pass. Whoever arrives at the moment with parts of the storm still inside him – where whatever is asked for is fulfilled – is unfortunate. There is danger. That is why my repeated emphasis is on exhausting the storm completely. Then only one desire will be left.

It is not right to call it a desire, it is a thirst. Even to call it a thirst is not right, because you won't even be conscious of it yourself. It is not as if you are thirsty, and are conscious of it. It is as if you have *become* the thirst. You are not separate, you have become the longing. Then those who ask will receive. Those who wish to read will read. Those who wish to learn will learn.

Peace be with you.

But the basis for all of this is that you have peace within you. Before that, all this has no meaning – it is simply a figment of your imagination. And if you do not have peace, then any journey in this direction is impossible.

9

THE VOICE OF SILENCE

Out of the silence that is peace
a resonant voice shall arise.
And this voice will say: It is not well;
thou hast reaped, now thou must sow.
And knowing this voice to be the silence itself
thou wilt obey.
Thou who art now a disciple,
able to stand, able to hear, able to see, able to speak,
who has conquered desire
and attained to self-knowledge,
who hast seen thy soul in its bloom
and recognized it,
and heard the voice of the silence –
go thou to the hall of learning
and read what is written there for thee....

To hear the voice of the silence
is to understand that from within comes
the only true guidance;
to go to the hall of learning is to enter the state
in which learning becomes possible.

Then will many words be written there for thee,
and written in fiery letters
for thee easily to read.
For when the disciple is ready
the master is ready also.

There are two chapters in the search for truth. First, when the seeker is searching, and second, when he shares. Do not think that your bliss is complete until you have also succeeded in sharing it with others. The search for bliss is not without greed, and to me, the desire for bliss is also self-centered. You are doing it just for yourself. As long as even the smallest part of you is there, desiring bliss just for yourself, your bliss will remain partial. A ray of darkness will always move by the side of such a bliss; a shadow of sadness will always remain there – because as long as you are present, total freedom from suffering is not possible. You may have a glimpse of bliss but it will remain only a glimpse. Your suffering will remain with you in some form or other because *you* are the suffering.

The day this second step happens, of sharing bliss, on that day *you* do not remain important: the other becomes important and you become unimportant. On that day, the seeker is not asking for bliss – he is giving it, he is sharing it. And as long as the bliss is not shared, it is not complete. When bliss is attained it is partial, when it is shared it becomes complete.

Think of it as inhaling and exhaling. The incoming breath is partial; you cannot live by just inhaling. If you try to hold the incoming breath, that breath which is the very basis of your life will become the cause of your death. If you inhale you will also have to exhale, and only when the breath is exhaled is the circle completed. The incoming breath is incomplete, the exhaled breath is incomplete: together, they complement each other. These are the two steps which keep life going.

When bliss enters you it is half of the cycle, and when it pours out of you and is shared, scattered, spread among others, spread to the farthest corners of the world, the breath becomes whole.

Remember, you inhale in direct proportion to the intensity with which you exhale. If a person exhales properly, then he is capable of inhaling to the same extent. The more a person lets go, the more he receives. And if after getting more he gives more, he gets still more. The chain becomes endless.

This should be rightly understood: that what you have is only truly yours when you are able to give it away. And as long as you are unable to give, know that you do not have it at all. As soon as you have something, sharing begins.

Understand one thing: if there is sadness in his life, a man contracts, he closes. He wants no one to see him, no one to meet him; he wants no one, not even his friends or companions, to come near him. He wants to sit in aloneness somewhere, to confine himself in some cave, with all the doors and windows closed. A sad man wants to close himself from all sides. Sadness is a constriction, a narrowing.

When you are sad you don't want anyone to talk to you, to speak to you. Even if someone expresses his sympathy it feels like a disturbance. When you are really sad even words of sympathy are nothing but an irritation. A loved one has died and you are surrounded by clouds of sorrow. When someone comes to console you, to offer you encouragement, it all sounds empty, meaningless. When he talks comfortingly of the soul being immortal, that there is no need to be sad, that no one really dies, and so on, he feels like an enemy. Sorrow wants to close in on itself from all sides like a seed. It wants to shrink.

Bliss is exactly the opposite. Just as one shrinks in sorrow, one expands in bliss. When bliss happens, a person wants to expand far and wide – to the farthest reaches of the winds, to the very ends of the skies – so that he can share what he has received. It is like when a flower blooms – its fragrance reaches far and wide. And when a lamp is lit, rays of light spread all around. In the same way, when the phenomenon of bliss happens it begins to share itself. If your bliss remains confined within you, then understand that it was not bliss, because the very nature of bliss is sharing, expanding.

That is why we have given the ultimate name to existence: *brahman*. *Brahman* means that which keeps on expanding. The word *brahman* has the same root as *expansion* and *growth*. It means that which goes on expanding, without limit. There is no point of limitation, it goes on expanding.

Only now, in this century, have the astronomers and physicists been able to say that the universe is an expanding reality. Before that, there was no such idea in the West. The theory was that no matter how big the universe might be, it had boundaries, limits; it was not expanding indefinitely. But with Einstein, a new theory has come into being, and this theory is very significant because it comes very close to the concept of *brahman*.

Einstein has said that this universe is boundless, that it is forever expanding. Just as your chest expands when you inhale, in the same way the universe is also expanding. There seems to be no end to its expansion – and it goes on expanding at a tremendous speed.

But this theory is a very ancient theory in India. We have given the ultimate truth the name *brahman*. *Brahman* means that which goes on expanding, infinitely expanding – that which has no boundary, which has no point where its expansion stops. And we have called the intrinsic nature of *brahman*, bliss. So bliss is an ever-expanding phenomenon. Bliss *is brahman*.

And the day bliss happens in your life, you won't be miserly. Only sad people are miserly. Try to understand this. It is so in all dimensions.

A sad man is miserly, he cannot give. He clings to everything, he grabs everything. He holds everything to his chest, he cannot let go of anything. You will be surprised to know that psychologists say a miserly man does not even breathe deeply, because to inhale deeply one has to exhale deeply. Psychologists say that it is almost certain that a miserly person will become constipated – because he cannot even eliminate waste from his body. He withholds even that. Psychologists say that constipation cannot occur unless there is a deep-seated miserliness in the subconscious. There is no other reason to stop the elimination of waste. The body eliminates it, it is the nature of the body to eliminate it, a very natural process, but the mind stops it. Remember, many people become interested in celibacy because they are miserly. Their enthusiasm for celibacy is not really a part of any search for the supreme reality. It is a part of their miserliness; that the energy contained in the semen should not be dispersed. Very few people become interested in celibacy from considered understanding. Mostly it is because of miserliness: whatever is inside should remain there, nothing should pass out.

That is why a miserly person cannot love. You cannot find a miserly person in love, because giving is a part of love. The very giving is love. And how can one who cannot give, love? That is why someone who is miserly cannot be loving. The opposite is also true: someone who is loving cannot be miserly, because someone who can give his heart for love can give away everything. There is no relation between bliss and miserliness; with sorrow there is.

So the day bliss happens you will really become a giver, your beggarliness will go. On that day, for the first time you will become capable of sharing. And you will have found a source which grows and does not shrink from being shared.

If you distribute wealth it decreases. It will decrease because the source of wealth is sorrow, not bliss. In some way or other accumulation of wealth will always depend on someone else's sorrow. Your wealth is created out of someone else's grief. So even though you are accumulating wealth, pain is also being accumulated. If you go around distributing wealth it will decrease, because wealth is not an inner state but a collection of things. If commodities are distributed they decrease.

I have heard:

A beggar was begging from a housewife. She gave him plentiful food and filled his begging bowl. She also gave him some clothes and some money. The beggar was good-looking, and appeared to belong to a good family. Although his clothes were torn and old, there was a brilliance in his eyes. His face, the contours of his face, his form, the beauty of him.... The housewife could not restrain herself, and she asked, "You look as if you come from a good family – how did this happen to you?"

The beggar said, "I did just what you are doing now – I kept giving. The condition I am in now will also be yours one day."

Material wealth has limits – if it is distributed it will diminish. There are no limits to bliss – if it is distributed it will increase. The source of bliss is within, and the more it is shared the more new sources will emerge. Under stand it this way. We dig a well, then pump the water out, and the springs fill the well. Have you ever thought where these springs come from? They are connected to the vast ocean, they will not dry up. The well will dry up if water is never drawn from it, but if it is used daily it will stay fresh and new. And the oceans to which these springs are connected are inexhaustible.

Remember, when we experience bliss, when we begin to draw on it, we realize that the streams of bliss are connected to *brahman*. However much we draw on them, they will never dry up. We are merely a well whose streams are connected to the faraway ocean. That ocean is *brahman*. That is why bliss increases when it is shared, and that is why it becomes whole only when it is being shared.

Now let us understand this sutra.

Out of the silence that is peace
a resonant voice shall arise.
And this voice will say: It is not well;
thou hast reaped, now thou must sow.

It is the opposite of what usually happens: first people sow and then reap. This sutra says:

...thou hast reaped, now thou must sow.

In this world, first we sow and then we reap. In the spiritual world, first we reap and then we sow. The laws in our world and the laws of the spiritual world are exactly the opposite of each other. Whatever is the law here, the law there will be just the opposite. If we reverse the laws of this world, they become the laws of the spiritual world.

Understand it this way: a man is standing on the shore of a lake that is full of fish. If those fish see the reflection of the man in the water, they will see him with his feet at the top and his head at the bottom, because the reflection in the water is inverted. But if the fish jump out of water and see the man, they will be very surprised: they may think he is standing upside down – because in the water his legs seemed to be above his head. The fish will inform their friends that the man was standing on the earth upside down.

This world is a reflection of the spiritual, it is a reflection of the truth. Reality is not the same way around as it appears to be, but in your world of thoughts, it is that way around. The day that you rise above the turbulent lake of your thoughts, on that day you will discover that in fact reality is exactly the opposite of how you thought it was, that just the opposite is the case. What was seen in the shadow of your thoughts, what was seen in the mirror of your thoughts, was incorrect. It was just the reflected image.

In the spiritual world, first we reap and then we have to sow. Why? First bliss is experienced – this means you have already reaped the harvest. First you take the breath in and then you exhale. You have reaped the harvest of bliss. The second phase is when you sow these seeds of bliss far and wide, so that other people may also reap its harvest. Someone else had sown and you have reaped that harvest.

Buddha sows, Mahavira sows, Krishna sows, Christ sows, Mohammed sows – he who attains bliss, sows it. First he reaps it and then he sows it – because you can only sow after you have reaped. You must have something to sow! How will you sow what you do not have? Only that which you have can be sown, so if you do not have bliss what will you sow?

All of us are making this mistake – that is why the world is in such a mess: we are all trying to give each other bliss, without bothering whether we have any of it ourselves in the first place. The result is that we all want to give happiness, we all want to give bliss, but we only succeed in making each other more miserable. No one is able to give happiness to anyone else.

The husband is trying very hard to make his wife happy but she is just becoming more miserable. The wife is trying very hard to make her husband happy, but he is thinking, "What sort of trouble have I landed myself into? How can I escape?" The father is trying to please his son and the son is thinking about when he will get a chance to escape from the clutches of the father. Sons are trying to please their fathers and fathers are hitting their heads and saying, "What sort of terrible sons were born into my family?"

We are all trying to please each other. It is not that we are not really trying – we are. There is no question about it, there is no doubt that we are trying. But we are trying without ever pausing to consider how we can give something to someone else which we ourselves do not possess. The wife herself is not happy and she is trying to make her husband happy. He himself is unhappy and is trying to make her happy. The father is unhappy and is trying to please his son. This is madness. What sort of arithmetic is this? I cannot give you what I do not have.

And this is also a part of it, that I do not have bliss but I am trying to get it from others. I never realize that those people I am expecting bliss from are expecting the same from me. When you are expecting happiness from someone and he is expecting it from you, then your state is like that of two beggars expecting charity from one another! How can there be any giving? Both are going to be disheartened, because both will be unsuccessful and will accuse the other one of cheating – that he could have given but he didn't. If he were capable of giving he would have.

Bliss is something which increases if given; hence one who is capable of giving is bound to give. He cannot withhold it, because by withholding, bliss rots; by withholding, bliss decreases; by withholding, bliss is lost. So when something increases by being shared, who won't share it? Everyone wants to share, but they don't have anything to share. Everyone wants to receive, but the very person they have gone to receive from is himself asking for something.

So a world full of beggars makes everyone suffer profoundly, the grief is acute. In the beginning everything seems joyous, but after a while everything becomes sorrowful. There is only happiness while there is still the hope that it is attainable. When hope is shattered, when every ray of hope is dimmed and every root is crushed, sorrow becomes visible.

First reap bliss, then sow its seeds. Then, someone else will reap its harvest. This means the harvest we reap has been sown by someone else. So even though Buddha may not be around today, we are reaping what he sowed. Jesus may not be here today but we are reaping what he sowed. This expanse, this existence is endless, and beginningless. Here, the whole of humanity is one continuous flow.

The sutra says that when you become calm after the storm, when the storm is over and peace descends, calmness descends on you and the flower of life blooms. Then, from that state of calmness, you will hear a voice clearly. When someone attains to calmness, he begins to hear it.

...this voice will say: It is not well;
thou hast reaped, now thou must sow.

You have taken, now share. You have received, now distribute. You have become the master, but the ownership is incomplete. Now give away what you have attained and become the complete master.

Have you ever thought that we are only the master of what we can give? This seems paradoxical. We can be masters only of those things that we can give. It is the giving which reveals that we were the owner. If you are not able to give, and hold on to things and find that giving is difficult, then you are not the master, the object is the master. When you are able to give, you are the master. Only the master can give – how can a slave give? And the day you are able to give bliss, you have become the master of it.

We give suffering – we give a lot of it without even being aware of it. We never come to realize that we inflict so many kinds of sufferings on so many people. We never become aware with what words, with what gestures, with what looks we manage to hurt someone. We go on inflicting hurt all around us. Standing, sitting – in all our actions – we go on spreading the poison of suffering. We are full of it, we cannot help it. Even if we try to stop it, it will not work. Even if we create walls around it, it will make no difference. It will find some other outlet and flow from there but it *will* flow. Rapids cannot be contained by force.

So we give out suffering. Our very life is nothing but a passing around of suffering. If only we could realize that we are spreading sorrow... but no one accepts it. No matter how much suffering you may be causing to others, if someone points it out to you, you never accept that it is true. You say, "That's totally wrong – there must be some misunderstanding. I am only giving happiness." And even though you also suffer at the hands of others, they will say the same: that they are only giving happiness, that if you are suffering then there must be something wrong with you.

Everyone is supposedly giving happiness but no one seems to be receiving it. And yet no one seems to realize that some basic mistake is happening. Keep this sutra in mind: that you can give only that which you have. There is no other way. It is only natural that we give suffering and receive suffering, and thus go on increasing it. This will continue until your suffering is swept away by the storm.

Why go on giving it to others? Conjure up the storm and allow it to wash away all manner of sufferings. You will continue to spread your suffering until you have learned the art of releasing it into the sky. Until then, you will go on releasing your suffering onto someone or other.

A young man came to me. He had run away from America, and he had reason to. Psychoanalysis had revealed that he was tempted to kill his own father, and he knew that this was true. He had only one thing on his mind, and that was that he should kill his father. His father had tormented him, then his mother had left and his father had remarried; the boy had faced all kinds of trouble. So in his mind there was a great hatred for his father.

When the psychologists made him aware of what was going on in his mind, and that it might really happen, he became very frightened. He came to India so that he did not have to live near his father, so that he could avoid the chance of killing him.

He came to me, and I told him, "No matter where you may run to, the day you decide to kill your father you will manage to reach him. You cannot go on running away like this, because how can you run away from yourself? You can run away from your father, but this mind of yours which wants to kill will still be with you, and it will only become even more aggressive."

He said, "What should I do?"

I told him, "You had better kill your father."

He said, "What are you saying? Are you mad? I have never met a man like you! I have come to you to find peace and you say I had better kill my father!"

So I told him that there was no need to kill his real father. There was a pillow in my room. I told him, "Take this pillow and imagine it is your father. Write your father's name on it, stick a photograph of your father on it – and buy a knife from the market."

He said, "You are joking!" but I saw that there was a glint of excitement in his eyes. His face, which was normally sad, brightened up!

I said, "Kill him and don't be worried. But how much can happen in just one day? Make a daily schedule so that for half an hour every day – first thing in the morning – you have to kill your father."

He said, "What will come out of this?"

I said, "Start doing this, and come and tell me about it after seven days."

After seven days he came back. He said, "What did you do to me? Just half an hour doesn't satisfy me. Sometimes for an hour or an hour and a half I beat him, then I stick the knife into him; and I feel so good after that...." And he said, "There has been a new development in the past two days; now I feel sorry for my father. The hatred has disappeared and now I have begun to feel sorry for him."

I said, "Keep it up for three weeks."

In the third week he came and told me, "Forgive me, and allow me to go and put my head at my father's feet and ask for his forgiveness. I don't have any hatred left in my heart. And now I feel that it was not really my father's fault, the circumstances were such.... Now I feel only pity, and I feel sad at the way I have treated my father for the last three weeks."

When I asked him, he said, "After three days I didn't see the pillow: my father took its place." The projection was complete. That which could not be cured through a whole year of psychological treatment was made possible by creating a storm for three weeks.

The young man went back, and his father wrote to me saying, "Thank you so much for returning my son to me. No matter how much I may thank you, it won't be enough. I never thought that my son would become so humble that he would put his head at my feet. This was beyond my imagining. I had accepted the fact that everything was over between us, and that it was not right for me to have anything to do with this child anymore."

Whatever is in you – grief, pain, anger – you should be capable of releasing it into the vast sky; then you will be free from your suffering.

There is no need to take it out on other people. What do you achieve by taking it out on people? People are just like pegs to hang things on. When a big peg like the sky is available, why take it out on small pegs like people? As it is, everyone is so full of grief; why load more on them? As it is, your wife is being crushed and is dying; as it is your husband is collapsing. How much more grief do you want to pile on? Why add more fuel to the fire? This open sky is very big, and its heart is so big that it will never tire of taking on your burdens. Let your grief fly away into this vast expanse, and there will be no trace left of – it will vanish.

All things dissolve in the sky. You too will vanish; what to say of your grief? You were not here yesterday – you were born out of this sky. When you cease to be tomorrow, you will once again merge with the sky. Earths are born and are destroyed, suns blaze and burn out, stars are born and then disintegrate, universes come and go... the sky absorbs everything. Your grief is nothing. Give it to the sky and it will absorb it.

Create a storm and let your grief be carried away. And then you will get a glimpse of bliss. In the void, in the silence that will come after the storm, you will feel it constantly.

...it is not well;
thou hast reaped, now thou must sow.
And knowing this voice to be the silence itself
thou wilt obey.

This instruction cannot be ignored, because it is not coming from the outside. This is the voice of your own inner being, this is your own command. You have given it to your own self, so you cannot escape from it.

Remember, someone else's command becomes a burden. You want to avoid it if at all possible. Even if you carry it out, you do so out of duty, and *duty* is an ugly word. It means you are being forced to do something, you are not happy about it.

Somebody came and told me that he is very respectful towards his mother, that he really looks after her. I told the man, "If you are merely doing so out of a sense of duty, then forget the whole thing. It means that you don't really love your mother – because whoever says that it is his duty to look after his mother does not really love her. Where there is love, there is no question of duty. It is a joy. You should say, 'I am looking after my mother because I love her. It is not a question of duty.' If you are doing it because you have to do it, then the whole thing becomes futile."

But there is a difference. Duty's commands come from without, and love's come from within. The dictates of love are your own, so you feel happy fulfilling them. The voice of duty is someone else's: the scriptures', society's, the teacher's, tradition's. The order comes from someone else, and you have to fulfill it. You do it, but your heart is not in it. You just get it done, you carry it like a burden.

And in this way whatever you are doing out of duty is poisoned. You think that you are doing some great service, but the person you are doing it for feels that you are doing nothing – because when your heart is not in what you are doing the other person can feel it at once.

Even small children can understand when their fathers are patting their back and smiling out of duty. Children know that the smile and the back-patting are false; that there is no heart in the hand which is patting them. Even a small child knows that no, his father's heart is not in it. Children understand these things.

We all know each other too well. There is no scope for cheating, because when the heart is present its juice can be felt. When it is not there, then everything feels dry. But you are bound to follow love's command, because it comes from your own inner being.

Thou who art now a disciple...

Meaning you who are now able to learn, you who have emptied your heart to a nothingness, you who have bowed down completely, will be...

...able to stand...

This is interesting: he who is ready to bow becomes capable of standing on his own feet, and he who is not ready to bow down, always remains dependent on others. This seems very paradoxical, but it is so – because all the strength of the universe starts flowing towards the person who is capable of bowing down. He who stands arrogantly and rigidly simply loses his own strength; such a person does not receive the strength of the universe.

Lao Tzu used to say that in a storm big trees stand rigidly and so they are uprooted. Small plants bend with the winds; the storm blows over them. The roots of big trees are overturned, they are laid flat on the ground; but small plants stand as straight as they did before. The storm gives new life to the plants, but it destroys the trees which are stubborn and proud. It is the same storm! The weak are saved but the mighty are destroyed.

It is amazing. The tree was very strong, that is why it stood up so stubbornly. And it said, "Let the storm come – I won't bend. I am the type which never bows down, even if my head is cut." But the small plants were neither stubborn nor offered any resistance to the storm; instead they bent with it. When the storm tried to bend them, they allowed it – just like a lover making his beloved yield, not out of any enmity but out of a feeling of love. The storm washed them clean, removed the dust from them; it rejuvenated them, removed their old leaves.

And when the storm was over, those same plants straightened up, more radiant than before, livelier and happier than before – their heads once again held high in the sky.

In our language they would be called weak, but in the paradoxical language of that other world of which I am talking, they proved to be stronger. Those trees that were strong in the language of this world, proved weak and fell flat on the earth. They could no longer get up, they had been uprooted. They were destroyed by their own egos, not by the storm – because if it had been the storm, it would have destroyed those small plants too. The storm did not do anything, it was just passing by. They themselves did something, and that caused their destruction. And the small plants did something else, and because of that they survived.

What we call strength in the language of this world is weakness in the language of spirituality. And that which we call weakness in the language of this world is strength in the language of spirituality. To bow down is weakness in this world: "Come what may, do not bow down to anything." In the language of spirituality, bowing down is an invitation for the energy of strength to fill you.

And one who bows down is filled from all sides: energy from the whole universe starts flowing towards him. He becomes like a vessel. His invitation is heard everywhere.

A conceited man is like the peak of a mountain. The rains come, they fall on the peak too, but the water cannot collect there. The peak is too full of itself. The rain waters collect in lakes. Lakes are empty so they get filled up. The peak is too full of itself, so it is left empty.

This sutra says, you who are a disciple, who can bow down, you who are humble, surrendered – you can stand on your own feet. Now you have that power in your legs...because this strength is not of the ego, but of humility. This strength is no longer yours, this strength belongs to the universal energy. The whole of existence is now giving you strength.

...able to hear...

The ego which would not let you hear is gone. The pride, which prevented you from hearing, is gone.

I see this happening quite often when scholars come to me. They cannot hear. I see this clearly; that although I am speaking, they do not hear. Even as I am speaking, they are continuously thinking to themselves about what they will say when I have finished speaking! Even as I am speaking, they are calculating all the time: what is right in what I am saying and what is not? Does what I am saying agree with what the scriptures say or is it against them? Does it fit with their objective or not? They are calculating!

Seeing their faces, I can clearly see that they are not listening; they are only preparing, they are simply getting ready for their turn to speak. And after I have finished speaking, the place they start talking from has no relation to the place where I finished – as if what I said had never been spoken at all, as if what I said had never reached their ears. They start talking from another world.

You should also pay attention to this. When you listen to somebody, are you really listening to them or are you chattering to yourself inside? If you are talking to yourself, you are not listening. Listening and talking cannot happen together. Yes, something will reach your ears and after the other person has finished talking, with the help of that little bit that you heard, you will speak. But the person who spoke will be surprised, because what you have understood is not what he said. If by some chance the other person is also muttering to himself while you are talking, the dialogue is taking place between two madmen.

No sense can come out of it; it is a useless debate, useless phrases are being hurled at one another. This is not a dialogue.

The sutra says that now you are able to hear because the voice of ego which resounded within you has stopped.

...able to see, able to speak...

And only one who can listen, can speak. And only one who can see, can speak. Before a person is able to speak, he needs to have learned the art of listening, because what you say will only have meaning after you have become capable of listening with an empty mind, what is worth talking about will only be heard in a state of emptiness. So what is said by those who have not yet perfected the art of silence will not have any value. The words of those who have not yet learned the art of silence are meaningless.

So there are two ways in which you can speak. A person can speak after having read the scriptures – that is speaking. Or if someone goes deeply into meditation, becomes silent, totally empty, and then speaks, that too is speaking. But the difference between the two of them is like the difference between earth and heaven. One is the speech of a pundit, and the other is the voice of a wise man. The pundit's speech may be very skillful and beautiful, technically perfect; it may be clear, logical, but it can never be the truth, because he has not experienced truth. And the speech which arises out of experience – and experience can be had only in silence, in emptiness, in calmness.... Experience is gained in that stillness which follows a storm. Only then does one become capable of speaking.

Mahavira remained in silence for twelve years – totally silent. Many people asked him to speak, but he did not. He only started speaking after twelve years. Until it had become clear to him that he had attained absolute peace, stillness, emptiness, there was no point in speaking. What was there to say, and to whom? When one has not yet heard that voice of emptiness for oneself, what will one say?

Thou who art now a disciple,
able to stand, able to hear, able to see, able to speak,
who has conquered desire
and attained to self-knowledge,
who hast seen thy soul in its bloom
and recognized it,
and heard the voice of the silence –
go thou to the hall of learning
and read what is written there for thee.

This is merely symbolic. But one who has become completely silent, totally empty, peaceful – to him the secret of the universe is revealed. The mysterious scripture of the universe, the secret keys of wisdom which lie hidden in the very core of existence...if we were to conceive that somewhere in the deepest core of this existence there lies a temple of wisdom, then this is how entrance is gained to that temple.

The sutra says it is this inner voice that will beckon you, it is this silence that will tell you that now you are ready: go into that *hall of learning*, go and read what is written there for you.

To hear the voice of the silence
is to understand that from within comes
the only true guidance...

Until you have become silent, your soul will not be able to guide you. Until then, you will have to take refuge in a master. The reason you have to seek this refuge is because you are still not capable of listening to the voice of your own inner master hidden deep within you. You are so full of noise that you are not able to hear that very fine, subtle voice which lies within you. It gets lost in the clamor of your mind with its racket, its turmoil, its crowd. It cannot be heard at all. That is why an outer master needs to instruct you, to guide you, to show you the way; otherwise there would be no need.

Your master lies hidden within you. But you cannot understand the inner voice; that is why you have to search for a master outside. It is useful – and it is necessary until you have become capable of listening to the voice of your own inner master. And the day you have heard the voice of your inner master, the outer master will have no meaning. But this does not mean that from that day you stop showing respect for the outer master; in fact you become even more grateful to him because he was the one who actually introduced you to your inner master.

Kabir has said, "The master and God are both present. Now whose feet should I touch first?" The outer master is standing there, but God, the inner master, has appeared alongside him. He has also appeared. And Kabir continues, "Now I am in a real dilemma, both are standing in front of me; my master and God are both present. Whose feet should I bow down to first?" Then Kabir says, "I touched my master's feet first because it was he who showed me the way to God. Without him, I would never have known about God. That is why I touch his feet first."

The outer master takes his leave once he has introduced you to the inner master. After that, the journey is purely an inner one. Then, apart from yourself, there is no one else there.

To hear the voice of the silence
is to understand that from within comes
the only true guidance;
to go to the hall of learning is to enter the state
in which learning becomes possible.
Then will many words be written there for thee,
and written in fiery letters
for thee easily to read.
For when the disciple is ready
the master is ready also.

The day you are utterly ready to be a disciple, on that day the supreme inner master becomes available to you. But first you will have to learn the process of becoming a disciple with an outer master. Once you have perfected your disciplehood, the outer master leaves and the inner one appears. That inner master was always ready; he was simply waiting for you to be ready. And the day that you are ready, you will find that he was always there. Once you have heard the inner voice, there is no more going astray in life, you will not make any mistakes in life. There is no scope left for that to happen because now, the one who travels and the one who guides are one and the same.

Understand this rightly: now the disciple and the master are one and the same. As long as the master was an outer master and you were the disciple, there had to be some distance, because no matter how intimate you are, no matter how much closeness, faith and trust you have in your master, still, there is bound to be a distance because on the outer, only relationships of distance are possible. The term *closeness* implies that there is also distance there. But you should keep on lessening this distance, and in this way you will reach a point beyond which there is no longer anything left to lessen. And the day you feel that now there is no distance left to make smaller between the outer master and you, you will discover that the outer master has disappeared and the inner master has appeared.

Just as water suddenly vaporizes at one hundred degrees, in the same way there is a particular point which, once it has been touched, means that the disciple is close to the master. There is a point in coming close to the outer master, a moment when if the outer master asks you to jump and be killed, then only "Yes" comes from within you. At that very moment, the outer master disappears and the inner master appears. As long as you can say no in any way to the outer master, the distance remains, the voice of the inner master cannot be heard.

The meaning of trust is precisely this – a state of total yes. The day this happens, the need for outer help ends. Now you have attained to that trust where the inner master is revealed.

10

THAT WITNESS IS YOU

PART II

1. Stand aside in the coming battle, and though thou fightest be not thou the warrior.

He is thyself,
yet thou art but finite and liable to error.
He is eternal and is sure.
He is eternal truth.
When once he has entered thee
and become thy Warrior,
he will never utterly desert thee,
and at the day of the great peace
he will become one with thee.

2. Look for the warrior and let him fight in thee.

Look for him,
else in the fever and hurry of the fight
thou mayest pass him;
and he will not know thee unless thou knowest him.
If thy cry reach his listening ear

then will he fight in thee
and fill the dull void within.

3. Take his orders for battle and obey them.

Obey him not as though he were a general,
but as though he were thyself,
and his spoken words were the utterance
of thy secret desires;
for he is thyself,
yet infinitely wiser and stronger than thyself.

In life there are two paths to victory.

One is that you try to win through fighting. But this way is just illusory. There will be plenty of fighting, but you will not be able to achieve victory. You will certainly fight, and many times it will seem to you that victory is near, but even then you will discover that in the end you cannot win. Victory eludes you. It will always seem that some time in the near future you will be able to win; your logic, your intellect will affirm that victory is possible – but it won't happen.

There is a reason for this: the one you are fighting is a part of you. It is as if someone were to make his two hands fight each other – how can there be a victory? Who will win? How? *You* are in both your hands. If you want, you can set your left hand up against your right one, but in doing so don't delude yourself into believing that you are only the right hand or only the left hand and not the other one. There can be a fight but it will be futile;

neither the right hand nor the left hand can win. Yes, if you want, you can befool yourself with the illusion of one winning over the other – by toppling the left hand with the right hand and thinking that the right hand has won. But this victory will be completely false, because at any moment you can simply let the left hand win instead.

Because it is *you* who is fighting through both your hands, there is no way of winning or of losing. There will never be a total victory, and there will never be a total defeat. One thing is certain: that in this struggle, in the fight between these two hands of yours, your energy will be diminished; it will go to waste and be exhausted. Anyone who follows this way will only miss the point. He will never win, nor will he ever lose completely – but he will always remain under the illusion that he *could* have won.

Let us try to understand this, because we have traveled on this path for life after life. That's why we have neither won nor lost. The place where you are standing right now is not a place of victory or of defeat. If you had really lost, then at least you would have chosen some other path. But no, the defeat is also incomplete and so the hope for victory remains. And you have never really won either.

You fight anger, and for a moment it seems as if you are going to conquer it – but then the very next day you discover that the victory was merely imaginary: anger takes hold of you again. You fight sexual desire: for a moment it seems that you are victorious, but then again you are defeated.

Now really try to understand this process. When do you fight your sexual energy? When it is on the ebb, you feel as if you are winning – and after making love, your sexual energy is naturally at the ebb. It is the same after you have eaten a meal – when your hunger has gone, you feel that you could fast. There is nothing surprising in this; after eating, after satisfying your hunger, one usually fasts. But this won't last much more than eight or ten hours, because hunger will return and you will find it difficult to continue fasting. On a full stomach a man can think of fasting – and even if he doesn't do it himself, he can at least sing its praises. But it is difficult to do so on an empty stomach.

When you are full of sexual energy, you become full of desire. After you have made love and your sexual energy is spent, your hunger has been satisfied, you repent. And then you say to yourself, "What kind of useless act am I doing? Why am I wasting my life's energy? What the hell is all this about? – it is behaving like an animal!" And then you begin to take vows of celibacy.

But such vows are false – because after some time, when your sexual energy has once again accumulated, you will find yourself breaking those vows. Once again a woman will appear very attractive, once again a man will begin to attract you, once again your mind will be full of sexual desire.

When your stomach is full you go to the other extreme – that of fasting, and when your stomach is empty you start dreaming of food. So you never win and you never lose.

Sometimes you feel as if you are winning, and sometimes you feel that you have lost, but neither of these ever really happens.

What is the reason for this? The one who is fighting and the one he is fighting with are part and parcel of the same energy. Who is this person who is fighting sexual desire, who is fighting the senses, who is fighting sin, who is fighting with anger?

Understand this rightly: the one who is angry is the same person as the one who is fighting anger. In the morning he becomes angry, in the evening he struggles against anger – the very same person! You divide yourself into two parts.

Some of you who are fond of playing cards may know that there is a card game which only one person plays. He deals out the cards for both sides; he plays on one side and then on the other. He plays all alone and takes great delight in being the winner and the loser! Now this is really hilarious, because who wins and who loses? He is the only player in the game! He is playing hide-and-seek with himself.

It is necessary for you to understand this rightly because we have been wasting energy on the path for many lives; always having the hope of winning – and yet we never win. Most people are destroying their energy this way. Their mistake is natural because the hope always remains.

I was a guest at the house of a multi-millionaire from Rajasthan. He was very old – he has died now – and very charitable. At the time that I was a guest in his home he must have been well over sixty-five. He told me that he had taken the vow of celibacy four times in his life. A friend of mine was there with me, and he was very impressed.

I told him, "Don't be so impressed! First, you had better ask him why he didn't take the vow for the fifth time, because what does taking the vow of celibacy four times mean? – just that you have broken your vow three times. And one who has broken it three times.... Don't jump to conclusions: go and ask him why he didn't take it for a fifth time too."

The old man started to cry, and he said, "You have put your finger right on the spot. No one I have told about taking a vow of celibacy four times has ever asked me, 'Why not the fifth time?' I did not take it a fifth time because I had already broken the vow four times and after that I couldn't gather enough courage to do it a fifth time. I understood by then that it was beyond me."

At least this man was honest. Even to understand this much is really very sincere. If only his understanding had had a little more depth.... But it could not mature. He thought that he was a weak person, and that was why he was not able to succeed. But it wasn't so; he wasn't weak. It was simply that the way he had chosen to fight is not the way to win.

Understand this difference correctly otherwise all your religious disciplines unknowingly end up giving you nothing but a feeling of inferiority, they fill you with feelings of inferiority.

Your holy men, your so-called saints, tell you to take the vow of celibacy. What they say impresses you because while you are under the spell of sexual desire you feel as if you have become a slave to something. Something is ordering you around; you are not your own master. That is why there is a sting in sexual desire. The anguish felt is not because of sexual desire, but because of the feeling of being a slave to something. It feels as if you are being pulled, as if you are being dragged into something against your will – and that you cannot do anything about it.

That is why what the so-called holy men and saints say appeals to you. We all want to be the master of ourselves – so that no one can order us around, so that we can behave in whatever way we wish. We don't want to find ourselves doing something that we don't want to do. This is what slavery is.

That's why we like to listen when someone says something against sexual desire. It appeals to us because we have experienced the slavery of sexual desire. That's why when someone talks about it we are very impressed, and in that moment we make the decision to put up a fight, to become celibate.

But you cannot achieve anything just by taking a decision. Just a decision is not enough. It is necessary, but you are not going to win just by making a decision. It will depend on the method you adopt, the way you go about it. If a path is not going to the place of victory, your decision, your vow, can only keep you wandering. And your vow can only result in what has been happening all along – that you become filled with feelings of inferiority. Time after time you will lose, and with every defeat you will feel that you are weak, impotent; that you won't ever be able to overcome your weaknesses; that this is something which only people like Mahavira can do.

But this has nothing to do with Mahavira. The difference between you and Mahavira is not that you are weak and Mahavira is strong, but that he is on the right path and you are on the wrong path. And no matter who someone is, if he is on the wrong path he cannot achieve anything.

So all the religions of the world have filled man with an inferiority complex. This is certainly very strange. All religions proclaim that you are God, that you are the manifestation of *brahman*, that nirvana is your nature, but the outcome appears to be just the opposite. Wherever religion has made an impression, man feels as if he is a sinner. Religions are preaching that you are the manifestation of God, but what they are really imparting to you, what becomes your experience, is that you are a sinner! What becomes your experience is that you are weak, you cannot do anything.

What is the reason for this? Religions talk about your utter sacredness, but the result is that you have an inferiority complex. Inferiority, guilt, helplessness and a sense of being weak are born in you, and in your mind a profound self-condemnation takes root, and you believe that "I am a bad person." And remember, for a person who feels this, it is very difficult to make contact with the divine, extremely difficult. That is why the more religious a country becomes, the more obsessed it is with sin. The opposite should happen, but this is what actually happens. The reason is that the path you are walking on simply does not lead to victory. There is a semblance of it – otherwise you would not have embarked upon it in the first place. Again and again it seems that you are winning, but the victory never really happens.

Even those so-called saints who go on preaching this to you – they themselves have not won. I know them very well; when they are alone with me, they ask the same questions that you are asking me now. That is why there is not even one iota of difference between you and your saints. If there *is* a difference, it is only this: that at least you are a little honest about it, and they are dishonest. Even where they have not succeeded, they will give you the impression that they have won.

Holy men, so-called saints come to me – and they are well-known preachers with hundreds of disciples; they have hundreds of monks as their followers. But when they are alone with me, even they ask me how they can overcome sexual desire. And can you believe it? – they have written books on celibacy! They preach celibacy and make up rules and vows of celibacy for people! It is a huge racket.

I ask them, "When *you* have not achieved celibacy, why do you suggest people take vows? Why are you getting people entangled in the very trap that you yourselves are caught up in? If you were at least to admit openly that you could not attain to celibacy, then perhaps a way could be found. You could all put your heads together and think about where you are going wrong and where the trouble lies."

And this is where you are going wrong: if a person has taken the wrong path, the result can only be disappointment. The right path...what is the right path? If you keep on fighting with yourself you will never win, because who is going to win and who is going to lose? And all these energies only belong to you. Sexual desire, greed, anger – all these energies are yours, all these forces belong to you.

So then what should we do? This sutra tells you.

You need to find a place within yourself which lies beyond them both. Then you will start winning. Sexual desire is there, and the greed for celibacy – they both exist. There is a struggle between the two but they are both at the same level, so neither can win. They are of equal strength, so neither can win. If you can find a point within you that is beyond both, that is neither eager for sex nor for celibacy – understand the difference: a point at which you are not interested in either sexual desire or celibacy – if you were to find such a point within you, it would lead you to victory.

We have called such a point the state of the witness. If you can find the witness within you which can impartially observe both states of mind then you will be well on the road to victory – because this third one, the witness, has no quarrel with anyone. It is not engaged in fighting with anyone. And it watches both desires, sexual desire and the desire for celibacy, as a witness.

I am using the word *desire* for celibacy. Understand this properly. Sex is a desire, celibacy too. Nobody has ever put it like this – that celibacy is also a type of desire. The opposite of sexual desire, is also a form of desire. When you have been harassed enough by sexual desire, you yearn for celibacy. Anger is a passion, and so is the desire not to be angry. When you are tired of being angry, when anger has burnt you and caused you wounds, you yearn for a state of no anger. But that too is a desire. The reverse of anger must also be a desire, the opposite of sex must also be a desire – they are on the same level. Just because something is the opposite, don't think that it is not a form of desiring. The world *is* desire. And if you take sannyas because you are unable to face the world, then your sannyas too is not separate from desire.

A sannyas that is born not from a fear of the world but from the state of being a witness to it is not a desire – it is a liberation. It is a little complex, but keep one thing in mind: that all opposites are of the same nature. Opposites cannot belong to different natures. If there is sexual desire then the opposite of it, which is celibacy, is also a desire. The difference is only this: it is as though at first you are standing on your feet and then you are standing on your head. But in both cases it is *you* who are standing. If sexual desire is like standing on your feet, then celibacy is like standing on your head. But it is just the other side of the same coin.

If you can find a witnessing point between both the desires, which watches them both – which does not side with one against the other, which does not choose this instead of that or that instead of this; which simply watches both of them, which is a watcher of the two – only this state of witnessing can achieve victory, because this witness doesn't have to strive to win; it is already the victor.

Understand this rightly. As this state of the witness goes on acquiring depth, it is already victorious. It doesn't have to win – there is nothing for it to win. It stands outside the struggle, it is not a part of it.

And the minute you stand apart from the struggle, you will realize what kind of madness you were involved in. From sexual desire to celibacy, from celibacy to sexual desire – you were swinging like a pendulum. First the pendulum swung to the left side; you thought it was moving to the left, but you did not realize then that while it was swinging to the left it was gathering momentum to go to the right. It swung to the left side precisely because it wanted to gather momentum to go to the right; it was collecting momentum.

The mechanics of a clock are such that when the pendulum is swinging to the left, it appears to you that it is moving to the left, but what you don't know is that it is actually gathering momentum to swing to the right.

Depending on how much it swings to the left, it will be able to swing to the right by precisely the same amount. And when it moves to the right side, you think that it is moving in the opposite direction; but when it is moving to the right, it is gathering momentum to go to the left again.

This means that when the idea of celibacy gets hold of you, what you are really doing is gaining energy to become sexually recharged. And when you are thinking of fasting, once again you are rekindling your desire for food. If you were only to go on eating, simply eating, then the desire for food would vanish. So fasting is necessary at intervals: through it your taste for food gets rekindled. If someone were to go on feeding you continuously, you would not like it, you would become sick of food. Likewise, if someone were to put you into such a situation that you had to indulge in sex all the time, you would run away from it so fast that you wouldn't even look back. In between a gap is necessary.

You move into sex and then abstain for a day or two...you observe celibacy. During that abstinence you rekindle enough interest to move into sex again. And if you don't understand this inner mechanism, you will continue to struggle and never be free from it. Your talk of celibacy just rekindles your interest in sex. All it does is rekindle your appetite for it.

The opposite of this is also true. It is because of going into sex that the issue of celibacy once again becomes important; after sex you will again repent. Then your mind becomes very saintly. After being angry you repent, and you think to yourself that this repentance is just the opposite of being angry. But no, all that your repentance is doing is giving fresh energy to your anger. That is why those who repent continue to be angry; they can never become free from it.

Repentance is not the enemy of anger, it is anger's friend. If you were to drop repenting, your anger would disappear. But you won't drop repenting. And after becoming angry you take a pride in the fact that you are repenting, that you are becoming a man of no anger. You have no idea that in repenting, you are once again gathering energy to move to the side of anger!

Opposites support each other. It is because of the opposite that the interest is generated. That is why when your tastes change.... The findings of those who conduct research on the mind say something different from what you understand. You think that if you adopt a new taste perhaps you are becoming the enemy of the old taste. But no, all you are doing is regenerating a desire for the former taste.

Only recently a western psychologist put forward a proposition. It is surprising, but it has a lot of truth in it. The proposition is this: the reason husbands and wives fight with each other so much is because they do not get a chance to have any variety in their relationships. This seems very shocking – at least to those who belong to the old ideology – but there is some truth behind it. In the West, experiments reveal that if the husband or the wife establish a relationship with another man or woman, their old relationship is not destroyed but on the contrary, it is rekindled.

But all along, our belief has been just the opposite. Our belief is that if the husband develops an interest in another woman, it means that he has lost interest in his wife. This is totally wrong. His showing interest in another woman and not making love to his wife for a while will rekindle his desire for his wife. If his wife only waits and is not in a hurry, then he will return. And the change refreshes them, it rejuvenates their interest in each other.

That's why in America they are experimenting with wife-swapping. There are small, exclusive clubs where they exchange wives. The experience of all those who have experimented with this bears out the fact that afterwards, interest in their spouses grows and conflicts decrease.

So no matter how dangerous it may appear to the person who belongs to the old morality, the future definitely belongs to these people. The old morality cannot last much longer, because it has already given enough trouble to husbands and wives – naturally so. If you were given only one type of food to eat every day – day in, day out – how long would you be able to eat the same stuff? Within seven days you would be fed up and feel that fasting is much better than this rubbish which you are eating. But each day you add some variety to your food so that your interest in it remains. You repeat the same food after five or six days, and that way you keep your taste alive.

In a deeper sense this holds true in all dimensions of life. So those of you who keep vacillating between opposites – please don't ever think that sometimes you are capable of being very saintly. There may be times when you become obsessed with the idea of celibacy, when you start using big words about wisdom and enlightenment, but it is nothing other than a way to get back into identification with your body again. When you begin to chatter on too much about the soul and suchlike, it just means that now you are fed up with the body, and a little diverting talk about the soul will help regenerate your interest in the body.

But apart from these two, there also lies a third point in man, and that point is the clue to victory. That point is the state of being a witness.

The first sutra:

Stand aside in the coming battle,
and though thou fightest be not thou the warrior.

The battle continues, but for the state of the witness this will be a battle with one important difference: you will fight, but you won't ever become a party to the battle. Don't become repentance, which is opposed to anger. Don't become celibacy, which is opposed to sexual desire. Don't become a warrior. The battle will continue, but become a witness. Watch them both from a distance, with no bias.

Maintain equilibrium; know that both sex and celibacy are forms of desire. Understand that both the world and sannyas are desires. Know that both bondage and freedom are forms of bondage. Put yourself beyond both, beyond the opposite. Say to yourself, "I am just a watcher, not a doer. I am not a doer, because the doer becomes a warrior." The moment you do something, you have become a warrior.

There is only one method of non-doing, and that is witnessing. Otherwise everything becomes a doing. Whatever we do, the feeling of the doer permeates it, and on the level of the doer, victory is not possible. On that level, we choose one party over the other – and once we have chosen a particular side, the other side automatically begins to strengthen. A day comes when we are forced to choose the other side. And when we favor the other side, the first side automatically begins to gain strength. And so we go on moving between this duality. The name of this duality is the world.

There is only one method for going beyond duality, and that is not to choose between dualities, but to watch them. What does this mean? This means that when a sexual desire comes up, you watch that it is there. When a sexual desire comes up, experience it and feel it taking you over from all sides. Don't fight it, but simply understand that it has taken hold of you. Whatever it makes you do, do it, but stand aloof and go on watching that it is making you do this and this – just as if you were a spectator watching a game. Have no quarrel with it.

Even after your sexual desire has reached its peak, even during this time, keep on watching – that now this and this is happening. When your sexual desire begins to wane and move down from its peak even then, watch: now sexual desire is disappearing and repentance is taking hold of the mind. Watch this also: repentance intensifying and thoughts of celibacy arising.

If you have watched this whole sequence from the state of a witness, you will understand that sexual desire and celibacy are not two separate things, but the rise and fall of the same wave. The day you understand this – that sexual desire and celibacy are both desires, that sex is the rising of the wave and celibacy is the falling of the wave, that anger is the rising of the wave and repentance is the falling, that the world is the wave rising, and sannyas is the wave falling – the day you see that these are connected, you will discover that you are beginning to win without even being a warrior. Choosing will stop, choicelessness will be born. What is there to choose between now? If they are one and the same, then there is nothing left to choose between. And when there is nothing left to choose between, you have started slipping out of the duality.

Choosing is duality, choicelessness is beyond duality. Learn the knack of this witnessing, and gradually go on immersing yourself more deeply in it. Suddenly you will find that the victory that could not be achieved through fighting is being won without a fight.

...be not thou the warrior.

This sutra is a very deep one:

...be not thou the warrior.

Yesterday, the sutra we were looking at said that you can now enter the hall of learning, and that on its walls are written fiery letters which you will be able to read.

This first sutra is from the hall of learning. It is written with fiery letters on the walls of the hall of learning:

Stand aside in the coming battle,
and though thou fightest be not thou the warrior.

That witness is you.

...yet thou art but finite and liable to error.

That witness is your innermost being. That witness is the deepest manifestation of your life. And right now you are standing on your periphery. You can make a mistake, but that witness cannot make a mistake. That witness is your highest reality. You are distorted: life's experiences, journeys, paths, the world and countless births, have conditioned and distorted you. You stand on the periphery full of dirt and dust; you can make a mistake, you cannot be relied upon. Don't trust yourself as the doer, because the doer stands on the periphery. He stands near the action, he is attached to the action. If you rely upon yourself, you will go on repeating the same things that you have always done. You are a circle, a vicious circle. You will keep going around in circles – which you have done time and again. Understand this a little.

Do you ever do something new? If you look back at your life and observe, you will find that you are always going around in circles. In the morning you are angry, in the afternoon you repent, by the evening you become loving, at night you are again full of anger, by morning hatred come. It keeps on moving in a circle. If you keep a diary for three months, you will be surprised – are you a man or a machine?

And if you were to write down everything in your diary, very honestly, you could even forecast what would happen on which day for the next three months! First thing in the morning you can put up your own calendar in the house: today I will be angry at such and such a time, and at such and such a time I will be peaceful. At such and such a time I will be full of despair and anguish.

It would be very helpful if every morning each member of a household were to hang up his calendar. Then the wife could warn her husband, "Please remember that when you return from the office at five o'clock I won't be in a good frame of mind." So then her husband can check the calendar and see what is going to happen that day, and act accordingly. The wife can also check her husband's calendar. And then both of them can come to some sort of a mutual understanding.

Right now, we are clashing with each other like blind people. And the funny part of it all is that whenever we clash, we always think that somebody is trying to harass us. Whereas the reality is that no one is harassing you, it is your own inner cycle working. It is just like when women have their period: nobody is drawing blood from their body, no one is trying to hurt them. It is their own inner cycle which is causing menstruation to happen. Your twenty-four-hourly cycles happen in the same way; no one is trying to harass you. But at some moment you become sad and in another moment you are happy, and when you are happy you think someone else is making you happy, and when you are sad you think someone else is making you sad.

And the most interesting thing about all this is that it all depends on your inner state of being. Something will make you sad if you are in a sad mood at the time, but that very same thing can make you happy if you are in a happy mood. If you examine yourself through all this, you will be very surprised, you will wonder. Then you won't go out and blame a single person in the whole world. You will find that the inner seasons keep on changing: at times it rains, at times there is sunshine, at times it is cold. Inner seasons keep on changing, and if you can be a witness to your inner seasons, you will become the master.

But instead you become the doer! When anger comes, you become angry. When sexual desire arises, you become full of lust. And when a desire for celibacy takes hold of you, you wave that flag. You become identified with everything. Stand aside. The further away you stand from the cycles of your moods, the more mastery you have.

Mastery is in the state of the witness. The defeat is in being a warrior. This will seem paradoxical. You will ask, "How can I win without becoming a warrior?" In this world you can only win by becoming a warrior. But if you become a warrior in the spiritual world nothing but defeat comes to you. And that defeat is not total: otherwise you would certainly become fed up. Even that defeat is incomplete, and a hope always remains, "I *will* win, I *will* win!" And victory never comes your way.

He is thyself...

This state of the witness is nothing but your own innermost being.

He is thyself,
yet thou art but finite and liable to error.
He is eternal and is sure.
He is eternal truth.
When once he has entered thee
and become thy warrior,
he will never utterly desert thee,
and at the day of the great peace
he will become one with thee.

There are two sides to you: one that is standing on the periphery, and one that lies hidden at the core. At your core you are godliness. There, you are the supreme power. At your periphery you are just a weak person. If you fight just at the level of your periphery, then you can only make use of as much energy as *you* possess. But as you move towards your center, your power will go on increasing. A person who stands at his very center does not have to fight at all. Such a person has become so powerful that under that power, desires burn away and turn to ash.

The important question is not how to fight, but how to become so powerful. In the presence of such power the periphery is suffocated and disappears. The clamor the periphery used to make simply vanishes. This sutra is about how to win without fighting. And victory only comes without fighting.

The second sutra:

Look for the warrior and let him fight in thee.

Remain a witness.

Look for him,
else in the fever and hurry of the fight
thou mayest pass him;
and he will not know thee
unless thou knowest him.
If thy cry reach his listening ear
then will he fight in thee
and fill the dull void within.

Search for this state of the witness. In this search you will meet the warrior who fights on the periphery. But there is a big difference: you will not become that warrior, you will not become a soldier, you will not go out and fight; you will just be simply present. What does this mean?

It means that right now when anger arises in you, repentance does not. If they were to arise side by side, they would cancel each other out and you would become peaceful. Right now, when anger arises in you, repentance does not, and when repentance arises, anger does not. They arise one at a time. Right now, when sexual desire arises, celibacy does not, and when celibacy arises, sexual desire does not. They never meet at any point. If they did, they would cancel each other out, they would cut each other off. Just as the negative and the positive neutralize each other, these two neutralize each other and you become peaceful. But when one of them arises, there is no knowing where the other one is. By the time the other one comes, the first one is gone. These two never meet anywhere.

Understand this a little, because it is one of the most profound innermost happenings which can lead to victory in life. If they were to appear at the same time, what would happen? When you are full of anger, if you were also filled with repentance – what would happen? Repentance and anger would cancel each other out. When you are full of sexual desire, if the desire for celibacy were also present in you, they would cancel each other out. And after that, there would be no celibacy and no sexual desire. Understand this difference.

That is why those who are truly celibate are never self-conscious of it. Anyone who has really and truly attained to celibacy does not have any pride or vanity about it. Anyone who has assumptions about his celibacy, who manages it, practices it, has merely chosen celibacy to counteract his sexual desire. Sexual desire has not been tamed, it is still waiting in the wings. Such a person is covering things up with his celibacy, but sexual desire is very much there – waiting. Soon his feelings will change, the season will change. In this world nothing stays the same, everything changes.

Apart from the witness, everything in this world is susceptible to change. Only one point in this world is eternal, constant, a place where no change takes place. Everything else changes. On the circumference the wheel goes on rotating. Only in the center where the axle is, where the witness abides – only there nothing revolves, everything is stationary.

So if you have chosen celibacy as a way of repressing sexual desire, the sexual desire still lies buried, waiting in the unconscious. When you get tired of celibacy it will catch hold of you by the neck; it won't let you go. Your holy men and saints are even afraid to sleep at night in case they have sexual dreams! They become so afraid, that if they come across a place where some woman has been sitting, they have to consult the scriptures – written by mad people like themselves – which stipulate that they shouldn't sit there until so many minutes have passed because if they do, sexual desire will arise.

Sexual desire does not arise because you are sitting where a woman has sat. But if you have repressed sexual desire so much, it can surface. Even the place where a woman has sat will feel wonderful! Now this is a sign of madness, not of celibacy. It is an indication of deep sexual desire.

An indication of true celibacy would be if a woman came and embraced you, and even then no sexual desire arose in you. And it would be an indication of madness if you sat where a woman had sat long ago, and it made you feel sexual. This is of your own making; the poor earth has nothing whatsoever to do with all of this. And this miracle only happens to the saints!

The miracle of experiencing sexual arousal by merely sitting in a place where a woman once sat happens only to saintly people. The woman has no hand in it, the saints can take full credit for it. The saint is so harassed inside from all his fighting and repressing that any excuse will do, any pretext whatsoever.

You must have heard or read about this: that as a holy man approaches the height of sainthood, beautiful *apsaras*, celestial nymphs, descend from the heavens to distract him. Now what sort of a business is this? – and going on in heaven! Who started it? And who could possibly be interested in corrupting the saints? Who is behind all this?

No. No *apsaras* descend from anywhere. This is simply a projection from the unconscious of the saints themselves. The thought of women has been so deeply repressed inside that it doesn't let go of them until the very last moment – and then these holy men claim they are being corrupted! Nobody is being corrupted: it is all a play of the mind. Nobody is corrupting them, but what they have repressed is gaining strength, and there comes a moment when it becomes so powerful that they will be defeated because of it. In spite of apparent earlier victories, in the end they will lose. Both sides, both hands are theirs. Your celibacy was an enforced celibacy, it was somehow forcibly managed. But your repressed sexual desire is lurking inside and waiting for an opportunity. A time will come when the pendulum starts to swing, and when it does…

Why doesn't this happen to you? Why don't *apsaras* come to *you*? For this to happen, you will first have to become a saint! If you want to invoke the *apsaras*, first you will need to go through the process of becoming a saint. The pendulum needs to go so far out to the left that when it swings to the right it reaches straight to heaven! That much energy needs to be generated to swing to the right. If you want *apsaras*, then you will first have to become a saint. Since the saints have vanished, so too have the *apsaras*!

Nowadays no *apsaras* come – not because there are none left, but because there are no saints left! Create some saints, and the *apsaras* will start coming once again. They are the madness of the saints' minds. What has been repressed will manifest itself. It will haunt you. And if you have repressed very much, this manifestation will be surreal. The saints have not been mistaken in saying this; they have reported rightly that *apsaras* came to them. And the *apsaras* must have been more beautiful than any woman could ever be.

That beauty is coming from their repressed desires. That beauty is a self-created one. When you are full of sexual desire, the deeper that desire, the more beautiful women will seem – or men, if that is the case. If you are full of desire then even an ugly woman will seem very beautiful. And if your desire has reached bursting point even an ugly old woman will seem beautiful.

This beauty that you see is merely your own projection. It is just like even a dry crust of bread appears to be a delicacy to a starving man. There is nothing delicious about that piece of dry bread – but you are ravenous. And if your stomach is full and a table of the choicest food is spread before you, you won't even notice it.

Try fasting for one day and then go to the market; that day you will only notice the signboards of hotels and restaurants, not of any other shop! And you will take great delight in reading those signboards, they will really attract you and it will seem as if you are seeing that tasty food and those sweets on display for the first time. Their rich colors, and the aromatic flavors floating up to your nostrils will open the doors to gastronomic secrets that you had never even dreamed of before!

But it is not them, it is the color that you give to them from what is inside you. A man projects his emotions onto everything around him. So your holy men and saints must have seen *apsaras* – but those *apsaras* were the creations of their minds, their very own creations.

If you become a witness, you will be able to view both sides at the same time. The more you distance yourself, the more clearly you will be able to see them side by side. Distance is needed to observe them simultaneously. If you are too close, only one can be seen.

From where I am sitting here, I can see all of you. If I were to move closer, then I would be able to see fewer people. And if I were to move even closer still, I would be able to see even fewer. Were I to sit right next to someone, I would only be able to see that person. The more distance there is, the bigger the area you can see.

So after a person has attained to the state of a witness, he is able to observe anger and peace, greed and contentment, hatred and love, sex and celibacy – he can observe them side by side. Then he is surprised to learn that they are part of one and the same wave – here anger, there repentance; here the world, there sannyas; here indulgence, there renunciation – these are two sides of the same wave. As he understands this fact, the simultaneous presence of the two cancels them both out. *This* is the warrior. There is no need for you to become a warrior.

It is necessary to seek out this warrior in whose presence opposites are canceled out. The mere fact of their simultaneous presence neutralizes them. This neutralization is a victory achieved without the violence of a battle, without fighting.

Look for the warrior and let him fight in thee.

The meaning of *warrior* is the simultaneous presence of opposites, the simultaneous realization of both.

Look for him,
else in the fever and hurry of the fight
thou mayest pass him...

Many times you are close to him. But you are less interested in understanding and so eager to fight, your mind is so full of hurry and worry about winning, that you pass by the warrior, who could have helped you win, without so much as glancing at him. If you are in a hurry, anxious to fight, impatient for a victory, you will go on missing him – because in order to see him you need to be patient, peaceful, silent and natural. Only then will you be able to see him. Only then will you be able to maintain such a distance that you are able to observe opposites simultaneously.

So don't ever be in a hurry to win – that is, if you want to win. If you want to win soon, then don't be hasty at all. If you want it to happen soon, don't be in a rush, because the more hasty you are, the more agitated you will be...and so you will go on missing.

The power that will liberate you is present within you. It is your energy that is enslaving you and it is your energy that will set you free. But don't ever be in a hurry. With patience; waiting, with no anxiety to win, our victory is certain.

...and he will not know thee
unless thou knowest him.

Bear in mind that that warrior is within you. But, ...he will not know thee unless thou knowest him. He will just continue sitting there, because you are not making any use of him. You are not making use of an immense energy! This immense energy lies hidden in the act of your seeing the opposites meeting simultaneously. And you go on missing this. You observe one, and when you get tired of it you observe the other one. But until there is a meeting there can be no neutralization. Until then, they cannot negate each other, they cannot erase each other.

If thy cry reach his listening ear
then will he fight in thee
and fill the dull void within.

The third sutra:

Take his orders for battle and obey them.

Obey him not as though he were a general,
but as though he were thyself,
and his spoken words were the utterance
of thy secret desires;
for he is thyself,
yet infinitely wiser and stronger than thyself.

Leave the whole war to the witness inside you. Don't try to turn him into a fighter. And as you become capable of using him, as you become capable of seeing through him, you will start receiving commands that will certainly lead you to victory. Don't take your orders from the scriptures or the holy books; take them from your own witness. It will always lead you in the right direction – there is no possibility of it ever making a mistake.

But we all take orders from God knows who! We don't even bother to find out if those from whom we are taking our orders have arrived anywhere or not. And the hilarious part of all this is that we take our orders from people who are just like us – because they fit with our intelligence.

For example, if you are troubled by sexual desire, the chances are that you will seek out a guru who is himself harassed by it, and as a result has forced himself to be celibate. The chances are that you will find such a person. You will not be able to find a master who is not troubled by sexual desire and whose celibacy is natural, because such an unaffected celibacy will be beyond your understanding. You are so harassed by sexual desire, you are so unnatural, that only an unnatural celibacy will make any sense to you.

If you ever come close to a natural person you will find a thousand excuses to run away from him. Why? – because you will not be able to accept that your master is untroubled by those things that trouble you. You will run away.

The situation is very difficult: you can only choose a guru just like you. And you will never be free of him because he will trap you in the same net. He will bundle you into a net that is exactly the opposite of the one you are trapped in – but it will be a part of the same trap. Sexual people choose celibates.

I continually see it, and people come and tell me, that this is exactly what happens.

Just a week ago, a member of parliament who also happens to be a big industrialist came to meet me. As he entered, he commented, "Your memory is very remarkable."

This made it clear to me that this man must have a bad memory, because this is something hardly worth talking about. Why is he so interested in memory, in whether it is good or bad? His memory must have been poor. He kept on repeating, "You are a remarkable person. You never forget the name of a book or the person you might be referring to, you never forget the name or face of a person you met years ago. Your memory is amazing!" Then he said, "Just recently when you were delivering your discourses on the epic, the *Ramayana*, at the Cross Maidan...." Now, I have never spoken on the *Ramayana*, I was speaking on the Gita, and he was saying that I was lecturing on the *Ramayana*! "what things you said! And I have heard talks on *Ramayana* from many a great pundit."

I said, "Sir, the minute you entered, I knew that you were afflicted with a bad memory."

Whatever makes an impression on you tells you something about yourself. It does not tell us much about the other, it says something about you. The moment you come to hear that so-and-so has been a celibate since childhood... and your poor mahatmas make it a point to have it known that they have been celibate since childhood. Sexual people are drawn to such lifelong celibates easily. There is no great reason for it; the only reason is their own weakness, their own problems. They are living at one extreme, and the other extreme calls them.

You are greedy, and if someone tells you he has renounced hundreds of thousands of rupees, you fall at his feet. This indicates something about you. Whether that person renounced hundreds of thousands of rupees or not doesn't matter much. But you are such a miser you won't give up even a *paisa*. That's why someone giving up hundreds of thousands immediately impresses you; you immediately fall at his feet.

In their scriptures the Jainas talk about Mahavira renouncing so many horses, so many elephants! This shows us something about the people who are discussing it; Mahavira renouncing wealth is not the important thing. Why talk about horses and donkeys – what have they got to do with us, what is the point in counting them?

But they go on raising the figures! This indicates their own clinging minds. That is why so many greedy people have gathered around Mahavira, that is why the Jainas have amassed so much wealth. There is a reason for their being so rich. Actually, greedy people became interested in Mahavira. He was a renunciate, so the greedy are immediately attracted.

Who you are attracted to entirely depends on you. But then a great calamity happens. Even the very great masters fail in this world because the people attracted to them are exactly the opposite type of people. You cannot understand Mahavira, but you are attracted to him because of your greedy nature. "Look what a great man he is! He has renounced so much!" Because you, as a miser, cannot even give up one paisa, and because he has renounced so many horses, so many elephants, so many chariots, so much jewelry, then: "This is the right master." But *you* are absolutely the wrong sort of person for such a master.

Life is very complex. If you are to receive the right command and save yourself from yourself.... Because when you seek a master, it is your periphery that is seeking and you will find the wrong one. Even if you are looking for the right one, you will seek under the influence of what is wrong in you. So it is better to fall back inside and stand in the witnessing self, because first of all you need to observe yourself with the eye of the witness. As your ability to watch as a witness develops, you will start receiving orders from within. Only these commands are true. These commands will take you on the right path.

It is essential to seek out your inner voice, your inner self, your interiority. Without it, you will go on drifting like a piece of wood tossed on the waves; sometimes being pushed here and sometimes being pulled there. Time will be wasted. First, you have to seek out your own interiority, because the master you choose after such a search will be entirely different. Then, it is not your peripheral self, your sick personality that chooses. Then, your inner voice has guided the choice.

If you can understand the state of the witness even a little, you can rely on the master you select to take you across. He becomes like a boat. But that should be the choice of your inner guide, not something chosen from your periphery.

Take his orders for battle and obey them.

Obey him not as though he were a general,
but as though he were thyself,
and his spoken words were the utterance
of thy secret desires;

for he is thyself,
yet infinitely wiser and stronger than thyself.

Within you lies a dimension of your own being that is much more powerful and much wiser than you are so far. Listen to it, follow it. But for that to happen, first you need to learn to wake up in the midst of the battle and become a witness.

II

LISTEN TO THE SONG OF LIFE

4. Listen to the song of life.

Look for it and listen to it first in your own heart.
At first you may say: "It is not there;
when I search I find only discord."
Look deeper.
If again you are disappointed,
pause and look deeper again.

There is a natural melody, an obscure fount
in every human heart.
It may be hidden over
and utterly concealed and silenced –
but it is there.
At the very base of your nature
you will find faith, hope, and love.
He that chooses evil refuses to look within himself,
shuts his ears to the melody of his heart,
as he blinds his eyes to the light of his soul.
He does this because he finds it easier
to live in desires.

But underneath all life is the strong current
that cannot be checked;
the great waters are there in reality.
Find them and you will perceive that none,
not the most wretched of creatures,
but is a part of it,
however he blind himself to the fact
and build up for himself
a phantasmal outer form of horror.
In that sense it is that I say to you:
all those beings among whom you struggle on
are fragments of the divine.
And so deceptive is the illusion in which you live,
that it is hard to guess where you will first detect
the sweet voice in the hearts of others.
But know that it is certainly within yourself.
Look for it there and once having heard it,
you will more readily recognize it around you.

In all his experiences of life, man is simply hearing the echo of his own heart. What you find on the outside is nothing but your own inner projection. The outer is just the screen: what you see reflected on it are your own shadows. If you feel that life is a suffering and you see unhappiness casting its shadow all around, know that it is nothing but the projection of your own troubled heart. If you see only anguish in life, it is you who has projected despair onto life. What you see on the outside is nothing but an extension of your inner state.

Think of the world as a mirror and what you see in that mirror as nothing but a picture of yourself. But we think that what we see actually exists in the world, and then we become engaged in trying to get rid of it. This effort only shows our ignorance, and takes us into deeper suffering, because the origins of what we are trying to erase do not lie there. It is just as if you feel that a mirror is projecting an ugly image of you, and so you break the mirror. You can break it if you want to, but this will not change your ugly face. By breaking the mirror you may not be able to see your ugly face, but not seeing it does not mean that it does not exist.

This is why so many people run away from the world because they can see their own ugliness reflected in the society. In relationships, in the mirror of relationships, all their innermost sicknesses become visible. In the jungle and in the lonely abodes of the Himalayas this mirror is no longer there; there, they cannot see themselves. And as long as they cannot see themselves reflected, they feel that some spiritual transformation is taking place. They are deluding themselves; they will have to return from the Himalayas. And only when they are back again in the midst of the crowd can they know if what they had felt to be erased in the Himalayas actually was, or whether they simply couldn't see it because there was no mirror there.

That's why once a person has run away to the solitude of the jungle he is very scared to return to society – because then he will again begin to see what he thought had been wiped away. You need someone else: without the other you are not able to see yourself. The presence of the other, the relationship with the other, makes it easier for you to be revealed. How will you become angry if there is nobody else around?

So there are two ways not to be angry: either you can become free of anger or you can run away from the presence of others. How will you have desires, how will you accumulate things, how will you create your ego if the other is not present? Suppose you were completely alone on the earth: what would you do, what would you be greedy for? What would be the relevance of greed? You would be the solemaster of the whole earth, the whole earth would be yours. Where would you put up fences? Where would you draw the boundary around your house? Where could you stake your claim, mark such and such a piece of land as yours? You would be all alone, and a claim would have no meaning. A claim is staked against somebody; the other needs to be there.

And to whom would you boast? Would you announce, "I am Alexander! I am Napoleon!"? Why would you bother? Who would you say it to? Who would be there to listen? Who would look on you as Alexander? No – ego would have no meaning. And even if you were to practice humbleness, what would be the sense in it? To whom would you declare that "There is nobody more humble than I am"?

If you are all alone, you are in great difficulty because then there is no means to express all those things that are hidden within you. You might never even become aware of them.

That is why the type of sannyas that evolves after a person leaves the society is unripe. It will disintegrate, it is gutless, it can survive only if it is protected. It can survive only under special circumstances. Under the open skies, in everyday life, its color will fade away.

I only call that sannyas which blossoms in the heart of society real – because mirrors are there. Rather than breaking the mirrors, you look at your ugliness full in the face: you try to change yourself and make yourself beautiful. Here, there are people who can make you angry, on whom you can let off steam, who can trigger your anger like burning fire. But you don't leave them and run away, you don't hold them responsible for causing your anger. You understand that they are merely an excuse, that the anger is actually within you and you used them as an excuse for your anger. You are grateful to them for giving you an opportunity to look at what lies hidden within you. They create the circumstances and enable your spirituality to grow.

If you transform yourself – if you do not escape from these excuses, if you do not break the mirror by leaving society and running away from it – you will be surprised. The day the anger within you disappears, you will immediately find that it has also vanished from the whole world. It is not that anger has really vanished from the world, because those who are hot-tempered will still be hot-tempered. But for you, this world will have become empty of anger, because now nothing of the world can make you angry. Now, there is no excuse that can provoke your anger because now there simply isn't any anger left inside you. Now, no mirror can reflect your ugliness because it is just not there.

The search for spirituality begins with this fundamental sutra, that whatsoever we find on the outside is actually hidden within us. If you assume that it is only on the outside, you can never become spiritual.

That is why Karl Marx, Frederick Engels and Lenin did not allow religion. There is a very significant meaning behind their denial, and it is very logical. Karl Marx said that it is the society which is diseased and not the individual. That's why society has to be changed, only then will the world be a better place. There is no point in changing the individual, because the disease is not in the individual.

This is the fundamental proposition of communism. That is why Karl Marx said that religion is pointless and useless. If his argument is right, religion *is* pointless. His conclusion is logical. If communism is right, religion becomes meaningless. The basic proposition of communism is that the disease lies without and not within, and the basic proposition of religion is that the disease lies within and not without.

That is why religion and communism are the greatest rivals on this earth. There is a deep clash between these two concepts, and it will continue. If the sickness lies without, then there is no need for the individual to do anything about himself. There remains no need for any meditation, religiousness or spiritual transformation. All these things are pointless. All we have to do is to bring about a change in the outer situation, and once that has happened, the mirror will have changed, and you will appear to be beautiful. There is no need for *you* to change.

But there is one fundamental flaw in this belief of communism. Who will change all this? Obviously it will be the people: the very people who were born into that society which is ugly, bad and exploitative. And these are the people who are going to create the new society! Since communism does not acknowledge that the individual has any potential – it believes that all potential lies in the society – then how will these same people who are born into the society be able to change it? And here communism finds itself in a difficulty. The very people who are born into this society are supposed to change it. And since an individual has no potential – all the potential is in the society – a society which is recreated by these people can never be a new society. How can something new happen? Those who were born into the old order will re-establish the old system. And this is exactly what has happened.

A revolution took place in Russia, and on the surface everything seemed to have changed, but inside exactly the same structure crept back in again. The labels changed, the system changed, there was a lot of commotion, killings took place on a large scale, but the original form of the society has remained the same as before. The capitalists and the poor have disappeared but now, in their place, there are the managers and the workers! The difference remains the same as it was before, the gap is the same – there is exploitation just as there was before. The proletariat are still the proletariat, and the affluent are still affluent. There is just a slight change in the mode of affluence; you no longer need a bank balance in Russia to be rich. What matters is how important a post you hold within the communist party hierarchy. That has now become the source of power.

What difference does it make whether you have paper money in your hand or the certificate of a powerful party post? It does not make any difference at all: the powerful are still powerful, the weak are still weak, and the difference between them is as great as it ever was before. Perhaps the distance has increased – because in a poor country even a poor man can become rich sometimes, but in Russia it is almost impossible for a person who is not a member of the communist party to rise in the hierarchy. For the past forty or fifty years, a small clique of about ten to fifteen people have been controlling the whole of Russia. A small group of people have captured the whole nation, the whole nation is in a state of slavery. No poor man was ever such a slave.

The basic proposition of religion is this: that the disease lies within the individual and not in the society. Only if the fundamental quality of the individual undergoes a change, can society be transformed. Society can be transformed only if a revolution takes place within the individual himself; there can be no other revolution.

What does it mean when we say the revolution of the individual? The revolution of the individual means:

"Whatever I find in my life has only come from inside me."

Look at it this way. Suppose you are hungry, you are unhappy, you are sad, your mind is full of anguish. The spring has come, the flowers are blooming, the birds are singing, but you don't hear the songs of the birds or see the blooming of the flowers; your nose does not breathe in the fragrance given out by the flowers. You don't even notice that spring has arrived – you are lost in your sadness, you are steeped in your depression. You may even find the blooming of the flowers disturbing; the song of the birds may sound like a noise. You may want everything to quieten down – what is all this noise about? The pleasant breezes of spring may sting you because the depression raging inside you colors your outlook.

It may also happen that you are full of love, you are in bliss, you are very cheerful. Then it is possible that if you see a plant which has no flowers on it but only thorns, still you may be able to experience beauty in those thorns. A thorny cactus plant can become a symbol of absolute beauty for you. If there is a feeling of love and joy inside you then even thorns can seem like flowers – because in reality it is the seer who sees, it is the listener who listens. So what the eyes see outside is of less importance; the one hidden within who sees through those eyes is more important.

It is your soul which reaches out to all around you and spreads itself over everything you come into contact with. So whatever you see, whatever you find, is nothing but an extension of your own interiority. Moreover, unless this is the case, there can be no possibility of transformation in life. Because it is only in transforming oneself that one transforms the whole world.

We can understand it like this too: that we don't all live in the same world. It seems to us that we do, but our psychological worlds are quite different. There are as many different worlds present here as there are people. One of you will be unhappy, another happy, one may be peaceful and another may be in turmoil – so you cannot all be part of the same world.

To one who is sitting peacefully here, the atmosphere around him will seem completely peaceful. Each and every breeze, each and every star, the leaves, the flowers, every tiny part of the trees, will seem to impart peace to him. Even a small movement of the wind will be a breath of peace for him. He will be filled with life. The same things will be happening around a person who is sitting next to him with a sad and a long face, but for him they have a different meaning.

The world is not made up of things, it is the interpretation you give that makes your world. How we interpret it, how we look on it – that is how your world is created. And we all have different ways of looking at things. Each and every person has a different philosophy. We all live in different worlds. Every person lives in his own psychological world, and that is the reason we clash with each other – our worlds are so different.

Two people get married, but they can never come to any sort of harmony because their worlds, that is the worlds created by their minds, are poles apart. That is why they are always at loggerheads with one other. The husband says one thing, the wife understands something totally different, something which her husband never said at all. He asserts a hundred times that this is not what he meant at all, but his wife just won't agree that he never meant it: "This was *exactly* what you meant!" And neither does the husband understand what the wife says. Communication seems to be impossible. You say something and it is taken to mean something else. Someone says something and you extract your meaning out of it. The other person may beat his head a thousand times trying to convince you that this was not the motive behind what he said, but you will never be convinced. You will reply that this was his motive but now he is changing things. Ways of looking at things....

No matter how close we come to each other, our worlds are quite different, and there is a constant struggle between them. As long as you do not understand that everyone is living in the world of his own mind, as long as you do not become so aware that you put yourself in his place and begin to see his way, the struggle will continue. Then, even a friendship is a type of enmity; a relationship is also a type of a nuisance. The family is also a kind of struggle, because so many worlds are born within it and there are struggles between them.

But it never crosses our minds that we are looking at things through a looking glass or a veil. The color of our looking glass affects everything that we see, and then we become engaged in trying to change things rather than changing our looking glass. In fact it would be better if we were to remove the looking glass altogether. Instead of trying to change ourselves, we are occupied in trying to change the outer situation: how we can make the world a better place to live in, how we can make the home a better place to live in, how we can have beauty all around us. But the inner person remains ugly and he makes everything around him ugly.

I stay in the homes of wealthy people and I am very surprised to see that although they have plenty of money they have no sense of beauty. And so they fill up their houses with all kinds of rubbish – very expensive rubbish. They go out and collect all sorts of expensive rubbish from all over the world, but they don't have any sense of aesthetics. They have plenty of money, but their homes look like junkyards! They buy whatever new things appear on the market and put them into their houses, but they have no idea of how to arrange them, they have no vision or poetic sense, no aesthetic experience. The only experience they have is of making money, which is the crudest thing in this world to do.

Their whole beings are ugly, but since they have money they can afford to buy beautiful things, so whatever seems to them to be beautiful.... If word gets around that a painting by Picasso is a must in the house nowadays, then they are willing to spend millions of rupees buying a Picasso! They don't have the slightest idea what the painting is all about; in fact they can't even tell whether the painting is hanging the right way around or upside down – but it is the done thing to have a Picasso in the house, so they have one. And then they hang it in some prominent place.

Picasso has expressed this in one of his letters, "My life is that of an unhappy man, because whatever I have made through great effort is hanging in the houses of those who have no vision of the beautiful, who do not have a sympathetic heart. Somewhere I am hanging in the bathroom, somewhere else in a sitting room. All my life's effort has passed into the hands of people who do not even have a moment to spare to look at it, to know what they have bought, to understand what the painting is all about!" No matter how many things you may collect, if you do not have any sense of the beauty inside you, you will always be surrounded by the ugly.

And even a hut can be beautiful, provided you have an aesthetic sense. An empty place can be beautiful. It is this aesthetic sense that spreads itself over the outer, it is this aesthetic sense that creates and lends color to the world around you. Then, even if the flowers arranged in your vase are not expensive, it doesn't matter. For you, beauty can emanate from a single stem, because beauty is something that comes from within you.

This sutra is worth understanding. For those who are on the path of self-transformation it is worth pondering over.

The fourth sutra:

Listen to the song of life.

Look for it and listen to it first in your own heart. At first you may say: "It is not there; when I search I find only discord." Look deeper. If you are still disappointed, pause and look even more deeply.

There is a natural music, a hidden source of treasure in every human heart. It may be covered, it may be concealed, it may appear to be silent – but nevertheless, it is there.

Listen to the song of life.

The first condition for listening is that you begin by listening for it in your heart. Without this, the outer music will not be heard. You listen to the outer music and perhaps you may even think that you understand it; you may sway your heads with joy, in bliss and affirmation. But if you have never heard the inner music, then all this will be just superficial and you will never really be able to enter into the world of music.

Music is spiritual. Until you have experienced the melody of your heart, until each and every breath is in a musical rhythm, until the very throbbing of your life has become a harp, until you can hear the melody of life which needs no creating but is already happening within you, which you already are...until you have heard it, you will never be able to recognize the eternal melody which goes on echoing in the very fabric of the universe. But once you have heard the melody of your heart, you will find it all around you; in the murmuring of the waterfall, in the wind passing through the leaves of the trees, in the falling of a stone, in the flowing of a river, in the silence, the stillness of the night, in the sound of the crickets.... Everywhere you will start hearing the reverberations of your heart. This whole world will become a song for you.

But this happens only on the day you are able to listen to the music of your heart. Why? Because the heart is so close to you: if you cannot listen to its melody, how will you be able to hear the music of all those things which are so far away from you? The stars are so far away – how will you listen to their music? As it is, you can't even hear the music of your own heart which is so close to you!

So begin your journey from that which is closest to you.

In the past, in very ancient times, those days which even history has stopped remembering, the teaching of music started with meditation. Because until you have experienced the music of your own heart, what can you do with an instrument, what can you do with your voice? The teaching of dance started with meditation, because what can happen by just shaking your body? As long as the vibration does not arise from within, as long as the electric current does not start flowing from within.... Until something within you has started dancing, shaking, the body will only be a form of exercise, it will not be dancing. And no matter how skillful you may become at shaking your body, it will only be a technical perfection, it won't come from your very being. It will have no soul in it, it will be just a skill. And the skill can be very profound, but it will still lack your essence, it will only be the body dancing. That is the difference.

The greatest of dancers can dance, a great musician can give birth to music – but the dancing of Krishna has something quite different about it. Technically, he may even be wrong; you may be able to find fault in his dance, and were you to ask an expert he would definitely find some fault. But still, Krishna's dance belongs to a different dimension.

You can find faults in the music of Meera, you can find some shortcomings in her poetry, her grammar may not be correct. Meera is not a poet, nor is she a dancer or a musician. Yet somewhere deep inside her, in her innermost core, dance happened, music was born, the birth of poetry took place. That same poetry and dance found an expression in her body radiating all the way to the outside. That's why there is something very different about her dancing. Her dance does not belong to this world, it is a ray coming somewhere from the beyond. It brings the message of some faraway land. That's why Meera has captured our hearts. Great musicians have come and gone, but they cannot be compared with Meera. Technically speaking she is no one, but while we go on forgetting musicians with time, it is impossible to forget Meera.

Chaitanya used to dance. There was no method or system to his dancing, it was totally raw. But there was life in his dancing, it had a soul, it was alive. Not only was his body shaking, something in his very depths was vibrating – and his body was simply an echo of these vibrations.

Long ago, the arts of music and dance were born in the temple, their birth took place in the temple, and then they spread among the people. At first, they were a part of the search for spirituality. But what happened happens with everything: we gradually become enamored with the outer form of things – only the outer holds enchantment for us. Then we become so engrossed with it that we completely forget the inner, from where all this came. It has died long before. And then all we do is to go on making the outer more and more glamorous.

Music has become very remote from spirituality, dance has moved far away from it. They have become so distant that now they are almost polar opposites. Now we have the situation where dance and music are serving the gratification of sensuality. Once they were born from the soul, now they are employed in the service of sensuality. That's why Islam had to reject music, declaring it to be a sin. This is a very surprising thing, but it is worth thinking about.

Hindus acknowledge that music is supreme, they take the experience of music to be the highest meditation. And thousands of years after the birth of Hinduism, the religion which came to the earth as the newest religion, Islam, prohibited music. It said you cannot play music in front of a mosque. It declared music to be a sin!

Islam is right and the Hindus are also right. When music was first born, it was part of the supreme understanding, part of meditation. But slowly, slowly it moved away from meditation and started serving the world of sensuality. And by the time Mohammed was born, music was completely in the service of sensuality, it was serving the world of sexuality. That's why Mohammed said that there should be no music played inside and around the mosques. This is how it came to be thought of as a sin. Both Hindus and Mohammedans are right, because music has both of these polarities in it.

So one thing has to be remembered: your music will fall into the service of sensuality if you have not first heard the music inside you. If you have heard it only on the outside, then its impact will be on your sex center; because the sex center is your outermost center, the lowest, the most peripheral. If you have listened to the music within, then it will reverberate within your very soul. But if on the other hand you have first heard music externally, its primary impact will be on your sex center – because that is what it is closest to. And then music is bound to become engaged in the service of sensuality. That is why sexual people like singing and dancing so much. In this way, music slowly, slowly became a part of the courts of kings and princes – and meditators moved away from it, because now it was primarily in the service of the non-meditators.

Music in itself is not the cause of this. If the journey does not begin from the inside, then this problem is bound to arise. If the journey begins from the inside, if once you have experienced the inner music, then whatever type of music is possible in the world – created, non-created, artificial, natural – all music will only resonate with the inner. But only if you have first heard the music within.

Nanak always used to keep a musician with him. He used to speak very little, instead he would sing, and Mardana, sitting by his side, would begin to play on his *ektara*. But first Nanak would talk about *ajapa*, the unstruck sound, so that the listeners could begin by hearing the soundless sound within. And when his devotees were immersed in listening to the silent melody within, he would start playing them outer music too, and then the outer music would become one with their profound inner music. And when the outer and the inner music become one, then the outer and the inner disappear and only the music remains. That moment of music is the moment of experiencing *brahman*.

Look for it and listen to it first in your own heart.
At first you may say: "It is not there;
when I search I find only discord."

Certainly, the first time you go within yourself you will find nothing there but the crowd and the marketplace, because so far the crowd and the marketplace are the only things you have allowed in. So naturally, you will hear such a hullabaloo, you will hear meaningless sounds, bits and pieces of unrelated conversations – what to say of music. What you will hear will be unrelated words without any context. If you sit down alone and start writing whatever is going on in your mind on a piece of paper, you will wonder, "Am I mad? Are there so many madmen inside me?"

Nowadays, scientists are thinking that if not today, then at least in the very near future, they will be able to invent an instrument which when attached to your head, will amplify all that is going through it, so others will actually be able to hear what is going on in your mind. Of course, no one will agree to this – that others should hear what is going on inside your head!...Because once people come to know, no one will believe you, because you have put up an absolutely false front. You appear to be very wise, but all this is totally false: whatever is going on inside you is the voice of sheer insanity.

So it is only natural that when you descend within for the first time, you will only hear this form of madness. At first you will only hear these voices. Don't be afraid of them, and don't become worried either. You need to go a little deeper within. If you listen to them as a witness, you will be able to move more deeply. Don't do anything to oppose them, because if you oppose them, you will get stuck with them. Don't fight them either, because if you do, you will become a part of the same mad crowd; the madness will increase even more. And don't even try stopping them – because in trying to stop them you won't be able to get rid of them and that which we stop, we have to constantly keep repressing; we cannot just leave it and move ahead. Just don't do anything with these voices. Keep moving deeper, with indifference....

Buddha has said: Move on with indifference. The clamor will continue – let it. It is just as if you are crossing a market place: so fine, it is a marketplace. You are not worried about it. In the same way don't become worried when you are crossing this inner marketplace. Just keep a sense of indifference, a feeling of neutrality that "Okay it is a marketplace. What is here is what I have accumulated so far." Continue moving silently inwards as a witness and searching more deeply.

Look deeper.
If again you are disappointed,
pause and look deeper again.

Don't be afraid, because the source is certainly there. Many people have found that source and you will find it too. And those who have found it are a proof that you can also find it, that it is within you, buried under layer upon layer. There can be many layers. But don't become afraid – continue your search. And no matter how much turmoil appears to be raging within you, just sit quietly, watching what is going on.

When Shri Aurobindo went into meditation for the first time, his guru told him, "Many thoughts will rage inside you, but just do one small thing: treat those thoughts as if they were flies, flies hovering all around your head. Don't worry about them, let them go on buzzing. Just treat them as if you were standing in the midst of them and they were hovering all around you."

Shri Aurobindo sat like this for three days continuously. In the beginning he became very afraid because there were many flies and if each fly was one thought, then thousands of flies were buzzing. But he was a man of determination. He said, "If I am to treat them just like flies, then what is there to be concerned about? All I have to do is to sit it out." He kept on sitting, the flies went on buzzing. He did not fight them or chase them away or remove them.

Slowly, slowly, after many hours had passed, he noticed that the crowd of flies was beginning to thin out. Then his trust grew stronger: by merely sitting, the flies were decreasing. So he thought, "Why not sit some more and see if they become even fewer?" This made him happy, it increased his confidence; he grew hopeful. So he kept on sitting, thinking occasionally that now was not the right time to get up because if he did, perhaps he would have to pass through that swarm of flies again. So he went on sitting – and he kept it up for three days without eating or drinking anything. He made up his mind that as long as there was even one fly left he wouldn't get up. And after three days the last fly had departed: no thought was left.

It is in this moment that the song of life is heard, it is in this moment that the source of life manifests. When you are in a state of no thoughts, then you become connected with the music of your heart. As long as you are full of thoughts, the clamor will continue. But it is not a very difficult task to pass through this clamor. You have only to maintain indifference and an attitude of not getting involved with the clamor. What is necessary is to slowly become more relaxed about it.

Just recently in the West they have invented biofeedback machines. These machines are cheap – they cost hardly a thousand rupees – very small and very useful. The machine is attached with wires to both sides of your head where the thoughts are being generated, and where the cells vibrate. The wires are put on your head and you are made to sit in front of the machine and then the machine is switched on. At once the needle of the machine starts to swing very fast. The more rapidly your thoughts move, the faster the needle swings. Then you are asked to become peaceful, to become still, and you will see that the needle in front of you becomes slower as you become quieter and more still. With this, your confidence increases. And as you keep becoming quieter the needle slows down more and more.

When you have achieved exactly the right state of calmness, which they call alpha waves, the machine begins to go "Beep-beep-beep." As it does, you are fully assured that the thoughts have calmed down, that now you are in the alpha state, a state in which meditation and sound sleep happen. If at that moment you look inside yourself you will not find even a single thought. Outside, the machine gives an indication that not a single thought is left inside. If you go on becoming more and more calm, you descend even more deeply than the alpha state, and the machine gives out another kind of sound.

What would have taken you years to achieve can be done in just a matter of a week by being connected with this machine. Because whatever you do, whether you are meditating or doing something else, you never come to know what is happening inside. And if you do, then it is a great help because then you are reassured that you are making progress; it is making some difference. They call this machine "biofeedback" because it supports you. It gives you the indication that yes, now you are becoming calmer; otherwise you would not come to know what is happening inside.

With this machine you know that you are becoming calmer, and the very thought that you are becoming peaceful acts like a suggestion. If you feel, "I am becoming peaceful," then you become even more peaceful. In this way, a sort of a communication is established between you and the machine. If you do nothing, but just let yourself be loose and become still, by just practicing five to ten minutes a day, after a few days you can achieve the alpha state.

This is the whole experiment of the inner world: to leave yourself calm and distance yourself from thoughts. This is the whole experiment proposed by all the religions, all the disciplines, the whole of Yoga and the whole of Tantra. The only significant thing is how you can get across the layer of noise and arrive at that place within yourself where the fountain of peace lies. That fountain lies within you. It is as much present within you as it was inside Buddha – not a fraction less. It is just a matter of your getting into contact with the source.

If again you are disappointed,
pause and look deeper again.

There is a natural melody, an obscure fount
in every human heart.
It may be hidden over
and utterly concealed and silenced –
but it is there.
At the very base of your nature
you will find faith, hope, and love.

From the day you establish contact with that source, your life will be full of faith, love and hope. This will be an indication.

People are told to have faith, but how can they? They are asked to have trust, but how can they? They are asked to believe, but how can they?...Because as long as one has not made contact with the inner bliss and the inner soundless music, faith, trust and belief are not born. They are the outer manifestations of the relationship with the inner melody. So with great effort people create a false belief, they forcibly cultivate faith. When it is being said again and again to believe, they start believing that it is okay. But this is harmful because then they remain deprived of real faith and then they end up having a pseudo faith – but thinking that they have real faith. We all have this type of faith. From our very childhood we are taught to believe, to have faith, and so we start believing.

There are also difficulties involved in not having any sort of a belief. It is very convenient to believe, because you are surrounded by a crowd of people who also believe. But it is a pseudo belief and it will not lead you to inner trust.

There is no way to reach to inner trust except through meditation. Education, information – nothing can help you there until you have started having a taste of the inner. Three things happen when you have had this taste.

Faith will come into your life. Faith does not mean trust towards someone, it means a trusting nature. It does not mean you will have faith in your master, or you will have faith in Mahavira. I notice that those who have faith in Mahavira do not show any faith in Mohammed. This is a false faith. The question is not in whom you have faith, rather there will be a natural quality of faith in your being. To have trust will be your natural state of being, the question will not be in whom. Your main characteristic will be to trust.

But what is happening right now? Your main characteristic is to mistrust. If some stranger comes to your home, the first look you will give him is to find out whether he is a thief or not. Is he some sort of a villain? If so, you will need to keep everything under lock and key. Is he going to walk off with something – or perhaps he has come to ask for a donation? Will he pester you for money? What will he do? You look at the clothes he is wearing to gauge his circumstances. His clothes will indicate his status. The first glance you give anyone is of mistrust. Even if you manage to trust, it is only after you have felt that doubting is not useful, because the man is not stealing anything, he is not running away with anything. When he is not doing anything of the sort, you start to trust him.

This trust of yours is not your natural state, it is a logical conclusion. Your natural state is to mistrust. The first thing that arises in you is to mistrust. If you happen to notice someone entering your house at night, at once you will shout, "Thief! thief!" You have no option, it is just your natural reaction. If you happen to see a shadow lurking in the darkness, the first thing that crosses your mind is that it is an enemy. It never occurs to you that it could be a friend!

What I am saying is this: that your natural state, without any logic supporting it, is of mistrust. This is the sign of a noisy mind – it is scared. In life it sees enemies all around: someone or other is always trying to seize something, someone or other is on the lookout to grab something. Everyone is dishonest, all are thieves, there is stealing everywhere. And the whole world has its eyes on you.

As a person becomes connected to his inner music, just the opposite happens and a natural state of trusting comes into being. Then, even if a thief enters your house, your first thought will not be that he is a thief. For your first thought to be on such lines is very bad – even if he *is* a thief. What is bad is your having such an idea as your first thought. It doesn't matter if you are right in your assessment of him as a thief. Even if he is proved to be a thief, the harm the thief could have done to you is nothing compared with the harm done by you in harboring this mistrust. Such a person can never become religious. Such a person remains deprived of God. Yes, he will have managed to save a few things, he will have avoided being robbed, he will have rid himself of a rogue – his pocket will be left intact – but what he is trying to save is worth next to nothing. And what he is losing is infinite.

And if you had trusted, what would you have lost? What do you have which can be lost? What could have been stolen? The person who has been deceived a thousand times, but still trusts on the thousand and first time is a saint, because to trust comes very naturally to him. No matter how much experience he may have to the contrary, he will not abandon his nature.

I have heard – Uma Swati has written it somewhere – that once a sage went into a river to bathe, and noticed that a scorpion had fallen into the river. He wanted to pick it up and put it on the bank. The scorpion stung him, but with that sting the scorpion fell out of his hand and back into the water. The sage picked it up again. A fisherman, who was standing close by and was observing all this, said, "Are you mad? This scorpion is biting you, it has just stung you, and you are still picking it up!"

The sage replied, "The scorpion is not abandoning his nature, so I will not abandon my nature either. I want to save him, but perhaps the poor scorpion is scared, and he is probably biting me because of his fear that I may try to kill him, or do something like that. But do you think I should lose out to the scorpion, that I should let the scorpion win? I will rescue him. I will do my very best until I can make the scorpion understand that I am not picking him up with the intention of killing him. Only then will I stop. I cannot lose to a scorpion!"

Try to understand this a little. Even if the scorpion were to bite, what could happen? It would cause some pain. But if the sage didn't lose to the scorpion, then you cannot even imagine the bliss he would experience.

This sutra is saying that in following your fundamental nature you will attain faith, hope and love.

Trust will become a natural state of being. Whom you trust is not the question; you will become trusting. Whether it is a thief or a sage, a mahatma or anyone else –

that is not the question. Whether it is a stranger or someone known to you, it will not matter, because your natural feeling will be to trust. This is the sign of a trusting person.

That's why those faithful who you see bowing their foreheads in temples, but walking with their heads held high past the mosques, are not faithful people, they are not anything of the sort. You will find the one who has faith bowing everywhere. Those who are protecting the mosque but burning the temples are not faithful people. You are showing your respect for the Koran by placing it on your head, but on the other hand you are kicking the Gita! Such a person is not a faithful person. This type of faith is false; it is dangerous and poisonous.

The meaning of having faith is that no matter what is happening around you, you still manage to find something to put your faith in. Such a person will always find something worthy of his faith. That is his natural quest.

...hope, and love.

Hopelessness disappears from the life of the one who has heard the melody of his inner music.

By hope, please don't take it to mean that he will start thinking, "Tomorrow I will be getting such and such a thing, and the day after I will get this or that." No, this kind of hope is nothing but a form of desiring. We have dealt with that and left it a long way back in the earlier sutras. The seeker has discarded it long ago.

Hope means that now, wherever he is in life, the seeker sees a ray of hope. If the night is very dark, he sees that the dawning of the day is close. If the skies are full of black clouds, he says, "How wonderful the flash of lightning will be!" If suffering comes to him, he says, "Let us wait a little: happiness must be just around the corner." No matter how much he is suffering, he manages to find a silver lining in it, and no matter how much you harass him, he will be able to learn something from it. No matter what happens in his life, life cannot disappoint him. He finds a ray of hope in every situation. He will discover that clear point everywhere and in everything. It is present everywhere.

A pessimist will find darkness everywhere. No matter what you do, if you ask a pessimist he will say that the world is a very bad place: between two dark nights there exists but one small day. But a hopeful person will declare that this world is a wonderful place: two bright and sunny days surround a short night. There are an equal number of days and nights; it all depends on how you look at things.

If a pessimist comes across a rosebush he will see only the thorns. When he sees that there are a thousand thorns, he says that the one flower that is there is a deception. "How can there possibly be a flower where there are so many thorns? In a plant which has so many poisonous thorns which can take your very life, how can there be a flower? This flower is nothing but a trick to get you entangled in thorns. This flower is a lie!" And he will say, "The flower blooms in the morning and by the evening it fades away, but the thorns last forever. The thorns are the truth. This flower is nothing but an illusion, a dream; don't get caught up with it, beware of it."

If an optimist goes near that rosebush, it will be the rose flower that will attract him first of all. He will be so lost in the beauty of the rose that even if someone comes and reminds him that there are thorns too, he will say, "How can there possibly be thorns where there is such a wonderful flower? And if there are, they must be for the protection of the flower. Even if there are thorns, it must be for a reason. In a plant on which such a wonderful flower is blooming, thorns cannot come as an enemy but only as a friend."

For the person who is able to immerse himself fully in the beauty of the flower, the thorns too will seem like flowers. And a person who focuses too much on the poison of the thorns will also see nothing but poison in the flower. This world takes on its color according to your vision.

The meaning of hope is that one sees only the bright side of life.

...you will find...love...

By *love* it does not mean love for one particular person. Love will be his natural state of being. All those who are ready and willing and open will be worthy to receive his love. His love will not be some kind of attachment, his love will not be some sort of lust. His love will not create any bondage – his love will be a spontaneous giving. He will share the bliss and peace which have happened to him. Because of his love he will go on distributing peace and joy. For us, love is a relationship, but for him love will be a state of being. It is not that he will love you, he will be simply loving.

There is a difference between the two. If you love somebody, love is a relationship, you are not simply loving. Buddha or Mahavira do not love someone in particular, they are simply loving. But this does not mean that everyone will receive their love in equal proportions. They are giving their love equally to all, but it all depends on how much one is capable of receiving. And if someone were to confront them as an enemy, he would remain deprived of their love. Someone who opens his heart fully to them will be completely filled with their love. Everyone will receive in different proportions, but from his side Mahavira is giving equally to one and all.

And it is not right to say that it is being *given*. It is something like when a lamp is lit; light automatically emanates from it. If you happen to be passing nearby, and if your eyes are open, you will see it. But if your eyes are shut, you won't see anything. On the other hand, the light is not shining out for you. The light is simply shining, emanating. If you pass by and your eyes are open, the light automatically becomes available to you. So in the life of such a person, love is a state of being.

He that chooses evil refuses to look within himself,
shuts his ears to the melody of his heart,
as he blinds his eyes to the light of his soul.
He does this because he finds it easier
to live in desires.

The choosing of evil means only this much: that you are not going towards yourself. By not going within yourself you choose to travel outwards, towards something outer. The meaning of evil is only one: that you are halting your inner journey and you are starting to move outwards. All outward journeys are an evil. Even if you were to give it a religious name, that would make no difference to it whatsoever. Whenever you go far away from yourself, you are treading the path of sin. And whenever you are moving closer to yourself, you are on the path of virtue. If a person wishes to go far away from himself, he needs to become deaf to his inner voice; otherwise that inner voice will pull him towards the inner. He who wishes to go far away from himself needs to turn a blind eye to his inner self – because the inner landscape will draw his eyes within.

Slowly slowly we die completely to the inner – so that we can easily move outwards and go far away from the inner without there being anything to prevent us. And the further we move away from the inner, the more we collect noise and hubbub around ourselves. And then after we have suffered and been harassed enough by this outer din and start longing to retrace our way back to the inner, we first have to pass through that same hubbub and marketplace din that we ourselves created. But if you remain calm and keep courage, you can pass through this crowd – because this crowd is very weak, and your inner voice is very powerful. If a contact is established even once, you will become the master of infinite sources.

But underneath all life is the strong current
that cannot be checked;
the great waters are there in reality.
Find them and you will perceive that none,
not the most wretched of creatures,
but is a part of it,
however he blind himself to the fact
and build up for himself
a phantasmal outer form of horror.
In that sense it is that I say to you:
all those beings among whom you struggle on
are fragments of the divine.
And so deceptive is the illusion in which you live,
that it is hard to guess where you will first detect
the sweet voice in the hearts of others.
But know that it is certainly within yourself.
Look for it there and once having heard it,
you will more readily recognize it around you.

Once you are able to hear it within yourself, then you will start hearing it all around you, in everyone. The more deeply you descend within yourself, the more deeply you will be able to see inside others. The day you recognize your center, people will no longer be just physical bodies to you. They become souls, because now their centers also become transparent to you.

You must bear one thing in mind, and that is that the more deeply you have descended within yourself, the more you will be able to observe the depth in others. If you have not gone within yourself at all – that is, if you are shallow – then you will see the same degree of shallowness in others.

That is why it sometimes happens that you may pass very close by a Krishna or a Buddha, but you are not able to recognize them – because your limited capacity to see within yourself also limits your capacity to recognize them. If you are shallow, you cannot behold their depths. You think only superficially; you accumulate only superficial ideas and yet you begin to think that you have known them, that you have recognized them!

And when I speak of your passing by a buddha, I am not just saying perhaps. You actually have, because you have been living on this earth, and some Buddha or Christ, some Mahavira, Rama or Krishna must have walked across your path at some time or other. You have passed them on so many paths in so many lifetimes but you have not recognized them! And if you had, perhaps today you would not be here – or you would not be in the situation in which you find yourself right now: full of pain and suffering.

The reason behind your not recognizing the enlightened ones is that your capacity for seeing is exactly in proportion to your own depth as it is known to you. What you do not see inside yourself, you can never see inside another. If you feel that you are surrounded on all sides by only bad people, the wrong sort of people; that you can see only darkness all around you, then one thing is certain – you have never seen the light within yourself. One thing is certain, that you have never seen the godliness within yourself. One thing is certain, that so far you have not heard the inner music.

12

THE LESSON OF HARMONY

5. Store in your memory the melody you hear.

Only fragments of the great song
come to your ears while yet you are but man.
But if you listen to it,
remember it faithfully,
so that none which has reached you is lost,
and endeavor to learn from it
the meaning of the mystery which surrounds you.
In time you will need no teacher.
For as the individual has voice,
so has that in which the individual exists.

6. Learn from it the lesson of harmony.

Life itself has speech and is never silent.
And its utterance is not,
as you that are deaf may suppose, a cry;
it is a song.
Learn from it that you are part of the harmony;
learn from it to obey the laws of the harmony.

If there is one thing that is worth learning more than anything else in life, it is a sense of music, a feeling for music. What music tells us is that the ultimate mystery of life is not a crowd of different notes, is not a chaos, is not a disharmony; rather, all the notes together are pointing to and indicating one thing. They are creating one wave, one rhythm; they are indicating that at the ultimate center of life everything is connected and in harmony.

The chaos that we may be seeing is because of our own blindness; and the turmoil that we hear in the notes, the tension that we perceive is because of our deafness. Because we cannot hear properly, we fail to experience that single harmony that is flowing between all the notes. We hear the notes, but we do not hear the bridge, the music that joins them all together. As our capacity for listening grows, the notes start disappearing and the music begins to manifest. Then a moment comes when all the notes disappear, all the waves disappear; when only the ocean of music, only the feeling of music remains.

Music is the relationship of love between the different notes, the path through which one note can connect with the next, the way in which one note can disappear into another note and become absorbed in it.

The space which exists between two notes is not empty. That space is full. Even though it is filled with absolute silence, even though it is filled with emptiness, it is full. To experience it is to experience the music of life.

You may have heard that truth cannot be expressed in words, but that it manifests itself in the space which lies between the words. You may also have heard that emptiness does not separate but unites; that a void is not merely a void, that even a void is filled with a unique music. But we are not able to hear the music of that stillness, of that void. The music of life is found there, but we are not able to recognize those spaces – rather, they appear to us to be dark valleys. We hear a sound which is followed by another sound, but we don't hear any connecting thread. This gives us the impression of chaos.

There are so many of us sitting here: we see first one person, then another, but we don't see the link that is there between the two. That's why each person seems separate to us. If we could only see the connecting link that exists between the two, then the individuals here would fade away and only a river of life would remain.

The way I see it is that you are not very important, neither is the person sitting next to you, but the life which is flowing between you, that *is* important. It is because of this very life that you are alive, and your neighbor too. But this life is invisible. You are seen on one side, and your neighbor is seen on the other; but this wave of life which lies in between you is not seen.

The one who sees only the visible sees only chaos in life. But everything that is visible is linked with the invisible. What you see is one side. What you do not see – the link in between – is actually the real existence. To experience that invisibility is to experience the music of life.

Let the meaning of music be well understood. It is that which is filling the gap, that which is filling the emptiness, that which is present as fullness – even in the void. It is that which is invisible but exists and can be experienced. The more sensitive we become within, the more we start experiencing it. Then, we do not see separate people, we see the divine which is the connecting link between them. Then, we do not look upon trees as this tree and as that tree; instead, we see the life that is flowing in them in the same way – both within and without.

And the day you see this, then the whole world becomes an expression of oneness. That is why so much emphasis has been placed on music in these sutras, because the one who has experienced music – not the notes, but the connecting wave which joins the notes, the invisible wave – the one who has experienced the harmony and rhythm which flows between the notes, has experienced *brahman*, the ultimate. And *brahman* is nothing but that which is holding everything together, connecting it, but which cannot be seen.

And one thing is certain: that which can be seen will fade away, will disappear. That which cannot be seen will not fade away; there is no way that it can. Like the waves we rise up and become visible. And then the waves fall back and are gone. But the ocean which is not seen…

You will be surprised, you will say, "No, the ocean can be seen, it *is* visible." But I say unto you that the ocean is never seen. It is always the waves that you see. You have never seen the ocean – because you can only see the surface of the ocean, and the surface is always full of waves. You are never able to see the ocean. What you see are the waves; the ocean is only inferred. The waves can be seen rising and falling, but the ocean from which they arise, and the ocean which they fall back into is actually the real basis, the music. The waves are the notes. But the notes are heard and the music is not heard; the waves are seen, but the ocean is not seen.

And what is even more interesting is that the waves cannot exist without the ocean – the notes cannot exist without the music. The ocean can exist without the waves, but the waves cannot exist without the ocean. Music can exist without notes, but notes cannot exist without music. Yet you do not hear the music or see the ocean. You see the waves, you hear the notes.

The impersonal, the *brahman*, the vast esoteric expansion of life does not lend itself to experience; it is people who are experienced. A person has a boundary, that's why he can be seen; waves are small, that's why they can be seen. The ocean is huge, eyes are small; that's why it cannot be seen. The note is small, it creates an impact, it is heard. The music of the ocean is vast, so it does not create an impact, it is not experienced. But if we start traveling inwards, we will begin to hear that music. Why? Why will it be heard if we move inwards?

Understand a little more about what I have said about the waves. If a wave were to rise up and look around, if that wave had eyes – and there is no problem about waves having eyes, because we too are waves and we have eyes – if a wave could think and were to look all around itself, it would see only waves and more waves. It would not see the ocean. And that wave would also be able to see that it was different from all the other waves.

Inevitably, one wave will just be forming, another wave will be rising up, and another wave will be falling back. One wave will be big, another wave will be small. So how can this one wave ever accept that it is a part of all the other waves? "A wave is disappearing right in front of me, but I am not disappearing. And if we were all one, then we would have all disappeared together. And a wave that is bigger than me is rising – so we cannot be the same. If we were, I would also have become bigger, and I would be just like him."

So one thing is certain: if the wave looks around it will never see the ocean, because the surface of the ocean is full of waves. The second thing is that to this wave, all the other waves will seem different. And the third thing is that to this wave it will seem that all the other waves are its enemy, that they are eager to destroy it. It will feel that they are anxious to get rid of it.

Struggle, competition, and the rat race – this is what we experience. But if the wave turns inwards, closes its eyes to the outer world and turns inwards, what will it find? If the wave turns inwards, it will begin to fall into the ocean – because within, the wave is nothing but the ocean; beneath the wave is nothing but the ocean. If the wave looks outside itself, all it can see is the other waves, but if it looks inside it will be able to experience the ocean.

And after looking inside, the whole situation will change. Once it has experienced the ocean, it will laugh: all those waves it was seeing were not real. The same ocean is inside them too! Now, by reaching within itself the wave can reach into others and see for itself that underneath it is all one and the same ocean. There is no barrier in the way, there is no wall anywhere, there is no obstacle to its going anywhere.

The one who can reach within himself can reach into anyone, because he has found a way to the depths, to the very innermost core where we are all one.

That's why, whenever you go to a person like Buddha or Mahavira, another, inner way, is available to them, from which they see your interiority. From there, they see you as you have never seen yourself; although you don't become aware of it because to you, it seems as if they are merely seeing you from the outside. That's why, in all the traditions, so much emphasis is laid on surrendering totally to the master – because the surrender itself can become the path. The master knows that which even you do not know about yourself. And what you say about yourself is hardly worth anything, the information you give about yourself has hardly any value, because, after all, what do you know of yourself? All you have seen is just the most superficial part of your own wave.

You may not be able to understand what he says because he sees deep within you, he sees you from a place that you have no connection with, that you have not yet established a relationship with.

Total surrender means letting go of your identity completely, dropping whatever ideas you may have. Now, you are ready to follow a path which only the master knows about – you don't.

So if a wave reaches inside itself, it also enters other waves. Then it comes to know that just to be a wave is not the reality, the reality is to be a part of the ocean. It knows that the other waves are not different from it, no matter how much they might seem to be; that we are all the play of the same ocean.

And the third thing it comes to know is that even though it will disappear as a wave, there is no way it can disappear as the ocean. This is precisely the experience of immortality. So if the sages have said that the soul never dies, don't take it to mean that *you* will not die. You will certainly die: since you are born, you will also have to die. But the soul doesn't die. The soul is that ocean within you which never dies. But of course the wave within you will certainly die.

But right now you think you are only the wave. That is why there is a lot of misunderstanding: people read somewhere that the soul never dies, and they take it to mean that they will never die. You have to die! There is no way you can escape from this. But when I say that you will die, I am saying: that which you *think* is you will die. But there is also a center within you that you do not know to be you and that will never die. As a wave, death is certain, as an ocean, deathlessness is certain.

Now let us enter these sutras.

The fifth sutra:

Store in your memory the melody you hear.

Only fragments of the great song
come to your ears while yet you are but man.
But if you listen to it,
remember it faithfully,
so that none which has reached you is lost,
and endeavor to learn from it
the meaning of the mystery which surrounds you.
In time you will need no teacher.
For as the individual has voice,
so has that in which the individual exists.

Store in your memory the melody you hear.

Right now, you are certainly not capable of really listening to that great music. In your present state, you cannot hear the whole melody. To hear that great melody, slowly you will have to start learning the inner melody – because only like can experience like.

Always remember these great words: only like can experience like.

If you want to hear that great music, you will have to become musical. If you want to see that great light, you will have to start becoming a light unto yourself. If you want to have a taste of deathlessness, you will have to go beyond the fear of death.

You have to become like that which you wish to experience, because only like can experience like. There is no way to know that which is not intrinsically the same.

That's why the ancient sages have said that your eyes are nothing but an extension of the sun within you, and that is why they are able to perceive the light. Your ears are an extension of the sound within you; that is why they are able to hear. Your sexual desire is a part of the earth; that is why it pulls you downwards to itself. Meditation is a part of the godliness within you; that is why it takes you towards existence.

Bear in mind that you become a channel for whatever you are connected to. So if you want to hear the supreme music, you will not be able to as you are right now – because right now you are so filled with noise, right now your life is so lacking in harmony. There is a great deal of clamor going on inside you, but no harmony at all. In the way you walk, in the way you sit, in the way you stand, in the way you live and think, there is great chatter and discord – as if you were a busy market road with traffic coming and going; a road which has no order, which is a chaos. If you think that you will be able to hear that great music in amongst this anarchy that is going on inside you, you are mistaken. It is impossible.

But if you make some effort, you will manage to hear some fragments of it – because no matter how chaotic a state you are in, you *are* alive. This is enough of an indication that there must be some kind of harmony within you. Otherwise you could not live, you would have broken down and disintegrated. If there were really so much chaos inside you that nothing at all remained there to join it together, you would have broken into pieces long ago. You would have fallen apart like a house in which the cement that holds the bricks together had cracked and broken. You would have collapsed.

But you are still alive, you are not dead and buried. That's why, no matter how great the turmoil inside you, no matter how much discord there is between the notes and no matter how great a clash there is between the voices, somewhere there is still something which is keeping you together. Otherwise how could you continue to exist? Something or other must be holding you together. Somewhere in the midst of all this din and discord some part of that melody is still alive – even if you only get a glimpse of it very rarely.

Sometimes, just watching a sunrise in the morning, you are overtaken by a wave of peace. Or sometimes at night, lying down on the ground and gazing up at the stars above, suddenly, all is filled with silence. Or in a moment of love, or listening to some music, or seeing a dancer perform, something becomes a dance within you too. In such moments you catch a glimpse of that music. It is this glimpse that you sometimes call happiness, sometimes peace, sometimes the juice of life. You have given it many names. But this glimpse is simply revealing that there are times when, in the presence of some outer phenomenon, you become integrated inside. For a moment, all your outer clamor ceases and the notes within you fall into a harmony. For a moment, the waves become the ocean and it is as if a door inside you opens. Even though it is only for a second, you have a glimpse, and the whole world becomes a different place. This is the potential. You will only experience fragments, you will only hear some far-distant echo.

That is why this fifth sutra says:

Store in your memory the melody you hear.

Whatever such incidents have occurred in your life – whenever you have had an experience of juice, of music, of harmony, nurture it in your memory, don't let it be lost.

There is an ancient sect of Christians, the Essenes, through whom Jesus received his initiation. The Essenes' school had a certain method of meditation: if ever a moment had occurred in your life that was free from all thought and filled with bliss, you were to recollect that moment again and again and meditate on it. Whatever the experience had been, you were to recall that moment again and again, and meditate on it; because at such a moment you were at your peak, at the highest point you had touched so far. So you were to continue going into it, and working hard at it.

In everyone's life there is such a moment. Man goes on living in the hope that perhaps such a moment will occur again, or that maybe this particular moment will grow bigger. It is difficult to find a person who cannot recall any such moment in his life. Sometimes it can happen for very commonplace reasons. You may be simply walking along, the sunrays falling on your head, and you find that all of a sudden you have become very peaceful. You didn't do anything for it – suddenly you entered into a space where tuning simply happened.

Sometimes in very commonplace situations... You are lying in your bed, and you wake up in the morning and suddenly find that you don't know who you are. The person who went to sleep the night before, who was full of worry and tension, is not there. For a moment you don't even know where you are. You are absolutely peaceful. You are so peaceful that you have even forgotten your own identity. So sometimes, in any trivial situation that seems to have no connection whatsoever with the experience of tuning, it happens. Life keeps on moving inside you. Sometimes, without your even being aware of it, the various divided parts in you fall into a harmony – just by chance. Then, no matter what may be happening outside, you become instantly peaceful.

Gather these reminiscences. If you meditate, these memories will go on increasing. Collect them, go on gathering them in some corner of your heart so that they make a lasting impression. Bring together all the memories that you have of when there was bliss in your life, of when you experienced that music. Bring them all to a focus at one particular point, so that with their support you can move on ahead.

Right now, you will find they are in fragments, but go on collecting these fragments. As their number goes on increasing, the possibility of finding bigger fragments will increase. This is how, slowly slowly, brick by brick, a great palace will be created, where one day you will be able to hear that great music which is called the music of life.

But man is an upside-down being: he collects memories of suffering! We show great interest in unhappiness, we discuss our unhappinesses time and time again. Just listen to people: they go on lamenting their suffering. They will lament about their suffering, but they will never sing when they are happy! Such an expression just doesn't exist in our language – that so-and-so is laughing his happiness. But there is an expression that so-and-so is lamenting his suffering. People go on talking about their troubles to one another – as if troubles are worth talking about, as if their trouble was some great news, as if they have performed some great feat by being unhappy!

But why does a person dwell so much on his suffering? He doesn't realize that by doing so he is only committing suicide, because by dwelling on your troubles they become even more substantial. By discussing unhappiness, unhappiness accumulates. By discussing your worries, your attention is diverted to problems; it becomes concentrated on them. By dwelling on suffering they only intensify, and in turn they give birth to new sufferings – because you become an expert on whatever you nurture, knowing more and more about it.

Nobody ever talks about happiness! We write it off as unmentionable. As it is, happy moments are anyway so few and far between. But one reason they are so few and far between is that we don't collect happiness, we collect suffering. Why? Why does man dwell on his sufferings so much? There are reasons for it.

Whenever a person discusses his troubles, it means only one thing, and that is that he is looking for some sympathy, he is looking for love from someone. And he does not talk about his happiness, because no one sympathizes with happiness. People feel jealous of a happy person; they do not love such a person. With this fear in his heart – that people will feel jealous of him – and afraid that no one will be sympathetic towards him, a person dwells on his sufferings. Man hungers for sympathy, he craves love.

But remember one thing: the sympathy which is expressed after hearing about someone's suffering is not love, and the kindness someone shows you after he has heard your troubles only confirms your wretchedness. This way you will go on becoming even more wretched. And if in your life you have cultivated only one interest – gaining sympathy from others. You will even start dwelling on imaginary sufferings, sufferings that have never happened – although slowly but surely you will create a way for them to happen.

Keep this in mind: never discuss your unhappiness. What is the purpose in doing so? By this I do not mean to say to talk instead about your happiness. I mean to say *express* your happiness. Release your unhappiness in solitude. Shut the doors, and then cry your heart out, weep as much as you want to, shriek if you have to, but don't go to someone else and discuss your misery. You do not seek out the other in your happy moments, but you unnecessarily pester him with your miseries, and you make him unhappy too. That's why, no matter how much sympathy we may show to someone who keeps going on about his troubles, the fact is that we are actually trying to avoid him! We would prefer not to meet him at all, because he manages to infect us with his wave of unhappiness. And even if we do lend an ear to his troubles, it is in the hope that he will stop soon, so that we will get a chance to talk about our troubles. In this way an exchange of miseries goes on.

Just put a full stop to talking about your suffering. Your suffering is your personal affair, it is better that you deal with it by yourself. Now I am not saying you should suppress it. You should definitely express it, but let it be to the empty sky above, where it will not become a burden on anybody's chest. And don't ask for sympathy by relating your sufferings. This is being a beggar. Let your misery be released in solitude, let it go.

Whenever someone is with you, let whatever happy memory you have within you surface. Whenever you are with someone, share your happiness, let your happiness sing and dance, and live your happiness – so that at least you reduce the suffering of the other person a little. The more you *live* this happiness, the more your happiness will increase.

The more you remember your happy moments, the more you will start moving into deeper happiness. Whatever we pay attention to, grows. Attention is a channel for growth.

Now the botanists say that if you pay proper attention to plants, they grow faster. Imagine, even plants! That's why in a garden, a plant that has received special affection from the gardener grows faster. The one he has given special care to grows faster, blooms faster – just by giving attention to it! These days a lot of experiments are being done on this. But a plant that no one has ever given any attention to.... Even if you were to give it everything – manure, water, sunlight, the right sort of earth, everything – just the fact that you were indifferent to it, did not give it attention, is sufficient to retard its growth.

Now scientists say that the reason for the speedy growth of a child is the attention the mother has given it. She may be some distance away, perhaps in another room, but her attention is tuned in to her child. She may be a hundred miles away, she may be caught up in a thousand and one things, but deep down her mind is always on her child. Even in her sleep, her attention is on the child. The sky may be full of thunder and her sleep will not be disturbed; but if her child makes even the slightest movement she wakes up. Her mind is always on her child.

Scientists say that when a child is growing, the attention that the mother gives to her child plays an even more important role than her milk. That's why children who grow up in an orphanage may get more and better milk than a mother's – and there is no problem in providing it – they may be looked after by trained nurses, and perhaps a mother may not be able to look after them any better because, after all, she has had no training.... In fact, they may be well looked after; they may get good food, medicines, clothes and so on, but for no apparent reason they do not seem to grow properly. They do not seem to be alive, they seem to lack something. They are not getting attention.

We seem to crave love so much. Do you know why? Because without love one gets no attention. The search for love is actually a search for attention. If someone gives you attention, then life within you blossoms, grows. If no attention is paid, the flower of life withers away. Hence the longing for love, for someone to love you, is not actually about love. When someone gives you attention, when someone looks at you with a loving, happy, smiling face, you grow. But sometimes this takes on a sick form. There is a sick side to everything.

To seek love is healthy, but when a person seeks attention by hook or by crook, then it becomes dangerous. If you weep bitterly and shout, then naturally, people's attention will be diverted to you. If the mother has not been giving attention, the child learns to do this. A child who receives loving attention does not weep and shout like that. A child who has not been given love and attention by his mother weeps loudly, cries and throws tantrums. Now he is learning the trick – that when he cries, his mother pays attention to him, when he throws things about, his mother pays attention to him, when he breaks something, his mother pays attention to him.

Have you ever noticed that when there are guests in your house, the children create much more trouble than usual? They are trying to attract the guests' attention: otherwise they would be sitting peacefully. You would like them to behave themselves and keep quiet when guests come, but how can they possibly keep quiet when there are guests in the house? What about attention? The guests are busy talking only to you and not paying them any attention. The children create many problems so that you will pay them attention as well as the guests. And all this is going on unconsciously.

Growth is an integral part of attention: the more attention you give, the more it grows. But then people turn it into a sickness. For example, the politician – he is not asking for anything else. What can he possibly get from his post? All that he will get will be a thousand abuses, he will be censured and insulted for a thousand and one things; that's about all he will get. But one thing is certain: while he holds that post he will get plenty of attention, people will flock to him from everywhere.

The search for a position is actually the search for attention, but it is a perverted one – because the way that you are seeking attention is by force, it is violent. Just as the child asks to be paid attention by breaking something, the politician asks for attention by becoming violent.

Watch: whenever a country gets involved in a war, whoever the leader of the country may be – he becomes a great leader. The reason is that during a war he has to be given much more significance than he ever had during peace time. That is why political scientists say that if someone wants to become a great leader, there must be a war while he is in office. Otherwise it is not possible.

India and Pakistan went to war over Bangladesh.... After that you started to hail Indira Gandhi as a great goddess; otherwise you would never have done so. If no war is waged during their time of office, leaders are lost into oblivion. If they lose a war, nobody ever bothers about them, but if they win, they receive all the attention. That's why a leader always strives for a victory in some war – because then his country's people, and the attention of the whole world, will come to him.

But this is perverted. This attention is not love, this attention is not coming from some creativity. This attention is being obtained from destruction, violence, hatred. But these are the very people who, as children, must have broken something at home to draw attention to themselves. Now they are trying to draw attention to themselves by becoming a member of the legislative assembly, an MP, a minister. These are the same children who must not have received their mother's love. If a person has received his mother's love, he never tries to draw attention to himself by violent means; he will do so in a creative way. Then he is full of joy. And if his joy attracts attention it is okay, but he doesn't weep and shout to attract it.

Don't ever link this thirst of yours for attention with your miseries, otherwise you will go on becoming even more miserable. Also don't try to attract attention by making someone else miserable, because then you will go on becoming even more miserable than you were before.

Just go on collecting the happy moments of your life, go on nurturing the memory of them. If you ever have any experience while doing meditation – if some refreshing breeze passes your way, or a ray of light penetrates your darkness, or a flower blooms inside you, some fragrance fills you, or you hear a piece of the great music – go on collecting it, go on nurturing it in the depths of your heart. And try to relive that experience again and again. Recall it as much as you can, and let that experience become more and more a part of your life.

Whenever you get an opportunity, a moment when you are all by yourself; close your eyes and go back to that moment, and relive it. By doing this you will help it to grow, you will be giving it life and attention. And like this, slowly slowly you will find that bigger fragments, longer moments are descending on you. Things will start becoming clearer; the experience of the music will become more intense.

Only fragments of the great song
come to your ears while yet you are but man.
But if you listen to it,
remember it faithfully,
so that none which has reached you is lost,
and endeavor to learn from it
the meaning of the mystery which surrounds you.

Anything sublime that has been attained can be lost. As long as the whole has not been attained, until then, anything attained can be lost.

Keep this in mind. Don't ever start thinking that what you have attained cannot be lost. Until you have attained the whole, you cannot afford to be careless; until then, whatever little you receive you must try to protect. As it is, you have plenty of miseries and only occasionally do you get a tiny moment of happiness. If you are careless, that small amount will get lost somewhere among all those miseries of yours. There is so much rubbish lying around in your house that even if you were to find a diamond, you would lose it amongst your own heap of rubbish. There is no need to lose it somewhere outside – it can be easily buried in the dirt of your own house. It is so small, and rarely do you find it. You have collected so much rubbish in your house; it will remain buried in it.

So clean out one corner of your heart, and in that corner nurture only happiness – that is, until you have attained to the whole. Once you have attained to the whole, your rubbish will be automatically swept away. Then, there is no fear of losing it. One can fall even at the last point: even a split second before the ultimate realization, it is still possible to go astray. But once the realization has happened, then there is no fear. You have plenty of rubbish in which it can be lost. So clean up one corner of your heart completely.

It is just like when someone makes a temple in some part of his house: then, he does not sleep there, he does not fight and shout in that part of the house, he does not eat his meals there. He goes into that temple only for prayer, for worship. No matter how much the rest of his house may be lacking in care, he always keeps that small part of it spotless.

In the same way, make a temple in some corner of your heart, and in that temple go on collecting only recollections of the moments of happiness you have experienced in your life. And whenever you get an opportunity, just close your eyes and enter quietly into that corner. Relive those memories, and let them come to life once again. A moment of love, some joyful moment, a moment of meditation – live these over and over again. Reliving does not mean only reminiscing about them. Reliving means to live them again. There is a difference between the two.

Suppose that you are remembering your childhood. You recollect that your childhood days were happy days. Or perhaps you recollect that one morning you went into the garden: the trees were silent, there was stillness all around, sunrays were filtering through the trees. Just then, you noticed a butterfly fluttering around, and you went after it, chasing it. You can remember this event even to this day.

There are two ways in which you can recollect this event. One way is to give an analytical description from your intellectual memory; that such and such a thing happened to you then. And the second way is that you just close your eyes, and once again you become a child. You are again standing under the shade of those trees where you stood twenty years ago, fifty years ago. You again feel the sunrays touching you...you have become a child once more. Forget about the fifty years that have come in between. Eliminate them; once again become that child. Don't just reminisce, relive it. Remembering only takes you to the surface – because if you are fifty years old, you are recalling it as a fifty-year-old man.

The meaning of reliving is that once again you became that five- or six-year-old child. It means that for a while you totally forget the existence of the forty-five intervening years. Now, you are just a five-year-old child, living out exactly that same moment. The sunrays have just begun to penetrate the trees, a butterfly is fluttering about, and you start running after it, following it, hot on the chase. Start to run! For a while you become like a five-year-old child. And when you come back, you will return rejuvenated.

If at the age of fifty you can once again become like a five-year-old child, then even at this age you have given your life a new freshness and vigor. And when you open your eyes, you will find that you have the eyes of a five-year-old – innocent. Of course, this may only last for a moment, but the reliving of this experience time and time again can be instrumental in changing your life.

Make it a point to relive a moment of happiness, a moment of bliss, a moment of music, so that it does not get lost.

In time you will need no teacher.
For as the individual has voice,
so has that in which the individual exists.

And if you keep catching hold of these fragments of music, and if these fragments harmonize together and start giving birth to a bigger music, then one day a time will come when you will be able to hear the inner voice – or the voice of God, or whatever name you may like to give it – and take orders from it directly.

Then, there will be no need for you to make anybody else your master. That is only necessary while you are unable to hear it directly. Until then, you will need a medium who can listen directly. What he is saying to you, you could have also heard directly. You are also capable of hearing it directly, but right now you are not in a position to do so because you are so full of noise. Gradually, as this noise dies down, as the dirt and the rubbish, the useless debris and weeds within you get cleaned out, and only the essential remains inside; as you become cleaner and tidier inside, you will be able to hear the melody of the infinite, the voice of the infinite, the sound of the infinite directly.

The day you start hearing it directly you will not need an outer master anymore. He was simply a medium; he could hear it, but you were not able to do so then. He was saying the very same things that your own inner voice would have said to you.

So grasp the happy moments, as many of them as you can, and go on gathering them.

It is necessary for you to keep one more thing in mind – because it generally proves to be a very big obstacle. Please don't make this mistake – many people do. They come to me and say, "Yesterday we felt great bliss while meditating, but today it wasn't the same." Someone comes and says, "In the beginning the meditation was a very joyful experience, but now it is not the same" – and he is very worried because of this.

Understand that this is not the meaning of this sutra. If you ask for a repetition of the same experience it won't happen, because you cannot force bliss to happen, nor can you have expectations about it happening. If you expect it, you will become so tense that it just won't happen.

That is why it often happens that when people meditate for the first time they experience such bliss the like of which they will never experience again. They themselves are responsible for this, because when they had that first experience they were not all tense with expectation, they were not waiting for something to happen. Nor did they feel that they would be disappointed if nothing happened. They had no preconceptions whatsoever. They were very naive – and bliss descended in that non-expectant innocence.

But once bliss has descended on them, they have expectations. Now, whenever they sit down to meditate, they have a condition: that bliss should happen. Now they are tense and tight. Now they are not meditating, now they are just demanding bliss. The first time it came, there was no demand for it. Now there is, so now it won't happen. The basis of what once happened has changed.

The meaning of this sutra is not that you demand that what you have received in the past happens again. The meaning is: whatever you have received – relive it, remember it. Don't demand a repetition, then it will happen again. Don't ask for it, then it will be given. Don't try to make it happen by force, because whatsoever is highest in life cannot be forced. Force can be used only on the trivial. You cannot force the highest. If you do, it will be destroyed.

You meet some stranger, you fall in love with him, and you feel very happy. But then you marry him, and it doesn't seem to be as perfect. Exactly the same thing is happening here. You are demanding, "Where is that happiness? Deliver it!" You want the happiness that you experienced on the first day to come back. Nobody in the world can bring it back. It is not something you can get back by pulling and pushing.

You ask your wife, "Where have the moments of happiness that you showered on me when I was your lover gone? Why aren't you giving them to me now? Is your love finished?"

And your wife replies, "You don't behave towards me in the same way as you did before. You are no longer as loving as you used to be! What is the matter with you? Are you involved with somebody else?" Now both the husband and wife are worried, they are upset. They are keeping an eye on each other, and they make demands on each other. And nothing comes from it. Life has become empty and is slipping by. Now, all that they do is to cause each other pain. And the reason behind this trouble is the same. What occurred on the first day happened without expectations.

On that day, she was not your wife, you had no power over her. On that day, you could not make any demands; whatever came was a gift. What you gave was also a gift, unasked for. It happened without expectations. And now you want what happened to you in your innocence to happen on demand. You are laying down a new condition, and that condition will ruin everything.

The flow of love that is there between a lover and his beloved is not there anymore between a husband and his wife. It is very difficult it is impossible. The experience of bliss which you had on the first day you started meditating will not happen on the second day, because on the second day you have come fully prepared to expect bliss. Remember, this expectation was not there on the first day. If on the second day too you come as you came on the first day, without any expectations, you will experience an even greater bliss. And on the third day, come with even fewer expectations. Have no demands whatsoever; just meditate. Simply don't ask when it will happen again, don't raise the question at all. Simply meditate, and it will go on growing.

The meaning of this sutra is to go on gathering your blissful moments. Relive them, but don't desire their repetition.

The meaning of reliving is tasting again and again what you have gathered; chewing it over. Cows and buffaloes know how to chew: learn from them! After they have eaten, they ruminate, they chew their food over again and again. Whatever experiences of happiness happen to you, ruminate on them.

And it is not as if you don't know how to, because you are continuously ruminating over your sorrows. If someone abuses you just once, you will repeat what he said at least fifty times to yourself. And all the time you are becoming more and more angry. Why are you so worried? He just abused you once, but you are replaying it fifty times! You cannot sleep at night thinking over how that fellow has abused you. You start to chew on it. What is so exciting about abuse? If you suffer a small hurt, you keep going on about it; about how it came to happen, about how it should not have happened like this, and so on.

Instead, ruminate on your happy moments. By dwelling on your sorrows, you have already multiplied them enough. So it is time to start dwelling on your happy moments, and your happiness will increase manyfold. But don't ask for it. Face the future with a free and open mind. Extract the essence from your past and inject it into your present life, but go forward into the future with a clean and empty slate – totally empty. That elixir which you have extracted from your past will prepare you well for the future. Then you need not ask; your happiness will multiply automatically.

The sixth sutra:

Learn from it the lesson of harmony

Life itself has speech and is never silent.
And its utterance is not,
as you that are deaf may suppose, a cry;
it is a song.

Learn from it that you are part of the harmony; learn from it to obey the laws of the harmony.

These fragments of music that you collect inside – don't treat them as just fragments, search for an interrelationship between them. It is difficult, and you will need to know the art of life.

In childhood you experienced joy in running after a butterfly, and that experience of joy is still there, present within you. And when you fell in love for the first time in your life and experienced a great, overflowing feeling of joy – that too is still present within you. Then one night, sitting by the side of the ocean, you were entranced by the sound of its roaring. That too is still there within you. Once, when you were just sitting and doing nothing, for no reason whatsoever you found everything becoming silent and peaceful. That too is within you. There are a number of experiences just like these lying within you but they are disconnected, and you have never bothered to find out what is common to them all, what is the point of harmony between them all.

What is the connection between the small child chasing a butterfly, and the young man sitting beside his beloved – what is the similarity between the two? Both occasions have given you happiness; in both, you had an experience of music and in both you experienced a similar ecstasy, so there is certainly a common element between them. They seem to be so different: the child chasing a butterfly, the young man sitting beside his beloved, and the old man chanting the mantra *Om.* On the surface they do not seem to have anything in common. But certainly there has to be something in common between them, because all three are saying that they are in great bliss. No matter how different the food, there is something similar about the taste.

So probe a little and find out: the happiness that a child felt while chasing the butterfly – what was it? It was the child being only aware of the butterfly and forgetting the rest of the world. The child had no idea he was running after the butterfly. He became one with the chase. His eyes were fixed on the butterfly; all the rest of his thoughts had evaporated. At that moment he had only one thought in his mind, and that was that somehow, he had to catch the butterfly. But it would be difficult even to call that a thought – it was more a feeling, and because of his single-pointedness towards that feeling, he experienced happiness.

Then, the same child who was chasing a butterfly grows up to be a young man, and now, one night when the sky is full of stars, he is sitting beside his beloved. There is no connection between the butterfly and the beloved. But sitting beside his beloved, his attention has once again become single-pointed. All his feelings have become single-pointed, the whole world has disappeared, and for him only his beloved remains. Now, he has no other thought in his mind. While his beloved is there, he drinks only from her. Now, no other feeling, no other thought catches hold of him. In this moment, he has again become totally immersed in the single-pointedness of his feeling.

And then the old man is reciting the mantra *Om*. These three events are worlds apart – the time of the butterfly, the world of the beloved, and now the old man reciting *Om* in a temple where the sacred lamps and the incense are burning. There seems to be no connection between these three. But no, in this chanting of *Om* he has again become single-pointed with his feeling. The world has disappeared for him: the sound of *Om* has become all. He has forgotten himself, he is not even aware of the one who is chanting the mantra. Only chanting has remained, only the sound of *Om* has remained. The feeling has again become focused at one point. Then he will understand that these three fragments are not fragments; he has found a thread moving through them. That is the music, that is the harmony.

So in the fragments that you collect from your life's experiences – from your glimpses of bliss, from your glimpses of the music – look for the harmony, the common thread between them all. And you will be very surprised to see that no matter how different those various experiences may appear to be, if they contain a feeling of happiness in them, they are similar. And no matter how different various experiences may appear to be, if they contain a feeling of suffering in them, they too are similar. There is only one language of happiness, and there is only one language of suffering.

So if you view these events as something separate from one another, you will never get an idea of what life is all about. You will think.... The old man reciting the mantra *Om* will look down on the young man and think,

"Why is this stupid young man running after girls?" And the young man sitting beside his beloved will consider the child to be foolish: wasting his time chasing worthless butterflies!

The three of them will not be able to understand each other. And the reason is that the old man never really understood his youth, he never really understood his childhood. Even though he is now an old man, he still doesn't understand that childhood, youth and old age are all a part of the flow of life – they are all one and the same thing. And whenever he experiences any happiness from anywhere, any feeling of bliss, no matter how different the outward circumstances may be, what is happening inside is one and the same thing.

Whether you are running after butterflies or reciting *Om*, it is the same thing. Running after butterflies is the child's way of reciting *Om*. And the old man's recitation of *Om* is his way of running after butterflies. Even the young man sitting beside his beloved is reciting *Om* and chasing butterflies. The day you are able to see this, all the parts will fit together and become a part of that one great music, and you will discover the deep secret within. Then the beads of a *mala* will not be so important to you, you will have discovered the inner thread that links them all. And that very thread can take you towards the supreme truth.

Then, the old man will never get angry with the child, because he will have understood his own childhood and assimilated it into his very soul. An old man who becomes angry with a child is not a very intelligent person.

His anger just shows that he is still resentful about his own childhood. Actually, he is just letting off steam on the child. The old man who tells a youth that he is just wasting his life and so on, has simply not understood life. The very fact that he is telling a young man off for wasting *his* life only proves that he himself feels that he wasted his life when he was young, and now he regrets how he lived. It has no other meaning. Old age and youth have not become one in the life of this old man; he is still living a fragmented life.

And suffering abides in the fragmentary. Otherwise, the old man would help the child to catch butterflies, he would help the youth to learn the art of love – because the old man knows that all these are also the resonances of the same divine sound, of *Om*, at different stages. Then he wouldn't be angry, he wouldn't be angry at anything, he would have no complaint about anything.

And remember: only an old man like this can be called a sage, a seer. Just any old man cannot be. With age, everyone grows old; but there are very few people who also grow in wisdom. To grow in wisdom as you age means to have experienced the whole essence of life.

That is why we have given so much respect to old people in this country – but it is not necessarily because of old age. We pay so much respect to an elderly person because, though the child may have had the experience of catching a butterfly, he doesn't have any idea of *Om*. The young man may have experienced what it is like to sit beside a beloved, but he too doesn't have any idea of *Om*. The old man has all three of them. He has them all.

That is why you have been asked to touch the feet of the old man, to bow down to him. It is not because he is older than you, it is because he has gone through all the beads of the mala, and perhaps he has found that connecting thread which runs through them all.

The person who has not been able to find that thread has not yet attained to old age. Even though his hair has turned white, it must have done so because of the sun. His life has passed within the confines of time, he has not experienced the timeless.

And what is the timeless? To have discovered the one connecting melody in all the diverse and endless experiences of life – *that* is the timeless.

And for the person who has caught hold of it, there is no unhappiness in this world. For such a person nothing in this world is a bondage. He has found the essence of life. And the moment you have found the essence, you become free from the bondage of life itself.

Life simply exists so that you can discover its essence. And if you don't, you will have to become a child again. You will have to be born again, you will have to chase butterflies again, you will have to sit with the beloved again, you will have to chant the mantra *Om* again. And if, even then, you don't find the essence of life, you will have to become a child all over again.

But if you can catch that one thread running through the whole of life, there is no need for you to become a child again. To become a child means that you have regressed to the lowest class. From high school you have been sent back again to the nursery. It is very sad. That's why in this country the yearning of our hearts has always been only one: how to be free from the cycle of birth and death.

The reason behind it is simple: what is the sense in growing old just so you can become a child again and again? It means that all that time was simply wasted; as if you had managed to reach the final grade and then you were pulled back and made to sit in the first grade again! It is good that this happens to you in a new body so there is not so much anguish.

If God were to create the universe again, he should be asked not to give us a new body, but instead to make the old man, in his same old body, a child again – so that he can catch butterflies. This would be more beneficial because when you get a new body you forget the whole story. You wonder what has been going on, what are you doing here. So it would be better if God were to make the old man chase after butterflies again in the same old body; it would be better if he were to make the old man run after women again in the same old body, it would be better if the old man were again to go back to the temple.

In a way, this is exactly what is going on, because even in your new body, the soul inside remains the same.

Learn from it the lesson of harmony

This very lesson is the whole essence of life.

13

REVERENCE FOR LIFE

7. Regard earnestly all the life that surrounds you.

Regard the constantly changing
and moving life which surrounds you,
for it is formed by the hearts of men;
and as you learn to understand
their constitution and meaning,
you will by degrees
be able to read the larger word of life.

8. Learn to look intelligently into the hearts of men.

Study the hearts of men,
that you may know
what is that world in which you live
and of which you will to be a part.
Intelligence is impartial;
no man is your enemy; no man is your friend.
All alike are your teachers.
Your enemy becomes a mystery that must be solved,
even though it takes ages;
for man must be understood.

**Your friend becomes a part of yourself,
an extension of yourself,
a riddle hard to read.**

In our search for the truth of life, the biggest difficulty that we come across is our irreverence for life. And we all carry this irreverence inside us. It will seem a little paradoxical, and it will be a little hard for you to understand, but it is all our so-called religions that have filled us with this irreverence. Real religiousness would have given us a reverence for life – because God himself is hidden in life; life is his very clothing, his covering. Life is his breath. So as long as we feel irreverence for life, it will be impossible to find God, because it is reverence that brings us to the door of the divine. By showing irreverence, we turn our backs on it.

Now a strange dilemma has been created. Religions exhort you to seek the universal reality, the ultimate source of life, and they also proclaim that it is hidden in each and every particle of life. But pathologically-minded people take the seeking of the ultimate source of life to mean a search in which the first condition is to negate life – as though the quest for godliness is anti-life, as though if you want to find the divine you will first have to renounce life. And if this is true, that if you want to find the supreme mystery of life you have first to renounce life, then you can never have any respect for life; you will rather denounce and scorn it. And when life is scorned, how can you show any reverence to the supreme mystery of life?

Krishna is full of reverence for life, Jesus is full of reverence for life, Buddha is full of reverence for life, yet a large number of their followers are full of irreverence for life. This is not because of the teachings of Krishna, Jesus or Buddha, but because of their followers' understanding. They all ask you to search for the supreme truth, and you too want to find it, but whenever you think of going on such a search, you always think that first, you must renounce this moment, first, you must renounce your present life for this search to become possible. You think you will have to distance yourself from your present life, that you will have to destroy it and only then can you undertake the search. And it is not that renouncing life is a prerequisite for the search – the truth is that we have become so fed up with life, so troubled by it, so unhappy and helpless in it, that whenever we get the slightest opportunity to leave it, to destroy it, we are always happy to do so. Any excuse, and we are ready to destroy life. We are suicidal, we are sick. And then all the pathologically-minded people get together and they change the whole definition of life, they change its color. They turn the whole context upside down.

Pathological people and people with sick minds very quickly become interested in religion. And there is a reason for this – the reason is that they are anti-life. They have never gained any peace or happiness from life, and the reason is not that life offers no possibilities for peace and happiness; the real reason is that the method that they have been using to find peace and happiness is wrong and so they became totally anti-life. Whenever they find any preacher who hints to them of a greater life, immediately they come to the conclusion that this life is full of sin; it is *this* life which is the cause of all suffering and only by renouncing it can they attain to the supreme life.

Unhappiness is not an intrinsic part of life itself, it lies in the way you look at life. If you behave like these sick people then even if you attain to supreme life, even there, you will find nothing but unhappiness. It is just the way you are – it does not matter where you are, it does not matter where you go; that trait will exist in you. No matter where you go, your way of looking remains with you. Even if you do find the divine, you will feel that it too is just making you miserable! You cannot ever be happy – unless you change your ways. But you don't want to change them; instead you become very eager to change the circumstances. You take great delight in condemning life, and it becomes very difficult for you ever to imagine that perhaps you could be wrong. And this community of condemners, even though it manages to inflict harm to your life, does not manage to help you to take even one step towards the divine.

It is necessary to understand one thing: that if a supreme life does exist, it is nothing but another name for the depth of this very life. And if there is a life beyond this life, the stairway to that life, the pathway to that life, starts from *this* life. This life is not your enemy. It is your friend, your partner; it is ready to support you. And if you are unable to see any path through this life, then you must change your way of seeing, you must change your method of looking at things. But who is ready to change himself?

I am very surprised to find that even the people who come and tell me that they are willing to change themselves are *not* ready to change themselves, they merely talk about doing so. Their wish is that everyone else should change, but they should not. To change yourself hurts your ego. It is very painful.

People come to me...they come up with plans to change me too! They tell me that if I were to do such and such a thing it would be very good, that if I were to speak like this or like that it would be very good, if I were to live in such and such a way it would produce very good results. I ask them, "Why did you come here? Did you come here to change yourself or to change me? I am happy just the way I am! For me there is no question of even making the smallest change. If you are unhappy, then worry about changing yourself. But if you too are happy, then the matter is closed."

But even when an unhappy person comes here, he forgets why he has come here. For what purpose has he come? To change himself!

People come to this camp, and the whole day long they torture me saying that such and such a person is doing this, somebody else is behaving like that. But why have *you* come? Have you come here to worry about everyone else? Who asked you to worry about other people? It seems that you have plenty of time, that you have a lot of energy. You are devoting your life to finding out who is doing what. What is the point? Which man is talking to which woman, which man is sitting next to which woman – why should it bother you? Who are you?

You came here to transform yourself but you start worrying how to transform others! You did not actually come here to change yourself – that's why you have become so concerned with others. Your idea that you came here to change yourself is false – you are just deceiving yourselves. You want to change the whole world, but you don't want to change the way you are in even the smallest way! And you want all your suffering to come to an end and for all your pain to finish. Your suffering will *not* end if you remain just the way you are! And why does it hurt you that someone is sitting lovingly with a woman, talking to her? Why should this cause *you* pain?

Someone sent word to me that such and such a person is sitting with a woman in a way which is not decent. Now, who can be the judge of what is decent and what is not decent? And the man who is informing me about all this has no idea why all this is causing him anxiety. I know this person very well: he is incapable of sitting with any woman, and it is not possible for any woman to sit close to him either. So he is disturbed.

He wanted to be in that man's place, that's why he brought me this news of indecent behavior. But he has no idea that it is his own sickness that is eating him; instead he is worried about reforming the other person! I told this man, "Have you ever noticed that the man sitting next to this woman is always happy, is always laughing, joyous? And you are always sad, unhappy and worried. Try to learn something from this man, and stop worrying about the woman sitting next to him. Then if you also become happy, maybe a woman will want to sit next to you too! But right now there is hell written all over your face. You look so worried and unhappy – who would want to sit next to you? And if two people are sitting together lovingly, what is indecent about it?"

It is a very strange thing: love appears indecent because of your irreverence for life. And love is the most profound flower of life. If two people are seen fighting on the road nobody will point out that it is indecent. But if two people are seen sitting lovingly under a tree with their arms around each other, it is deemed indecent! Violence is not indecent, but love is! Why is love indecent? And why isn't violence? Violence is destruction, love is life. So it means that you have reverence for death, and irreverence for life.

It is surprising: when films are made on war, no government raises any objection to them. These films are full of violence and destruction, but no government in the world will declare these films to be indecent. Yet whenever love is depicted in a film, all the governments become worried. The government decides how far away you need to be from each other before you can kiss: whether the distance should be six inches or four inches. It decides that the kiss becomes indecent after so many inches, and is decent from so many inches apart! But if you knife someone on the screen, then it is not thought to be indecent, then no one says that the knife should be at least six inches away.

It is worth looking at where the problem lies. Why is kissing considered sinful and knifing not? A kiss is a friend of life, and a knife is a friend of death. No one has any objection to the knife. We are all suicidal, we are all murderers. We are all enemies of love. Why this enmity? If we were to go deeply into it, we would find that we do not have any reverence for life.

Moreover, if two people are sitting lovingly together, not harming anyone, it is their personal affair, their personal joy. And if this is causing you trouble, you should search within yourself. There is a lack of love in your life; your sexual desire has not been gratified yet, it remains unfulfilled. Your sexual desire has become a disease, it has become a wound. But the people who are bringing me this news will not admit that they are troubled by sexual longings. Instead, they complain: "What is all this that is going on?"

Focus on yourself, examine your own way of looking at things. Don't worry about others. And always bear one thing in mind: what do you respect? Is it life?

Two people who are in love, standing hand in hand is one of the most beautiful phenomena on this earth. And if love is not beautiful, then the flowers cannot be beautiful, then the songs of the birds cannot be beautiful either because a flower is also a manifestation of love and a manifestation of the tree's sexuality. Through it, the tree is creating its seeds, creating its sperm. If it is not beautiful then the morning song of the birds cannot be called beautiful, because it too is either a call for the beloved, or the search for a lover – it too is a sexual longing.

If a person is full of irreverence for life then he finds nothing beautiful in the world. Everything becomes obscene. And if you don't see your so-called obscenity in the flowers, it is only because you have no idea about the sexuality of the flowers. When the spring comes, the earth becomes youthful. That joy which you see being manifested all around in nature, that festival and dance of color, that celebration, is also this sexual energy.

Sexuality is one of the reasons people condemn life. Who can say in how many ways we have opposed sexual energy, and called it a sin? But it can be sinful precisely because it has the potential to be sacred. Bear one thing in mind: only that which also has the potential to become sacred can be sinful.

If a small child makes a mistake, we condone it. We do not say he has committed a sin; instead we say he is only a child, that right now he is not capable of choosing right from wrong, so let us forgive his mistake. If a person commits a crime while he is drunk, then even the court pardons him – saying that he was drunk at the time, that if he had been in his right senses he would have been capable of doing the right thing, but since he was not in his right senses he cannot be blamed for the deed. And if a person is proved to be insane, he is absolved of even the biggest crime, because how can you blame a mad person? He is incapable of deciding what is right, so he cannot be held responsible for doing wrong.

A situation where sin is possible is also a situation where virtue is possible. Without there being this potential for both, sin alone cannot happen. The same energy that can become sin can also become sacred.

The reason the wise have opposed sex is very different from the reason why the ignorant have jumped on the idea. The wise ones ask you not to fall into sexual desire so that your sexual energy can be directed upwards, towards the divine. In this, there is no condemnation of sexual desire; they are simply saying there is a higher use for it. And the truth is, that in this lies its very greatness – because by indulging in sexual desire you will only enter the world and into deeper darkness. But if you don't indulge in sexuality, then this very same energy can become a ladder to take you upwards, beyond darkness.

Why should you want to use a ladder which can take you upwards for a downwards journey?

This approach shows respect towards sexual energy, not disrespect. Sexual energy can take you towards the ultimate truth, so don't waste it unnecessarily.

But the sick-minded have understood this to mean that one should become an enemy of sexual energy. They don't use the ladder to take them upwards, in fact they don't want to use the ladder at all! All that they do is roam around carrying the ladder on their shoulders – they don't use it at all.

Taking sexual energy upwards is a very joyful experience, very blissful. But if you cannot do that, then at least don't carry it around on your shoulders, because by doing so you are only becoming sick and you are unnecessarily carrying a burden.

This antagonism to sex also creates an irreverence for life in our minds, because life is born from it, life arises out of it, because life is an expansion of sexual energy.

The act of love is done in secret, in the dark, because somewhere there is guilt, the feeling that it is a sin. If love is a sin, then children born from love cannot be sacred. And if love is a sin, then the whole of life is a sin.

These sutras are very valuable, they are worth understanding. The first one for today, the seventh sutra, says:

Regard earnestly all the life that surrounds you.

Respect all life in its totality: not death, not violence, not destruction, but life, creation, love. From where life arises, from where life is born, from where life unfolds – whether in plants, or in birds, or in humans – respect it, the whole of life.

Regard the constantly changing
and moving life which surrounds you,
for it is formed by the hearts of men;
and as you learn to understand
their constitution and meaning,
you will by degrees
be able to read the larger word of life.

There is a creative aspect in reverence for life. Look all around, and you will find that everything has been created by the heart. The person sitting beside you also has a heart beating inside him. The life force is pulsating even in a tree, the earth lying beneath your feet is also breathing. From a tiny insect to a big constellation in the sky – everywhere the same life is being manifested in different forms.

So how can you gain entry into existence if you do not have reverence for all of this in your heart? How will you enter, how will you find the door? If you are against it, if you are antagonistic, condemning, then you will turn your back on the door. Wherever you come across life, worship it. Wherever you come across a bud of life blooming, welcome it. Destruction, condemnation should not arise in your mind. Let reverence become your state of being.

Schweitzer has written a book, *Reverence for Life* – respect towards life. He dedicated the whole of his life to respecting and revering life. Schweitzer has said, "It is through reverence for life that I came to realize the divine." And he has said, "I have not worshipped in any other way, neither with prayer nor with meditation. But wherever I saw life, I did whatever I could to respect it, to serve it, to greet it. And whenever I felt that I was on the side of death, I immediately removed myself. Wherever I felt that I was about to destroy something, I immediately removed my hands away from that place. I never used my energy in the service of destruction, I never used my energy to spoil anything. If I could mend something, make or create something, give some support, make some way for life – that is what I did. This was my only worship, and this gave me fulfillment because I have found that which seems worth finding – and there is nothing else left to seek."

But this can only happen after your vision has changed. Right now, you are occupied in looking for ways to destroy, and there is no end to your satisfaction if you are able to find something, somewhere to destroy. Nobody seems to derive any thrill from creating something, but everyone is very keen on destroying things.

Look within yourself for the causes of this eagerness. There is a strong sense in you to condemn. If I were to say something condemning of someone, you would immediately accept it without any argument. But if I were to start praising someone, your mind would be immediately taken aback, you would not be willing to accept it. You would say, "But where is the proof, what is the proof? You are mistaken!" But you don't say this when someone is being condemned.

Have you ever noticed that when someone comes to you and criticizes somebody else, how willingly and happily you accept it? You never ask if the criticism is true or not. You never ask if there is any proof to support it. You don't even bother to find out whether the person who has brought you this piece of news is trustworthy or not. And you do not even want to know the reasons for believing it, or the purpose in believing it.

No, whenever someone starts condemning somebody, you immediately come alive, your energy blossoms and your mind is so eager and willing to absorb each and every bit of the slander! And it doesn't stop there; you immediately run out to tell someone else about it, because you can hardly control yourself. At the most you can keep it to yourself for perhaps half an hour or an hour, and then you will rush to tell someone about it. Such is your joy in slander; it holds great fascination for you. This is violence, and it is a violence which does not appear to be violence.

If you threw a knife at someone you would be sentenced in a court of law, but no one will arrest you if you hurl slander at someone. There are no grounds for doing so and so no trouble involved for you. Without a shadow of a threat or of harm to yourself, you have managed an act of violence – and at the same time you have also indulged your joy in being destructive. You will be only too eager to tell the story to someone else. And remember one thing: when you relate it to another person, your story will have twice as much abuse in it as it had when it was related to you. If you were told the figure fifty, you will say the figure one hundred. And you won't even notice how and when you raised it to a hundred. The joy of slandering is so great that man goes on exaggerating the details.

But if someone praises someone in front of you, you cannot bear it. Your heart simply closes; all your doors and windows shut tightly and you already know that this is wrong, that this praise is not possible, that this person is not worthy of it. You will try your very best to put forward all sorts of arguments to the contrary, to use whatever means are at your disposal to support the contrary before you are forced to agree that what the other person is saying is true. And more often than not you will find something or other from somewhere that can prove that it is not so. You will reassure yourself that this thing is not true, and you will never go to anyone to broadcast this deed which is worthy of praise. This shows that you have a disrespect for life, that you respect death.

If by some chance you find that the day's newspaper does not have news of any violence – that nothing has been set on fire anywhere, that there has been no looting or riots, that no war is being waged anywhere, no bombs have been dropped anywhere – you will throw the newspaper away in disgust and declare that today there is no news at all! Is this what you were waiting for all the time? Is this what you were anticipating since the early morning – news of violence? Saying that there is no news at all today, feeling that the two rupees you spent on buying the newspaper has gone to waste...did you ever reflect on what you were expecting in return for your two rupees on how much you wanted from the world so that your two rupees were not wasted?

Newspapers are printed for people like you; so the press never prints any good news. Good news has no readership; it is not exciting, it is not sensational. The newspapermen print exactly what you want them to print; they only look for what you desire. So they collect and put together all the rubbish and meaningless filth of the world, and from first thing in the morning you relish all of this. It makes your day. And then you spend the whole day spreading whatever rubbish you have gathered from the newspaper. Your knowledge is no deeper than the newspapers', and you go on repeating it.

Have you ever thought about why this interests you so much? People read detective novels – why? Why do they read detective novels and spy stories? Why do they go and see films that depict war and violence? If you come across two people fighting on the road, you will forget the hundred and one things that you have to do and watch them instead. Maybe you are on your way to buy medicine for your mother who at that very moment is dying, but even then your feet will refuse to move from the spot. You will say, "Never mind about my mother, she can wait a while. What is the hurry? But these two people quarreling, who knows what will happen?" And if they go on quarreling but nothing much does happen, you leave there very disappointed.

That is why I am telling you to examine this tendency. It will show you your outlook towards life. What do you want from life, what is your state of mind? First recognize it, and then change it. Watch and see: wherever you are drawn towards death, violence and destruction – withdraw that interest, and extend it towards life. If you pass a flower, a bud becoming a flower, stop for a few moments and look at it. Pause there for a while, and gaze at this flower unfolding – because life itself is unfolding on that very spot. And if you see a child at play, joyously laughing and dancing and shouting, stop there for some moments and watch him.

What is the point in observing two people with knives drawn, fighting each other? You may not be aware of it, and perhaps you may never have thought about it: that because you are paying them attention you have a hand in those two people fighting and trying to knife each other. If a crowd does not gather, the fighters themselves will lose interest in the fight. If no one comes to watch them, then those who are fighting will also think, "What is the fun in fighting now that no one is even looking? Let's leave it for some other time." But if a crowd gathers, then the fighters are encouraged. The bigger the crowd that gathers, the more excited they will become about the whole affair, because then it is a question of prestige, a matter of pride.

So don't ever think that because you were simply looking on you were not a party to it. You were, because your eyes took part in those acts of violence. If there were a really unique court in this world, then not only would the person who used the knife be found guilty of the crime, but you too would be found guilty, along with him, because *you* were also standing there. Why were you standing there? Your presence may have encouraged those people. Your presence may have provoked them, and because of your presence something happened that otherwise might not have.

So look what your attention usually focuses on and then divert it towards life. And wherever you come across life, be filled with reverence, be filled with gratitude. And then whatever you can do for life, do it!

If you are able to achieve this state of mind, you will suddenly find that a thousand and one worries have disappeared, because they were nothing but a product of your sick nature. Thousands of diseases will disappear, because those diseases were being supported by your violent feelings. Many of your wounds will vanish, because the act of wounding others was keeping your own wounds alive.

In this world, only he who is capable of enjoying bliss happening anywhere, to anyone, can truly attain to bliss.

As it is, whenever you see anyone being happy you become unhappy and your sole concern becomes how to make that person unhappy too. Perhaps you may not be doing this consciously; but all this goes on unconsciously within you: that you cannot bear to see anyone happy. And when you see someone suffering, a glint comes into your eye, your feet start dancing. And then you show a lot of sympathy. Perhaps you think that you are a great friend of those who are suffering – because look how much sympathy you are showing! But remember one thing: if you are not capable of becoming happy at someone else's happiness, then all this sympathy which you are expressing at their suffering is false. It cannot be otherwise. If you are incapable of becoming happy because of someone else's happiness, you cannot be sad because of his suffering.

When the other's happiness makes you unhappy, look within yourself and you will certainly find that his unhappiness makes you happy. This is simple arithmetic; it cannot be otherwise. Your sympathy is not really for others; you are just deriving joy from it. Today someone has taken a tumble. Look how he has slipped on the banana peel and is now lying flat on his face! Inside you feel very happy that it is not you who has slipped, but someone else. But what you show on the outside is a very civilized and well-mannered face: great sympathy. Helping him to get up, brushing down his clothes.... But deep down in your heart you are very happy that it is not you but your neighbor who fell. So many times you wanted to put him down, and now that banana peel has done it for you! When you go to offer your condolences about someone else's misfortune, just look within yourself and see if you are not really feeling happy.

Once I was staying in the house of a certain woman. She was always on the lookout to discover who has died where. It could be anybody, even someone she didn't know. And she always managed to go there to offer her condolences. Whenever I saw her going to commiserate, I noticed that her walk had a joyous quality to it, which was not normally there. I inquired, "What is the matter? When someone dies, or when something happens to someone – how is it that you go out with such a happy face?"

She replied, "One must express sympathy with another's misfortune."

I said, "From your face and your manner I cannot see any signs of sorrow. It seems as if you were just waiting for someone to die. This eager interest and brisk walk make me doubtful."

Observe yourself when you offer your sympathy to someone. Just for a minute shut your eyes and look within: isn't all this giving you some pleasure, aren't you enjoying all this? Aren't you deriving some pleasure from all this sympathy? If you are, know that this is perverted. And when you come across someone who is happy, does it make you jealous? When you see someone happy, does it sting you? And if it does, then at heart you do not have any reverence for life.

Wherever you find life blossoming and smiling, that should make you happy.

I am not saying this because somebody will benefit from it; I am saying this because it will free you from your sickness. Your wounds will disappear, you will stop creating miseries for yourself – because a person who is creating suffering for others is actually only creating it for himself, but he is not aware of it. And he who tries to make others joyous is actually creating a basis for an even greater happiness for himself.

If you are unhappy, then you yourself are responsible, and only when you are aware of this will you begin to feel your responsibility. Now every man wants to be happy. It is difficult to find a man who doesn't want to be happy. It is a very curious thing that there are nearly six billion people on this earth who all want to make themselves happy, but they are all miserable! There must be some mistake somewhere. And the mistake must be a big one, a fundamental one; otherwise how could six billion people go on repeating the same mistake over and over again? Everybody wants to be happy and no one is.

Your mistake is that even though you want to be happy, you want to make others unhappy. And a person who wants to make others unhappy can never be happy himself. Your mistake is that you want to see yourself happy, but you do not want to see others happy. And one who cannot see others happy will always remain unhappy; he can never be happy.

As you sow, so will you reap. Whatever we do to others comes back to us. This world is one big echo. Here, whatever you give showers back on you. If you call someone names, it comes back to you. If you share joy and happiness, then joy and happiness are given to you too. Whenever you are prepared to give to the world, it gives back the same to you. If you have shown reverence for life, this whole creation, the whole of existence becomes full of reverence for you. And if on the other hand you disrespect life, then this whole existence is disrespectful towards you.

This creates a difficulty. If you disrespect the world, if you disrespect life, then life and the world disrespect you. And when they disrespect you, you begin to feel that you were right after all in thinking that this world is only worthy of disrespect. Then you will be caught in a vicious circle and it will be very difficult for you to get out of it. You will feel that you were right in thinking that the world is really a very unhappy place to live in; that it is not a celebration, it is a sorrow. If you had any doubts, now they will be confirmed, because now the world has become a problem for you. It will never occur to you that the seeds of this misery were sown by you alone, and that now you are just reaping the crop.

If there is any fundamental meaning to the doctrine of karma it is this: that whatever you do, it comes back to you. Whatever you give, you receive back. Your actions become your destiny and then you have to carry that destiny with you. If it consists of unhappiness, then know well that your actions were the kind that bring suffering. And if the outcome is happiness, then your actions were the kind that bring happiness.

These sutras are the sutras for supreme happiness.

Regard earnestly all the life that surrounds you.

Regard the constantly changing
and moving life which surrounds you,
for it is formed by the hearts of men;
and as you learn to understand
their constitution and meaning,
you will by degrees
be able to read the larger word of life.

The eighth sutra:

Learn to look intelligently into the hearts of men.

Study the hearts of men,
that you may know
what is that world in which you live
and of which you will to be a part.

Learn to look intelligently into the hearts of men.

Never mind intelligence, we don't even bother to look – what to say of intelligence? We don't want the bother of looking inside another's heart. The truth is that we form opinions about others without ever having understood them. We are only driven by our own ideas, we make up our minds as to how people are, without ever bothering to look into their hearts first. And once our minds are made up, we seek out facts to support them. We have hundreds of strategies which help us avoid looking into the human heart. This saves us trouble; we don't have to worry about it.

You are sitting next to someone, and you ask him, "Please sir, what is your name? What religion do you belong to? What is your caste, what are your credentials, where do you live?" and so on. You ask all this so that you can save yourself the trouble of actually looking inside him. If that person replies, "I am a brahmin," and if you are also a brahmin, this reassures you, and you feel that now there is no need to probe any further: you already know all about brahmins. But no two brahmins are ever alike, every man is different.

And if the same person were to say, "I am a Mohammedan," you would definitely feel that now there is no point in conversing any further. The man is a Mohammedan, and for a Hindu a Mohammedan is a bad person. If the questioner were a Mohammedan, for him a Hindu is a bad person. The thing is settled; now there is no need to look into the individual. We have already stuck a label on that person, that he is a Mohammedan. In our hearts we already know that this person is bad, that now it is not right to have any further relationship with him. And had that man said, "I am a communist," you would have thought it wise to move your seat even further away. We try to avoid knowing other people; we put labels on them.

Are two Mohammmedans ever alike, are two Hindus, or are two communists? Every human being is unique, nobody else can be like him. But it is not convenient to think like this – because if we acknowledge that each person is a unique being, we will have to study each and every one of them. Who is going to be bothered with all this? So instead we ask about the person's business, his occupation and so on, and leave it at that. We feel that this much information about him is enough for us to know what sort of a person he is. On the basis of this we make up our minds about him, this little bit of introductory chit-chat settles what sort of a person the other is.

Even a whole life is insufficient to find out what sort of a person the other really is. But we make up our minds after only two minutes of chit-chat, and then act according to that information. We form an image of him. These are all tricks of ours.

You have an image of your wife in your mind, and your wife has an image of you, her husband, in her mind. We operate with that image in our minds and we don't bother to know the person directly. The wife knows how a husband should behave. If he acts accordingly, it is okay, and if he doesn't, then it is wrong. But she is not bothered to understand who her husband really is – the yardstick has already been decided. And by those yardsticks we measure people and put them in such and such a category. It seems that categories are not for people, but people are for categories! So she doesn't see who the husband standing in front of her really is. In her mind she has a concept of what a husband should be and she lives by that concept. If he corresponds to that concept then it is okay, and if he goes against it, then it is wrong!

But no person ever corresponds to or goes against a concept. Each person is just what he is, all concepts fall short. All concepts are like ready-made clothes: they are not tailored exactly for you, they are made on the principle of the average, and every person is different from the average. There is no such thing as the average person – each person is unique.

For instance, if you were to measure the height of each and every person in your village: children, old people, young people, tall people, short ones – in all a total of say, five hundred – and then you were to divide the sum total of the heights of those five hundred people by five hundred to arrive at the average height of a person in that village.... If you were to go looking for the person whose height matches that average, you might not find even a single person in the village who is that height, because in reality the average does not exist, the average is a lie. Each person has his own particular height; there is no such thing as the average. The average is only a mathematical calculation, it has nothing whatsoever to do with real life.

So we go on living according to the concepts and images we have made. Nobody ever looks directly, nobody ever looks straight into the heart! And no one is really bothered to find out exactly what is happening in the heart either! It is a little dangerous to do so, because if you do, you may find yourself in a predicament. So it is better to maintain a distance. It is dangerous to explore anybody's depths, because if you do, the other person's depths will also change you. And then it will not be so easy to brush things away.

Supposing you have a servant: how can you look into his heart? Because if you do, it will create problems, it will become difficult for you to treat him as a servant. You will see that he too is human. So if you want to treat him as a servant then it is better not to look into his heart.

Have you ever noticed that if a stranger enters your room while you are reading the newspaper, you get up at once and ask him to take a seat? You would also do the same if someone you knew came in. But when the servant comes and cleans the room and then leaves, you don't even realize that someone has come and gone – as if the servant were not a human being at all, but just some sort of a machine. His role is functional, directly related to work. It is dangerous to get to know him well, because then you may learn that perhaps he has an ailing mother, that he has children who need to be educated, that he too has the same human heart as you have, and all that passes through any human being's heart passes through his too.

So if you were to look into his heart you would find yourself in trouble, you would have to do something about it. You would even begin to wonder how he gets by on the salary of fifty rupees that you pay him. He has an aged mother, children, a wife and a house to run: how is he managing on just fifty rupees? So if you were to look into his heart, one day or other you would have to put yourself in his place and think, "How would I manage on just fifty rupees?"

So it is better to keep some distance, and not to make an effort to know his heart. "It is enough for me to know that this man works for me and is paid fifty rupees for the job. To know more about this man is dangerous." That is why we have built so many walls around us. We never look inside anyone's heart, we stay as far away as we possibly can. We all live and behave with each other as untouchables.

This sutra is saying, "Learn to look intelligently into the hearts of men..." because until you have learned to look inside the hearts of other people, you will not melt, you cannot disappear. Until then, it will be difficult for you to get rid of your ego. If you gradually make yourself flow with the rhythm of another's heart, slowly but surely your ego will melt away by itself – because then you will find that a heart just like yours is also beating in the other person. You will realize that a being just like yours is also present in the other. You will know that the fear which you harbor is meaningless. You will also be able to see clearly that the differences between one person and another exist only on the surface. Deep down inside perhaps there is only one universal heart beating in us all. Once you have learned the art of looking into another's heart, the pure depths of the heart become visible to you, and then you find that there is only one heart beating in amongst the many hearts. There may be many physical hearts present, but the heart will be one. And this realization will prove to be a big step in taking you towards the universal reality.

Study the hearts of men,
that you may know
what is that world in which you live
and of which you will to be a part.

Intelligence is impartial;
no man is your enemy; no man is your friend.
All alike are your teachers.
Your enemy becomes a mystery that must be solved,
even though it takes ages;
for man must be understood.
Your friend becomes a part of yourself,
an extension of yourself,
a riddle hard to read.

To study the hearts of others you must look impartially, otherwise you will not be able to study them. If you are already biased, then whatever you find will only be a reinvention of your own preconceptions; it will be simply the repetition of your own ideas. And if you have a preconception, all that you will be doing is proving yourself to be right. And this is exactly how we live: we decide beforehand which side we are going to take, and after that we embark on the search for truth.

So right from the beginning this search for truth is a phony one. If you have already decided beforehand which side you are going to take, the whole thing is meaningless.

There is a teacher in Rajasthan University who conducts research on dead souls and reincarnation. Once someone brought him to meet me. He said he wanted to prove scientifically that there is such a thing as rebirth.

So I told him, "Right from the start you have put me in a difficult position, because you are saying that you wish to prove scientifically that rebirth takes place. This means that you have already decided that such a phenomenon as rebirth does, as a matter of fact, exist and that now you just want to prove it scientifically. This means that you have already made up your mind about it. But if you really possessed a scientific outlook, it would have been better for you to say that you wish to know scientifically if there is such a thing as reincarnation or not. You are saying you want to *prove it!* This means that you have already made up your mind beforehand that rebirth happens.

"Now all that is left is to prove it scientifically – and this you will manage to do somehow or other, because now you will only take into consideration those events which bear out your belief and you will leave out all those events which are contrary to it. You will select only those things which suit you, and leave out all those which do not. In this way a man can prove anything."

A man has written a book in which he has proved that the number thirteen is unlucky. And he says that he has proved it scientifically. How has he done it? From court records all over the world he has gathered the numbers of horrifying cases that were under trial on the date of the thirteenth. He has discovered the number of times people were sentenced to death or hanged on the thirteenth, he has counted the number of accidents that took place on the thirteenth, he has found out the number of people who have died on the thirteenth. And he has collected the statistics of the number of people who were born on the thirteenth but have been unhealthy their whole lives. He has collected all these statistics of calamity and written a big book. If you were to read that book, even you would be scared of the number thirteen, and you would think it wise to avoid it.

And the funny thing is that exactly the same figures are also available for the fourteenth and the fifteenth. Evidently, he never bothered to find out about them but only concentrated on gathering data for the thirteenth. It is not as if accidents only occurred on the thirteenth; some nice things must have happened too, but he left those out! Not only calamities happen on the thirteenth; some success stories must also happen on that date. And on the thirteenth not only deaths occur, but also births. If some people were hanged on the thirteenth, others must have been successful in having court cases repealed, and thus have avoided being hanged.

The writer has ignored all this. And just the same happens on the fourteenth too. But if you read the book you will feel worried, because he has gathered so much evidence to support the fact that many, many people have taken their lives by jumping from the thirteenth floor. People have jumped from the twelfth floor and also died! And for a person who wants to die, does it matter to him whether the number of the floor is thirteen, fourteen, or twelve? He never goes to find out!

This book had such an impact in America that hotels dropped the number thirteen when they numbered their floors. That is why in big hotels in America you will find that after the twelfth floor you arrive directly at the fourteenth. No one is willing to risk stopping at thirteen, because already so much tragedy has taken place there – why ask for more! It seems that the number thirteen is jinxed. If somebody constructs a building, he skips the thirteenth floor. They don't number it thirteen; otherwise no one will buy it, the floor will remain empty. If you have already decided the side you are going to take, it can only add to this kind of madness.

This sutra is saying that if you are really interested in studying the hearts of people, you must remain unbiased. Impartiality is the first sign of intelligence. If you are intelligent, you will be impartial; and if you are partial, it means you are not intelligent. The meaning of intelligence is that you don't come to any conclusions until you have examined all the facts. "Until something has been proved conclusively, we will not take any side; until then, we will remain in the middle. We will not decide in favor of this side or that."

It is difficult to be intelligent, because to be intelligent one needs to be patient, to be tolerant. To be a fool is very easy, there is no problem at all. A person is generally in a hurry to take sides. But if you are impartial you will realize that no woman is your enemy, no man is your friend.

All alike are your teachers.

This sutra is wonderful: All alike are your teachers. Your friend is teaching you something, and your enemy is also teaching you something. And at times your enemy teaches you much more than a friend. Many times you can learn much more from an enemy, much more than you could have ever imagined. But if you can remember that an enemy as well as a friend is your teacher, then you will be able to descend into the heart of the enemy as well. Then even the heart of the enemy will not be closed to you. Nothing in the world will be closed to you, everything will be opened to you, because *you* will be open.

Your enemy becomes a mystery that must be solved...

After all why is someone your enemy? Generally we have already decided beforehand that since so-and-so is a bad person, then he is our enemy. You are a nice person, and that fellow is bad; that's why he is your enemy. And this is exactly what he also thinks: that he is a nice fellow, and you are bad. That's why you are his enemy.

No, you are not achieving anything by thinking yourself a good person, and calling the other a bad person; nor are you increasing your understanding through this. You are standing in exactly the same place as you have always stood. If he is an enemy of yours, then try to find out *why*. What is it that makes him your enemy? You also have a hand in his enmity. The way you are also plays a part in it. And what type of person he is also plays a part in it. This is the mystery.

This sutra is saying that your enemy becomes a mystery, a mystery which you must solve. You must solve it, and it can only be solved if you remain impartial.

When Jesus was on the cross, his dying words were, "Father, forgive them, for they know not what they do. Heavenly Father, forgive them." This is what is meant by looking into the heart of the enemy.

Jesus is dying; he is on the cross, he is being crucified, and he is told if he has any last prayer to say to God he had better say it now – because the last moment is near. So what does Jesus pray? It is a wonderful prayer. No man in human history has ever made such a significant prayer. Jesus prayed, "Heavenly Father, I only ask one thing of you: that you forgive these people who are crucifying me because they do not know what they are doing! They are doing so out of ignorance, so they should be forgiven. They are acting out of ignorance. They are doing so because they feel I am their enemy. They are foolish, so don't punish them for my crucifixion."

This is what is called looking into the heart of the enemy. This is what is meant by taking an impartial attitude. Otherwise, how can you pray for the person who is crucifying you? You would have prayed to put all these people in hell, to destroy them completely from their very roots.

And it is not as if only *you* behave in this particular manner. No, even your sages, your so-called sages, have been like this – and they curse! If Durvasa had been in the place of Jesus, can you imagine what would have happened? Just try to imagine a little… the whole world would have been sent to hell!

And we even call such a person a sage! The blame for this does not lie with the sages, it lies with us. We do not understand what we are doing. We say that the sage Durvasa made a curse. A sage giving a curse! So what is the difference between you and a sage? And if a sage can curse, then what are you waiting for? You can curse and become a sage too!

But the people who call Durvasa a sage are only saying something about themselves, about what sort of people they are – not about Durvasa. All this only tells us about them. Even in a person like Durvasa they can behold a sage. It only means they have no idea that destruction, hatred and violence can have nothing in common with sagehood.

For a person who has an impartial mind, even an enemy is a mystery. Even though it may take ages to solve it – that doesn't matter. Don't hurry, remain impartial. And no matter how long it takes, don't rush into taking sides. You must get to know what a human being is like.

Your friend becomes a part of yourself,
an extension of yourself,
a riddle hard to read.

It is difficult to understand an enemy, because he is a mystery. It is difficult to understand even a friend, because he too is a mystery! It is difficult to understand an enemy because he stands at a great distance from us and a friend is difficult to understand because he gets to be very close.

You don't even understand your friends. You don't even bother to understand someone, to see that the human heart is a book which has to be opened and read, that the human heart is a musical instrument which you have to learn to play, that the human heart is a seed which has to be provided with soil, light and water and made to sprout. No, we don't give any thought to the human heart.

Keep these two sutras in mind:

Regard earnestly all the life that surrounds you.

Learn to look intelligently into the hearts of men.

These can become steps that take you to the supreme heart, to the heart of existence.

14

RESPECT YOUR HEART

9. Regard most earnestly your own heart.

For through your own heart
comes the one light which can illuminate life
and make it clear to your eyes.

Only one thing is more difficult to know –
your own heart.
Not until the bonds of personality be loosed
can that profound mystery of self begin to be seen.
Not till you stand aside from it,
will it in any way reveal itself to your understanding.
Then, and not till then, can you grasp and guide it.
Then, and not till then, can you use all its powers,
and devote them to a worthy service.

It is impossible to help others
till you have obtained some certainty of your own.
When you have learned the first twenty-one rules
and have entered the hall of learning
with your powers developed and senses unchained,
then you will find there is a fount within you
from which speech will arise.

**These notes are written only for those
to whom I give my peace;
those who can read what I have written
with the inner as well as the outer sense.**

Thousands and thousands of years of conditioning have made your mind so distorted that whatever you see is never the truth in its natural form but your own distorted version of it. So whatever conclusions your mind may reach, they will always lead you into illusion. Your life can only be transformed with the help of nature, and not by going against it – because you yourself are a creation of nature, so there is no way you can flow against it.

At whatever point in your nature you find yourself, from that very point you can grow. It is only through the laws of this same nature that you can transcend it as well. It is with the help of the ladder that man goes beyond it. It is through the support of the path that one can reach a destination and abandon the path. But no one can ever arrive at the destination by being against the path.

But logic can often be misleading. If I were to tell you, "This path will take you to your destination, but remember one thing: once you have reached your destination, you must abandon the path, because if you keep on clinging to it you will never be able to enter there" – you can also deduce from this that since the path has to be discarded anyway at the end, why not leave it from the very start? But if you do this you will never be able to reach your destination.

You have to take up the path – and discard it too. In the beginning you have to stay with it, and then ultimately you have to discard it.

But this can be misinterpreted in two ways. Firstly, why adopt a path that you will have to discard in the end? It seems logical to say, "Why take on something that you have to ultimately let go of?" But you will not be able to let go of something that you never took on in the first place. And without letting go of it you will never gain entry to the destination.

A second difficulty is also possible: that you will never discard the path once you have taken it. Now that you have taken it, what is the sense in leaving it? If this is the case, then too, you will never reach. The path can only take you to your destination; it cannot take you inside it. Only when you let go of the path can you gain entry to it.

Stairs can take you up as far as the roof, but not onto it. If you remain standing on the stairs, you will have managed to come as far as the roof, but that doesn't mean that you have arrived on the roof. And if you discard the stairs right from the start, you won't even manage to get near the roof. At some point you will have to abandon the steps, but this doesn't mean that you become their enemy. You need the help of the staircase, but this doesn't mean that you become attached to it. You have to learn to *use* the staircase.

Right now, nature is your stairway, you are standing on it. This sutra applies to nature. The first sutra was about reverence for life, which is reverence for nature. You have to understand this if you want to transcend nature – and it is necessary to transcend nature, because if you remain *in* it you will not attain to supreme bliss. In nature, there is both suffering and happiness.

In nature there is duality; its very existence is based on duality. In nature you can attain to happiness as well as to suffering. And however much happiness you desire, you will also have that much suffering. Your capacity to experience happiness will be exactly the same as your capacity to experience suffering. Nature is duality, and in a state of duality the sides are always equally balanced, always even. If this were not so, nature would be perverted, everything would go haywire.

So as you are moving more to one side, you are gaining momentum to move to the other side. If you wish your reputation to grow, be aware that your notoriety will also grow. It goes along with it. If you wish for good health, know that sickness too is standing just around the corner. And if you want life, you will also have to accept death. You will always have suffering as well as happiness in nature. Nature is duality.

You have to go beyond, because it is duality that is creating all the problems. You have to attain to that moment when duality vanishes. We call such a moment bliss, we call such a moment peace, we call such a moment *moksha* – when both happiness and suffering disappear. *Moksha* means being beyond duality – when you are not being pressurized from either side, when the opposites are not squeezing you, where neither side is pulling you, when the banks vanish and the river is absorbed into the ocean. That is why we know the banks as friends, because they help us to reach the ocean. But we should not become such friends with them that we remain attached to them and hold back from becoming one with the ocean.

So reverence for nature is reverence for life, and a sensitive use of the laws of life.

A friend came to me. He is young, so naturally he has to be interested in women. But his mind was full of thousands of years of conditioning, and he must have been in the company of holy monks from an early age, because he thought that taking an interest in women was sinful. The more he thought that it was sinful, the more interested he became in them. He even started avoiding women – but the more he tried to run away from them, the more desperate he became about them. He tried to suppress his desire, but it just took on new forms and started troubling him even more. During the day he had thoughts, at night he had dreams – and they were all full of sensuality.

Then he went and consulted some saint, who advised him to see the mother in all women. Now this created a big problem: how to see the mother in all women? And all the time this strongly suppressed sensuality was pushing him from inside. So the saint advised him: "Look! If you can't see the mother in all women, it is better to worship a goddess, to see the mother in a goddess. And slowly slowly as your feelings for the goddess become stronger, you will be able to perceive the goddess in all the women you see."

The intentions of the saint were honorable, he really wanted to help, but without understanding a problem you cannot be of much help. And life is complex: without first understanding the laws of life, even if you do offer help, and with good motives, only bad will come out of it.

You cannot imagine what happened. The outcome of all this was that the man started worshipping a goddess and carrying a picture of her wherever he went. The saint had never even dreamed that such a thing could happen – saints, as you know, are incapable of thinking for themselves! The sad result of all this was that now the young man was sexually attracted to the goddess herself, and at night in his dreams he started having a sexual relationship with her. All this scared the poor fellow out of his wits! When a person who is used to treating sex as a sin suddenly finds himself sexually attracted to a goddess, you can imagine what kind of a hell he must go through. He felt that he had committed the greatest of sins; a sin for which he could never, ever be forgiven. He felt that now there was nothing left for him to do but to die. That poor fellow came and said to me, "Sir, you cannot imagine the terrible sin I have committed. Even when I think of the goddess, I am aroused!"

So I said, "Doesn't the person whom you asked for help have any sense at all? This was bound to happen. You can only transcend sexual desire once you have understood what it is all about. All this talk of accepting all women as your mother is nothing but foolishness. What can change just by accepting that you should focus yourself on the goddess? Only what is inside you can be focused onto the goddess! How can something which is not inside you be projected onto her? The goddess is not the question, the question is you.

"Right now you are tormented by sexual desire. And this sexual desire is so strong that it will be projected – no matter where you go or whom you see. So in trying to escape from a small sin you have ended up committing an even bigger one." The poor fellow had become so helpless and weak because he thought that the goddess would be angry with him. So I told him not to worry about this: that no one would be angry, that the goddess was more intelligent than your so-called saints, that she wouldn't be angry.

But you can well imagine the pain and the anguish that this boy was going through, what kind of a hell he was in. Yet no one would ever see that it was the saint was responsible, that it was he who had landed the boy into this hell. And he *was* responsible. He must have been living in a similar kind of hell himself; otherwise how could he give such advice, so full of foolishness and total ignorance about the whole matter?

Now what could I possibly say to this boy? I would not have asked him to do what he was doing. So I advised him, "Instead of getting involved in all this stupid nonsense, it would be better for you to love a woman. Don't be scared of it, and let your love be natural. All this business about loving the goddess is dangerous, because it is all very unnatural and imaginary. Fall in love with a real woman, and don't be frightened. Fall in love, and then try to understand what love is all about. But first, you must free your love from all these distortions and make it very natural. And then with the help of nature it is possible to go beyond it. Make your love a meditation and purify your love as much as you can. Bring as much meditation into your love as you possibly can, so that you can feel love is something which is not sinful but sacred. Develop such a feeling, and live by it.

"And don't feel guilty, because sensuality too is given to you by existence. That too has given to you by existence. And no saint whatsoever can take it away from you – *not ever*. Make proper use of whatever nature has given you and then try to rise above it. But you will never be able to transcend it if you treat it as some kind of an enemy. Enmity will only bring about this sort of undesirable result. And you cannot imagine the lengths to which enmity can go."

During the Victorian age in England, in their homes people used to cover even the legs of their chairs, because at that time it was felt that naked legs provoked sexual desire! Just imagine – chair legs! And if you went into a house and found that a chair's legs were not covered, you would think that the person was doing something indecent, leaving the legs of the chairs naked like that! Just imagine! Queen Victoria was very strict about such things; it was thought to be something immoral. So in all their homes, people would cover the legs of their chairs with cloth. Now, if you cover up the legs, your mind will be even more filled with sexual thoughts. What type of foolishness is this?

It is not as if all this only happened in Victorian times. Such types of people are present everywhere, in all ages. Even today, there is a society of women in England – and these women have definitely been deprived of love, must never have experienced love in their lives – which proclaims that even animals, when they are taken out onto the road, must be covered with clothes! Dogs, horses, oxen – they must never be seen around naked because if they are, they will create sexual desire!

If, when you see an ox, the idea comes into your mind that it is naked, then your mind is sick. There is some sort of a sickness inside you, you are not healthy. Otherwise this would not occur to you. And if you were really healthy, then even to see a human being naked would not trouble you. But if you are sick, then even an uncovered chair will pose a problem for you. That is just a sign of your sickness.

You can make laws to make sure that animals are covered with clothes, that even the chairs are covered, but the mind which is active in all this is going against nature. And this mind will weave even more webs. This mind is losing courage, it will become a criminal.

There was a time in this country when we made temples such as you see in Khajuraho, Puri, Konark and Bhubaneshwar. They must have been very courageous, magnificent people – fully accepting the ways of nature. Outside the temple walls they carved naked figures; naked men and women making love. Just imagine – carving naked statues of men and women having sexual intercourse, and that too on the temple walls. They must have been very brave people to have done so, splendid people. Such an acceptance of life: that even their temples were within the realms of nature. The outside temple wall was consecrated to nature, and God resided within the inner wall.

The builders of the temples of Khajuraho and Konark believed that as long as the outer walls held a fascination for you, you could not enter the inner sanctum. So first, you should satisfy your curiosity with the outer walls, you should meditate on the naked figures. The day you found that those walls no longer held any fascination for you, the day you could pass by without giving them so much as a glance – as if the figures did not exist at all – you would know that now you had the right to enter the temple, now you could enter. But you would not be able to enter if you tried to avoid the outer walls. Even if you did enter, your mind would still be fixed on the outer walls, your mind would continue to feed on them.

And there is no need to suppress your interest either. The carvings of naked figures making love on the outer walls must have been the work of amazing psychologists; they must have possessed a very deep understanding of life. But later on, a weakness took hold of this country and then a long, impotent era followed. India became a slave, and this took away all our courage. The sad result of all this was the proposal of Mahatma Gandhi and Purshottam Das Tandon to bury all these temples under clay, because they thought it was dangerous for them to be seen.

Those brave people who carved these statues, who fully accepted the ways of nature are one kind. And another kind is these weak people. Covering them up is a sign of weakness. If you want, you can cover up the statues of Khajuraho, you can even destroy them, but how will you destroy man's very nature? You cannot. You can make use of man's nature but you cannot destroy it.

Always remember one law: no energy can ever be destroyed. It is impossible. It can only be transformed. Your nature can transform and become godliness, but it cannot be destroyed.

So always remember this great sutra – to show respect for all that life has given to you, both the outer and the inner. And remember one thing: you can only show respect outwardly when you feel it inside too. You insult something outwardly, because in your heart you don't have respect for it. If you hate something from inside, then if you come across it on the outside you are bound to insult it. And if you have respect for it from within, then you are bound to show it respect on the outside.

You should try to find your own nature. You should search for your inner being, you should try to find your own intrinsic nature.

Remember two words: *nature* and *intrinsic nature*. Nature is a part of the physical reality and intrinsic nature is godliness. Until you have known your nature you will not be able to move into your intrinsic nature. As you go within yourself, first you will come across your nature. If you move even deeper within, you will find your intrinsic nature: the godliness which is beyond nature. But if you become afraid of nature itself, then you will never go within, you will only move on the surface, on the periphery. And if you become afraid of your nature, you will go against it and create a wall around it. That wall is what is called personality.

Now try to understand this sutra, the ninth sutra:

Regard most earnestly your own heart.

Just to think about this creates a difficulty for us, because we are bound to say that yes, of course we respect the wishes of our own hearts. But this is not so. This friend who came to me did not respect his sexual desire; instead he insulted it, he tried very hard to suppress it, he tried to get rid of it. And then that urge took its revenge on him. He tried to seek the help of a goddess to get rid of it, but it assumed the form of the goddess herself. The goddess proved to be weaker, and his sexual desire more powerful. This is the revenge. He did not understand his nature, so he was bound to get into difficulties.

Regard most earnestly your own heart.

Whatever is inside you. And it is your nature that you will encounter first of all. When you close your eyes, what is the first thing you meet? You will encounter the nature of your body, and then the nature of your mind. And when you have gone beyond both of them, you will meet the nature of your soul. These are the three levels.

Your body has its own nature: learn to respect it. But we disrespect even that! Either food fascinates us, or we swing to the other extreme and fasting attracts us. Either we take so much interest in food that it actually becomes the cause of our death.... And this is not showing respect for your body. By overeating, you are simply insulting your body, because you are unnecessarily forcing something into it that the body doesn't need. You are just creating a poison for it.

Doctors say that more people die from over-eating than from under-eating – although it should be otherwise, because there are many hungry people in the world. But the doctors say that very few people die from hunger compared with those who die from over-eating! A hungry person can survive, but an overfed person dies because of the large amount of toxic elements he collects in his body through his habit of over-eating.

So don't ever think that a person who over-eats loves his body. Actually, he is his body's enemy. He is insulting it, he is not respecting the natural signals that his body is giving out. Even when his body tells him to stop eating, he goes on eating. This is one way of destroying the body. And it is this type of person who, sooner or later, will show a great deal of interest in fasting – because it is only natural that someone who has made his body suffer from overeating will one day find his body taking revenge and starting to trouble him. So then he swings to the other extreme and starts fasting. Fasting too is an insult to the body, because when the body is hungry you are not providing it with food. One type of insult is to stuff the body with food when it does not need it, and the other type is not providing food when the body asks for it.

So what does it mean to respect it? To respect the body is to show a regard for it, and to completely fulfill its natural, spontaneous demands whenever they arise – that is, to fulfill them with reverence and respect. Because the body is just like a machine, and it is only with the help of this magnificent machine that you will be able to experience the world, it is only with its help that you will reach to the threshold of the divine. That is why it is necessary for you to respect it.

But we don't bother about it. We don't even bother about the mind. For the mind we create all sorts of trouble. We swing from one extreme to another. Reverence lies in the middle.

That is why Buddha summed up his whole philosophy of life as being the middle way. He said all extremes are an insult to life. Therefore, always remain in the middle, don't ever go to the extreme. Then you will be able to live reverently.

If you show disrespect for the mind and body, you develop a false personality. In the English language there is the word *personality*; it is a very valuable word. In Greece, when plays were performed, the actors had to put on a mask to cover their faces. That mask used to be called a *persona*. And personality has come from that very word *persona*. Personality means the mask you have put on, your acquired personality; not what you actually are, but the face that you put on for others to see.

So if a person goes against his inner nature, he will have to acquire an appropriate mask to suit this opposite nature. He will cover himself up with a shell of personality. This shell will never let him meet with his inner being. It is not nature that is against you, but your personality. And everyone has developed a personality for himself that he keeps on reinforcing.

People come to me and say that they would like to experience their souls – but at the same time they are not ready to drop their personalities even one little bit. They would like to attain their souls without dropping their personalities! This is impossible. First you have to understand this personality; only then will you be able to progress in your search for the soul. Otherwise, you will keep on wandering – because the very thing you are holding onto is the obstacle.

Put it like this: supposing a person wishes to get out of jail, but at the same time he keeps clinging to the prison walls and declares that he will never let go of the walls because he has spent so many days inside them. He is not willing to break his own chains. He says, "These chains are my ornaments, they are very valuable! I will not be able to sleep without them. Without them, sleep will be impossible. Without them, I will feel empty, naked! I cannot leave them. But I want to be free, I want to be liberated!"

Your situation is very similar. The thing you want to save is the wall, and without breaking it you will never be able to enter the soul.

Try to understand:

Regard most earnestly your own heart.

For through your own heart
comes the one light which can illuminate life
and make it clear to your eyes.

Only one thing is more difficult to know –
your own heart.
Not until the bonds of personality be loosed
can that profound mystery of self begin to be seen.

What are the bonds of personality? All of us are born, and with that birth we are given a mandatory society, a family, and we are educated and civilized in a particular way. We form certain concepts: how to live, how to sit, how to stand, what is right and so on. All the concepts are given to us readymade, and then we grow up according to them. And we *have* to grow according to them, because those among us who are grown-up are very powerful. And whatever they teach us, we have to learn, because if we do not learn what they teach us, they won't let us live. We have to bow down to what they believe, because they are powerful and they have all the influence. The society belongs to them, they control almost everything. The state belongs - to them. They will make the small child agree to everything they want.

This small child will grow up with a personality which others have given to him. And because of this personality, sooner or later a dreadful anxiety and anguish will be born in him – because he is phony. Anguish is born out of phoniness.

Bliss can only be born from truth, from that which is your true nature. Then this man will go in search of spirituality, of the divine, of wisdom, of yoga, of meditation. But he does not even know that first he has to get rid of his personality. It is as though a hedge has grown all around your spring, or a big stone is obstructing your fountain. So if you want to attain to the divine, to attain to peace with your personality intact, then you will be in trouble.

And it is a very difficult thing to demolish the personality, because we become greatly attached to it. We even feel that our personality is our very nature, we think it is what we really are. This identification with our personality is what is called ego.

A lot of talk goes on about ego. People often say, "Drop your ego" but you don't even know what ego is. This identification that you form with your personality – that you and your personality are one and the same thing – this is ego. Someone has got hold of a Hindu personality, someone else, a Mohammedan one; someone has a Jaina personality, and someone else, a Christian one. This is what creates the problem. And we are stuck with it, and we feel, "This is what I am."

It is necessary to demolish it. Even if you manage to make just a few holes in it, you will feel a small fresh breeze coming from your true nature. It is not necessary for you to demolish it and go against the society, because were you to demolish it and throw it away completely, you *would* find yourself against the society. It is not necessary to become an enemy of society. It is enough for you to become capable of taking off and putting on this mask as you want.

You must understand what I am saying. It is not that you should throw away all the layers of your personality. If you do, you will get into big trouble, because the people you live amongst have not thrown away their personalities. They will create problems for you, because you will be destroying their system. And they have a vested interest in carrying on with their system – it is very convenient for them.

Dropping your personality means only one thing: you have realized that you are not your personality, and whenever you wish, you can take it off and put it to one side. This much is sufficient. Now, for carrying out your work in society, you can keep it on. But it has become a play for you, you are no more a slave to it. Now, for the sake of society, you can put on the cloak of your personality, but for yourself you can take it off and put it to one side. When you are meditating, you no longer remain a personality, you become only a soul. In this way, the outer world becomes a drama for you and you start acting in it. An intelligent person will inevitably live in the society only as an actor acting, and in no other way. His relationship with society is only that of being an actor in a play.

But if you start being dramatic and unreal with yourself, then the problem arises. You put on a face for others; others like that face, so what is the problem? But when you are all alone by yourself then, at least, you should drop that facade. Because then for whose sake are you wearing that mask? Who are you trying to deceive?

If all this is done with full awareness, then personality is no more a bondage. Personality becomes an efficient thing, a good thing. It acts as a kind of lubricant to smooth out relationships in society, it eases the friction. Unnecessary friction is avoided.

But if you keep it wrapped around you even when you are all alone, then you will be simply destroying yourself. In society, yes, a personality; but with yourself, no personality. And until these shackles of personality are loosened, the mystery of the soul will not start to be revealed, because in this very knot of your personality the secret of your soul lies hidden.

Try to understand what personality is and how it can be loosened. You forget very easily.

A friend of mine is forever smiling, but I know he is an unhappy man. And there is nothing so bad in it because why should you interfere with someone else's sadness? One day he came to stay with me. At around midnight I got up to go to the bathroom. I put on the light and saw that, even in his sleep, his mouth was stretched into a smile. I became a little worried. I know this man is unhappy and that the smile which he has on his face the whole day is forced, because now and then he pours out his heart to me and confesses that he is so unhappy, and that his smile is nothing but a social habit. But even during the night, when he was fast asleep, there was a smile on his face!

When he got up in the morning, I asked him about it. He replied that it has become such a habit that even if he wanted to remove it, for example when he was alone by himself, he couldn't. He said, "It seems as if my jaws have become permanently fixed in this position. I can't relax them."

Just ponder a little over your own face. Just after you have returned from meeting somebody, immediately go and stand in front of the mirror and relax your face. Suddenly you will see two faces: the one you had when you first entered, just as you had come back from your meeting, and the other one – which will be the face you have after relaxing it.

I watch your faces here. When you begin a meditation you have one face. And during the second stage when you become completely mad, then your face undergoes a thousand rapid changes – one face, another face, a third face; you have a long row of faces! I get a glimpse of all those faces of yours that you put on and use for various occasions. And in the fourth stage, when you are standing quietly, then all the faces disappear, then you assume a kind of facelessness. It is as if it is not your face at all; all the lines of worry have disappeared from it Then, your face is perhaps just like it was in childhood; as it was before the society began to distort you; or it may have been like that in your mother's womb, when no one had taught you anything yet. And if you were to enter into it a little more deeply, you would come to that face which is really yours – a face which has not been given to you by others.

In Japan, Zen masters will often tell you to seek out your "original face" the one you had at the time of your birth, or the one that you will have after your death. All the faces in between are borrowed ones. But one has to learn these faces.

You have a small child at home, and some guest comes to your house and you tell the child, "Go and touch his feet." The child does not want to do so at all, but he has to obey your orders.

When I am a guest in some house, the parents will touch my feet, and then they will catch their small children by the scruff of their necks and make them bow down too! The children don't want to; they refuse to move, it doesn't mean anything to them, they want nothing to do with it – but their father is pushing them to.

Soon the child will learn that it is better to bow down and touch someone's feet. And this ritual will become an integral part of his personality. Then, he will touch people's feet as and when the situation demands, but there won't be any spirituality involved in it. His life will be deprived of a very significant phenomenon. He will touch anyone's feet and it will be artificial, formal. And that supreme experience of life that comes from touching someone's feet will not be available to him. Now, touching someone's feet will be simply a part of a ritual: he has learned that it is more convenient to do so. Being stubborn won't do: "My father forces it on me anyway. It is better to please him, otherwise he is capable of making my life a hell in a thousand and one ways" – and he does. An intelligent child will soon find out that the most sensible thing to do is to touch a person's feet. He will understand.

But this bowing down will be a purely mechanical affair. And the danger is that one day, if he *does* come across someone whose feet he would really like to touch – even then, it will be just a mechanical act, because the truth of it is now so deeply buried, and the weight of his personality is so heavy.

Parents keep on telling their children, "Look, she is your mother. You must love her." Is this something you can insist on to someone? Or that this person is your father, and so you should love him? What does all this mean? It simply means that the parent and the child do not get along well, and that is why the child is being forced to love. The mother says, "I am your mother – you must love me." Is this something she should need to say? No, the mother should be a mother and the love should happen by itself. And if it is not happening, then the fault is the mother's. What mistake can a small child make? As yet, the child knows nothing.

But a mother who has to remind her son that she is his mother so he should love her, is not really a mother, even though she may have given birth to him. She may have given birth, but motherhood is a totally different matter. Every woman does not automatically attain to motherhood. Yes, any woman can give birth to a child, but to be a mother is very difficult, because being a mother is one long process of loving.

She tells her son, "You must love me – I am your mother." Slowly slowly the son will learn to fake love. What else can he do? He has to get milk from this mother, he has to get money from her: he is totally dependent upon her, completely helpless. The mother is his sole help, security and protection. So a bargain is struck: the son will learn to fake love. He will smile when he sees his mother – even though he may not feel like smiling. He will learn to compliment his mother. He will remark, "My mother is the loveliest mother in the world" and so on. And all this will make the mother very happy. And the child is learning how to deceive, the son is learning how to lie, and such a supreme phenomenon as love is being made false. And the longer the son stays with his mother, the more faked and phony that love will become. It will now become a part of his personality.

And then later on when he falls in love with some woman, that love will not come from within, will not be intimate.

He will still be telling lies. In the same way he will tell the woman, "You are the prettiest woman in the world." He will try to please her by making declarations of love. He will try to show her how much in love with her he is. Ten times a day he will make assertions of love. But all this will be false.

Think about this sometimes. When you tell your wife, "I love you so much," do you really feel some sort of love inside? Very often it is said out of fear. You often say it because it is better to go on repeating it many times: it sticks in the memory. Your wife is reassured, you are also reassured. In the same way, the wife keeps on repeating it. That too is a sham. Your personalities are talking to each other, but your inner beings are not coming together. This type of falseness does not bring any bliss, it doesn't bring any contentment. It is simply not possible to derive contentment from something that is bogus. Have you ever seen a false seed sprouting? Have you ever heard a song being born from an artificial throat? Has anybody ever been able to see something beautiful through artificial eyes? False means something that does not exist. Nothing can be born out of it. False means something that appears to be, but that doesn't actually exist. Nothing can come from it. Then life becomes an empty affair. Try to understand this personality. Whatever inside you is false and phony, recognize it.

I am not asking you to stop telling lies because it harms the other person; of course that happens. I ask you not to tell lies because, first and foremost, it is you who will be harmed by doing so. You are becoming a false entity, a deception. To say "becoming" is not correct. You have already become so. You have become skilled at it! You have become so clever at playing this game that it never even occurs to you what you are actually up to.

I know people who tell lies. I don't really blame them, because by this time they are not doing it consciously. By now, lies come out of them automatically. And sometimes they tell lies for no rhyme or reason whatsoever; lies that won't be of any help to them, which they can't profit by. And it is not as if they lie knowingly – lies have become so deeply ingrained in them that now they cannot help telling them. As soon as they speak...and no matter what they may be thinking at the time, once it passes through their phony structure, it comes out as a lie. Even if they want to speak the truth, they cannot without some lies being added to it. Try to recognize this fake structure of yours. Become aware of it. And try to get rid of it.

Let me tell you how these lies become deeply ingrained in us. A friend came to see me. He said, "You tell us to go completely mad in the second stage of Dynamic Meditation, so I dance, jump, shriek, weep and so on, but it has just occurred to me today that all I am doing is nothing but pretending. I am not really crying, I am not really dancing or shouting or jumping. In fact, all I am doing is utterly false." It took this fellow three days to realize it! This is what I mean when I say how lies become so deeply ingrained in us. For three days he was dancing and jumping around. After three days it struck him that whatever he was doing was utterly false. But still he realized in time – his personality structure has not as yet become so solid. It should take you only a second to realize, "What is all this I am doing?"

And no matter what you do, no matter how much you may jump and dance, if it is false it will be just a physical exercise. Of course you will feel good after doing it, just as you feel good after doing some exercise. But it will not be meditation. Meditation only happens after the authentic in you starts to emerge.

But there is a difficulty. From our very childhood we are told, "Don't cry." Especially men have been told never to cry under any circumstances. So they have simply forgotten the art of crying. They have been made to understand that to cry is to be a weakling, that only women cry – as if crying is only the prerogative of women, as if men do not have the right to cry! If this were true, then why has God made tears? Why has he made tear glands behind the eyes of men? And if men have been given them as well, then what is their purpose? But no, each boy is told that he is doing a girlish thing – as if he were committing some sin. And the funny thing about all this is that even women and mothers will say, "Stop behaving like a woman!" – as if this is something bad which only women can do. Do women have the sole copyright on bad behavior?

Society's whole emphasis is on making men hard. They have to be made hard so that they can be cruel, so that they are able to fight, kill and beat others. If a man cries, if he is mellow and gentle, he will not be able to do all these things. Then, if he is sent to fight in a war with a gun in his hand, he will start crying and exclaim, "How can I kill a human being? It is not right to kill." So a man must be made hard, as hard as a stone. His soul must be destroyed completely. That is why he is brainwashed in this way: his ego is persuaded by calling on his manhood. He is told that he is a man, that he should not cry, that weeping is for girls.

And whenever men come across tough women, they praise them to the skies! They say, "Look, what a tough woman! She is like the Queen of Jhansi!" – as if being hard is something to be proud of. A woman who has gone wrong – and they praise her to the skies! But if by some chance a man proves to be gentle, they ridicule him by calling him womanish.

Men have been brainwashed, prepared for war. That is why you are not able to weep. Your tears have dried up. For years together you have not wept, your tear glands have become lifeless. Even if you scream and cry out, tears do not come! But I would like your tear glands to be reactivated; you *should* be able to cry. Once those blocked tears find their way out, they will wash away those three decades of personality that society has imposed upon you, and you will return to those moments of your childhood of thirty, forty years ago when you were a small child, when you were able to weep and nobody taunted you for behaving like a girl. You will return to those moments. If your tears are able to flow, if real tears flow, tears that come from within, you will find that your personality has fallen away. You will find that you have become very light, you will find an opening has been created.

That's why I lay so much emphasis on crying, shouting, laughing – because everything has been taken away from you. You cannot even laugh wholeheartedly, because people say that to laugh so loudly is very impolite. See how badly they have damaged man? – to laugh joyously is considered to be bad manners. If four people are seen laughing happily together, people will give them such looks – as if to say that they are country bumpkins! Not educated – country bumpkins! Yes, you can smile politely, but make sure you don't make any noise. It is like telling a waterfall to move quietly and stop its uproar, like telling the winds that they should blow in such a way that they do not make any sound amongst the leaves.

When you laugh exuberantly you don't realize how much all the rubbish accumulated inside you is also being swept away with your laughter. But since you cannot even laugh properly that rubbish remains stuck inside. Right now you are not being allowed to express anything wholeheartedly. And the reason is very simple: if you were to express yourself wholeheartedly then the society would not be able to make you its servant.

If your nature is totally suppressed, you can be easily made a slave. But if, on the other hand, you give expression to your nature in all its dimensions, you will be so fresh and alive that no power on this earth can make you its slave. And society wants you to be a slave and not a master. Yes, a slave! You should dance to its tune, do exactly as you are told. If you are asked to sit down, then you should sit; if you are asked to stand, then you must stand. But above all, you should never be allowed to be free, to do as you please – because a free person will become a rebel. That's why society takes all your freedom away from you and puts a shield around you. Then, once you are stuck behind that shield, even if you want to laugh or cry, you cannot, because it won't move even an inch to give you enough space to do so.

Once a woman was brought to me. Her husband had died, and she had been having fits of hysteria for the last three months, fainting fits. After seeing her, I asked whether she had wept or not when her husband died. The people who had brought her to me praised her highly and said, "Sir, she is a very brave woman, a very intelligent woman, a university professor. She did not cry at all."

I replied, "These hysterical fits are a result of this. And you foolish people must have praised her for putting on such a brave face, saying, 'Look how brave she is, what a strong heart she has,' and so on."

Can a heart ever be strong? The beauty of the heart, its strength, lies in its very softness. It is as delicate as a flower. What do you mean by a strong heart? Is it some sort of a flower that is made out of stone?

They all showered praises on her, and turned her into a hysteric. And nobody ever thinks about who will have to face the consequences of these foolish acts. The woman kept fainting, and she could not cry.

I told her, "Don't get taken in by what these foolish people are saying. Please cry if you feel like it. Being a professor does not mean that you are no longer a woman."

But she was a great professor, head of a department. How could she cry? She was intelligent. Is there any conflict between intelligence and crying? An intelligent person will cry from deep within the heart – that's the only difference.

She replied, "What are you saying? – that I should have wept?"

I said, "Yes, you should have wept. The person you loved, the person who gave you happiness is gone. Do you think someone else should receive this sorrow? You did not give your happiness to someone else; who do you think should receive your sorrow? This world is a duality; you received happiness and now you will have to receive sorrow. Only then will both sides be balanced, only then will there be an equilibrium. So cry your heart out, roll on the ground, lament!"

She said, "What are you saying?"

I replied, "So then this hysteria will continue." This hysteria was an overflow, caused by what had been forcibly suppressed. "The sorrow which is not being allowed to flow out of you is strangling your nervous system, is taking hold of your nervous system. You are in exactly the same state as a car would be if its accelerator and brakes were put on at the same time. The condition that car would be in is called hysteria." And this woman's heart needed to cry.

I asked her, "Were you happy with your husband?"

She said, "Yes, I was very happy with him, I was very happy indeed."

"In that case," I replied, "you will have to suffer in equal proportion. Your heart is crying out to go with the pain but your professorship, your knowledgeability; this herd of fools surrounding you, their praise that you are such a great person, that this is the behavior worthy of you – all this is just putting the brakes on it. You are pressing on the accelerator and the brakes at the same time! Whenever the accelerator and the brakes are pushed at the same time in someone, hysteria is born. Either you just put on the brakes, and don't touch the accelerator. But that would only be possible if you had never found any happiness with your husband. You found happiness, so you will have to face the other side too."

The woman began to weep right then in front of me. I told her to remain sitting there for half an hour, and to cry her heart out. After half an hour she said, "Now I know that I won't have fits of hysteria."

And I told her, "Don't listen to anyone. It will take about four to six months, but go through your suffering completely. Suffering too has its value. It is necessary; it is also a part of the education of life."

The hysteria did not happen again. It is now almost eight months and she has not had a fit. But as for those so-called wise ones…it is difficult to find such a foolish lot of people anywhere!

First, recognize your personality, and then break it.

My meditation technique is a system to break down your personality. It is not meditation but the removal of your personality! And once it is removed, meditation is a very natural thing. Once the rock is removed, you don't have to do anything to make the spring flow. The spring flows by itself; it is only a question of removing the stone.

Meditation is your nature. If the rock of your personality is not there, it will come automatically. But at least you should let something there be natural. Whether it is tears, or laughter, or dancing – at least let something natural happen. Then what is supremely natural is also bound to happen.

Not till you stand aside from it,
will it in any way reveal itself to your understanding.

Until then, that which is your nature will not be revealed.

Then, and not till then, can you grasp and guide it.
Then, and not till then, can you use all its powers,
and devote them to a worthy service.

This has to be understood: that people start offering their services to others without first having any sort of understanding about themselves. Our country has many social workers like this – in fact far too many for our needs. People who have no knowledge about themselves, people who do not have even the smallest spark of self-realization, even these people are placing themselves at the service of others. And this type of service can only give bad results. Nobody can inflict damage like these so-called servants can, because whatever they do is supposedly done for your benefit – so it is difficult to avoid them.

You can avoid a murderer, but how can you escape from someone who wants to do you some good deed ? A killer goes straight for your neck, so immediately you are careful, but a servant starts by first massaging your feet. This makes you relax, and say, "Well done, carry on with the good work!" But be careful – because he will slowly work his way up from your feet to your neck. After all, progress has to be made! Have no doubt, he will certainly reach your neck! He may take a little time to cover the distance between your feet and your neck, but once he has reached your neck, you can't say, "Don't massage my neck" – because all this time you have been thinking that the poor fellow is only serving you. Keep in mind that all such servants ultimately grab you by the neck.

A hoard of such servants gathered around Gandhi, and now they have taken hold of this country by the neck. Now they are all occupying high offices and the whole country is at their mercy. Originally, their mission was to serve others, but see how they are managing to be served themselves now – and greatly served! And those who could not manage this are miserable. Poor fellows; they are lamenting, they are saying, "We gave our whole lives in the service of this country, and what have we got in return? If you can do nothing else for us, then at least give us a bronze medallion to certify that we served! If nothing else, at least give us a pension because we served! Once in a while honor us at some function or other because we served!" And what service did they give? If you come to understand these servants you will be very surprised.

These servants sometimes visit me. One of them will proclaim that he has been serving the tribal children, looking after their education for almost thirty years. Just recently, a woman came to me and said that she has sacrificed thirty years, her whole life, in the service of the tribal people.

After listening to her I said, "It is all very well and good that you have spent thirty years serving them, it is a very fine thing that you have sacrificed your entire life; but these children you have spent your entire life trying to educate, tell me, have they profited from your education or were they harmed by it? The real test is, did they become more peaceful or not, did they become happier or not, did their joy increase or decrease?"

She became a little restless when I said to her, "At the most, what you will achieve by teaching tribal children to read and write is to make them like our children. But it is not as if our children were living in some sort of paradise. As it is, we are fed up with the way our young people are behaving in the universities. They are burning the buildings, beating up the principals, stoning the vice-chancellors, going around with naked knives in their hands – and all this because of the education we have given them! You say you are taking a lot of trouble with the tribal children, you say that you have devoted your entire life to them. And if you succeed in your work, then these very children will do exactly the same thing. What else can they do? What benefit are they deriving from your service?"

But she is not bothered about any benefit; she is busy, and that's enough! And to keep yourself busy is a trick to avoid yourself. She feels that she is doing something noble, and this does not give her a chance to look inside herself. Actually, she is a very agitated woman, very tense, very suppressed; all the energies within her have become diseases. But somehow or other she has managed to divert her attention from all this by keeping herself immersed in the service of others. And she is so occupied in helping others that it never even crosses her mind that she too may have a problem.

Often people become involved in others' problems just in order to forget their own. And if by chance you suggest they take a few days off from their busy schedules of service – because even in those few days they will be able to see their own problems.

Man is very cunning: he knows many ways to escape. He will start showing interest in others so that he does not have to think about himself. He will always keep himself busy doing something or other. Opening a school here, making a center for personal growth and social advancement there, visiting Delhi... and so on. This woman was busy in exactly the same way: busy collecting funds, busy purchasing a bus – so busy. What time is left?

I asked her, "Are you at peace?"

She replied, "No, I am not. Please tell me some way to become peaceful." I told her to come to the camp at Mount Abu. She replied that this would be very difficult because she had to be in Delhi at that time. And why did she have to go to Delhi? She had to open a hospital in the tribal area!

So I told her, "First consider whether people are healthier where there are hospitals, or whether they are healthier where the tribal people live, where there are no hospitals. First, worry about this – because with hospitals come diseases as well as treatment. Tribal people are much more healthy."

But all she is bothered about is opening a hospital. She replied, "All you are saying is right, but still it is not right to be without a hospital. A hospital is necessary, progress has to be made." She acknowledges that tribal people are healthier, but she still maintains that a hospital is necessary. What is the need for a hospital?

I said to her, "The right way to give help would be to get rid of the hospitals, wherever they are, and convert people to the aboriginal way of life instead – that is, if you are *really* interested in making people healthy. But if your motive is something else, then that is a different matter altogether. As far as health is concerned, the aboriginals are more healthy."

She replied, "What you say is correct, but right now I have to go to Delhi. Perhaps I can join another camp!"

She is not at all interested in meditation or peace. This business of serving the aboriginals is a trick of hers to get rid of her worry.

In the same way, someone is letting off steam in his shop. He is busy making money; he has no interest in anything else. Someone else is caught up in politics; he is worrying about winning an election, becoming a minister. This person is not at all concerned with whether there is such a thing as a soul or not. Someone else is busy serving people; he too is not at all concerned with the soul.

But remember one thing: if a person starts serving others without first knowing about himself, he will only cause harm to them. How can a person who as yet knows nothing about himself know what is good for another person? To become a servant of the people before you have explored your own inner self can only mean one thing – that you will do some mischief or other. In this world, we are less harassed by bad people than by the so-called do-gooders. They present their good intentions in such a way that you simply have to go along with them. Even if they are taking you to hell, you will have to go along with them, because their intentions always seem to be so honorable. They are going to so much trouble on your behalf that you simply cannot refuse them and ask them why they are dragging you into hell! To refuse would appear to be very impolite because, after all, the poor fellows are taking so much trouble.

There is an old Arabic saying: The road to hell is filled with good intentions. Full of good intentions!

Only the person who has gone deeply into meditation has a right to serve others. And before that, you don't have any right to do so at all. How can you give bliss to others when you yourself do not have it? You can only give suffering, no matter what name you call it by. But yes, if there is bliss within you, then that bliss can be made to flow in others too.

Then, and not till then, can you grasp and guide it.
Then, and not till then, can you use all its powers,
and devote them to a worthy service.

It is impossible to help others
till you have obtained some certainty of your own.

How will you help? How can you help with something you know nothing about? But you don't even consider whether you know anything about it or not. If someone comes to you for advice, do you ever say, "I'm sorry, I won't be able to advise you because I don't know anything about this." No, you are so generous in giving advice that it doesn't matter who the person is – as long as it is somebody! And forget about someone coming to you, even if you *hear* of someone who is in need of advice, you at once run to his house to offer yours. Even if that person tries to avoid you, you still give it anyway.

I notice that even in this camp, people are going to each other's rooms to counsel and advise, to impart knowledge. They are waking each other up, they are trying to make one another peaceful! They can't sit down quietly, but they won't let anyone else sit in peace! Who wants your advice? Do you have any advice to offer?

But they get a great thrill from doing so. It's great fun to be a guru, and no one is interested in becoming a disciple. It's great fun to be a guru, because it gives a big boost to your ego. If you were to go and see the state of these so-called advisers, these people who are your advisers right now...

But if something were to happen to them tomorrow, then you would find yourself advising these very same people; they themselves would be in need of your advice, and they would be in the same helpless state that you are right now. If by chance they see you becoming angry, they will advise you how to get rid of your anger – but just try abusing them a little and then see what happens! In one second they will have forgotten about the advice they were giving you. Then you will have to counsel them.

Why? Why are people so eager to advise others? – because they want the pleasure of being wise without actually becoming wise. If you go to a truly wise person to ask for his advice, the chances are that ninety-nine times out of a hundred he will tell you, "I'm sorry, I don't know anything about this subject at all." The one time he may know something about it, he will politely put forward his suggestion but at the same time he will also make it quite clear to you that though it may have been useful for him, that does not necessarily mean that it will be useful for you too. He will say, "All men are different from each other, and everyone's circumstances are also different. That's why I can only say this much: that this advice was very helpful to me, it was of great use to me. But the same thing can also harm you, so please do think it over. There is no infallible law."

But you even advice to the other that has proved to have been of no use to you...

I was reading a letter a psychologist's wife had sent me. She informed me that her husband is a marriage counselor: he straightens out the fights and quarrels between married couples. "But," she says, "he has no solution for our own fights and quarrels. He sorts out the differences between hundreds of married couples. Fighting couples come to him with their problems. He listens to them and sorts out all their arguments. He always manages to find some way of bringing them together again. God knows how many couples he has saved from divorce. But *we* will definitely divorce – that much is certain!"

So she asked me, "What is the problem? After all, I know for a fact that my husband is very intelligent, because I myself have seen him bring many wayward couples back onto the right path. But when it comes to dealing with his own problems, his advice just doesn't seem to work."

It may sometimes happen that the advice you give others proves to be helpful. The reason for this is that while giving the advice, you distance yourself from the person and adopt an impartial attitude. But when it comes to yourself, you are not able to maintain a distance, you are not able to see the matter in an impartial light – so you are bound to take sides.

So I had a letter written to the psychologist's wife and I told her, "Don't worry. Take your problem to some other marriage counselor, and you will see that he will definitely find some way to sort out your problems. In this blind world, blind people are also showing the way. Anything goes! The other counselor will definitely find a way out. But if you insist on taking advice only from your husband it will be very difficult, because your husband will not be able to advise you. Your husband cannot give you impartial advice because he himself is a party in this dispute. So both of you should go to someone else."

This type of wisdom, which is so useful in helping each other, is only skin-deep. This wisdom is not born from deep experience. It is just bookish, only superficial. You have to get away from it.

Until you have had some glimpse of the soul, it is essential that you avoid giving any sort of advice about God, the soul and so on – because by giving such advice you will only be creating problems for others. If you cannot bring bliss into the life of another person, then the least you can do for that person is not to create any trouble.

When you have learned the first twenty-one rules
and have entered the hall of learning
with your powers developed and senses unchained,
then you will find there is a fount within you
from which speech will arise.

These notes are written only for those
to whom I give my peace;
those who can read what I have written
with the inner as well as the outer sense.

15

INQUIRE OF THE HOLY ONES

Having obtained the use of the inner senses,
having conquered the desires of the outer senses,
having conquered the desires of the individual soul,
and having obtained knowledge,
prepare now, O disciple,
to enter upon the way in reality.
The path is found; make yourself ready to tread it.

10. Inquire of the earth, the air and the water of the secrets they hold for you.

The development of your inner senses
will enable you to do this.

11. Inquire of the holy ones of the earth of the secrets they hold for you.

The conquering of the desires of the outer senses
will give you the right to this.

Before we go into the sutras, a few questions asked by some friends. All the questions relate to being naked during the morning meditation.

One friend has asked, "Why has nudity been banned? Does it have no usefulness?"

No, nudity has much usefulness, because nudity is not just nudity. Your culture, your education, your conditioning – all of them are associated with your clothes. And the moment you put your clothes aside, along with them it is also possible to put aside all those things which are covering you like clothes. The very fear of being seen going around naked is the fear of being seen as one really is. The outer form of nakedness is only the first step. Actually, the real nakedness has to happen within – showing yourself exactly as you are, not wearing any mask, not putting on any face, not being covered by anything that is false.

But because man lives basically in the outer world, even physical nudity will help him towards the inner nakedness. And to be seen going around naked also creates fear, because clothes mold you into a shape and form that your body does not really possess. Clothes cover you up, clothes hide you. By wearing clothes, you are saved from the eyes of others.

Standing naked means that you reveal yourself just as you are; ugly or beautiful, good or bad. You don't hide anything at all. This is symbolic. And in the morning meditation, during the second stage when I ask you to express whatsoever there may be inside you, then it is natural that the idea of taking off your clothes comes into your minds. And it becomes easy for whoever takes off his clothes to express his madness during the second stage – because whoever is ready to be seen naked will not worry about others' opinions of him. Now he is able to shriek, to cry out loud, to dance. By shedding his clothes it is as if he has also dropped worrying about what others think of him. Someone who is afraid of what other people may say about him will never be able to take off his clothes.

It is helpful if a person can remove his clothes before entering the morning meditation. But some meditators are not able to summon up that much courage, so if during the second stage of the meditation they feel the need to take off their clothes, they can do so. It is still helpful.

It would not be so helpful if clothes were just clothes, but much more is associated with them. When you were born you were naked, and now whenever you stand naked, you return to your childhood. Clothes were imposed on you from the day you became aware of your body. From that day, you felt that there was something sinful about the body, that some parts of the body should be hidden, clothed; that there was something bad about the body. A small child is scolded by his parents if he ventures outside naked, so clothes have become associated with a condemnation towards the body: there is something bad about the body, particularly about the genitals, so they should be hidden.

As well as all this, your body has become divided into two parts. The lower part of your body is considered to be bad, and the upper part, good. This division of the body has also divided your consciousness into two parts. So generally people only identify themselves with the head, and treat the rest of the body as if it does not belong to them!

At the most, they will condescend to include the top part, but the lower part they will treat as some kind of a necessary evil.

Having this attitude breaks your life energy into pieces. In a child, this energy is integrated, it forms a circle. But this circle is not present in you. So the moment you summon enough courage to shed your clothes, from that moment onwards, all the bad feelings you may have been harboring regarding your body – that is, from the first day you were forcibly made to clothe yourself to the present day – all this condemnation about your body falls away.

Because you are always wearing so many clothes it never even occurs to you that slowly slowly, you have even forgotten what your body is like without them. When we are clothed, we are in a kind of prison, and the minute we remove our clothes we become free. We become free like the birds and the animals. And that freedom can be put to use.

So being naked is of use, but there are some restraints regarding this camp. And the restraints are such that if nudity had been allowed, then it would not have been possible to have had the camp. For the camp to happen, nudity had to be done away with. And I thought it right to choose the lesser evil.

Only two days before the camp began, the government of Rajasthan informed us that it could not lease us any of its grounds, buildings or institutions. And it was difficult to make some kind of alternative arrangement in just two days. Seekers from all over the world had already arrived. Seekers from within India were on their way, but those from outside India had already arrived. So there was no other way. And the government has at least this much right: that it can refuse permission to use its premises to ensure that there is no nudity on its grounds. And there is nothing wrong in its exercising this right. After all, the property belongs to them; we don't own any property here. So these arrangements have been made with this hotel, the Palace Hotel, and its managers understandably have their limitations. They too don't have the courage to allow people to go naked, because for them it means that their business will be at stake.

So these are the reasons why banning nudity has been necessary during the morning meditation. But don't take this to mean that we have altered our meditation technique in any way. And also don't take this to mean that we have bowed to government pressure in any way. It is nothing of the sort. There is no question of bowing down, nor is there any question of changing the technique. In fact, in a way the government has provided us with a reason – and this will only benefit us – that we should soon be able to have some place of our own where nobody will be able to impose any restrictions on us.

The government has its own restraints: it has to face its own pressures: from the society, from the public, from their conditionings. If we had a private place of our own, then nobody could pressurize us. That would be our own private setup, and within our own compound anyone could be naked if he wished – it would not be a public place. But this hotel is a public place; other people can also come here, and where other people are also allowed to come, then you have to think about them too.

Any process which helps to bring about a transformation in one's life generally goes against the crowd. It is not simply a question of nudity. Nudity is only symbolic. All that we are doing will certainly go against the ideas of the crowd, because the mob lives like a blind man, without any thought or evaluation. The mob follows the path of tradition very strictly. Whatever tradition says is correct, it just follows that – no matter how much suffering it may have to go through because of doing so. It never even occurs to the crowd that its concepts could be causing its sufferings. But those people who want to bring about a revolution in their lives will naturally have to rise above the concepts of the crowd.

This is the actual meaning of *sannyas*. Leaving society is not the meaning of sannyas, because it is not possible to leave society. Sannyas means to rise above the concepts of the crowd. If whatever the society thinks to be correct is also proved by your own experience, only then agree with it. Otherwise, look for something else.

Even so, an intelligent person should always remember that although he himself can drop the concepts and ideas of those among whom he lives, it is not right to demolish them. One can break them for oneself, one can be free of them – that is one's personal freedom – but I will not ask you to go and stand naked on the road, because the road does not belong to you. It is not right to do anything which hurts and causes trouble to those who live around there. But at the same time I also want to say to those people, and make it very clear to them, that they too have no right to interfere and create any problems if someone wants to be naked in a lonely, desolate place within his own setup. It is necessary that the individual's freedom is respected.

At the same time, freedom of the individual does not mean licentiousness. Even if I have said that you can shed your clothes during the morning meditation, it does not mean that I have given you license to roam around naked wherever you feel to. And if you wish to become naked everywhere it simply means that you are interested in nakedness and not in meditation. This too is a sickness – it has just become a contrary sickness. Someone is mad about clothes, and you have become mad about nakedness. What is the difference? Stupidity has simply been reversed, as if it has made a headstand. There are some who insists on never taking off their clothes – and they are also mad.

I have read about a Christian nun who used to wear clothes even while she was taking a shower in her own bathroom! Her friends told her, "You are mad! There is nobody in the bathroom except you, so why do you wear your clothes while having a shower? Then there is no fun in having a shower!"

The nun replied, "Ever since I have read that God is everywhere, I cannot bring myself to take off my clothes, even in the bathroom."

This is a sort of madness. And if God can see everywhere, then how come he can't see inside your clothes? How can the clothes be any hindrance to him? When a wall is not creating any problem for him, how can the clothes? And is God some kind of Peeping Tom who has nothing better to do than peep into bathrooms? If this is so, then your God is perverted. If man is perverted, then he is bound to make his God perverted too. Your perversions are bound to dominate your deities, because you create the concepts about them.

If horses were to create their God, that God wouldn't have a human face, he would have the face of a horse. When Africans make their God they color him black. Their God will have the lips of an African, his hair will be that of an African. When the Chinese make their God, they take away the bones from his cheeks, they make his nose flat. We make our God in our own image. Whatever our insanities are, we also impose them on our God. Now take the case of people who have to peep into other people's bathrooms. This is a perversion of man. So then they make a God who is peeping everywhere!

So if a fascination for nudity takes a hold of you, that too is a perversion, a sickness. Remember, your being naked is one thing, but showing off your nakedness to other people – that is another thing. There is a difference between the two. Your being naked can be a natural thing, but if your interest in nudity lies in parading it in front of others, then in psychology such a thing is called exhibitionism. An exhibitionist is a pervert.

Try to understand this. Psychology talks of two types of sickness connected with this. One sickness it calls voyeurism – that is when you get a thrill out of seeing other people naked. The other it calls exhibitionism, when you get a thrill from other people seeing you naked. Both are sicknesses, neither one is natural. Men are often voyeurs. The sickness which generally afflicts men is to peep and see women naked. Women are generally exhibitionists. Their sickness is that they want other people to peep at them when they are naked. That's why women think of all those ways and means to make people look at them. They will put on such clothes and such jewelry that others cannot help looking at them. And men find ways in which they can peep. But both are sicknesses.

And you will be surprised to know that both these sicknesses have been born because of clothes. If you ever happen to visit a tribal society where both men and women usually go naked, you will not find either a voyeur or an exhibitionist. There, no one is bothered about seeing anything, because what is there left to see? What is there to be curious about? Everybody is naked; what is there to see? Your curiosity is only aroused when something is being hidden. When everything is out in the open, what is there to see? So in a tribal society, where both men and women are naked, no one is curious to see anything, no one is eager to show off anything. This sickness of peeping and exhibiting happens because of clothes. And you just cannot imagine the lengths to which these perversions can go.

So many pictures, so many stories, so many films and magazines are printed and sold only because they contain photos of naked people. Governments the whole world over are trying to ban them, but it cannot be stopped. There are underground presses; there is a big racket involving millions of rupees which goes on producing huge amounts of such literature, and all this is sold underground. No power on this earth is able to prevent it. Instead, the more they try to ban such items, the more such things are sold on the black market. But it is very surprising: why is man interested in seeing someone naked?

You will be amazed to know that you only become interested in seeing those parts which are covered up. You are not interested in those parts which are uncovered. You may perhaps think that the people who invented clothes are against sexuality and that's why they invented them – but in that you would be very much mistaken. No, the people who invented clothes created a great device for making man more sexual. A lot of interest has been generated, in fact sick interest, in those parts of the body which have been covered. There is no reason for this interest, because the body is a natural phenomenon. But by constantly hiding them, by continuously forbidding them, we have generated a lot of interest in them. Now the whole world has become obsessed with such things.

So keep both things in mind. An intelligent person will not be curious to see anyone naked, nor will he be interested in others seeing him naked. Both are sicknesses.

And both of these sicknesses should be discarded along with your clothes. Only then will spirituality be a part of your nudity. Only then will your nudity not be indecent.

But this will be so only as far as you are concerned. Society will not necessarily agree, because society is full of those same, old, perverted attitudes. The newspapers will not agree. The person who is publishing those newspapers and the journalists; they all have the same, old, perverted ideas. Their problem is the same, their difficulty is the same. The governments will also not agree. Because if those who are occupying high positions in the government had any idea of spirituality they would not be where they are now, they would be somewhere else. So it is not a question of any of these people agreeing. And there is no need to persuade them to agree, there is no point in trying to do so. There is no need even to pay any attention to what they are doing. But one thing is certain: they can create obstacles and hindrances for us, but they can only do this if we hold onto nudity obsessively. Otherwise they cannot create problems. This matter concerns our personal spiritual practice, and it is in a private place.

I don't even agree that a Jaina *muni* should go about on the road naked. Because the road not only belongs to the traveler, but also to the people who live around there. It also belongs to those people who can see what is happening on the road. And if they don't want to see something, then no one has the right to invade their vision. It is not a question of whether they are right or wrong. My eyes belong to me, and if I don't want to see you naked, then you have no business standing naked in front of me. But if you persist in standing there, it only means that you are less interested in nudity and more interested in someone seeing you naked. In that case, the whole thing becomes meaningless. You are letting go of one sickness only to catch hold of another – in other words avoiding the well only to fall into a deeper ditch.

I am not some kind of a nudity propagandist. Nakedness can be of use in meditation, and it has my support. But it is always necessary to consider the society. Not out of any fear of it – there is no question of any fear. But it is as if a public bus is blowing its horn at you, and you remain standing in front of it saying, "Do you think I am afraid of you and will move aside?" If this is the case, you are mad! If a bus is approaching, blowing its horn, and if someone moves out of the way, it is not out of some cowardice. If someone moves out of the way, will you call him a coward, and ask him, "Why did you move away when the bus was approaching? You should have remained standing there while the driver was blowing his horn." Only someone who is mad will keep standing there!

In life there is no reason to bow down to something unnecessarily, but at the same time there is also no reason to be unnecessarily stubborn about anything either. It is necessary to find a middle way.

So there was only one option left if we were to hold the camp here, and that was to put a stop to nudity – otherwise the camp would not have been possible. Out of the two options, I found it more appropriate to put a ban on nudity. Of course this will create some hindrances, but it won't be as harmful as having no camp at all. I don't behave like a blind man in any matter, and I have no madness of any kind regarding anything. Whatever is appropriate, whatever is simple, and in whatever way most people can benefit, it is always right to consider just that.

Having obtained the use of the inner senses,
having conquered the desires of the outer senses,
having conquered the desires of the individual soul,
and having obtained knowledge,
prepare now, O disciple,
to enter upon the way in reality.
The path is found; make yourself ready to tread it.

The tenth sutra:

Inquire of the earth, the air and the water
of the secrets they hold for you.

The development of your inner senses
will enable you to do this.

The tenth sutra deserves great attention. Only after a long journey, only after having understood and lived the sutras that we have been discussing so far, does it become possible to experiment with the tenth sutra – not before that. Because before that it will sound very strange; this sutra will seem very puzzling. If someone tried very hard to understand it, he might think it were some sort of poetry – a beautiful metaphor. But this is not some kind of poetry, it is not a metaphor. It is a scientific fact. But this scientific fact can only be understood when you have experimented with all of the earlier sutras.

Inquire of the earth, the air and the water of the secrets they hold for you.

This is one of the fundamental tenets of the esoteric wisdom of spirituality. Let us try to understand it. In this world, whatever suprememost proclamation of truth takes place, it is of course compiled in the form of scriptures, but apart from that, it is also compiled within existence itself. A mistake can be made in the scriptures because, after all, they are compiled by man. But no mistake can be made in existence, because no one is compiling. It is compiling itself.

Buddha spoke. His first statement was made under the bodhi tree, but even before that, the phenomenon of his enlightenment had already taken place under that same bodhi tree. Buddhists have tried to save that bodhi tree – it is still alive even today. Ashoka the Great sent a branch of that bodhi tree to Sri Lanka with his daughter, Sanghamitra, and his son, Mahendra. The followers of Buddha, who could see into the future, had the vision that Buddha's religion would not survive in India anymore. Even Buddha himself had declared that his religion would not continue in India longer than five hundred years. Why? The reason was that women had gained entry into his monastic order.

For a long time, Buddha did not give initiation to women and he remained stubborn about it. For many years

Buddha kept on avoiding it, denying women sannyas initiation and saying that his commune of monks should be only for men. But this seemed a little hard, and it was – because hundreds of thousands of women wanted to receive initiation, and their requests became stronger and stronger. And finally, because of their pressure and his compassion for them, Buddha agreed. He initiated women into sannyas. But the day he initiated them he said that his religion, which could have lived for thousands of years if he had not initiated women into the commune, would now only be alive for five hundred years.

I also used to think that Buddha was a little hard on women, that he shouldn't have banned them for so long. But as I come more and more in contact with women, I realize that he was right in doing so.

The emotional state of women and their manner of working is very different from that of men. And just because of this, many problems are created that otherwise could have been avoided. They create problems in such a way and end up weaving such webs of emotion and imagination – believing them to be real – that it becomes impossible to pull them out of this mesh. They drag others into their imaginary web too. Thoughts work in a very different way in men and women, in fact, in the opposite way.

Man is guided by intellect, by thought, by logic; that is why there is a system, a planning in his work. Women go by feelings, by imagination, by dreams; there is no system or method in their work. Using intellect, logic, a dozen people can arrive at a consensus, but using imagination you cannot convince even one person. Imagination is always personal; logic can belong to a multitude. If I were to put forward an argument, we could take a decision on that basis as to which direction to adopt. But if it were simply a matter of feelings, then there would be no way for us to arrive at a decision, because feelings are a very personal thing.

That is why women are never able to form a fraternity. Even to bring four women onto a joint platform is a very difficult thing. It would be impossible to raise an army of women because each woman would want to be the commander; no one would want to be a soldier. Each woman would start issuing orders, and nobody would be left to obey them. Each woman would hold onto her opinion so strongly that she wouldn't give way to anything else.

And there is no possibility of making her give way, because it is not a question of logic. In logic, there is at least the possibility that we can think things over, we can talk about them, we can arrive at some conclusion or other as to what is right. But as far as feelings are concerned, there is no such possibility. If ten or twenty women gather together, they can create such turmoil and commotion that even fifty thousand men could not manage. And their way of working is different, their approach is different.

So sometimes I also feel that Buddha was right, and that perhaps it wasn't right to have forced him. Earlier, I used to think that stopping women was not compassionate of him, but now I feel that perhaps, after all, it would have been more compassionate of him to have stopped them, because then at least his religion would have lasted for thousands of years. It is hard to decide which would have been the more compassionate – to have allowed women in and let the religion be destroyed in five hundred years, or not to have allowed them in and let the religion live on for thousands of years. It is very difficult to say.

Ashoka sent a branch of that bodhi tree to Sri Lanka with his son and daughter so that the tree could be kept alive – because the day the Buddhist religion would end in India, that bodhi tree would also be burned down, would be destroyed, would die. The bodhi tree remained alive in Sri Lanka. And only a few years ago, a branch of it was brought back and replanted in Bodh Gaya.

The reason for having such an attachment to that tree is not merely an emotional one. That tree has absorbed the supreme enlightenment that took place in Buddha's life. It has drunk of the light. The explosion that took place in Buddha's existence has seeped into each and every pore of that tree.

So there are errors in what man has collected about Buddha – there have to be. It is a very difficult task. When Buddha speaks, twenty-five different people who are listening to him take twenty-five different meanings from what he is saying. After Buddha left his body, when the *sangha* gathered to compile his teachings, there were a lot of problems, there was no agreement on anything. There were differences even amongst those people who had always been with him. Someone would say that Buddha had always said this, then someone else would say that Buddha had never said it. Someone would say that this is the meaning of a statement, then someone else would refute it by saying Buddha could not have possibly meant that. There were a lot of problems. Then, somehow or other, they managed to put together a compilation distilled from amongst them all that was agreeable to them all.

But if Buddha were to return he would disown it all, because it is not the original: firstly, because it was put together by a group of people, and secondly, because those parts that they disagreed about were excluded. They put together something which no one disagreed with. If Buddha were to return, he would say, "I never said this."

It is just as if I were saying something here, and then all of your opinions were taken as to what I actually *did* say. And then a common thread were sought from amongst them all, which would not offend any one of you, and which none of you would disagree with. One thing is certain: that it could be anything, but it would definitely not be what I had said! So many of you together – you would have destroyed it.

But this bodhi tree has no mind, this bodhi tree is silent, is quiet. The phenomenon of enlightenment that happened beneath it has entered the tree itself. Not only has it entered the bodhi tree, but also it has entered the River Niranjana flowing nearby. And it has also entered the particles of the earth, around which so much light happened.

And it has also entered the sky, which was a witness to this phenomenon.

This sutra is saying:

Having obtained the use of the inner senses,
having conquered the desires of the outer senses,
having conquered the desires of the individual soul,
and having obtained knowledge,
prepare now, O disciple,
to enter upon the way in reality.
The path is found;
make yourself ready to tread it.

Inquire of the earth, the air and the water
of the secrets they hold for you.

The need to consult the scriptures arises because we do not know the art of asking directly from existence itself. Otherwise, the bodhi tree could tell you what had happened, the Niranjana river could tell what had happened. The earth too could tell you the memories it has collected of Buddha walking on it, Mahavira sitting on it, Krishna dancing upon it.

Gradually, this phenomenon is gaining a scientific basis too, so now it may be easier for you to understand. The scientists say that whatever I am saying – right now, for instance – this sound can never be lost. It will not be lost, it will go on and on resounding, it will remain present in the folds of the air. There is a distinct possibility of developing an instrument that can capture these past sounds – and it is merely a question of time, if not today, then definitely sometime in the near future. Whether Krishna really preached the Gita on the battlefield or not can be decided, because the voice is not destroyed, it goes on resonating. It becomes very faint, but it keeps on resounding. It becomes very far away, but keeps on resounding. It can be caught.

It is just like a radio station in New York making some announcement that you listen to in India. But it takes some time for it to reach here from New York. You are able to listen to an announcement made in New York a fraction of a second later here. What does this mean? What was said a fraction of a second ago can be heard now. The announcement has become a thing of the past – it occurred a fraction of a second ago, but is heard now, this much time later. If it can be heard after a fraction of a second, then why can't it be heard after two days? Because, in principle, it has become clear that the past can be caught. What happened a fraction of a second ago can be caught a fraction of a second later. Before the existence of radio, we could not catch the announcement even after that short gap of time. Now we can.

Work is happening on this in scientific laboratories. And they are saying that it is not impossible for us to catch past sounds; sounds of two thousand years ago, even two million years ago. Of course there are complications, but the voice *is* present.

This sutra is talking about the same thing. We don't know when science will be able to tune in to the sounds of the past. But the person who has achieved mastery over his outward and inward senses – who after following all these sutras has entered the state of nothingness, who has attained to meditation – such a person, just by focusing his attention and becoming peaceful, without the help of any instrument, just by centering his attention on that very point where Krishna said the Gita, can once again listen to it as an inner voice. This is because for the inner world there *is* no time gap, in fact, there is no time there. There is no distance of space, in fact there is no space there. That inner center is eternal. From that center you can travel into the past or into the future. There, you will come to know the secrets that are hidden in the air.

The sutra says:

Inquire of the earth, the air and the water...

These three have kept many secrets hidden. And there is a special reason why the Hindus have made their temples on the banks of rivers. The Hindus' places of spiritual discipline were all near the banks of rivers, and for special reasons. And all the Hindus' places of pilgrimage are also on the banks of rivers for special reasons. The Hindu sages and seers have hidden the most profound processes of Hindu meditation in water; that is why these pilgrimage places are of so much value.

People keep going to the Ganges and to Yamuna without any understanding. They go to all the pilgrimage places; they gather at Sangam, the confluence of the three rivers, they hold fairs and festivities there – but they have no idea that when all this happened for the first time there were a lot of mystical reasons behind it. The Hindus have hidden all their experiences of life's innermost secrets in the Ganges. And whoever becomes capable of asking from the Ganges, is given the answers by her. So sitting on the banks of the Ganges is not merely something traditional. Sitting beside the Ganges has great meaning.

The Jainas have built all their temples and places of pilgrimage on the mountains, and they too have done this purposely. The Hindus had already laid down their concepts far and wide along the banks of the rivers, so there was the possibility of the two becoming entangled and mixed up. That's why the Jainas chose to build all their places of pilgrimage on the mountains. And they have charged the mountains with all their concepts.

On one small hill, Parshva Nath Hill, twenty-two out of the twenty-four the Jaina *tirthankaras* chose to leave their earthly bodies. It cannot be accidental. Out of a total of twenty-four prophets, twenty-two chose, in a period stretching over thousands of years, to leave their earthly bodies there. And the remaining two were not able to do so because of some accident; otherwise the original plan of all the twenty-four was to surrender their bodies on that one particular hill. The light which is released from the tirthankara at the time of leaving his body becomes imprinted on the stone forever. And whoever knows the secret can even today go to Parshva Nath Hill and ask the hill, "When Parshva Nath left his body, what took place on this hill, what did you experience?"

There is a difference between the methodology of the two religions. Making a record on water has to be done in a certain way because water is always in a continuous flow. If something is to be recorded on a mountain, it has to be done in a different way. The whole process, the whole methodology is different, because the mountain is stationary.

All the religions have not only created scriptures, they have also discovered much more profoundly reliable ways, because a scripture is a very papery thing, not very reliable. For example in Egypt, the religious people constructed pyramids. They hid everything in the fabric of the pyramid, in the architecture of the pyramid, in each and every stone, in the very plan and layout – they hid everything they knew. Those who understand the pyramids.... Now, all kinds of research work is being done on them and the researchers are amazed to see how many secrets they possess!

It is said that the Egyptians put all they knew into the pyramids – but the keys have been lost. Now and then some key is found somewhere which brings a few secrets to light. Throughout the world, none of the ancient religions ever simply relied on books; they used other means too. But the pyramid is also a man-made thing, and no matter how strong it is, it can be destroyed. That is why in India, instead of trying to put everything into manmade repositories, we made arrangements to hide them in the elements of nature itself.

Inquire of the earth, the air and the water of the secrets they hold for you.

In a particular state of meditation, contact is established and the answers start flowing in. But before that, your heart should have become so peaceful that you don't bring your own answer in; otherwise everything will become distorted. You should have become so silent that from your side there is no way left to add something to it. Only then are you able to know what is being said; otherwise you will create your own mixture.

People come and tell me that I came to them in their dreams and said such and such a thing. I tell them, "First, you should learn how to be silent. Otherwise, not only is the dream yours, but the one who appears in your dream is also a part of you – it is not me. Not only are you generating your own dream, you are also projecting me into it, and the words you are putting into my mouth are yours too." But you are very clever! Because you will not trust your own utterances, you are getting me to say it all – and you are making me say whatever you wish.

There is no end to the ways in which man tries to deceive himself. There is no limit. People come and tell me that they have done such and such a thing because I ordered them to do so! And when did I give them the order? They say, "In our dreams you asked us to do it!" But what they did was exactly what they wanted to do. And many times I am very surprised that when I am telling them straight to their faces not to do something, they are just not listening at all! They say they have done what I told them to do in their dream, but when I tell them something straight to their faces, they pay no attention to what I am asking them to do – what to say of carrying it out!

This is what I call cheating. But they are simply not aware of what they are doing. When I ask them in person to do something, they shake their heads and say that it is not possible. But when I tell them something in a dream, they carry out my instructions very well! So it is very clear that they are doing exactly what they want to do.

Until your mind has become completely peaceful, you will only hear what you want to hear. Until then, you will only do what you want to do. Until then, the secrets of existence will not be revealed to you, because you are so full of your emotions and your passions and your desires, that even if existence wanted to reveal itself to you, it couldn't. But if your meditation keeps on deepening, and you reach to a point when you can actually experience that there is no thought, then make a little experiment.

Try this small experiment. When you have reached this state of meditation, sit under a tree and experiment with this for a few days. It can be done under any tree, but if it is some special tree, then the results will be very clear and they will come soon – for example if you meditate continuously under the bodhi tree in Bodh Gaya for seven days.

If your meditation has settled and you feel it is going well, then for seven nights go and meditate continuously under the tree. When you feel you have become a complete void, just tell the tree that if it has any message for you, it should tell you. Then you should wait silently for the answer. You will be amazed that the tree will say something, and it will say something which can totally transform your life.

The tree has absorbed something, it is safeguarding something, but it is doing so only for those who are capable of asking. If they ask, they will receive the answer. But it is not really necessary to go that far. This sky contains all the buddhas that have ever been; all the Mahaviras, every Jesus, every Krishna that has ever been, that has ever walked on this earth. But why not ask the earth itself?

In a state of complete meditation, stretch yourself naked on the earth, as if you were a small child lying on his mother's breast. And just feel that the whole earth is your mother, and that you are lying on her chest, fondling her breasts with your hands. Become totally calm and empty. And when you feel a complete oneness between your physical body and the earth, when you both have become one and a state of nothingness has settled in you, go ahead and ask. If this earth has any message for you, you will receive it. And you will find that you have never received such a powerful message from anywhere before in your life. After receiving it, you will not remain the same person that you were before. And then it is possible to go even more deeply into this process. In this way you can reclaim many things which had otherwise become lost.

This book of Mabel Collins' has been found through a similar search. Its original version in Sanskrit had been lost, it was lost thousands of years ago. No original version of it exists today. Mabel Collins has reclaimed these sutras through similar mystical methods. So she is not the author of this book. This book has not been written by Mabel Collins, it has been read by her. She has read this book through some secret doors of life, and she has compiled it. She has mentioned only this much: that these sutras are from a long-lost Sanskrit volume. "...I am not the author of this book, I have not created these sutras, I have merely heard them. And I have compiled them exactly as they came to me."

Many books have been lost. Whatever man creates is bound to get lost. But there are also ways and means of retrieving what has been lost. Many books have been interpolated; much has been inserted in them, added by people who came later on. These are not the original versions, because much has been added to them. Until the original versions are retrieved from the earth or the sky, they cannot be relied upon. We have no idea which keys can open the secrets hidden in the air.

But one key is very obvious, and I call it the master key. All the locks can be opened by this key. This key is your state of emptiness. Then, if you wish, you can talk with all the Mahaviras, you can meet all the buddhas, you can again hear the flute of Krishna. But for this to happen it is necessary that you first become a void.

The development of your inner senses
will enable you to do this.

The eleventh sutra:

Inquire of the holy ones of the earth
of the secrets they hold for you.

The conquering of the desires of the outer senses
will give you the right to this.

Inquire of the holy ones of the earth...

This matter of inquiring from the holy ones of the earth should also be understood.

This world does not only consist of beings who possess a physical body. This world also consists of beings who do not possess a physical form, who are bodiless spirits. Whenever someone dies, if he happens to be an ordinary person who is full of commonplace desires and passions, who is full of the everyday traits of good and bad that are found in the average man, who is good in an everyday sort of a way, it does not take even a second for him to be reborn.... Because for the ordinary person, ordinary wombs are constantly available; there is no shortage, he never has to wait in a queue. But if there is a person who is extraordinarily evil, he has to wait – because it is difficult to find an extraordinarily evil womb. If a Hitler dies, waiting becomes necessary. Sometimes it takes hundreds of years before an appropriately evil womb can be found from which a Hitler can be reborn. Or, on the other hand, if the person has been extraordinarily good, a very saintly soul, then too it can take thousands of years – because to find such a worthy womb is also very difficult. Extraordinarily good and extraordinarily evil are equally difficult to find. But the ordinary, the commonplace is readily available. Those bad souls who are held back from taking on a new body we call evil spirits. And those good souls who are held back from taking on a new body we call gods. This sutra is talking about these gods:

Inquire of the holy ones of the earth
of the secrets they hold for you.

If you can become peaceful, you will soon find that you are entering another world – a world in which many bodiless spirits are only too eager to help you. These spirits can reveal many secrets to you, secrets which you would not be able to attain through your own efforts – even after many lifetimes. These spirits have not as yet attained nirvana – it is extremely difficult to establish contact with the ones who have – but they are bodiless and are just waiting for a favorable birth. And it is very easy to establish contact with them, it is simply a matter of tuning – just like moving the knobs on a radio so that the needle stops at exactly the right station. If there is even a slightly wrong movement to this side or to that side of the station then much noise is created, much noise is heard. But if the needle stops at the right place, you have tuned into the right station.

In exactly the same way, if you can learn the art of tuning your meditation to the right point, then you can connect your meditation to any source. Many spirits are only too eager to help you to accomplish a lot of your work. And there are also many spirits only too eager to harm you and to spoil much of the work you have already done. Those who are evil-natured take delight in causing trouble for other people. And those who are good-natured delight in making others happy.

There are many spirits around you that can be helpful to you, and there are many spirits that can cause you harm. If you are full of fear, if you are very worried, if your mind is in a lot of turmoil, the chances are that you will come into contact with evil spirits – because then you are like an open door for them. It often happens that you see ghosts when you are very scared. It does not mean that they are born out of your fear. It means that because of your fear, contact is made with them. Fear makes you available to them.

And when you are fearless, blissful, peaceful – in such a state, contact with the evil spirits cannot happen. As far as that is concerned, your doors are closed. But in these moments your contact with good spirits is possible. It is what I am constantly saying to you during the meditations: that only in a moment of bliss, in a moment of absolute bliss, can you meet the divine. There is no other way. This is tuning. When you are filled with bliss, then you become connected to the universal source of bliss.

When you are full of misery, you become connected to the vast expanses of misery – wherever they are in the world.

We say a miserable person goes to hell. He doesn't actually go anywhere, a miserable person only opens up towards hell and hell comes to him. A happy man opens up towards heaven and heaven comes to him. A blissful person opens up towards the ultimate reality, and the ultimate reality enters him.

It all depends which side you are open to. Your life starts expanding in that very direction.

This sutra says:

Inquire of the holy ones of the earth
of the secrets they hold for you.

The conquering of the desires of the outer senses
will give you the right to this.

16

INQUIRE OF THE INMOST

12. Inquire of the inmost, the one, of its final secret, which it holds for you through the ages.

The great and difficult victory,
the conquering of the desires of the individual soul, is a work of ages;
therefore expect not to obtain its reward
until ages of experience have been accumulated.
When the time of learning
this twelfth rule is reached,
man is on the threshold of becoming more than man.
The knowledge which is now yours
is only yours because your soul has become one
with all pure souls and with the inmost.
It is a trust vested in you by the most high.
Betray it, misuse your knowledge, or neglect it,
and it is possible even now for you to fall
from the high estate you have attained.
Great ones fall back, even from the threshold,
unable to sustain the weight of their responsibility,
unable to pass on.

Therefore look forward always
with awe and trembling to this moment,
and be prepared for the battle.

Before we take up the sutra, two small questions:

Someone is asking why Meera did not die even after drinking poison. What sort of devotion did she have, what sort of love? A similar thing is said about Prahlad: that he could not be burned by fire. But how is it then that Socrates died after consuming poison, and why was Jesus not saved on the cross?

It will be useful to understand a few things. One: never ever make the mistake of comparing two enlightened people, because no one is a replica of someone else. A person like Jesus never existed before and will never be born again. A person like Meera will also never be born again. Socrates is unique, and so is Prahlad. But our minds have this trivial habit of comparing. Since they are not replicas of each other, their individualities, the way they flow and the way they live and die will be different from one another.

Meera did not die after consuming poison because no poison could enter into the rapturous state in which she was living. In the deepest state of love, poison cannot enter, poison will not be able to enter the body. The path of Meera is the path of love – and love is an antidote for poison.

If you are too full of love, poison will not be able to enter your bloodstream. For poison to enter there already needs to be some poison in your bloodstream. Like begets like. If you are full of anger, poison can very quickly and easily enter your bloodstream, because anger activates the poison glands within you. Poison is already present there.

All of us are full of anger and hatred, so poison is already present in our bloodstream. Because of this inner poison, outer poison is able to enter the body. If there is no trace of something already inside you, then it cannot enter your body.

A person like Meera is living in such love that any inner sources of poison have ceased to exist long ago. Her blood is totally influenced by love, it is full of love; so poison will not be able to enter, it will be thrown out of her body. But Meera is not even aware of all this. If she did know it, then poison would enter her body. Meera does not know that she is being given poison, that she is drinking poison. She is so immersed in her love that she is simply not aware of what is happening to her at the bodily level; she has no knowledge of it.

Try to understand it this way. Supposing a rat bites you and you think that a snake has bitten you; in a case like this, symptoms of a snake's poison will manifest even though the rat was not poisonous. You can even die. Delusion is enough to kill you.

You will be surprised to know that those people who have studied snakes say that only three percent of snakes are actually poisonous. That is, out of a hundred different species, only three have poison sacs and ninety-seven have none. But the miracle is that a person can still die from the bite of a non-poisonous snake.

That is why snake charmers are so successful. The snake that has bitten a person is not poisonous, but the person's imagination makes it poisonous. That is why the snake charmers' charms work. These charms can cure you of your imagination. The snake that bit you was not poisonous, but the *feeling* that a snake has bitten you acts like a poison. You can even die – because if you are in such a state, the poison glands inside you will release poison. This emotional state can be cured by charms – that's why the snake's bite can be neutralized.

And just the opposite also happens. Even if a poisonous snake bites you, if the snake charmer is able to reassure you that the effects of the bite have been warded off by his charms, this assurance can act as a barrier inside you between you and the poison. It can prevent the poison from entering your bloodstream.

You are simply not aware of how much power your mind exercises over your body. The people who have conducted research on hypnosis have obtained miraculous results. They say that if you are put into a hypnotic trance, put to sleep, and an ordinary piece of stone is placed in your hand but you are told that is a burning ember, you will immediately scream and throw the stone away. And I can also confirm this from my own personal experiments, because I have done a lot of work on hypnosis. You will cry out in pain, as if it really were an ember – even though it is an ordinary cold stone. It is understandable that since you were unconscious you believed what I told you, but that your hand should also have a blister – and that blister will be exactly the same as if an ember had really been held in your hand. That blister will last long after you have regained consciousness, it will last just as long as if the mark had been made by a real ember.

And just the opposite also happens. If you are put in a trance and a real ember is placed on your hand but you are told that it is only a cold pebble, then you will not shriek or throw the pebble away, and it will not leave a blister on your hand. Now all the scientists are unanimous in saying that your body simply follows what is going on in your mind.

So Meera is so charged with love that she just doesn't see the poison at all. Please remember one thing: what you see simply reflects your state of being. To Meera, the whole of creation seems to be full of nectar; she sees Krishna in everything. She must have seen Krishna in the poison too, and drunk of it fully. She must have found the flavor of Krishna in that too. Being in such an inner state the poison cannot have any effect. It will be ineffectual, it will not reach Meera.

And if no blister appears on the hand when an ember is placed on it, then the matter can be settled scientifically. Prahlad, too, can remain unburned by the fire. It is a question of your inner state. God saving Prahlad is just a tale, it is not scientific. If some God were to go around saving someone here from being burned, and someone there from being poisoned, protecting someone here, consoling someone there, it would become an unmanageable maze for him. There is no God doing all this; it is the inner state of Prahlad. He is full of trust that he won't be burned, that God will save him. God saving him is not the issue. But remember one thing: if you have the idea that there is no God who can save you, your trust cannot be total. Prahlad has a total trust that there is a God, and that God will save him. He has put himself completely in the hands of God, come what may, and in such a state the fire cannot touch him.

You must have heard of those people who do fire dancing; they walk on fires and emerge intact, without burning their feet. There is nothing miraculous about it. Yes, the miracle is the power that their minds have over their bodies. One can escape the fire, but if you have even the slightest doubt, you will get burned.

That is why it is difficult to find someone like Prahlad nowadays. Those days are gone when people had so much trust that there wasn't even an iota of doubt. There used to be so much simplicity, so much innocence. Today, even a small child will raise questions and say, "No, this is not possible." Today, even a small child is no longer a child. In the past, even an old man was just like a child. Life was very simple; people lived close to nature. Civilization was not so much advanced, there was no formal education, so naturally there was not much skepticism either. The more educated the personality is, the more skeptical it becomes – because with education, questions arise. And they should arise, otherwise education cannot make any progress.

Put it this way: if scientific knowledge continues expanding in the world, then doubt will also keep on growing, because without doubt, science cannot make any headway. Science thrives on questions. Only if you ask will you get the answers. You search, but in that search doubt is essential, curiosity is essential, but trust is not needed.

Religion lives on trust, just as science thrives on doubt. If there is a predominance of religion in the world, it is difficult for science to thrive, very difficult, because the two are based on very different fundamentals. But if your trust is total and you have no doubt inside, then there is no law in this world that your trust cannot vanquish. And there is nothing in this world that your trust cannot make possible. But your trust must be total – even the smallest hole in it will sink the boat.

That is why if someone tries to make such experiments through effort, he will soon land himself in trouble. Never try such things through effort – even by mistake. You think that Prahlad was not touched by fire, so why shouldn't you also be saved – and then you put your hand in the fire to see! But you are putting your hand into the fire as a scientist and not as a religious man. You are simply experimenting to find out, to see what happens. And this experimentation only shows that you still have doubts about whether it will happen or not – and so you will get burned.

That's why religious experiments can never be repeated but scientific experiments can. Whatever scientific experiment has been carried out in any corner of the world, you can repeat it again in any other part of the world, because it stands on doubt; trust is not its component. But if you ever try to repeat what happened to Prahlad you will land yourself in trouble, because it cannot be repeated.

Religious happenings are a personal and individual thing. You can never have the same inner state as Prahlad. And how can someone who is trying to imitate reach such an inner state? Prahlad was not imitating anyone's experiment, he was not trying to test God in some way or other. Testing means that doubt is present. He was merely giving himself up to God. He had no doubt whatsoever in his mind about the outcome: that it could not be any different from what he thought. For him, there was simply no question of things being otherwise. This complete trust, total faith, can save you from the fire.

But the situation of Jesus is completely different. That Jesus could not be saved from the cross is not the point. But if you understand it rightly, you will find that the people who really know about Jesus believe that this whole plan to be crucified was actually masterminded by Jesus himself. The whole plan was his. Jesus wanted to be crucified – this was a part of his plan. Jesus had a vast plan. But Prahlad and Meera had no such plan. That's why Prahlad has hardly any followers. And how much of a following does Meera have?

Jesus has made half of the world Christian. There is a vast plan behind all this. Jesus had the idea of transforming the world, and right from the beginning he understood very clearly that if he was crucified for his teachings, they would be engraved on the hearts of mankind for ever. The cross was just a game: for Jesus there is no question of dying. For Jesus, the cross was just a game, but this game could be put to good use. That was the plan. The game Jesus was playing was all well-planned before hand. People generally think that Jesus fell into the hands of his enemies. But those who know, know that it was his enemies who fell into Jesus' hands. In fact, they never knew what was going on!

Judas, a disciple of Jesus, informed Jesus' enemies about him. People think that Judas was an enemy of Jesus, but this is not true. In fact, he was Jesus' most loyal disciple. He was so loyal that when Jesus ordered him to make plans for his crucifixion, he even carried out those plans. Jesus' orders had to be carried out.

That's why when Judas was leaving to go and inform Jesus' enemies, Jesus touched his feet and kissed him. People think the reason behind this gesture was to show love even towards the enemy – but this was not the case. The inside story is something totally different. In fact, Judas was the most intelligent disciple of them all. And perhaps you are not aware of this: that on the day that Jesus was crucified, the other disciples ran away, but Judas committed suicide. He hanged himself.

People think that he did so out of repentance, that he felt guilty for betraying Jesus, that he felt responsible for Jesus' crucifixion. No. It was because of the very deep and intimate love he had for Jesus; a love so strong that when Jesus asked him to make preparations for his crucifixion, he went ahead and did so. But love brings tremendous difficulties. He made those arrangements, and then he hanged himself, because after that, life ceased to have any meaning for him.

All this was preplanned. Jesus wanted to be crucified because only through his crucifixion could something take place which would transform people's lives. That's why the symbol of the cross is much more important for Christianity than even Jesus himself. They don't hang a statue of Jesus around their necks, they wear a cross – because it was through the cross, because of the crucifixion, that the birth of Christianity was able to take place.

Søren Kirkegaard was a very devout Christian mystic. He went so far as to say that Christianity should not be called Christianity but Crossianity, because the concept of Christianity is based solely on the cross. That's why the cross is more important than Christ. It was because of the crucifixion that Jesus could become a Christ. That's why the picture of Jesus hanging from the cross has become the most well-loved one. This was a historical plan.

And the inner state of Socrates is yet again different. In fact, you should never make comparisons. I am not comparing, I am merely pointing out their individual traits and telling you why events happened the way they did.

Socrates was told that if he stopped giving his discourses he would be set free. The judges told him this. But Socrates replied, "If I stop speaking, what is the point of my living? The sole reason for my existence is so that I can speak the truth. My life and speaking the truth are one and the same thing. So please don't impose this ban. Either allow me to speak the truth, and let me live, or if you ban me from speaking the truth, it is better that you kill me, it is better that you give me poison. And if you give me poison, remember one thing: I will never die. Because of your poison I will become immortal. If people ever remember you, it will be because of me, because you gave Socrates poison. You will be remembered for nothing else, for one thing only – that you administered poison to Socrates.

"But," said Socrates, "I want to make one thing very clear, and that is: truth is more dear to me than life. Death has no importance for me whatsoever, but truth is very important. And for the sake of truth, I am willing to accept death."

He who is willing to accept death for the sake of truth will achieve immortality. And until you are willing to accept death for the sake of truth, truth does not have any value. Only when truth becomes so priceless to us that we are willing to lay down our lives for its sake, does it become authentic truth.

So whatever Socrates was saying, his life was reflecting it. Socrates was on the threshold of death, the poison was being made ready. The person who had been put in charge of preparing the poison was even slowing down the procedure, because he had started to love this man, Socrates. When Socrates was put in jail, whoever came into contact with him started loving him. Even the jailer had started loving him. This man was grinding the poison very slowly, because the longer Socrates was able to live, the better. The longer such a beautiful flower was allowed to remain blossoming on this earth, the better.

But Socrates tells him, "Why are you taking so long? You are not doing the job that has been entrusted to you properly. It appears that you have become attached to me and that you are favoring me. This is not right. Please do your duty, and get on with the job. Please make up the potion fast. It is nearly six, and you have to administer it at six o'clock."

The person who was grinding the poison says, "Socrates, what kind of a madman are you? I am purposely taking some time so that you can live a little longer, and here you are shouting! What is the hurry?"

Then Socrates replies, "I have known what life is; now I want to know what death is."

Socrates is an explorer. There has never been such an explorer on this earth. He is not a devotee; he is an explorer, an adventurer. He says he is in a mood to see what death is like: "I want to see what death is. What is death like?"

Someone says, "Socrates, aren't you a little afraid? You are about to die, aren't you afraid?"

Socrates replies, "I don't know whether I will survive or not – that is why there is nothing to be afraid of. If I knew that I would survive, there would be nothing to worry about because I would know that I would survive. And if I knew that I wouldn't survive, then too there would be nothing to be afraid of, because how can one who will not survive be afraid? As things stand, I don't know anything. When I enter my death, only then will I know."

Socrates says, "I will not say anything about something that I do not know."

Such a natural quest for truth, which does not favor one side or the other, is very difficult. For Meera it is a question of feeling, for Jesus it is a question of feeling, but for Socrates it is a question of finding out. Remember: if you have absolute faith that the soul is immortal, it is easier to die fearlessly. But the fearlessness of Socrates is certainly unique.

He says, "I don't *know* if the soul is immortal or not; I will be able to find that out only when I die. And before that, there is no way of knowing! First, I will have to go through the experience and then I will know. If I die, there is no reason to be afraid, because if I am dead who is there to be afraid? Who is there to be unhappy? Who will suffer? And if I survive, even then there is nothing to be afraid of, because then I will have survived." Socrates says, "It is useless to be afraid of death – in either case. If you are a believer, it is useless, because you will survive. If you are a non-believer it is also useless to be afraid, because you won't survive. So why be afraid? Who will suffer?"

The hands of the man who came to administer the poison were trembling. When poison has to be given to a person like Socrates, your hands will certainly tremble! Seeing all this, Socrates tells the man, "Your hands shouldn't shake so. Do whatsoever you have been asked to do calmly. Don't let your hands tremble – because when I am not afraid of dying, what are you afraid of? Look at me!"

Though Socrates is an old man, his hands don't shake when he holds the cup of poison. He drinks the poison and then lies down. All his disciples are weeping. Seeing them in such a state he says, "Stop crying! I am still alive. You can do all your crying after I am gone. What is the hurry? Right now, why not feel this death that is about to descend on me? Perhaps you will learn something from it."

Then Socrates starts to give a running commentary. He says, "Now my feet are turning cold: it seems my feet have become dead. Now my thighs are becoming cold: it seems my thighs have become dead." He says, "Death is creeping over me, but the one thing I find very surprising is that my feeling of existing seems to be fully intact. The poison has not made the slightest impression on it. Even now I can feel my is-ness just as much as I did before."

Then his hands become cold. Then he says, "My heartbeat seems to be weakening." Then, "My lips are becoming lifeless. It seems that now I will not be able to speak any further, so remember my last words – that I am still completely alive. So it seems that as my whole body is so close to being lifeless and yet I am still completely intact, I can see no reason why I will not be completely intact when my whole body is lifeless. I think that even though my body will die, I will not. But I cannot say anything for certain yet because I am still in the process of finding out."

Now, this is a very different kind of personality. Never compare them, and never try to make one smaller or bigger than the other. That is the sign of a mediocre mind. They are all different summits. There are many mountain peaks on the Himalayas, and each one of them has its own beauty. Similarly, human consciousness has given rise to many heights, and each height has its own beauty. In a way, it is good that they are not all alike, otherwise you would become bored and fed up. If there were too many Meeras, her significance would be lost. If there were too many Prahlads around, if every village had one, they would be worthless. We don't need too many men like Socrates either.

Each person should always remember that he is born to be himself. And the day he touches his peak he becomes unique. On that day, no one like him was ever born before, and no one like him will ever be born in the future. He is a unique phenomenon. Existence loves an original. To existence, the borrowed, the carbon copies, have no value whatsoever.

Another friend has asked about a statement that was given yesterday in the Neo-Sannyas International meeting, saying that we believe in free sex. Do I agree with it?

I believe neither in free sex nor in repressed sex. There is really no need for such beliefs. Sex is a private and personal matter, and to have any point of view about it only shows the meanness of one's mind. You never ask me what is my point of view regarding food, what is my point of view regarding washing – whether washing should be done freely, as you like, or whether it should be controlled. If you were to ask such questions, you would look foolish. So why do you ask about sex? It is a personal matter, absolutely personal. There is no question of anyone giving their opinion.

Society believes in repressing sex; it believes in putting up walls around sex, tying it up with laws, patrolling it with the police and the courts; never letting anyone make his own decisions regarding it. And as a reaction against this, there are some people who go to the other extreme. They say that sex should be free, that no one should place any obstacles in the way, that no one should make any laws regarding it. They want licentiousness. This too is a reaction, but of another sort, and it takes you to the other extreme.

My own view is this: that sex should be considered as something very natural; that we should not have any preconceived ideas about it. Viewpoints make everything unnatural. Each and every person should be guided by his own understanding, his own feelings and his own sensibilities towards life. And I do not give guidelines for small matters because I believe that if you have intelligence, if you have meditation, if you have some expanded understanding, you are quite capable of taking decisions on small matters for yourself. And if you are dependent on me for making decisions for each and every thing, it will be as if I am helping a blind person. How long can I go on helping you? And who can help you?

Supposing a blind man comes to me and asks me, "Does the road lie to the left or to the right? If I want to go to the railway station, which way should I turn, and if I want to go to the river, then which way should I turn?" Even if I were to explain everything to him in great detail, he still would remain blind. It can also happen that he may learn to walk on certain roads quite satisfactorily.

But in this world there are many roads, and the roads keep changing daily. Sometimes you may have to go to the river, sometimes to the railway station, sometimes to this village and sometimes to another village. Circumstances change daily, paths change daily, villages change daily. So I will advise the blind person not to ask me for directions but instead to ask me how his eyes can be treated – because once his eyesight is cured he will be able to find his own way no matter where he is.

I call meditation your life's eye.

Don't ask me about small, petty things. People ask me what to eat, what not to drink. Don't ask me about all these useless things. You should have your own eyes to see – they will tell you what to eat and what not to eat. Nothing will happen by my saying something. Even if I were to tell you what not to eat, what not to drink, even then, if you were blind and ignorant and not capable of awareness you would still manage to find some way to get around it.

People asked Buddha whether they should eat meat or not. So Buddha replied, "It is not a good thing to kill someone, or to do violence to anyone, so don't kill any bird or animal for food." And do you know that all Buddhists eat meat, but they claim that they only eat the meat from animals that have died naturally! Buddha said, "Violence is a form of sin, so don't kill for food" – so they even found a way to get around that, saying that there can be no harm in eating a cow which has died a natural death, because Buddha did not forbid them from eating the meat of an animal that has met with a natural death.

So in China and Japan there are big signboards on hotels, just like the ones we have on certain shops in India, which proclaim "Pure Ghee – pure purified butter – sold here." It is very clear what this implies. What is the need to mention the word *pure*? Isn't saying "ghee" sufficient? But since *pure* is especially mentioned, it means that it must not be pure. In China and Japan there are similar signboards on hotels which claim to sell only the meat from animals that have died a natural death, that have not been killed by anybody! How so many animals can die a natural death every day is very difficult to say – the whole country is meat-eating.

There is always a way out, and you will find it. Whatsoever you want to do, you will certainly do it, because your actions emerge from the space of your darkness. There is hardly any way in which you could avoid it.

Then there are the Jainas. Mahavira said, "Don't consume living, growing vegetables, green vegetables, on certain days of religious significance." So what do the Jainas do? They dry and preserve the vegetables before the stipulated days, and then they eat them! Some people are really too much!

I was once a guest at someone's house – it was the period of *Paryushan*. My host came and offered me some bananas. I asked them, "Do you people eat bananas during Paryushan?"

They replied, "Bananas are yellow, only green food is forbidden!"

You are quite capable of deceiving even Mahavira. All you know is deceiving, you simply cannot do anything else. Right now, as you are, you will always manage somehow to find the wrong way to go about doing things, because you yourself are wrong.

If I were to say that I am in favor of controlling sex, you would find ways to bypass that statement. And if I were to say that I favor free sex, then too you would find ways to draw your own conclusions. And since it will be you who will be finding the ways to cheat, I don't say that I am in favor of free sex or against it. I am in favor of you having a discerning eye. Your eyes should be opened, your awareness should grow. Then, out of such an awareness, you should be able to decide for yourself what you should do and what you should not do. Do whatever you have to do with complete awareness. Be completely aware, do everything consciously. Then a path will open up in your life.

Understand what I am saying correctly. I am not at all in favor of giving you some kind of a detailed guideline, a map – because when it is detailed, any sort of guideline will only succeed in turning you into a slave; you are almost certain to follow it. And when anything turns you into a slave, at the same time you will try to find ways and means to get around it. You will find some way to get out of it.

That's why I do not make you dependent on anything, and in that way, force you to find ways to cheat around it. Instead, I want to give you eyes. Eyes will make your path clear. Then, whatever you feel to be right – act accordingly. And if you take a wrong step, you will face the consequences, but if you take the right step again, you will gather its fruit. If you want to put yourself in suffering, you will opt for the wrong step. But then who am I to stop you from putting yourself in suffering? – because that too would be interfering with your freedom. And on the other hand, if you walk on the right path, you will reap the rewards of happiness, of bliss.

So all the decisions are in your hands so that you can clearly begin to see the relationship between cause and effect. You should be able to see very clearly for yourself which of your actions cause you suffering, and which give you bliss. Then your path is clear, then the search for bliss is yours. Go on using your own eyes and keep walking on that path.

And always remember one thing: never come to me for any kind of guidance on trivial matters. If some master does give guidelines for trivial matters, then he isn't a master. He is only trying to bind you to him and make you a slave.

Now let us take up the sutra.

The twelfth sutra:

Inquire of the inmost, the one, of its final secret,
which it holds for you through the ages.

The great and difficult victory,
the conquering of the desires of the individual soul, is a work of ages;
therefore expect not to obtain its reward
until ages of experience have been accumulated.
When the time of learning
this twelfth rule is reached,
man is on the threshold of becoming more than man.

The knowledge which is now yours
is only yours because your soul has become one
with all pure souls and with the inmost.
It is a trust vested in you by the most high.
Betray it, misuse your knowledge, or neglect it,
and it is possible even now for you to fall
from the high estate you have attained.
Great ones fall back, even from the threshold,
unable to sustain the weight of their responsibility,
unable to pass on.
Therefore look forward always

with awe and trembling to this moment,
and be prepared for the battle.

**Inquire of the inmost, the One, of its final secret,
which it holds for you through the ages.**

Inquire of the earth, inquire of the air, inquire of the sky, of the water – but all these lie outside you, and whatever they have hidden is outside you. They will be able to tell you about the buddhas, the *tirthankaras,* the Christs, the Krishnas – but the real secret lies hidden within you.

Your innermost self has been journeying since time immemorial. Its experiences are countless. Is there anything you have not been? There were lives in which you were a stone. You have been a plant; at times a bird, an animal, a woman, a man; at times a saint and at times a thief. There is nothing that you have not experienced, there is no state through which you have not passed. You have known hells as well as heavens, you have experienced suffering as well as happiness. You have borne the burden of much pain and guilt and many times you have committed suicide. You have created much havoc and destruction and indulged in much violence. You have also tasted the joys of creativity. You have given birth to many creations, you have made many things. There is nothing that has not crossed your path, nothing that you have not had something to do with.

This legacy lies safely hidden in your innermost being. Whatever you have lived through, whatever you have known, and whatever you have done – the essence of all of this is preserved. The essence of all this experience lies hidden in your innermost self. You should inquire from it, you should open it up. And the moment it is opened, the secret of life will be revealed to you, because you have lived life – you yourself *are* life.

There is nothing in this world that you are not acquainted with – but you go on forgetting. And with each new body you build a new ego. With each new ego you forget your past, you do not remember what has occurred on your journey. That is why you have been continuously forgetting your legacy. You are not even able to make use of the experience you have gathered. That's why you go on repeating the same things over and over again; the very things that you have already done hundreds of times.

Mahavira used to insist on the value of *jati-smaran*, past life remembrance, to his disciples. He would say: "First, recollect your past lives." He made this the fundamental basis of his system. He used to say, "Until you are able to remember your past lives, you will keep repeating the same mistakes now, because you have forgotten that you have already done the same things."

You have amassed wealth many times; this is not the first occasion. And it is not as if amassing so much wealth in the past gave you success – but now you are doing the same thing again. Many times you have built big mansions that were destroyed, and today there is not a trace of them left. But you are again making big houses, you are again thinking that they will last forever – as if you will live in them forever!

You have loved many men and women in the past, and all those loves came to nothing; you did not gain anything from them. But you are doing the same thing all over again. Do you think that the treasures of life can be found in the relationship between a man and a woman? You have raised children before, and then, too, you had great expectations of them – but they all came to nothing. They never really brought you any contentment. How can anyone else make you contented when you cannot manage to be content yourself? But you are doing exactly the same thing again and again!

You are revolving like a wheel with the spokes moving from the top to the bottom, from the bottom to the top. The wheel keeps on revolving. And whenever some spoke comes to the top you feel as if something new is happening. But these events have happened to you an endless number of times before.

So Mahavira used to say, "Go back a little, go back to your past lives and try to remember them; then you will not repeat the same mistakes again. Then, you will come to know that what you are bent on doing is nothing but a repetition of what you have already done. And repetition is a useless thing, it is meaningless."

On the other hand, everything you need to know is lying within you. Everything is there; nothing ever gets lost. Whatever you come to know, even once, becomes an integral part of you. Of course all of this is hidden there, but something even greater is also hidden there within you, and that is the very beginning of the universe.

You were only a witness before the birth of this universe. When this creation started, you were a witness to it, because you were always there. You are a part of that which has no beginning, which is eternal. Creations come and go, universes are made and destroyed, but you are a part of that consciousness, you are a ray of that consciousness which is already present at the moment of creation – in fact one should say which *creates* the universe. And when the whole of creation dissolves, even then it is present as a witness.

Consciousness is never destroyed. You are a part of that supreme consciousness. You even know the moment of the birth of creation, because you yourself have given that birth, you participated in it. That event is lying hidden deep within your innermost self. And here you are asking others, "Who is the creator of this universe?" You are not even aware that you yourself participated in its creation. But you can only come to know all of this when you enter your innermost being.

The ending of this universe is also hidden within you, because it is you who has written this tale. You are the creator of it, you are a participant in this whole play. This supreme mystery of the ending of the universe is also present inside you. You become scared of death because you are not aware that the center of immortality is within you. You are afraid, you tremble about trivial things, when really nothing can make you tremble. There is nothing that can make you afraid because there is nothing that can destroy you. But that essence lies hidden very deep within you.

This sutra says:

Inquire of the inmost, the one, of its final secret, which it holds for you through the ages.

Inquire of yourself.

Ramana Maharshi's whole system of meditation was based on only this. He used to say, "There is only one form of meditation, and that is to ask yourself, 'Who am I? Who am I? Who am I?'" He would say, "Put all the energy that you possess, put your whole life's energy at stake in asking just this one question, 'Who am I?' Ask this question as if your life depended on it. Let each and every cell of your body cry out for this answer. And go on asking this question, but don't give any answers, because all the answers you give will be false. Let the answer come by itself, don't give the answer. You are always in such a hurry to supply the answer, and all your answers born out of your hurry are false – because such answers are already present in your head even before the question has been asked."

People come to me and they say, "I ask myself, 'Who am I? Who am I?' And then the answer comes, 'I am the soul, I am *brahman*, the ultimate reality.'"

The answer doesn't come so fast. You must have read it in some book, you must have learned it from some scriptures. And the funny thing is that you already knew this long before you put the question to yourself! So what is the need to ask? Why are you asking? Who are you asking? You already know that you are a soul, and if you already know that, then what is there to ask?

No, the answers that your memory gives you will not be of any use. The answers given by your mind will be of no use. The real answer will come from your innermost self and that is very different. When that answer comes, it will sound as if it is someone else's voice, as if it is not yours. The difference will be very clear. Though you will be asking the question, someone else will be answering. That speech will not be yours, those words will not be yours, that voice will not be yours. It will seem to be totally unknown.

That is why the mystics, the Sufis, the devotees, have said, "We asked and God gave the answer." There is no God giving the answer, it is your own innermost self speaking to you; and in that place you yourself are God. But the voice is unfamiliar, you have never heard it before. You have never heard such words before. It has nothing to do with your lips, it does not arise from your throat, it has nothing whatsoever to do with your memory system, your mind, your intellect. It seems to be coming from some far-off place, from some place that is far away. That's why everyone feels that the answer was given by somebody else. It is not someone else who gives you the answer; the answer comes from your own innermost being, but you have wandered so far away from it, you have gone so far away, the gap between you and your innermost being has become so big, that your own answer seems to have been given by somebody else.

Ask, "Who am I?" but don't give any answer. Use all your energy in asking the question, and don't save any of it for answering – because your answer does not have any value. Your answer will be something which you have heard somewhere or read in some book or other; coming either from the scriptures or the sayings of some sages or from your social conditioning. It will be like dust which has gathered on you from the outside: it will have no value. Ask as if you do not have any answer left to give. In your process of asking the question, all your answers should have dropped away and only the question should be left. And the day that only your question remains, your question will shoot like an arrow into your innermost self – because then there aren't any answers on the periphery to stop it. Then, you will travel inwards.

That's why all previous knowledge has to be dropped before attaining to supreme wisdom – that is, all the knowledge that you have accumulated up until now. Before it becomes possible to realize the supreme wisdom, it is necessary to throw all the scriptures into the river. All forms of burden have to be dropped, all doctrines and theories have to be done away with – because whatever has been acquired from the outside cannot take you inwards.

And if you become capable of asking just this one pure question, "Who am I?" with all your heart and soul; and if you are in no hurry to get an answer, if you do not feel any expectation whatsoever – rather you feel you cannot possibly answer, because in the first place you do not know the answer – then one day you will suddenly realize that your question is taking you inwards. It will have become a boat on which you can sail inwards. Then, one day a point will also come when after constantly asking the question, the question too will drop – because the periphery, which gives meaningless answers, cannot have a meaningful question. This is a little complicated to understand – but how can the periphery, whose answers are meaningless, have a meaningful question?

First, your answers will drop away, your knowledge will be dropped and you will become ignorant. And in such a state of ignorance, only your question will be left; answers cannot survive. Then, a stage will come when even your ignorance falls away – and your question too. After constantly asking, after all answers have fallen away, a moment comes when you suddenly find that even the question does not arise anymore. Even if you wanted to formulate the question, you would not be able to do so. You have become a void. By constantly asking, "Who am I? Who am I?" a state of emptiness has been born. And in that emptiness your innermost voice is heard for the first time, and you can hear the answer.

This sounds very paradoxical. As long as you keep on asking, you will not get the answer. When the questioning is dropped, you will get the answer. But now don't say, "Then why should I ask? Let us just sit down and close our eyes, and we will get the answer." No, because even though you may say, "I am not questioning at all," actually, you are still in the process of questioning. It is not possible as yet. And questions are helpful in taking you away from the periphery.

It is exactly like when you use a second thorn to remove a thorn from your body. What do you do with that second thorn? Do you keep it safely in the old wound? No, you throw it away too. Right now, your mind is full of questions; that's why Ramana says to ask. Use this questioning as a thorn to remove the thorn of knowledge.

And then what will you do with this second thorn? After all, it was quite helpful in removing the thorn of knowledge, so because of this will you keep it safely? Now that you have been released from the bondage of knowledge, why worry about hanging on to ignorance? Why should a person who is willing to let go of knowledge still be attached to ignorance? Someone who could drop the answers such as "I am a soul, I am *brahman*, I am this and I am that," and all such nonsense – will he hold onto the question, "Who am I?" A moment will come when he will let go of that too. Both the thorns will be thrown away.

Knowledge is a thorn, so is ignorance. And when both knowledge and ignorance are absent, then supreme wisdom is attained, then understanding blossoms. Then you know, "I am *brahman*." Then, whatsoever you know will be from your own experience, it will be your very own discovery, you will be seeing it. This seeing will be your own personal experience. Then, what you say will not be something that you have heard from another person. What you say will be from your own experience. And the power of the whole world cannot take that experience away from you.

The knowledge that you had before, for example, "I am the *brahman*," was such that, even if a small child questioned you about it, he would put you into all kinds of trouble. All he would have to say would be, "So, sir, you proclaim that you are the *brahman*? See this small stone? Can you destroy it?" This would be enough to get you into trouble – and all your talk about being the *brahman* would disappear! Or he could say something like, "Okay, since you call yourself the *brahman*, the supreme reality, can you make this tree blossom even though it is not the season for it to give flowers? After all, you are the *brahman*!"

A Jaina *muni* often comes to see me. The poor fellow has only one problem: he feels that he has attained to supreme wisdom, that he has attained the state of *kaivalya*. But there is one small problem: in the Jaina holy scriptures it is written that anyone who has attained to *kaivalya* automatically becomes clairvoyant; that he can see the past, the present and the future. And everyone creates trouble for him around this issue. But still he maintains that he has attained to the wisdom of *kaivalya*. And people say, "Ah! Do you know all about the past, the present and the future?" And so the poor fellow comes to me and says this is creating a big problem for him.

"Is it necessary for *kaivalaya* wisdom to be clairvoyant as well?" he asks. "Is it possible that there is a state of *kaivalya* without all this clairvoyance business? Though I have attained to the supreme wisdom of *kaivalya*, still, these people manage to get me into trouble. They come and say, 'Okay, supremely wise one, do you see this closed fist? Now, tell us what is in it.' This puts me in great difficulty. So please, will you say something in your talks to the effect that one can have the supreme wisdom of *kaivalya* without needing to be a clairvoyant at the same time?"

Now this man has taken this part about *kaivalya* wisdom straight from the scriptures! And in the same scriptures it is also written that once a person has attained to *kaivalya* wisdom, he automatically becomes omniscient too, so his problem is that he cannot deny that either.

I said to him, "It would be better not to think of yourself as such a wise person. Don't be in such a hurry to achieve *kaivalya* wisdom – because the day you do, you won't need to ask me for validation, you won't need to come and ask me for some sort of a certificate verifying that yes, you have attained to *kaivalya* wisdom and being a clairvoyant is not a necessary part of doing so. When you do attain to *kaivalya* wisdom, it will be your own realization and then all such things will have no meaning. And if you do attain to *kaivalya* wisdom without also becoming a clairvoyant, you will say, 'It is all right. Although I have not become clairvoyant, I have still attained to *kaivalya* wisdom.'

"But what is the need to tell someone else about it? Why should you try to convince others? When you try to convince others, it is only natural for them to raise doubts, they will raise certain questions. Then you will have to answer them, and this will create problems for you."

Often people who are a little out of their minds seem to know a lot about *brahman*, *kaivalya* and so on; they seem to have a particular knack for grasping such things very fast! But actually, it is only a symptom of madness and these people should be treated, they should be kept in an asylum. The illusions they have are only because of their egos.

The sutra says:

The great and difficult victory,
the conquering of the desires of the individual soul,
is a work of ages...

This is not something which can be achieved in a moment. Many people come to me and say, "My kundalini has arisen! A holy woman placed her hand on me and it has arisen!"

I ask, "What else has changed in your life?" and they reply, "No, nothing. Everything else is just the same."

These days there is a holy woman in Bombay, and the ten or twenty people who go to see her have all become enlightened! She has made around twenty-five people buddhas – instantly! And if you ask those people who are supposed to have become buddhas, "Please tell us what else has happened to you," they reply, "Nothing else has happened. It is simply that we have now become buddhas!" – because she has told them, "You have now attained supreme wisdom."

Man is always on the lookout for an easy way, and he is always eager for someone to tell him that such and such a thing has happened to him. He agrees at once! Actually, he has just been waiting for someone to tell him.

Life is not so cheap. It is only after ages of hard work, effort and dedication, lifetimes of wandering, that something comes into one's hand – and even then, not much, only very little.

This sutra says that even one who has done everything, even a person who is standing on the very threshold, at the very doorstep of the divine, can still fall back. A small mistake, and the door which seemed to lie within the reach of your hand will be lost for ages. And the closer you come, the more fatal the mistake becomes, because when you are far away from the destination, you are not so afraid of getting lost. As it is, you are so far away that even if you do get lost, it hardly seems to matter much. You are so far away – a little more distance won't make that much of a difference. But the closer you get to your destination, the more arduous it suddenly seems to become, because now, even if you take one wrong step, you will miss your goal. The stakes become very high; the responsibility increases. Now, much more awareness is required. The nearer you get, the more difficult it becomes. But there are people who pretend to have reached without ever having taken a single step! All that someone has to do is to give them the illusion that they have reached, and at once they will agree, "See, what did I tell you?"

There is a man in America.... One of his disciples has written to me informing me that various people have already confirmed that his guru has attained enlightenment. Some wise people from India have even issued written certificates saying that he has attained the state of enlightenment: "Now all that we need is a certificate from you."

What madness! And those who have given something in writing, they have proved one thing – that they themselves know nothing about enlightenment.

Is it a question of some sort of a certificate? Is there any need to ask someone? Will someone else decide that you have attained? Even after reaching, are you still waiting for someone else's decision?

But man wants to become something without having to do anything! And in no other sphere of life is it possible for you to become something so easily, without doing anything, as it is in the sphere of religion! In all other spheres of life you will have to do something first; only then can you become something. But in the case of religion, there seems to be no problem in becoming something; there is no criterion, no one can create any hindrances for you.

But please remember one thing: as your meditation deepens, as you come closer and closer to *samadhi*, the more your responsibility increases. The danger also increases, because earlier, even if you had made a mistake, it would not have made much of a difference. You had already wandered so far: what harm could a little bit more wandering do? You were so far away: how much further away could you possibly get? But now, missing even by an inch can make the difference of thousands of miles. Now, even a small step in the wrong direction may mean endless wandering. Many people go astray or fall back when they are very close. And once you are so close, if you still have even a small trace of ego left inside you, it will make you go astray. It is this ego that will make you proclaim that you have achieved *samadhi* long before you have actually done so. It is this ego that is responsible for your announcing that you have achieved meditation long before you have actually done so. And once you feel that you have; then at that very moment the journey stops.

The knowledge which is now yours
is only yours because your soul has become one
with all pure souls and with the inmost.
It is a trust vested in you by the most high.
Betray it, misuse your knowledge, or neglect it,
and it is possible even now for you to fall
from the high estate you have attained.

I see this happening every day: as people get very close, their ego has one last, final attempt at asserting itself. Before, their ego was concerned with wealth, with status; now they develop an ego about being very religious – that they have mastered the art of meditation! The moment this ego begins to assert itself, know that you are betraying your knowledge, you are misusing it, you are neglecting it.

And it is possible even now for you to fall back from the heights you have attained.

Great ones fall back, even from the threshold,
unable to sustain the weight of their responsibility,
unable to pass on.
Therefore look forward always
with awe and trembling to this moment,
and be prepared for the battle.

Always stay alert with awe and trembling: you must understand this. What does it mean? Why have awe and trembling been linked together? Awe and trembling seem to be two totally opposite things. Why should the one who is in awe, in trust, be trembling? How can one who is trembling be in awe and trust? But there is a great purpose behind saying this. It is not a question of harmonizing them both; in fact the two are present in two different dimensions: awe towards the future, and fear about falling back.

Awe relates to making future progress, and trembling to the possibility of falling back, even at this stage. They do not exist on the same plane; their dimensions are different.

Always remain trembling. It is still possible for you to fall back. The fear of this will keep you alert: that you can still fall back. Wherever you hear the voice of your ego, immediately tremble. You can still be pulled back; the bridge has not yet been demolished completely, the way back is still in place. You can still take the path back.

Have a trust about the future – a complete trust in the future, and a trembling about the past – have no trust at all in the past. Be mindful of both these things: that there is still much to happen, that everything has not yet happened – this awareness towards the future – and that although the past may have been erased, it has not been totally wiped out – it is still possible to fall back. The roads are still in place. A small mistake and you can fall back a long, long way.

To climb is very difficult but to descend is not. Within a split second you can fall way back, you can fall a long way down, whereas it takes a very long time to rise. This is the fear. And to have a total trust towards the future, a hope.

Keep these two things in mind.

17

THE MANIFESTATION OF THE INVISIBLE

It is written that for him who is on the threshold
of divinity no law can be framed, no guide can exist.
Yet to enlighten the disciple,
the final struggle may be thus expressed:

13. Hold fast to that which has neither substance nor existence.

14. Listen only to the voice which is soundless.

15. Look only on that which is invisible alike to the inner and the outer sense.

Peace be with you.

In the pursuit of truth, the journey to the temple of the divine is already arduous. To talk about it is even more arduous. The moment the experiences that happen on the path are put into words they become false, because words are very small and the experience is so vast. It is like someone trying to hold the sky in his fist and failing in the attempt. The same failure happens when you try to put truth into words. It can be said through emptiness, but never through words. Perhaps it can find an expression through silence, but with speech it fails. Of course, all this is true when you are still traveling on the path, but when you stand at the threshold of the temple, then the words *really* create difficulty. Because to be at the door of the temple of the divine means the end of all duality, and all our language is created through duality.

In language, the existence of opposites is essential. We can understand what darkness means only because of the existence of light – otherwise to say "darkness" would be meaningless. If someone asks you, "What is the definition of darkness?" what will you say? You will say, "It is an absence of light," won't you? It is really out of helplessness that you have to bring in light to define darkness. You can't help it! And you will feel even more helpless if someone asks you, "What is the definition of light?" Then you will have to say, "It is an absence of darkness." This is really a vicious circle: you have to drag light in to define darkness and darkness in to define light! They seem to be dependent on each other; and neither of them can exist independently, on its own. One cannot even be defined without referring to the other one.

Language is full of duality because language has been created for a world of duality; a world in which the meaning of birth is bound up with death, and in just the opposite way, the meaning of death is bound up with birth. Even the meaning of love is hidden in hatred – and if hatred were to disappear from the world, love would also disappear.

At the threshold of the temple, all duality disappears. There, the language of duality is of no use. Then what can be said? Supposing we say that God is light; in that case we will have to bring in darkness. And what sort of a God is this, that we have to bring in darkness to define him? Then what shall we call God? If we say that God is love, then we have to bring in hatred too. If we say that God is eternal, then we have to explain him in terms of the momentary, the transitory. If we speak of God as the creator, then too we will have to refer to his creation. What kind of a creator is someone whose very existence is dependent on his creation?

Once the concept of opposites has been left at the door, then there really remains nothing to say about that which is inside.

This is why this sutra starts with:

It is written that for him who is on the threshold of divinity
no law can be framed, no guide can exist.
Yet to enlighten the disciple,
the final struggle may be thus expressed...

For one who has reached the threshold of the divine, there can be no law made – because all laws are meant for the world. Outside the temple they are effective and can have results, but inside the temple they serve no purpose.

What is right and what is wrong – all this is relevant only in the world of duality. It is dependent upon definitions and interpretations. At the doorway of the temple even right and wrong disappear. Here, not even good and bad remain. Religiousness and irreligiousness, morality and immorality are no longer there. Here, we have to leave behind whatsoever we have learned in the world of duality. So what laws can there be inside this temple where there is no duality, where there are no opposites?

That is why we have said the *paramahansa,* the supremely wise one, is beyond the domain of any rule. We cannot make any kind of rule for him. We cannot say anything about what he should or should not do. Whatever he does is right, and whatever he doesn't do must be wrong. For us it is the other way around: we are not supposed to do what is wrong and we are supposed to do what is right. It is said that whatever the *paramahansa* does is right and whatever he doesn't do is wrong. No rules apply to him, because he who has already entered the temple has moved beyond all rules.

Laws exist only at the periphery; at the center there are no laws. As long as we are at the periphery the laws apply to us, but as we reach to the center they don't apply anymore. Even then, the *paramahansa* may choose to abide by the laws – but then that is his freedom. On the other hand, if he chooses to, he may live by breaking all the laws – in which case that too will be his freedom. His responsibility is to no one, he is not answerable to anything – because now there is no one above him to whom he is answerable.

Now, he is standing in the place beyond which there is nothing.

So this sutra says that there is no law. No law can be framed, no guideline can be given. One cannot be told how to enter the temple. Yes, only this much can be said: that whatsoever you have learned up until now from the world of duality will have to be left at the threshold. At the entrance to the temple only a negative guideline can be given. This is why the Upanishads say, *neti-neti* – not this, not that. This statement can be made only at the threshold of the temple. Beyond this, nothing can be said.

Neti-neti means it is not this, but it is not that either. Whatever you can say, it is not that. You have to deny everything; nothing that belongs to you can remain with you. Whatever you may have learned from the world, from all your experiences, proves to be useless: leave it all at the door. Don't try to bring any of it with you when you are about to enter – otherwise you will never be able to enter.

So if there is any rule, it will only be one of negation: to leave all that you have learned at the door, to become totally ignorant, innocent, like a piece of blank paper; as if you have never ventured into the world, as if you have never learned anything, as if you have never lived, as if you are totally raw, as if you have not even had a trace of experience. With such purity, enter the temple. This purity can only be defined in negative terms: that you have wiped away whatever you may have learned. Because what you have learned from the world of duality cannot be taken with you inside the temple. And if you try to save even a small part, you will not be able to enter the temple, you will not even be able to find the door. No laws can be framed, no guidelines can be given. No maps of any kind can be given to you that would be useful inside the temple of the divine, that would tell you that these are the paths that you can travel on.

This should be rightly understood.

The sky of consciousness is, in a way, very similar to the outer sky. If you walk on the earth, marks are made, footprints are made. But when birds fly in the sky, no trace is left. On the earth there are paths, but in the sky no paths exist. Those who may have gone before you leave no trace behind for you to follow. There are no footprints in the temple of God, in the ultimate experience of awareness, in the ultimate experience of consciousness. Buddha walked there, Jesus walked there, but they have left no footprints.

That is why no map is possible. It cannot be said, "Just keep this map carefully and follow it, and you too will be able to enter." Even your map will have to be left behind – because this is not the material world where maps can be used. Marks can be drawn on matter, but no marks can be made on the divine. You can draw lines on something which is tangible, but you cannot draw lines on the soul. This is why no road exists there, no guidelines are given. This is why no guidance of any kind can be given.

Only those who have the courage that is necessary for moving into the unknown can enter there. Those who ask for maps will have to stop outside the temple. Those who say, "What will happen to us if we go any further? Until we are reassured about this, we will not go on" – those people simply cannot go any further. Only those who are very courageous can enter there, only those who say, "We are not afraid or worried. Let whatever comes, come!" Only those who say, "We are not bothered at all about safety and security; even if death comes, we are ready," can enter.

At the gateway of the temple, only the one who can show that much daring – even to disappear – can enter.

Knowledge acquired from the outside can be of no help whatsoever, because that kind of knowledge cannot comprehend or even touch the supreme experience. This is why whoever reaches to that state has an original experience. Even though thousands of buddhas have reached there, the experience is always original and untouched: the experience is new. Whenever a person enters the temple, he finds that nothing there is stale. If it were possible to give you maps, scriptural scholars and guides, and if you could then enter the temple with their descriptions of the experience, your own experience would be false.

American psychologists say that today, wherever American tourists travel, they feel that they have already seen it all before. Everything appears stale to them. And the funny part of all this is that today, it is Americans who have the greatest possibility to travel all over the globe. All over the world, eighty percent of the vast crowd of tourists that you come across are Americans. It is the Americans who travel to every nook and corner of the world. And a very interesting thing has happened: wherever they go, they feel as if they have seen it all before. Everything appears to be stale to them.

They have seen the Taj Mahal a thousand times already on the television, at the movies, in pictures and so forth, so when they arrive at the *real* Taj Mahal, it is a Taj Mahal that they have seen thousands of times before. It is stale. They have pinned great hopes on seeing it, but when they arrive they feel that they have already seen it many, many times. And the fact is that the Taj Mahal seems to be so beautiful in photographs, on the TV and in the cinema, that it can never be so beautiful when it is seen by the naked eye. That's why the real Taj Mahal appears to pale a little. The Taj Mahal that you saw in the photos was much more colorful, it appeared to be much more precious. They went to see it thinking that the original must be even more beautiful, but the original seems pale in comparison. Because they have already been seen it so many times before, there seems to be nothing original about it.

This is why, even though the American tourist travels so much, he never seems to arrive anywhere, he doesn't experience anything. Wherever he goes, he feels that he has seen it all before. Everything looks stale, everything seems boring.

It is good that there is no map for the temple of God; otherwise even there you would hit yourself on the head with disappointment. You would say, "Oh my god! It is the same thing that I read about in the Gita," or "It is the same thing that Buddha has already explained!" There too, you would be bored. But fortunately, no map could ever be made of it – and no map will ever be made. Whatever information has been told to you about it so far, none of it is of any use inside the temple; it is only helpful in taking you as far as the entrance. This is why the temple always remains virgin and untouched. This is why, whenever you enter inside the temple, the experience is always unique, incomparable. Even after you have experienced it, you will not be able to tell anyone about it. After the experience you will suddenly realize that anything that can be said will bear no resemblance whatsoever to what the experience really is. What you have seen simply cannot be put into words.

This is why this sutra says that:

...no law can be framed, no guides can exist.
Yet to enlighten the disciple,
the final struggle may be thus expressed...

This final happening, this ultimate phenomenon of life that happens, when you enter the temple leaving everything behind, this experience at the threshold can be described. But this too is only an attempt at describing it. It cannot be completely successful. Some hints can be given, but even those hints will be very difficult to make.

The thirteenth sutra:

Hold fast to that which has neither substance nor existence.

The difficulty is mainly caused by its dual nature.

Hold fast to that which has neither substance nor existence.

We know very well what substance is, what matter is, what has form. We know about matter, but we know nothing about the non-material. That's why people say that the soul is non-material, that it is beyond matter. Matter has form, it has certain attributes. The soul has no form, no attributes. It is formless, without any attributes, so we describe the soul in the language of matter. Matter has substance, soul is without substance. But we know only about what has substance; we have no idea about the non-substantial.

This sutra says that if you want to enter the ultimate truth, then not only will you have to let go of all that which has substance, you will also have to let go of the non-substantial. Not only will you have to let go of form, you will also have to let go of the formless.

Why? It is a little difficult to understand. That's why these sutras were written after much hesitation. You will have to let go of both the form and the formless. Even the formless has some form, because it can be defined only in the language of things that have a form.

If someone were to ask, "What is formless?" then you would say, "Something which has no form." The formless too is part of form. Even the formless can never be free of form because it can't be described without mentioning the word *form*. So much controversy is happening all the time about whether God has a form or whether he is formless; whether he is someone with attributes or whether he is without attributes. There are many arguments about all this and they have gone on and on for thousands of years.

This sutra says that neither does God have attributes, nor is he without attributes. It is saying that if the attribute-less can only be defined in terms of attributes, then how much meaning can the attribute-less have? So if God is truly without attributes he cannot be *called* attribute-less because then you are only negating attributes. You cannot define your God without mentioning attributes. You will have to concede one thing: that your God may be without any attributes, but you still cannot define him without making some kind of reference to attributes. And how can you call someone attribute-less if he cannot even be defined without referring to attributes?

The sutra says that neither attributes nor non-attributes, neither form nor formlessness, neither manifest nor unmanifest, neither matter nor spirit can enter there.

It is a complicated matter. It seems to be very difficult to understand because in the first place it is difficult to rise from matter to soul – and then it becomes even more difficult to rise from the soul to something beyond the soul. Matter and soul are also part of duality, matter and soul are also opposites. Consciousness and matter are opposites. Not only will matter have to be left behind, but consciousness too. This does not mean that you will become unconscious. It only means that whatsoever you had understood to be your consciousness has become useless. And something very new has happened which goes even beyond consciousness, which extends beyond consciousness, which transcends consciousness.

Hold fast to that which has neither substance nor existence.

Leave everything else at the threshold.

In order to understand this, let us divide the journey into two parts. The first part of the journey is to let go of form and substance. Whatever has shape or form – let go of it so that you can enter the formless that dwells within you. This is the first discipline. Then, on the day that you have completely entered within – having first left the outer behind in order to enter the inner... When the outer has been left behind completely, let go of the inner too, because the inner is nothing but a part of the outer. Matter was dropped to become spiritual, and once matter has been dropped completely, then let go of the spiritual too.

That's why Buddha has said that there is no soul. And what Buddha said could not be understood; it was a statement of absolute wisdom. He has said, *anatta*: no-soul – not even the soul exists there. It is said only in this sense: that in order to know the soul, matter has to be dropped, and then, even the soul has to be dropped. Buddha did not use any word for what will remain after that. He has said, "If I use any word it will only complicate matters even further. To say anything at all will create a boundary, to say anything at all will mean that an opposite is also possible. Therefore, I will say nothing."

All his life people kept asking Buddha questions about what happens in the ultimate moment. And Buddha would say, "It is just like when a lamp is extinguished, that is all. You will be extinguished, just like the flame of a lamp. Nobody asks where the flame has gone. In the same way, you will be extinguished." To question where the flame has gone then becomes meaningless. That's why Buddha never used the word *moksha*; instead he used the word *nirvana*. *Nirvana* means "extinguishing of the flame." The word *moksha* suggests that you will continue in some lofty, liberated state – but *you* will still continue. Buddha says, "*You* will not survive, because this 'you' is part of a duality." But this does not mean that nothing will survive. Everything survives. All that is worthy of surviving will survive. "But to describe this," the Buddha said, "I will not use any words, because all words are drawn from opposites, and opposites are a part of the world."

Hold fast to that which has neither substance nor existence.

The fourteenth sutra:

Listen only to the voice which is soundless.

The sounds that we hear are produced through friction, they are produced by the impact between two things. They are born out of duality. When you strike two cymbals, only then is a sound produced. And when you hit both your hands together, the sound of clapping is created. When the winds pass through the trees, there is a rustling sound. If I am speaking, it is only because of the friction created in my throat that sound is made. The speaking we know is a sound in some form or other. It is created through an impact, a friction between two things.

But there won't be two in this temple. This is why there cannot be any sound there, there cannot be any words there. There cannot be an impact between two things, because how can there be any impact or collision where duality does not exist in any form? There is only empty sky there. What kind of voice or sound can there be if there is no other? The sound that is created out of impact simply cannot be created.

So then there are two things: either we can call it a soundless voice, a soundless sound, a sound which is not created out of an impact, which is not produced by striking two things together, or we can call it what the seers have chosen to call it – and they have chosen a very beautiful phrase to describe it – *anahat nad*. *Anahat* means unstruck, something which has not been produced by any sort of impact.

Is there such a thing as an unstruck sound? Is there any sound that is made, without any sort of an impact whatsoever? If there is such a sound, then this is the basic note of life. In this there are many things to be understood. Anything that is created through an impact will be destroyed, will disappear – because an impact has only a limited power. How long can that energy last? The energy created by the clapping of hands has a limit – it will fade away, it will disappear.

Buddha used to say that what is created from an impact cannot be eternal. How can it be eternal? Something which did not exist until a moment ago, which has just been born, cannot last forever. A stick that has one end must surely have another end? Anything that is born must die. Only that which has never been born can be eternal. Only that which is unborn, which is without a beginning, can be infinite. So is there such a voice, such a sound, such a melody which can be called the music of life – which was never born and will therefore never die? Until we come to know of such a phenomenon, we have not known the ultimate source of life.

Listen only to the voice which is soundless.

This is the real power: "Listen only to the voice which is soundless." This is the ultimate music. But how will you hear it?

The science of mantra has created the method for doing this. It says: begin with the chanting of a mantra. In the beginning do it loudly, with force. Start chanting *Om* in such a way that you can also hear it, that it resonates in the air. And when you have perfected this chanting and it resonates in such a way that no other word or thought moves in you, only then will your chanting of *Om* be pure. But if it happens that any other thought is moving in you at the same time, then traces of it will also enter the resonance of *Om*.

Try to understand this. Suppose you are chanting *Om*, and at the same time a thought is going on in your mind – to go to the market and buy something. With this, the *Om* which you are chanting is becoming impure, because at the back of it a note is being tagged on – to go to the market – and this note is distorting your *Om*. Your *Om* will be pure only when it alone is reverberating inside you, when there is no other thought, when there is nothing there to distort it. The day your chanting of *Om* becomes pure, on that day you can close your mouth and let the sound of *Om* reverberate within you.

Then, don't say it out loud, just let it go on reverberating within. Close your lips, making sure there is no meeting with the air and then go on chanting *Om* inside. And when *Om* begins to reverberate within, make sure that you do not have any other thought in your mind – even at some other deeper level – that you don't have any sort of desire, impression, emotion. But if there is some emotion, thought or desire happening at some other, deeper level, then it will make your *Om* impure – so get rid of it. And once only the reverberations of *Om* are left within you, then you can take the third step.

Now, don't chant *Om* loudly at all, just close your eyes and try to listen to it – as if *Om* is resonating inside you all by itself and you are not doing anything to make it happen. This happens only if you have reached a level of complete purity in the previous stages; that is, you have chanted *Om* and let it echo inside, but there is no other thought at the same time; the process of thinking has come to an end in your conscious mind. Now, close your mouth and let *Om* reverberate within. At this stage, thoughts will start troubling you at the unconscious level, so what you should do then is to intensify the reverberations to such an extent that they start to echo in your unconscious too – until no thought is left there either. In this way, your unconscious will also become peaceful. In this way, both the layers of your mind will calm down. Now, stop chanting *Om*; because once the mind has calmed down, the echo that is already going on naturally, by itself, in the innermost depths of your heart, can be heard by you. In fact it has always been there – you are made of it, it is your basic essence. You could not hear it before because of your thoughts. Now it can be heard.

So your first chanting of *Om* was not the real sound of the mantra. It was only a means to help you get rid of your thoughts. Now, become silent and just listen. Don't chant. Until now you have been chanting. In the beginning you chanted *Om* very loudly, then later you did it very softly inside. Now, don't chant; just listen. Now, you should just listen. Is *Om* echoing there, within you? You will be amazed to feel that vibrations of *Om* are actually emanating from your very being and spreading out to each and every fiber of your body. As this realization becomes more and more clear to you, you will learn that *Om* is the very music of your life.

This music that you will hear is *anahat*, unstruck, because it has not been created out of any friction or clash whatsoever. This is the sound which Nanak and Kabir have called the unchanted sound, the silent sound. They have said this because this sound is not born from any chanting. This sutra calls it "the voice which is soundless."

Listen only to the voice which is soundless.

The fifteenth sutra:

**Look only on that which is invisible
alike to the inner and the outer sense.**

We have observed the world, the dimension of the senses. We have seen what is outside. Then we have opened up the senses on another level and seen what is within. The eyes have looked at the world which lay outside, the world of matter, and then they have looked within, and seen the soul.

This sutra says: now you should close your eyes to both the outer and the inner. Now, have a look at that which cannot be seen with the eyes, which cannot even be felt by the senses. Now, free yourself from the outer as well as the inner and look at that ultimate reality which is neither outer nor inner, and is in both the outer and the inner.

This third – neither outer nor inner, or both outer and inner – this is the One. And in the search for this One you will have to let go of both ways of using the senses.

You can understand it in this way: what we see with the external senses is the world, is matter; what we see with the inner senses is the soul, consciousness; and what we see when we let go of them both, is godliness. Or you can say: what we see with the outer senses are thoughts, what we see with the inner senses is meditation, and what we see after leaving behind both the outer and the inner senses is *samadhi,* no-mind, enlightenment.

What you saw from the outside was only half. What you saw inside was also half. What you see after having let go of both the inside and outside is the whole, the entirety. And until you have seen the whole, there is no liberation. The incomplete imprisons, the complete liberates.

Peace be with you.

Supreme peace is attained only in the moment when you are no longer there. As long as you are, you will remain in turmoil.

That's why one more, final thing needs to be taken note of. You can never be peaceful as long as *you* are, because in this very "is-ness" is the problem. Your very is-ness creates the disturbance, the whole turmoil. Only when *you* are not will you become peaceful.

This is why when the sutra says, "Peace Be With You," it has a wealth of meaning. It means that you should cease to be, that you should be finished, so that all that remains is peace. *You* are the problem.

A storm arises in the ocean and then calms down. We say that the storm has calmed down, but what does it mean? Is a calm storm still present there? No, in saying that the storm has calmed down, we are saying that the storm no longer exists.

A person falls sick, then he recovers. We say that the sickness has been cured. What does this mean? Does it mean that now a cured sickness exists? Saying that the sickness has been cured means precisely this: that the sickness no longer exists. There was a sickness but it is not there now.

All that you are right now is just a sum total of "diseases." You can never become peaceful until this "you" falls silent, until this "you" disappears.

"Peace Be With You" means only one thing, and it is that you reach to that place where you are not. As long as *you* are, you will go on playing your tune of turmoil. That is why religion is the ultimate death. In it, you are completely erased, you don't survive. What survives is your innermost core, your center. But right now you are not acquainted with it.

It *is* peaceful. It is peaceful right now. Right now, if *you* can become quiet, if *you* are not; you will be able to hear that peace in this very moment. But you are a tumult, a crowd, full of turmoil and madness. It is because of this "you" that you are unable to hear this inner, peaceful, soundless sound, this voice which arises out of nothingness.

If, even for just one second, *you* disappear, you will be able to see the divine. And once you have seen it, you will not be able to turn back – because then you will know that it is pointless to invite the same old diseases back again.

But right now you make efforts, you make efforts to become peaceful without even bothering to see that "I am the unrest." Right now, you make efforts to become free, without even bothering to see that "I am the bondage." This is why I say to you that it will not be "your" freedom, but freedom from yourself. What will happen is not your freedom but freedom from yourself. And on the day when you are able to let go of yourself, just as a snake slips out of its skin, you will suddenly realize that you were always free. But you are holding on very tightly to your skin, you are holding on very tightly to your covering, you are holding on very tightly to your body, you are holding on to that outer covering so tightly that you have forgotten that it can be discarded, dropped.

All the techniques of meditation are nothing but ways to help you discard this covering, even if it is only for a second. Once you have had even one glimpse, then there is no need for meditation. Then, that glimpse will start pulling you, that glimpse will become a magnet. Then, that glimpse itself starts beckoning you and taking you along the path to where this sutra, Peace be with you, can be realized.

About Osho

Osho defies categorization, reflecting everything from the individual quest for meaning to the most urgent social and political issues facing society today. His books are not written but are transcribed from recordings of extemporaneous talks given over a period of thirty-five years. Osho has been described by the *Sunday Times* in London as one of the "1000 Makers of the 20th Century" and by *Sunday Mid-Day* in India as one of the ten people – along with Gandhi, Nehru and Buddha – who have changed the destiny of India.

Osho has a stated aim of helping to create the conditions for the birth of a new kind of human being, characterized as "Zorba the Buddha" – one whose feet are firmly on the ground, yet whose hands can touch the stars. Running like a thread through all aspects of Osho is a vision that encom-passes both the timeless wisdom of the East and the highest potential of Western science and technology.

He is synonymous with a revolutionary contribution to the science of inner transformation and an approach to medita-tion which specifically addresses the accelerated pace of contemporary life. The unique Osho Active Meditations™ are designed to allow the release of accumulated stress in the body and mind so that it is easier to be still and experience the thought-free state of meditation.

Osho International Meditation Resort

Osho International Meditation Resort has been created so that people can have a direct experience of a new way of living – with more alertness, relaxation, and humor. It is located about 100 miles southeast of Mumbai in Pune, India, on 40 acres in the tree-lined residential area of Koregaon Park. The resort offers a variety of programs to the thousands of people who visit each year from more than 100 countries. Accommodation for visitors is available on-campus in the new Osho Guesthouse.

The Multiversity programs at the meditation resort take place in a pyramid complex next to the famous Zen garden park, Osho Teerth. The programs are designed to provide the transformation tools that give people access to a new lifestyle – one of relaxed awareness – which is an approach they can take with them into their everyday lives. Self-discovery classes, sessions, courses and meditative processes are offered throughout the year. For exercising the body and keeping fit, there is a beautiful outdoor facility where one can experiment with a Zen approach to sports and recreation.

In the main meditation auditorium the daily schedule from 6:00 A.M. up to 11:00 P.M. includes both active and passive meditation methods. Following the daily evening meeting meditation, the nightlife in this multicultural resort is alive with outdoor eating areas that fill with friends and often with dancing.

The resort has its own supply of safe, filtered drinking water and the food served is made with organically grown produce from the resort's own farm.

An online tour of the meditation resort, as well as travel and program information, can be found at: www.osho.com

This is a comprehensive website in different languages with an online magazine, audio and video webcasting, an Audiobook Club, the complete English and Hindi archive of Osho talks and a complete catalog of all Osho publications including books, audio and video. Includes information about the active meditation techniques developed by Osho, most with streaming video demonstrations.

The daily meditation schedule includes:

Osho Dynamic Meditation™: A technique designed to release tensions and repressed emotions, opening the way to a new vitality and an experience of profound silence.

Osho Kundalini Meditation™: A technique of shaking free one's dormant energies, and through spontaneous dance and silent sitting, allowing these energies to be redirected inward.

Osho Nadabrahma Meditation™: A method of harmonizing one's energy flow, based on an ancient Tibetan humming technique.

Osho Nataraj Meditation™: A method involving the inner alchemy of dancing so totally that the dancer disappears and only the dance remains.

Vipassana Meditation: A technique originating with Gautam Buddha and now updated for the 21st Century, for dissolving mental chatter through the awareness of breath.

No Dimensions Meditation™: A powerful method for centering one's energy, based on a Sufi technique.

Osho Gourishankar Meditation™: A one-hour nighttime meditation, which includes a breathing technique, gazing softly at a light and gentle body movements.

Books by Osho in English Language

Early Discourses and Writings

A Cup of Tea
Dimensions Beyond The Known
From Sex to Super-consciousness
The Great Challenge
Hidden Mysteries
I Am The Gate
The Inner Journey
Psychology of the Esoteric
Seeds of Wisdom

Meditation

The Voice of Silence
And Now and Here (Vol 1 & 2)
In Search of the Miraculous (Vol 1 &.2)
Meditation: The Art of Ecstasy
Meditation: The First and Last Freedom
The Path of Meditation
The Perfect Way
Yaa-Hoo! The Mystic Rose

Buddha and Buddhist Masters

The Book of Wisdom
The Dhammapada: The Way of the Buddha (Vol 1-12)
The Diamond Sutra

The Discipline of Transcendence (Vol 1-4)
The Heart Sutra

Indian Mystics

Enlightenment: The Only Revolution (Ashtavakra)
Showering Without Clouds (Sahajo)
The Last Morning Star (Daya)
The Song of Ecstasy (Adi Shankara)

Baul Mystics

The Beloved (Vol 1 & 2)
Kabir
The Divine Melody
Ecstasy: The Forgotten Language
The Fish in the Sea is Not Thirsty
The Great Secret
The Guest
The Path of Love
The Revolution

Jesus and Christian Mystics

Come Follow to You (Vol 1-4)
I Say Unto You (Vol 1 & 2)
The Mustard Seed
Theologia Mystica

Jewish Mystics

The Art of Dying
The True Sage

Western Mystics

Guida Spirituale (Desiderata)

The Hidden Harmony
(Heraclitus)
The Messiah (Vol 1 & 2) (Commentaries on Khalil Gibran's The Prophet)
The New Alchemy: To Turn You On (Commentaries on Mabel Collins' Light on the Path)
Philosophia Perennis (Vol 1 & 2) (The Golden Verses of Pythagoras)
Zarathustra: A God That Can Dance
Zarathustra: The Laughing Prophet (Commentaries on Nietzsche's Thus Spake Zarathustra)

Sufism

Just Like That
Journey to the Heart
The Perfect Master (Vol 1 & 2)
The Secret
Sufis: The People of the Path (Vol 1 & 2)
Unio Mystica (Vol 1 & 2)
The Wisdom of the Sands (Vol 1 & 2)

Tantra

Tantra: The Supreme Understanding
The Tantra Experience
The Royal Song of Saraha
(same as Tantra Vision, Vol 1)
The Tantric Transformation
The Royal Song of Saraha
(same as Tantra Vision, Vol 2)
The Book of Secrets: Vigyan Bhairav Tantra

The Upanishads

Behind a Thousand Names
(Nirvana Upanishad)
Heartbeat of the Absolute
(Ishavasya Upanishad)
I Am That (Isa Upanishad)
The Message Beyond Words
(Kathopanishad)
Philosophia Ultima (Mandukya Upanishad)
The Supreme Doctrine (Kenopanishad)
Finger Pointing to the Moon
(Adhyatma Upanishad)
That Art Thou (Sarvasar Upanishad, Kaivalya Upanishad, Adhyatma Upanishad)
The Ultimate Alchemy, Vol 1&2
(Atma Pooja Upanishad Vol 1 & 2)
Vedanta: Seven Steps to Samadhi (Akshaya Upanishad)
Flight of the Alone to the Alone
(Kaivalya Upanishad)

Tao

The Empty Boat
The Secret of Secrets
Tao:The Golden Gate (Vol 1&2)
Tao:The Pathless Path (Vol 1&2)
Tao: The Three Treasures (Vol 1-4)
When the Shoe Fits

Yoga

The Path of Yoga (previously Yoga: The Alpha and the Omega Vol 1)
Yoga: The Alpha and the Omega (Vol 2-10)

Zen and Zen Masters

Ah, This!
Ancient Music in the Pines
And the Flowers Showered
A Bird on the Wing
Bodhidharma: The Greatest Zen Master
Communism and Zen Fire, Zen Wind
Dang Dang Doko Dang
The First Principle
God is Dead: Now Zen is the Only Living Truth
The Grass Grows By Itself
The Great Zen Master Ta Hui
Hsin Hsin Ming: The Book of Nothing
I Celebrate Myself: God is No Where, Life is Now Here
Kyozan: A True Man of Zen
Nirvana: The Last Nightmare
No Mind: The Flowers of Eternity
No Water, No Moon
One Seed Makes the Whole Earth Green
Returning to the Source
The Search: Talks on the 10 Bulls of Zen
A Sudden Clash of Thunder
The Sun Rises in the Evening
Take it Easy (Vol 1 & 2)
This Very Body the Buddha
Walking in Zen, Sitting in Zen

The White Lotus
Yakusan: Straight to the Point of Enlightenment
Zen Manifesto : Freedom From Oneself
Zen: The Mystery and the Poetry of the Beyond
Zen: The Path of Paradox (Vol 1, 2 & 3)
Zen: The Special Transmission
Zen Boxed Sets
The World of Zen (5 vol.)
Live Zen
This. This. A Thousand Times This
Zen: The Diamond Thunderbolt
Zen: The Quantum Leap from Mind to No-Mind

Zen: The Solitary Bird, Cuckoo

of the Forest
Zen: All The Colors Of The Rainbow (5 vol.)
The Buddha: The Emptiness of the Heart
The Language of Existence
The Miracle
The Original Man
Turning In

Osho: On the Ancient Masters of Zen (7 volumes)*

Dogen: The Zen Master
Hyakujo: The Everest of Zen–
With Basho's haikus
Isan: No Footprints in the Blue Sky
Joshu: The Lion's Roar
Ma Tzu: The Empty Mirror
Nansen: The Point Of Departure

Rinzai: Master of the Irrational
*Each volume is also available individually.

Responses to Questions

Be Still and Know
Come, Come, Yet Again Come
The Goose is Out
The Great Pilgrimage: From Here to Here
The Invitation
My Way: The Way of the White Clouds
Nowhere to Go But In
The Razor's Edge
Walk Without Feet, Fly Without Wings and Think Without Mind
The Wild Geese and the Water
Zen: Zest, Zip, Zap and Zing

Talks in America

From Bondage To Freedom
From Darkness to Light
From Death To Deathlessness
From the False to the Truth
From Unconsciousness to Consciousness
The Rajneesh Bible (Vol 2-4)

The World Tour

Beyond Enlightenment (Talks in Bombay)
Beyond Psychology (Talks in Uruguay)
Light on the Path (Talks in the Himalayas)
The Path of the Mystic (Talks in Uruguay)
Sermons in Stones (Talks in Bombay)

Socrates Poisoned Again After 25 Centuries (Talks in Greece)
The Sword and the Lotus
(Talks in the Himalayas)
The Transmission of the Lamp
(Talks in Uruguay)

Osho's Vision for the World

The Golden Future
The Hidden Splendor
The New Dawn
The Rebel
The Rebellious Spirit

The Mantra Series

Hari Om Tat Sat
Om Mani Padme Hum
Om Shantih Shantih Shantih
Sat-Chit-Anand
Satyam-Shivam-Sundram

Personal Glimpses

Books I Have Loved
Glimpses of a Golden Childhood
Notes of a Madman

Interviews with the World Press

The Last Testament (Vol 1)

Intimate Talks between

Master and Disciple – Darshan Diaries
A Rose is a Rose is a Rose
Be Realistic: Plan for a Miracle
Believing the Impossible Before Breakfast
Beloved of My Heart
Blessed are the Ignorant
Dance Your Way to God
Don't Just Do Something, Sit There
Far Beyond the Stars
For Madmen Only
The Further Shore
Get Out of Your Own Way
God's Got A Thing about You
God is Not for Sale
The Great Nothing
Hallelujah!
Let Go!
The 99 Names of Nothingness
No Book, No Buddha, No Teaching, No Disciple
Nothing to Lose but Your Head
Only Losers Can Win in This Game
Open Door
Open Secret
The Shadow of the Whip
The Sound of One Hand Clapping
The Sun Behind the Sun Behind the Sun
The Tongue-Tip Taste of Tao
This Is It
Turn On, Tune In and Drop the Lot
What Is, Is, What Ain't, Ain't
Won't You Join The Dance?

Compilations

After Middle Age: A Limitless Sky
At the Feet of the Master
Bhagwan Shree Rajneesh: On Basic Human Rights
Jesus Crucified Again, This Time in Ronald Reagan's America
Priests and Politicians: The Mafia of the Soul
Take it Really Seriously

Gift Books of Osho Quotations

A Must for Contemplation Before Sleep
A Must for Morning

Contemplation

India My Love

Photobooks

Shree Rajneesh: A Man of Many Climates, Seasons and Rainbows
through the eye of the camera
Impressions... Osho Commune International Photobook

Books about Osho

Bhagwan: The Buddha for the Future by Juliet Forman
Bhagwan Shree Rajneesh: The Most Dangerous Man Since Jesus Christ by Sue Appleton

Bhagwan: The Most Godless Yet the Most Godly Man by Dr. George Meredith
Bhagwan: One Man Against the Whole Ugly Past of Humanity by Juliet Forman

Bhagwan: Twelve Days That Shook the World by Juliet Forman
Was Bhagwan Shree Rajneesh Poisoned by Ronald Reagan's America? by Sue Appleton.
Diamond Days With Osho
by Ma Prem Shunyo

For any information about Osho Books & Audio/Video Tapes please contact:

OSHO Multimedia & Resorts Pvt. Ltd.

17 Koregaon Park, Pune–411001, MS, India
Phone: 020 4019999 Fax: 020 4019990
E-mail: distrib@osho.net Website: www.osho.com

JAICO PUBLISHING HOUSE

Elevate Your Life. Transform Your World.

ESTABLISHED IN 1946, Jaico Publishing House is home to world-transforming authors such as Sri Sri Paramahansa Yogananda, Osho, The Dalai Lama, Sri Sri Ravi Shankar, Robin Sharma, Deepak Chopra, Jack Canfield, Eknath Easwaran, Devdutt Pattanaik, Khushwant Singh, John Maxwell, Brian Tracy and Stephen Hawking.

Our late founder Mr. Jaman Shah first established Jaico as a book distribution company. Sensing that independence was around the corner, he aptly named his company Jaico ('Jai' means victory in Hindi). In order to service the significant demand for affordable books in a developing nation, Mr. Shah initiated Jaico's own publications. Jaico was India's first publisher of paperback books in the English language.

While self-help, religion and philosophy, mind/body/spirit, and business titles form the cornerstone of our non-fiction list, we publish an exciting range of travel, current affairs, biography, and popular science books as well. Our renewed focus on popular fiction is evident in our new titles by a host of fresh young talent from India and abroad. Jaico's recently established Translations Division translates selected English content into nine regional languages.

Jaico's Higher Education Division (HED) is recognized for its student-friendly textbooks in Business Management and Engineering which are in use countrywide.

In addition to being a publisher and distributor of its own titles, Jaico is a major national distributor of books of leading international and Indian publishers. With its headquarters in Mumbai, Jaico has branches and sales offices in Ahmedabad, Bangalore, Bhopal, Bhubaneswar, Chennai, Delhi, Hyderabad, Kolkata and Lucknow.

SINCE 1946